MISS LESLIE'S
LADY'S NEW RECEIPT-BOOK

MISS LESLIE'S LADY'S NEW RECEIPT-BOOK

ELIZA LESLIE

ISBN: 978-93-89582-35-2

Published: 1850

© 2020
LECTOR HOUSE LLP

LECTOR HOUSE LLP
E-MAIL: lectorpublishing@gmail.com

MISS LESLIE'S
LADY'S NEW RECEIPT-BOOK;

A USEFUL GUIDE FOR LARGE OR SMALL FAMILIES,

CONTAINING DIRECTIONS FOR

COOKING, PRESERVING, PICKLING,

AND
PREPARING THE FOLLOWING ARTICLES ACCORDING TO THE MOST NEW AND APPROVED RECEIPTS, VIZ.:

SOUPS,	CONFECTION-	PUDDINGS,
FISH,	ARY,	PIES,
MEATS,	SWEETMEATS,	TARTS,
VEGETABLES,	JELLIES,	CUSTARDS,
POULTRY,	SYRUPS,	ICE CREAMS,
OYSTERS,	CORDIALS,	BLANC-MANGE,
GAME,	CANDIES,	CAKES,
	PERFUMERY, ETC.	

THIRD EDITION, ENLARGED,

WITH ONE HUNDRED AND TWENTY ADDITIONAL RECEIPTS FOR PRE-PARING

FARINA, INDIAN MEAL, FANCY TEA CAKE, MARMALADES,
ETC.
BEING A SEQUEL TO HER "COMPLETE COOKERY."

"Let these receipts be fairly and faithfully tried, and I trust that few, if any, will cause disappointment in the result." —Preface

1850.

PREFACE.

The present volume is designed as a sequel to my book, entitled "Directions for Cookery in all its Branches." Since the first appearance of that work, I have introduced into the new editions so many improvements and additional receipts that its size can no longer be conveniently increased. While obtaining fresh accessions of valuable knowledge on this and other subjects connected with the domestic improvement of my young countrywomen, I have been induced to note down, as they presented themselves, these new items of information. And I now offer them, arranged in due form, to that most efficient of all patrons, the public.

Families who possess the means and the inclination to keep an excellent table, and to entertain their guests in a handsome and liberal manner, will, most probably, find in this book and its predecessor all that may be wanted for such purposes. A large number of these new receipts are of French origin; obtained from French cooks, or from persons instructed by them. And I have endeavoured to render the directions as intelligible and practicable as possible; so as to be easily understood, and easily followed. I have not thought it necessary to give their titles in French, as foreign designations can rarely be comprehended, or indeed accurately pronounced, except by those who are familiar with the language. Let these and the other receipts be fairly and faithfully tried, and I trust that few, if any, will cause disappointment in the result.

ELIZA LESLIE.

Philadelphia, Oct. 15th, 1846.

CONTENTS

WEIGHT AND MEASURE.

Wheat flour	one pound of 16 ounces	is one quart.
Indian meal	one pound 2 ounces	is one quart.
Butter, when soft,	one pound 1 ounc	is one quart.
Loaf-sugar, broken up,	one pound	is one quart.
White sugar, powdered,	one pound 1 ounce	is one quart.
Best brown sugar	one pound 2 ounces	is one quart.
Eggs	ten eggs	weigh one pound.

LIQUID MEASURE.

Four large table-spoonfuls	are	half a jill.
Eight large table-spoonfuls	are	one jill.
Two jills	are	half a pint.
A common-sized tumbler	holds	half a pint.
A common-sized wine-glass	holds about	half a jill.
Two pints	are	one quart.
Four quarts	are	one gallon.

About twenty-five drops of any thin liquid will fill a common-sized tea-spoon.

Four table-spoonfuls will generally fill a common-sized wine-glass.

Four wine-glasses will fill a half-pint tumbler, or a large coffee-cup.

A quart black bottle holds in reality about a pint and a half; sometimes not so much.

A table-spoonful of salt is about one ounce.

DRY MEASURE.

Half a gallon	is	a quarter of a peck.
One gallon	is	half a peck.
Two gallons	are	one peck.
Four gallons	are	half a bushel.
Eight gallons	are	one bushel.

Throughout this book, the pound is avoirdupois weight—sixteen ounces.

THE LADY'S RECEIPT-BOOK.

SOUPS, ETC.

SPRING SOUP.—Unless your dinner hour is very late, the stock for this soup should be made the day before it is wanted, and set away in a stone pan, closely covered. To make the stock, take a knuckle of veal, break the bones, and cut it into several pieces. Allow a quart of water to each pound of veal. Put it into a soup-pot, with a set of calves-feet, and some bits of cold ham, cut off near the hock. If you have no ham, sprinkle in a table-spoonful of salt, and a salt-spoon of cayenne. Place the pot over a *moderate* fire, and let it simmer slowly (skimming it well) for several hours, till the veal is all to rags and the flesh of the calves-feet has dropped in shreds from the bones. Then strain the soup; and if not wanted that day, set it away in a stone pan, as above mentioned.

Next day have ready-boiled two quarts or more of green peas, (they must on no account be old,) and a pint of the green tops cut off from asparagus boiled for the purpose. Pound a handful of raw spinach till you have extracted a teacup-full of the juice. Set the soup or stock over the fire; add the peas, asparagus, and spin-ach-juice, stirring them well in; also a quarter of a pound of fresh butter, divided into four bits, and rolled in flour. Let the whole come to a boil; and then take it off and transfer it to a tureen. It will be found excellent.

In boiling the peas for this soup, you may put with them half a dozen sprigs of green mint, to be afterwards taken out.

Late in the spring you may add to the other vegetables two cucumbers, pared and sliced, and the whitest part or heart of a lettuce, boiled together; then well-drained, and put into the soup with the peas and asparagus. It must be very thick with vegetables.

SUMMER SOUP.—Take a large neck of mutton, and hack it so as nearly to cut it apart, but not quite. Allow a small quart of water to each pound of meat, and sprinkle on a table-spoonful of salt and a very little black pepper. Put it into a soup-pot, and boil it *slowly* (skimming it well) till the meat is reduced to rags. Then strain the liquid, return it to the soup-pot, and carefully remove all the fat from the surface. Have ready half a dozen small turnips sliced thin, two young onions sliced, a table-spoonful of sweet-marjoram leaves picked from the stalks, and a quart of shelled Lima beans. Put in the vegetables, and boil them in the soup till they are thoroughly done. You may add to them two table-spoonfuls of green nasturtian seeds, either fresh or pickled. Put in also some little dumplings, (made of flour and butter,) about ten minutes before the soup is done.

Instead of Lima beans, you may divide a cauliflower or two broccolis into sprigs, and boil them in the soup with the other vegetables.

This soup may be made of a shoulder of mutton, cut into pieces and the bones cracked.

AUTUMN SOUP.—Begin this soup as early in the day as possible. Take six pounds of the lean of fine fresh beef; cut it into small pieces; sprinkle it with a tea-spoonful of salt, (not more); put it into a soup-pot, and pour on six quarts of water. The hock of a cold ham will greatly improve it. Set it over a moderate fire, and let it boil slowly. After it comes to a boil skim it well. Have ready a quarter of a peck of ochras cut into very thin round slices, and a quarter of a peck of tomatoes cut into pieces; also a quart of shelled Lima beans. Season them with pepper. Put them in; and after the whole has boiled three hours *at least*, take six ears of young Indian corn, and having grated off all the grain, add them, to the soup and boil it an hour longer. Before you serve up the soup remove from it all the bits of meat, which, if the soup is sufficiently cooked, will be reduced to shreds.

You may put in with the ochras and tomatoes one or two sliced onions. The soup, when done, should be as thick as a jelly.

Ochras for soup may be kept all winter, by tying them separately to a line stretched high across the store-room.

WINTER SOUP.—The day before you make the soup, get a fore-leg or shin of beef. Have the bone sawed through in several places, and the meat notched or scored down to the bone. This will cause the juice or essence to come out more freely, when cooked. Rub it slightly with salt; cover it, and set it away. Next morning, early as possible, as soon as the fire is well made up, put the beef into a large soup-pot, allowing to each pound a small quart of water. Then taste the water, and if the salt that has been rubbed on the meat is not sufficient, add a very little more. Throw in also a tea-spoonful of whole pepper-corns; and you may add half a dozen blades of mace. Let it simmer slowly till it comes to a boil; then skim it well. After it boils, you may quicken the fire. At nine o'clock put in a large head of cabbage cut fine as for cold-slaw; a dozen carrots sliced; the leaves stripped from a bunch of sweet-marjoram; and the leaves of a sprig of parsley minced fine. An hour afterwards, add six turnips, and three potatoes, all cut into four or eight pieces. Also two onions, which will be better if previously roasted brown, and then sliced. Keep the soup boiling steadily, but not hard, unless the dinner hour is very early. For a late dinner, there will be time to boil it slowly all the while; and all soups are the better for long and slow boiling. See that it is well skimmed, so that, when done, there will be not a particle of fat or scum on the surface. At dinner-time take it up with a large ladle, and transfer it to a tureen. In doing so, carefully avoid the shreds of meat and bone. Leave them all in the bottom of the pot, pressing them down with the ladle. A mass of shreds in the tureen or soup-plate looks slovenly and disgusting, and should never be seen at the table; also, they absorb too much of the liquid. Let the vegetables remain in the soup when it is served up, but pick out every shred of meat or bone that may be found in the tureen when ready to go to table.

In very cold weather, what is left of this soup will keep till the second day; when it must be simmered again over the fire, till it just comes to a boil. Put it away in a tin or stone vessel. The lead which is used in glazing earthen jars frequently communicates its poison to liquids that are kept in them.

RABBIT SOUP.—Begin this soup six hours before dinner. Cut up three large, but young and tender rabbits, or four small ones, (scoring the backs,) and dredge them with flour. Slice six mild onions, and season them with half a grated nutmeg; or more, if you like it. Put some fresh butter into a hot frying pan, (you may substitute for the butter some cold roast-veal gravy that has been carefully cleared from the fat,) place it over the fire, and when it boils, put in the rabbits and onions, and fry them a light brown. Then transfer the whole to a soup-pot; season it with a very small tea-spoonful of salt, a tea-spoonful of whole pepper, a large tea-spoonful of sweet-marjoram leaves stripped from the stalks, and four or five blades of mace, adding three large carrots in slices. Pour on, slowly, four quarts of hot water from a kettle already boiling hard. Cover the soup-pot, and let it simmer slowly (skimming it well) till the meat of the rabbits is reduced to shreds, and drops from the bones, which will not be in less than five hours, if boiled as gently as it ought. When quite done, strain the soup into a tureen. Have ready the grated yolks of six hard boiled eggs, and stir them into the soup immediately after it is strained, and while it is very hot. Add, also, some bread cut into dice or small squares, and fried brown in fresh butter. Or substitute for the fried bread, buttered toast, with all the crust removed, and cut into very small bits or mouthfuls.

Hare soup may be made in this manner. It is also an excellent way of disposing of old fowls. A similar soup may be made of fresh-killed venison.

For hare or venison soup, add, (after straining it,) about half an hour before you take it up, two glasses of sherry or Madeira, and a lemon sliced thin.

CHICKEN SOUP.—Cut up two large fine fowls, as if carving them for the table, and wash the pieces in cold water. Take half a dozen thin slices of cold ham, and lay them in a soup-pot, mixed among the pieces of chicken. Season them with a very little cayenne, a little nutmeg, and a few blades of mace, but no salt, as the ham will make it salt enough. Add a head of celery, split and cut into long bits, a quarter of a pound of butter, divided in two, and rolled in flour. Pour on three quarts of milk. Set the soup-pot over the fire, and let it boil rather slowly, skimming it well. When it has boiled an hour, put in some small round dumplings, made of half a pound of flour mixed with a quarter of a pound of butter; divide this dough into equal portions, and roll them in your hands into little balls about the size of a large hickory nut. The soup must boil till the flesh of the fowls is loose on the bones, but not till it drops off. Stir in, at the last, the beaten yolks of three or four eggs; and let the soup remain about five minutes longer over the fire. Then take it up. Cut off from the bones the flesh of the fowls, and divide it into mouthfuls. Cut up the slices of ham in the same manner. Mince the livers and gizzards. Put the bits of fowl and ham in the bottom of a large tureen, and pour the soup upon it.

This soup will be found excellent, and may be made of large old fowls, that cannot be cooked in any other way. If they are so old that when the soup is finished they still continue tough, remove them entirely, and do not serve them up in it.

Similar soup may be made of a large old turkey. Also of four rabbits.

DUCK SOUP.—Half roast a pair of fine large tame ducks; keeping them half an hour at the fire, and saving the gravy, the fat of which must be carefully skimmed off. Then cut them up; season them with black pepper; and put them into a soup-pot with four or five small onions sliced thin, a small bunch of sage, a thin slice of cold ham cut into pieces, a grated nutmeg, and the yellow rind of a lemon pared thin, and cut into bits. Add the gravy of the ducks. Pour on, slowly, three quarts of boiling water from a kettle. Cover the soup-pot, and set it over a moderate fire. Simmer it slowly (skimming it well) for about four hours, or till the flesh of the ducks is dissolved into small shreds. When done, strain it through a sieve into a tureen over a quart of young green peas, that have been boiled by themselves. If peas are not in season, substitute half a dozen hard boiled eggs cut into round slices, white and yolk together.

If wild ducks are used for soup, three or four will be required for the above quantity. Before you put them on the spit to roast, place a large carrot in the body of each duck, to remove the sedgy or fishy taste. This taste will be all absorbed by the carrot, which, of course, must be thrown away.

PIGEON SOUP may be made as above. It will require one dozen tame pigeons, or two dozen wild ones.

Wild pigeons may be made very fat by catching them alive in nets, at the season when they abound; clipping their wings to prevent their flying away; putting them into a field where there is a stream of water convenient for them to drink, or into a large yard; and feeding them twice a day with corn. When fattened in this manner, they will be found profitable articles for sale; the objection to wild pigeons being that they are usually so poor and lean.

FINE CLAM SOUP.—Take half a hundred or more small sand clams, and put them into a pot of hard-boiling water. Boil them about a quarter of an hour, or till all the shells have opened wide. Then take them out, and having removed them from the shells, chop them small and put them with their liquor into a pitcher. Strain a pint of the liquor into a bowl, and reserve it for the soup. Put the clams into a soup-pot, with a gallon of water, and a half pint of the liquor; a dozen whole pepper-corns, half a dozen blades of mace; but no salt, as the clam-liquor will be salt enough; add a pint of grated bread-crumbs, and the crusts of the bread cut very small; also a tea-spoonful of sweet-marjoram leaves. Let the soup boil two hours. Then add a quarter of a pound of fresh butter, divided into half a dozen pieces, and each piece rolled slightly in flour. Boil it half an hour longer, and then about five minutes before you take up the soup, stir in the beaten yolks of three eggs.

As the flavour will be all boiled out of the chopped clams, it will be best to leave them in the bottom of the soup-pot, and not serve them up in the tureen. Press them down with a broad wooden ladle, so as to get as much liquor out of them as possible, while you are taking up the soup.

This soup will be better still, if made with milk instead of water; milk being an improvement to all fish-soups.

EXCELLENT CLAM SOUP.—Take forty or fifty clams, and wash and scrub the outsides of the shells till they are perfectly clean. Then put them into a pot with just sufficient water to keep them from burning. The water must boil hard when you put in the clams. In about a quarter of an hour the shells will open, and the liquor run out and mix with the water, which must be saved for the soup, and strained into a soup-pot, after the clams are taken out. Extract the clams from their shells, and cut them up small. Then put them into the soup-pot, adding a minced onion, a saucer of finely chopped celery, or a table-spoonful of celery seed, and a dozen blades of mace, with a dozen whole pepper-corns. No salt, as the clam-liquor will be quite salt enough. If the liquid is not in sufficient quantity to fill a large tureen, add some milk. Thicken the soup with two large table-spoonfuls of fresh butter rolled in flour. Let it boil a quarter of an hour or twenty minutes. Just before you take it from the fire, stir in, gradually, the beaten yolks of five eggs; and then take up the soup, and pour it into a tureen, the bottom of which is covered with toasted bread, cut into square dice about an inch in size.

FRENCH WHITE SOUP.—Boil a knuckle of veal and four calves' feet in five quarts of water, with three onions sliced, a bunch of sweet herbs, four heads of white celery cut small, a table-spoonful of whole pepper, and a *small* tea-spoonful of salt, adding five or six large blades of mace. Let it boil very slowly, till the meat is in rags and has dropped from the bone, and till the gristle has quite dissolved. Skim it well while boiling. When done, strain it through a sieve into a tureen, or a deep white-ware pan. Next day, take off all the fat, and put the jelly (for such it ought to be) into a clean soup-pot with two ounces of vermicelli, and set it over the fire. When the vermicelli is dissolved, stir in, gradually, a pint of thick cream, while the soup is quite hot; but do not let it come to a boil after the cream is in, lest it should curdle. Cut up one or two French rolls in the bottom of a tureen, pour in the soup, and send it to table.

COCOA-NUT SOUP.—Take eight calves' feet (two sets) that have been scalded and scraped, but not skinned; and put them into a soup-kettle with six or seven blades of mace, and the yellow rind of a lemon pared thin. Pour on a gallon of water; cover the kettle, and let it boil very slowly (skimming it well) till the flesh is reduced to rags and has dropped entirely from the bones. Then strain it into a broad white-ware pan, and set it away to get cold. When it has congealed, scrape off the fat and sediment, cut up the cake of jelly, (or stock,) and put it into a clean porcelain or enamelled kettle. Have ready half a pound of very finely grated cocoa-nut. Mix it with a pint of cream. If you cannot obtain cream, take rich unskimmed milk, and add to it three ounces of the best fresh butter divided into three parts, each bit rolled in arrow-root or rice-flour. Mix it, gradually, with the cocoa-nut, and add it to the calves-feet-stock in the kettle, seasoned with half a grated nutmeg. Set it over the fire, and boil it, slowly, about a quarter of an hour; stirring it well. Then transfer it to a tureen, and serve it up. Have ready small French rolls, or light milk biscuit to eat with it; also powdered sugar in case any of the company should wish to sweeten it.

ALMOND SOUP is made in the above manner, substituting pounded almonds for the grated cocoa-nut. You must have half a pound of shelled sweet almonds, mixed with two ounces of shelled bitter almonds. After blanching them in hot water, they must be pounded to a smooth paste (one at a time) in a marble mortar; adding frequently a little rose-water to prevent their oiling, and becoming heavy. Or you may use peach-water for this purpose; in which case omit the bitter almonds, as the peach water will give the desired flavour. When the pounded almonds are ready, mix them with the other ingredients, as above.

The calves' feet for these soups should be boiled either very early in the morning, or the day before.

SOUP-MEAT.—To make the soup *very good*, the meat (of which there should be a large proportion, rather more than a pound to a quart of water) must remain in, till it drops entirely from the bones and is boiled to rags. But none of these fragments and shreds should be found in the tureen when the soup is sent to table. They should all be kept at the bottom of the pot, pressing down the ladle hard upon them when you are dipping out the soup. If any are seen in the soup after it is taken up, let them be carefully removed with a spoon. To send the soup to table with bits of bone and shreds of meat in it, is a slovenly, disgusting, and vulgar practice, and should be strictly forbidden; as some indifferent cooks will do so to save themselves the trouble of removing it. A mass of shreds left at the bottom of the tureen, absorbs so much of the liquid as to diminish the quantity of the soup; and if eaten is very unwholesome, all the nourishment being boiled out of it.

Mutton, however, need not be boiled to pieces in the soup, which will have sufficient strength if the meat is left whole. A piece of loin of mutton, that has been cooked in soup, is to many persons very palatable. It is well worth sending to table.

SAUCE FOR MUTTON THAT HAS BEEN BOILED IN SOUP.—Mutton that has been boiled in soup is very generally liked, particularly the loin. Take two large boiled onions; cut them up, and put them into a saucepan with a piece of fresh butter, slightly rolled in flour; a table-spoonful of mustard, (French or tarragon mustard will be best); a very little salt and cayenne; and some pickled cucumbers, chopped small; green nasturtian seeds will be still better than cucumbers. Put all these ingredients into a small saucepan, and add to them a little of the soup. Set the sauce over the fire, and when it has come to a boil, take it off, and keep it warm till the meat goes to table; then send it in a sauce-boat.

SUBSTITUTES FOR CAPER-SAUCE.—Take some pickled string-beans, or pickled cucumbers, or gherkins; cut them into small bits, and put them thickly into a sauce-tureen of melted butter, adding a spoonful of vinegar; or, what is still better, the juice of a lemon Serve it up as sauce to boiled mutton.

A still better substitute will be found in nasturtian seeds plucked from the stems, and pickled by simply putting them (when green, but full-grown) into a jar of cider-vinegar. Add a few table-spoonfuls of these to the melted butter before it goes to table. Their flavour is superior to that of capers.

FISH, ETC.

FRESH SALMON STEWED. — Having cleaned and washed the fish, cut it into round slices or fillets, rather more than an inch in thickness. Lay them in a large dish; sprinkling a very little salt evenly over the slices; and in half an hour turn them on the other side. Let them rest another half hour; then wash, drain, and wipe them dry with a clean towel. Spread some of the best fresh butter thickly over the strainer of a large fish-kettle; and lay the pieces of salmon upon it. Cover them nearly all over with very thin slices of fresh lemon, from which the seeds have been removed. Intersperse among the lemon a few slices of shalots, or very small mild onions; a few sprigs of parsley and some whole pepper-corns. Set the kettle over a large bed of live coals; and spread very hot ashes thickly over the lid; which must be previously well-heated on the *inside* by standing it up before the fire. The heat should be regularly kept up, while the fish is stewing, both above and below it. It will require an hour to cook thoroughly. When dishing it, remove the sliced lemon, shalots, parsley, &c., leaving them in the bottom of the kettle. Put a cover over the fish, and set the dish that contains it over a large vessel of hot water, while you are preparing the sauce. For this sauce, mix thoroughly a quarter of a pound of fresh butter with a table-spoonful of flour. Put it into a quart tin vessel with a lid, and add a table-spoonful of water, and the seasoning that was left in the bottom of the fish-kettle. Cover the vessel closely, and set it in a larger sauce-pan or pot of boiling water. Shake it about over the fire till it comes to a boil. If you *set it down* on hot coals the butter will oil. When it has boiled, remove the lemon, onion, &c.; pour the sauce into a sauce-boat, and send it to table with the stewed fish, garnished with sprigs of curled parsley.

This is a French mode of cooking salmon. Fresh cod, or halibut, may be stewed in the same manner.

ROASTED SALMON. — Take a large piece of fine fresh salmon, cut from the middle of the fish, well cleaned and carefully scaled. Wipe it dry in a clean coarse cloth. Then dredge it with flour, put it on the spit, and place it before a clear bright fire. Baste it with fresh butter, and roast it well; seeing that it is thoroughly done to the bone. Serve it up plain; garnishing the dish with slices of lemon, as many persons like a little lemon-juice with salmon. This mode of cooking salmon will be found excellent. A small one or a salmon-trout may be roasted whole.

BAKED SALMON. — A small salmon may be baked whole. Stuff it with force-meat made of bread-crumbs; chopped oysters, or minced lobster; butter; cayenne; a little salt, and powdered mace, — all mixed well, and moistened with beaten yolk of egg. Bend the salmon round, and put the tail into the mouth, fastening it with a skewer. Put it into a large deep dish; lay bits of butter on it at small intervals; and set it into the oven. While baking, look at it occasionally, and baste it with the butter. When one side is well browned, turn it carefully in the dish, and add more butter. Bake it till the other side is well browned. Then transfer it to another dish with the gravy that is about it, and send it to table.

If you bake salmon in slices, reserve the forcemeat for the outside. Dip each slice first in beaten yolk of egg, and then in the forcemeat, till it is well coated. If in one large piece, cover it in the same manner thickly with the seasoning.

The usual sauce for baked salmon is melted butter, flavoured with the juice of a lemon, and a glass of port wine, stirred in just before the butter is taken from the fire. Serve it up in a sauce-boat.

BOILED TURBOT OR SHEEP'S-HEAD FISH.—Having cleaned and washed the fish, soak it an hour or two in salt and water to draw off the slime. Then let it lie half an hour or more in cold water. Afterwards drain, and wipe it dry. Score the back deeply with a knife. The whiteness of the fish will be much improved by rubbing it over with a cut lemon. The fish-kettle must be large, and nicely clean. Lay the fish with its back downward, on the strainer of the kettle. Cover it well with cold water, (milk and water in equal portions will be better still,) and add a small table-spoonful of salt. Do not let it come to a boil too fast, and skim it carefully. When the scum has ceased to rise, diminish the heat under the kettle, and let it simmer for about half an hour or more; not allowing it to boil hard. When the fish is done, take it up carefully with a fish-slice; and having prepared the sauce, pour it over the fish and send it to table hot.

For the sauce mix together very smoothly, with a broad bladed knife, a quarter of a pound of fresh butter, two tea-spoonfuls of flour. Put them into a clean sauce-pan, and hold it over the fire, and stir them till melted. Then add a large salt-spoonful of powdered mace, and as much cayenne as will lie on a sixpence. It will be much improved by the addition of some boiled lobster, chopped small. When the sauce has simmered two or three minutes, add very gradually, half a pint of rich cream, and let it come almost to a boil, stirring all the time. After the fish is taken up, pour the sauce over it hot. Or you may send it to table in a sauce-boat. In this case ornament the fish with the coral of the lobster put on in a handsome figure.

Another way of dressing this fish is, after it has been boiled to set it on ice to get cold; and then, having carefully removed the bones, cut the flesh into small squares, put it into a stew-pan, and having mixed the above sauce, add it to the fish, and let it stew slowly in the sauce; but do not let it come to a boil. When thoroughly hot, take it up, and send it to table in a deep dish.

BAKED TURBOT OR SHEEP'S-HEAD FISH.—Having cleaned the fish, soak it an hour or two in salt and water, and afterwards wash it well through two or three fresh waters. Then dry it in a clean towel. Score it deeply, across the back; and then lay it in a deep white baking-dish. Mix together a large tea-spoonful of powdered mace and nutmeg; add a salt-spoon of cayenne; a few sprigs of sweet-marjoram and sweet basil finely minced; two large table-spoonfuls of fresh butter; and two table-spoonfuls of grated bread-crumbs. Stir this mixture into a pint of rich cream.

Pour this marinade over the fish, cover it, and let it stand half an hour. Then bake it in the marinade; and send it hot to table.

If the fish is too large to be baked whole, cut it into fillets; extracting the bone.

Salmon-trout may be baked in this manner.

SEA BASS WITH TOMATOES.—Take three large fine sea-bass, or black-fish. Cut off their heads and tails, and fry the fish in plenty of lard till about half done. Have ready a pint of tomatoes, that have been pickled cold in vinegar flavoured with a muslin bag of mixed spices. Drain the tomatoes well from the vinegar; skin them, and mash them in a pan; dredging them with about as much flour as would fill a large table-spoon heaped up. Pour the mixture over the fish while in the frying pan; and continue frying till they are thoroughly done.

Cutlets of halibut may be fried in this manner with tomatoes: also, any other pan-fish.

Beef-steaks or lamb-chops are excellent fried thus with tomatoes.

BAKED SALMON-TROUT.—Having cleaned the fish, and laid it two hours in weak salt and water, dry it in a cloth, and then rub both the inside and outside with a seasoning of cayenne pepper, powdered mace, nutmeg, and a little salt mixed well together. Then lay it in a deep baking pan, turn the tail round into the mouth, and stick bits of fresh butter thickly over the fish. Put it into an oven, and bake it well; basting it frequently with the liquid that will soon surround it. When you suppose it to be nearly done, try it by sticking down to the back-bone a thin-bladed knife. When you find that the flesh separates immediately from the bone, it is done sufficiently. Serve it up with lobster-sauce.

Any large fresh fish may be baked in this way.

CREAM TROUT.—Having prepared the trout very nicely, and cut off the heads and tails, put the fish into boiling water that has been slightly salted, and simmer them for five minutes. Then take them out, and lay them to drain. Put them into a stew-pan, and season them well with powdered mace, nutmeg, and a little cayenne, all mixed together. Put in as much rich cream as will cover the fish, adding some bits of the fresh yellow rind of a small lemon. Keep the pan covered, and let the fish stew for about ten minutes after it has begun to simmer. Then dish the fish, and keep them hot till you have finished the sauce. Mix, very smoothly, a small tea-spoonful of arrow-root with a little milk, and stir it into the cream. Then add the juice of the lemon. Pour the sauce over the fish, and then send them to table.

Turbot or sheep's-head fish may be dressed as above; of course it will require a large proportion of seasoning, &c., and longer time to cook.

Carp is very nice stewed in this manner.

STEWED COD-FISH.—Take a fine *fresh* cod, and cut into slices an inch thick, separated from the bones. Lay the pieces of fish in the bottom of a stew-pan: season them with a grated nutmeg; half a dozen blades of mace; a salt-spoonful of cayenne pepper, and a small saucer-full of chopped celery, or a bunch of sweet herbs tied together. Pour on half a pint of oyster liquor diluted with two wine glasses or a jill of water, and the juice of a lemon. Cover it close, and let it stew gently till the fish is almost done, shaking the pan frequently. Then take a piece of fresh butter the size of an egg; roll it in flour, and add it to the stew. Also, put in two dozen large fine oysters, with what liquor there is about them. Cover it again; quicken the fire a little, and let the whole continue to stew five minutes longer. Before you send it to table remove the bunch of sweet herbs.

Rock-fish may be stewed in this manner. Fresh salmon also.

FRIED COD-FISH.—Take the middle or tail part of a fresh cod-fish, and cut it into slices not quite an inch thick, first removing the skin. Season them with a little salt and cayenne pepper. Have ready in one dish some beaten yolk of egg, and in another some grated bread-crumbs. Dip each slice of fish twice into the egg, and then twice into the crumbs. Fry them in fresh butter, and serve them up with the gravy about them.

Halibut may be fried as above.

STEWED HALIBUT.—Cut the fish into pieces about four inches square, of course omitting the bone. Season it very slightly with salt, and let it rest for half an hour. Then take it out of the salt, put it into a large deep dish, and strew over it a mixture of cayenne pepper, ground white ginger, and grated nutmeg. Lay among it some small bits of fresh butter rolled in grated cracker. Add half a pint of vinegar, (tarragon vinegar if you have it.) Place the dish in a slow oven, and let the halibut cook till thoroughly done, basting it very *frequently* with the liquid. When nearly done, add a large table-spoonful or more of capers, or pickled nasturtians.

STEWED ROCK-FISH.—Take a large rock-fish, and cut it in slices near an inch thick. Sprinkle it *very slightly* with salt, and let it remain for half an hour. Slice very thin a dozen large onions. Put them into a stew-pan with a quarter of a pound of fresh butter, cut into bits. Set them over a slow fire, and stir them continually till they are quite soft, taking care not to let them become brown. Then put in the sliced fish in layers; seasoning each layer with a mixture of white ground ginger, cayenne pepper, and grated nutmeg; add some chopped parsley, and some bits of butter rolled in flour. Pour in a pint of water, and, if you choose, a small wine-glass of vinegar, (tarragon vinegar will be best.[1]) Set it over a good fire and let it cook about an hour. When done, take out the fish carefully, to avoid breaking the slices. Lay it in a deep dish that has been made hot, and cover it immediately. Have ready the beaten yolks of two eggs. Stir them into the gravy. Give it one boil up; and then either pour it over the fish, or serve it up in a sauce-boat.

Halibut, fresh cod, or any other large fish may be stewed in this manner.

TO KEEP A SHAD WITHOUT CORNING.—By the following process, (which we can highly recommend from experience,) a shad may be kept twenty-four hours, or indeed longer, so as to be perfectly fresh in taste and appearance. For instance, if brought *fresh* from market on Saturday morning, it may be broiled for

[1] To make this vinegar,—half fill a bottle with tarragon leaves, and fill it quite up with the best cider vinegar. Cork it tightly, and do not remove the tarragon, but let it remain always at the bottom. The flavour is very fine.

breakfast on Sunday, and will seem like a fresh shad just from the water. Immediately on bringing it in, let it be scaled, cleaned, washed, split, and wiped dry; cutting off the head and tail. Spread the shad open on a large flat dish. Mix well together in a cup, a heaped table-spoonful of brown sugar; a heaped tea-spoonful of cayenne pepper, and a tea-spoonful of fine salt; and then rub the mixture, thoroughly and evenly, all over the inside of the fish; which, of course, must be spread with the skin or outside downwards. Cover it closely with a large tin cover or with another dish, and set it immediately on ice or in a very cold place, and let it rest till next morning, or till it is wanted for cooking. Immediately before you put it on the gridiron, take a clean towel and carefully wipe off the whole of the seasoning, not letting a particle of it remain round the edges, or anywhere else. Then put the shad on a previously heated gridiron, over hot coals, and broil it well. Butter it, and send it hot to table, where every one can season it again, according to their taste. If these directions are *exactly* followed, no one, without being told, could possibly guess that the shad was not fresh from market that morning.

Any fresh fish intended for splitting and broiling may be kept till next day in this manner, which will be found very superior to what is called corning.

EXCELLENT STEWED OYSTERS.—Take fifty fine large fresh oysters, and strain the liquor from them into a saucepan. Season it with equal portions of cayenne, black pepper, and salt, all mixed together in a small tea-spoon, and add half a dozen blades of mace. Set it over the fire, and let it come to a hard boil, skimming it well. Mix together in a pan or bowl, a quarter of a pound of fresh butter and a table-spoonful and a half (not more) of flour. Beat and stir the butter and flour till it is quite smooth, and free from lumps. Having taken the oyster-liquor from the fire, stir into it the beaten butter and flour. Set the sauce-pan again over the fire, and give it another boil up. Then put in the oysters, and when they come to a hard boil take them off. Have ready in the bottom of a deep dish, two nice slices of toasted bread with all the crust trimmed off. Cut the toast into dice or small squares. Pour the oysters and their gravy hot into the dish. Cover them closely, and send them to table. There is no better way of stewing oysters than this, when you cannot conveniently do them with cream. If you *have* cream, (which for this purpose must be very rich,) add half a pint of it to the gravy, and season it with grated nutmeg. The cream must be stirred in at the last, just before the oysters are taken from the fire.

FRENCH STEWED OYSTERS.—Take a hundred large fine oysters. Set them over the fire in their own liquor, (skimming them well,) and when they begin to simmer take them out with a perforated ladle, and throw them directly into a pan of cold water to plump them. When they are quite cold, place them in a sieve, and drain them well. Having saved their liquor, add to it a quarter of a pound of fresh butter divided into four pieces, (each piece rolled in flour,) a dozen blades of mace, a powdered nutmeg, and a small salt-spoon of cayenne. Set this mixture over the fire, and stir it till the butter and flour is well mixed all through. Then put in the oysters, and as soon as they have come to a boil, take off the sauce-pan, and stir in immediately the beaten yolks of three eggs. Serve them up hot.

OYSTER LOAVES.—Take some tall fresh rolls, or small loaves. Cut nicely a round or oval hole in the top of each, saving the pieces that come off. Then carefully scoop out the crumb from the inside, leaving the crust standing. Have ready a sufficient quantity of large fresh oysters. Put the oysters with one-fourth of their liquor into a stew-pan; adding the bread-crumbs; a large piece of fresh butter; some powdered nutmeg; and a few blades of mace. Stew them about ten minutes. Then stir in two or three large table-spoonfuls of cream; take them off just as they are coming to a boil. If cooked too long the oysters will become tough and shrivelled, and the cream will curdle. Fill the inside of your scooped loaves with the oysters, reserving as many large oysters as you have loaves. Place the bit of upper-crust carefully on the top of each, so as to cover the whole. Arrange them on a dish, and lay on each lid one of the large oysters kept out for the purpose. These ornamental oysters must be well drained from any liquid that is about them.

OYSTER OMELET.—Having strained the liquor from twenty-five oysters of the largest size, mince them small; omitting the hard part or gristle. If you cannot get large oysters, you should have forty or fifty small ones. Break into a shallow pan six, seven, or eight eggs, according to the quantity of minced oysters. Omit half the whites, and, (having beaten the eggs till very light, thick, and smooth,) mix the oysters gradually into them, adding a little cayenne pepper, and some powdered nutmeg. Put three ounces or more of the best fresh butter into a small frying-pan, if you have no pan especially for omelets. Place it over a clear fire, and when the butter (which should be previously cut up) has come to a boil, put in the omelet-mixture; stir it till it begin to set; and fry it a light brown, lifting the edge several times by slipping a knife under it, and taking care not to cook it too much or it will shrivel and become tough. When done, clap a large hot plate or dish on the top of the omelet, and turn it quickly and carefully out of the pan. Fold it over; and serve it up immediately. It is a fine breakfast dish. This quantity will make one large or two small omelets.

Clam omelets may be made as above.

An omelet-pan should be smaller than a common frying-pan, and lined with tin. In a large pan the omelet will spread too much, and become thin like a pan-cake.

Never turn an omelet while frying, as that will make it heavy and tough. When done, brown it by holding a red-hot shovel or salamander close above the top.

Excellent omelets may be made of cold boiled ham, or smoked tongue; grated or minced small, mixed with a sufficiency of beaten eggs, and fried in butter.

ANCHOVY TOAST.—Cut four slices of bread and toast them; having first pared off the crust. Butter the toast on both sides. Wash, scrape, and chop ten anchovies and put them thickly between the slices of toast. Beat the yolks of four eggs, and then mix them with half a pint of cream. Put the mixture into a sauce-pan, and set it over the fire to simmer till thick; but do not allow it to boil. Stir it well, lest it should curdle. When it is *near* boiling, take it off, and pour it hot over the toast.

Tongue toast may be made in this way.

OYSTER TOAST may be made as above; substituting minced oysters for the anchovy; seasoning them with cayenne; and boiling a few blades of mace with the egg and cream.

BROILED OYSTERS.—Take the largest and finest oysters. See that your gridiron is very clean. Rub the bars with fresh butter, and set it over a clear steady fire, entirely clear from smoke; or on a bed of bright hot wood coals. Place the oysters on the gridiron, and when done on one side, take a fork and turn them on the other; being careful not to let them burn. Put some fresh butter in the bottom of a dish. Lay the oysters on it, and season them slightly with pepper. Send them to table hot.

FRENCH OYSTER PIE.—Having buttered the inside of a deep dish, line it with puff-paste rolled out rather thick, and prepare another sheet of paste for the lid. Put a clean towel into the dish (folded so as to support the lid) and then put on the lid; set it into the oven, and bake the paste well. When done, remove the lid, and take out the folded towel. While the paste is baking, prepare the oysters. Having picked off carefully any bits of shell that may be found about them, lay them in a sieve and drain off the liquor into a pan. Put the oysters into a skillet or stew-pan, with barely enough of the liquor to keep them from burning. Season them with whole pepper; blades of mace; some grated nutmeg; and some grated lemon-peel, (the yellow rind only,) and a little finely minced celery. Then add a large portion of fresh butter, divided into bits, and very slightly dredged with flour. Let the oysters simmer over the fire, but do not allow them to come to a boil, as that will shrivel them. Next beat the yolks only, of three, four, or five eggs, (in proportion to the size of the pie,) and stir the beaten egg into the stew a few minutes before you take it from the fire. Keep it warm till the paste is baked. Then carefully remove the lid of the pie; and replace it, after you have filled the dish with the oysters and gravy.

The lid of the pie may be ornamented with a wreath of leaves cut out of paste, and put on before baking. In the centre, place a paste-knot or flower.

Oyster pies are generally eaten warm; but they are very good cold.

CLAM PIE.—Take a sufficient number of clams to fill a large pie-dish when opened. Make a nice paste in the proportion of a pound of fresh butter to two quarts of flour. Paste for shell-fish, or meat, or chicken pies should be rolled out double the thickness of that intended for fruit pies. Line the sides and bottom of your pie-dish with paste. Then cover the bottom with a thin beef-steak, divested of bone and fat. Put in the clams, and season them with mace, nutmeg, and a few whole pepper-corns. No salt. Add a spoonful of butter rolled in flour, and some hard-boiled yolks of eggs crumbled fine. Then put in enough of the clam-liquor to make sufficient gravy. Put on the lid of the pie, (which like the bottom crust should be rolled out thick,) notch it handsomely, and bake it well. It should be eaten warm.

CLAM FRITTERS.—Put a sufficient quantity of clams into a pot of boiling water. The small sand-clams will be best. When the shells open wide, take them out, extract the clams from the shells, and put them into a stew-pan. Strain their liquor, and pour about half of it over the clams; adding a little black pepper. They will require no salt. Let them stew, slowly, for half an hour; then take them out; drain off all the liquor; and mince the clams as fine as possible, omitting the hardest parts. You should have as many clams as will make a large pint when minced. Make a batter of seven eggs, beaten till very thick and light; and then mixed gradually with a quart of milk, and a pint of sifted flour, stirred in by degrees, and made perfectly smooth and free from lumps. Then, gradually, mix the minced clams with the batter, and stir the whole very hard. Have ready in a frying pan over the fire a sufficiency of boiling lard. Put in, with a spoon, the batter so as to form fritters, and fry them light brown. Drain them well when done, and serve them up hot.

Oyster fritters may be made as above; except that the oysters must be minced raw, and mixed into the batter without having been stewed.

LOBSTER PATTIES.—Make some puff-paste, and spread it on very deep patty-pans. Bake it empty. Having boiled well two or three fine lobsters, extract all their meat, and mince it very small, mixing it with the coral smoothly mashed, and some yolk of hard-boiled egg, grated. Season it with a little salt; some cayenne; and some powdered mace or nutmeg; adding a little yellow lemon-rind grated. Moisten the mixture well with cream, or fresh butter, or salad oil. Put it into a stew-pan; add a very little water, and let it stew till it just comes to a boil. Take it off the fire, and the patties being baked, remove them from the tin-pans, place them on a large dish, and fill them up to the top with the mixture.

Similar patties may be made of prawns, or crabs.

A SEA-COAST PIE.—Having boiled a sufficient number of crabs or lobsters, extract all the meat from the shells, and cut it into mouthfuls. Have ready some fine large oysters drained from the liquor. Cover the bottom and sides of a deep dish with puff-paste; and put in a thick layer of crab or lobster, seasoned with a little cayenne pepper, and a little grated lemon-peel; and mixed with some hard-boiled yolk of egg, crumbled fine, and moistened with fresh butter. Next, put a close layer of oysters, seasoned with pounded mace and grated nutmeg. Lay some bits of butter rolled in flour on the top of the layer. Proceed in this manner with alternate layers of crab or lobster, and of oysters, till the dish is nearly full. Then pour in, at the last, a tea-cupfull of more of the oyster liquor, with an equal quantity of rich cream. Have ready a thick lid of puff-paste. Put it on the pie; pressing the edges closely so as to unite them all round; and notch them handsomely. Make a wreath of leaves cut out of paste, and a flower or knot for the centre; place them on the top-crust; and bake the pie well. While it is baking, prepare some balls made of chopped oysters; grated bread-crumbs; powdered nutmeg, or mace; and grated lemon-peel; with a little beaten yolk of egg to bind together the other ingredients. Having fried these balls in butter, drain them, and when the pie is baked, lay a circle of them round the top; between the border of paste-leaves and the centre-knot.

This pie will be found so fine that it ought to be baked in a dish which will contain a large quantity.

LOBSTER RISSOLES.—Extract the meat of a boiled lobster; mince it as fine as possible; mix with it the coral pounded smooth, and some yolks of hard-boiled eggs pounded also. Season it with cayenne pepper, powdered mace, and a very little salt. Make a batter of beaten egg, milk, and flour. To each egg allow two large table-spoonfuls of milk, and a large tea-spoonful of flour. Beat the batter well, and then mix the lobster with it gradually, till it is stiff enough to make into oval balls, about the size of a large plum. Fry them in the best salad oil, and serve them up either warm or cold.

Similar rissoles may be made of raw oysters minced fine; or of boiled clams. These should be fried in lard.

Very young Indian corn, grated from the cob, prepared in the above manner, made into balls, and fried in fresh butter, is excellent. Previous to grating it is best to boil the ears of corn.

TO DRESS A TURTLE.—The turtle should be taken out of water, and killed over night in winter, and early in the morning in summer. Hang it up by the hind fins, and before it has had time to draw in its neck, cut off its head with a very sharp knife, and leave the turtle suspended. It should bleed two or three hours or more, before you begin to cut it up. Then lay it on its back upon a table: have at hand several vessels of cold water, in which to throw the most important parts as you separate them; also a large boiler of hot water. Take off the fins at the joint, and lay them by themselves in cold water; next divide the back-shell from the under-shell. The upper part of the turtle is called the calipash—the under part the calipee. In cutting open the turtle, be very careful not to break the gall, which should be taken out and thrown away; if broken, its bitterness will spoil all around it. Take out the entrails, and throw them into a tub of cold water. When well washed, open them from end to end with a small penknife, scrape off the inside skin, and, to cleanse them thoroughly, draw them several times through a woollen cloth. Wash, also, the liver, lungs, heart, kidneys, &c., and lay them in cold water; the liver in a pan by itself. If there are eggs, put them also into cold water. Having extracted the intestines, stand up the turtle on end, to let the blood run out. Afterwards cut out all the flesh from the upper and under shells, and remove the bones. Cut the calipee (or meat belonging to the under-shell) into pieces about as large as the palm of your hand, and break the shell. The calipash, or meat next the back-shell, may be cut smaller—the green fat into pieces about two inches square. Put all the meat into a large pan, sprinkle it slightly with salt, and cover it up. Lay the shells and fins in a tub of boiling water, and scald them till the scales can be scraped off with a knife, and all the meat that still adheres to the shells easily removed, as it is worth saving. Clean the fins nicely, (taking off the dark skin,) and lay them in cold water. Wipe the back-shell dry, and set it aside. Then proceed to make the soup. For this purpose, take the coarser pieces of flesh with the bones and entrails. Put them into a pot with a pound of ham cut into pieces, and eight large calves'-feet (two sets) that have been singed and scraped but not skinned. If you cannot conveniently obtain calves'-feet, substitute a large fore-leg or knuckle of veal. Add four onions sliced thin; two table-spoonfuls of sweet-marjoram leaves; a large bunch of parsley; a dozen blades of mace; and a salt-spoon of cayenne. The ham will make any other salt unnecessary. Pour on as much water as will completely cover the whole, and let it simmer slowly over a steady fire during five hours, skimming it well. If after a while the soup seems to be boiling away too much, replenish it with a little hot water from a kettle, kept boiling hard for the purpose. When it has simmered five hours, take up the whole, and strain the soup through a sieve into a deep pan. Wash out the soup-pot with hot water, and return the strained soup to it, with the entrails cut into small pieces, and some of the best of the meat and a portion of the green fat. Have ready two or three dozen force-meat balls about the size of a boy's marble, and made of the usual proportions of minced veal, bread-crumbs, butter, grated lemon-peel, mace, nutmeg, and beaten yolk of egg. Put them into the soup, and let it boil an hour longer; also the eggs of the turtle, or some hard-boiled yolks of eggs. After it has thus boiled another hour, add two sliced lemons and a pint of Madeira. Boil the soup a quarter of an hour longer, and it will then be ready for the tureen. It must never boil hard.

In the mean time, stew in another pot the finest of the turtle-meat, seasoned with a little salt, and cayenne, and a liberal allowance of sweet-marjoram leaves rubbed fine, and mixed with powdered mace and nutmeg. Add a pound of fresh butter, cut into quarters and rolled in flour. When the turtle-meat has stewed an hour, put in the green fat, add the grated peel, and the juice of two lemons, and a pint or more of Madeira, and let the whole stew slowly an hour longer. While the meat is stewing, take the shell off the back; wash it clean, and wipe it dry, lay a band of puff-paste all round the inside of the shell, two inches below the edge, and two inches above it. Notch the paste handsomely, and fill the shell with the stewed turtle. Have ready the oven, heated as if for bread. Lay a large iron baking-sheet or a square pan upon four bricks (one at each corner) to elevate the shell from the floor of the oven. Place on it the turtle-shell with its contents, and let it bake till well browned on the surface. Send it to table in the shell placed on a large dish. At the other end set the tureen of soup. Have ready as two side dishes the fins stewed tender in a little of the soup; and the liver fried in butter. Garnish with lemons cut in half.

This receipt is for a turtle of moderate size. A large one will of course require an increased proportion of all the articles used in seasoning it—more wine, &c. In serving up turtle at a dinner-party, let it constitute the first course, and have no other dishes on table with it. There is no need of any other fish or soup.

VEGETABLES, ETC.

AN EXCELLENT WAY OF BOILING CABBAGE.—Having trimmed the cabbage, and washed it well in cold water, (examining the leaves to see that no insects are lurking among them,) cut it almost into quarters, but do not divide it entirely down at the stem, which should be cut off just below the termination of the leaves. Let it lie an hour in a pan of cold water. Have ready a pot *full* of boiling water, seasoned with a small tea-spoonful of salt. Put the cabbage into it, and let it boil for an hour and a half, skimming it occasionally. Then take it out; put it into a cullender to drain, and when all the hot water has drained off, set it under the hydrant. Let the hydrant run on it, till the cabbage has become perfectly cold all through. If you have no hydrant, set it under a pump, or keep pouring cold water on it from a pitcher. Then, having thrown out all the first water, and washed the pot, fill it again, and let the second water boil. During this time the cabbage under the hydrant will be growing cold. Then put it on again in the second water, and boil it two hours, or two and a half. Even the thickest part of the stalk must be perfectly tender all through. When thoroughly done, take up the cabbage, drain it well through the cullender, pressing it down with a broad ladle to squeeze out all the moisture; lay it in a deep dish, and cut it *entirely* apart, dividing it into quarters. Lay some bits of fresh butter among the leaves, add a little pepper, cover the dish, and send it to table hot.

This receipt for boiling cabbage was obtained from a physician, and on trial has been found very superior to any other. Cabbage cooked in this manner loses its unpleasant odour, and its unwholesome properties, and may be eaten without apprehension, except by persons decidedly dyspeptic. The usual cabbage-smell will not be perceptible in the house—either while the cabbage is boiling or afterwards.

If you like it boiled with corned pork or bacon, the *second boiling* (after the cabbage has been made cold under the hydrant) may be in the pot with the meat—skimming it well.

TO STEW RED CABBAGE.—Having stripped off the outer leaves, and washed the cabbage, quarter it, remove all the stalk, and cut the cabbage into shreds. Slice some cold ham as thin as possible, and put it into a stew-pan, alternately with layers of shred cabbage; having first laid some bits of fresh butter in the bottom of the pan. Add about half a pint of boiling water. Cover the pan closely, and let it stew steadily for three hours, till the cabbage is very tender, and the liquid all wasted; taking care not to let it burn. If you find it so dry as to be in danger of scorching, add a little more *boiling* water. When done, press and drain it through a cullender, and serve it up with the cabbage heaped in the middle of the dish, and the ham laid round.

It may be improved by adding, before it begins to stew, a jill of red beet vinegar.

White cabbage may be stewed as above. Also cauliflower or broccoli, omitting the vinegar.

YOUNG CORN OMELET.—To a dozen ears of fine young Indian corn allow five eggs. Boil the corn a quarter of an hour; and then, with a large grater, grate it down from the cob. Beat the eggs very light, and then stir gradually the grated corn into the pan of eggs. Add a small salt-spoon of salt, and a very little cayenne. Put into a hot frying-pan equal quantities of lard and fresh butter, and stir them well together, over the fire. When they boil, put in the mixture thick, and fry it; afterwards browning the top with a red-hot shovel, or a salamander. Transfer it, when done, to a heated dish, but do not fold it over. It will be found excellent. This is a good way of using boiled corn that has been left from dinner the preceding day.

CAULIFLOWER OMELET.—Take the white part of a boiled cauliflower after it is cold; chop it very small, and mix with it a sufficient quantity of well-beaten egg, to make a very thick batter. Then fry it in fresh butter in a small pan, and send it hot to table.

FRIED CAULIFLOWER.—Having laid a fine cauliflower in cold water for an hour, put it into a pot of boiling water that has been slightly salted, (milk and water will be still better,) and boil it twenty-five minutes, or till the large stalk is perfectly tender. Then divide it, equally, into small tufts, and spread it on a dish to cool. Prepare a sufficient quantity of batter made in the proportion of a table-spoonful of flour, and two table-spoonfuls of milk to each egg. Beat the eggs very light; then stir into them the flour and milk alternately; a spoonful of flour, and two spoonfuls of milk at a time. When the cauliflower is cold, have ready some fresh butter in a frying-pan over a clear fire. When it has come to a boil and has done bubbling, dip each tuft of cauliflower twice into the pan of batter, and fry them a light brown. Send them to table hot.

Broccoli may be fried in this manner.

CAULIFLOWER MACCARONI.—Having removed the outside leaves, and cut off the stalk, wash the cauliflower, and examine it thoroughly to see if there are any insects about it. Next lay it for an hour in a pan of cold water. Then put it into a pot of boiling milk and water that has had a little fresh butter melted in it. Whatever scum may float on the top of the water must be removed before the cauliflower goes in. Boil it, steadily, half an hour, or till it is quite tender. Then take it out, drain it, and cut it into short sprigs. Have ready three ounces of rich, but not strong cheese, grated fine. Put into a stew-pan a quarter of a pound of fresh butter; nearly half of the grated cheese; two large table-spoonfuls of cream or rich milk; and a very little salt and cayenne. Toss or shake it over the fire, till it is well mixed, and has come to a boil. Then add the tufts of cauliflower; and let the whole stew together about five minutes. When done, put it into a deep dish; strew over the top the remaining half of the grated cheese, and brown it with a salamander or a red hot shovel held above the surface.

This will be found very superior to real maccaroni.

BROCCOLI AND EGGS.—Take several heads of broccoli, and cut the stalks short, paring off from the stalks the tough outside skin. Trim off the small outside shoots or blossoms, and tie them together in bunches. After all the broccoli has been washed, and lain half an hour or more in a pan of fresh, cold water, put the large heads, with a salt-spoonful of salt, into a pot of boiling water, and let them boil till thoroughly done, and the stalk perfectly tender. When the large heads have boiled about a quarter of an hour, put in the small tufts, which of course require less time to cook. In the meanwhile have ready six beaten eggs. Put a quarter of a pound of butter into a sauce-pan, and stir it over the fire till it is all melted; then add gradually the beaten eggs, and stir the mixture, or shake it over the fire till it becomes very thick. Toast sufficient bread to cover entirely the bottom of a deep dish, cutting it to fit exactly, having removed the crust. Pour the egg and butter over the hot toast. Then place upon it the broccoli; the largest and finest head in the middle, the lesser ones round it; and having untied the small sprigs, lay them, in a circle close to the edge.

FRIED CELERY.—Take fine large celery; cut it into pieces three or four inches in length, and boil it tender; having seasoned the water with a very little salt. Then drain the pieces well, and lay them, separately, to cool on a large dish. Make a batter in the proportion of three well-beaten eggs stirred into a pint of rich milk, alternately with half a pint of grated bread-crumbs, or of sifted flour. Beat the batter very hard after it is all mixed. Put into a hot frying-pan, a sufficiency of fresh lard; melt it over the fire, and when it comes to a boil, dip each piece of celery *twice* into the batter, put them into the pan, and fry them a light brown. When done, lay them to drain on an inverted sieve with a broad pan placed beneath it. Then dish the fried celery, and send it to table hot.

Parsnips, and salsify (or oyster plant) may be fried in butter according to the above directions. Also the tops of asparagus cut off from the stalk; and the white part or blossom of cauliflower. Cold sweet potatoes are very nice, peeled, cut into long slips, and fried in this way.

FRIED ARTICHOKES.—The artichokes must be young and tender. Cut them into quarters, remove the choke part, and strip off the leaves. Having washed the artichokes well, and laid them an hour in cold water, put them into a pot of boiling water, and keep them boiling steadily for a long time, till you find by trying them with a fork that they are tender all through. Then take them out immediately, and drain them. Have ready a sufficiency of batter, made in the proportion of the yolk of one egg to a large table-spoonful of milk, and a tea-spoonful of flour. The eggs must be well beaten before they are mixed with the milk; then beat in the flour a spoonful at a time. Have ready over the fire some fresh butter, or lard, in a frying-pan. When it has boiled hard, dip the artichokes into the batter, (each piece should be twice dipped,) and fry them brown. Then drain them well, and send them to table hot.

Parsnips may be fried as above. Salsify also.

Another way of frying artichokes, parsnips, and salsify, is, after they have been boiled tender, to dip each piece first in beaten yolk of egg, (without milk or flour,) and then roll it in finely-grated bread-crumbs. Then put them into the pan and fry them in butter or lard, or a mixture of both.

In boiling artichokes, observe to take them out as soon as they are tender. If they remain in the water after they are done, they turn blackish and lose their flavour.

MUSHROOM OMELET.—Take some fresh-gathered mushrooms; remove the stalks, and rub the flaps or heads very slightly with a little salt, mixed with cayenne. Then stew the mushrooms in a small sauce-pan, with barely sufficient cream or rich milk to cover them. Put in with them a small onion; and if the onion is found to turn blackish, throw away the whole; it being proof that there is among them a false or poisonous mushroom. Stir them with a silver spoon, and keep on the lid of the pan closely; unless when you are stirring. If the spoon turns black, the mushrooms should not be eaten.

After they have come to a boil, take them off the fire; drain them, and when cool, chop them small. To a pint or more of the minced mushrooms, allow six or seven eggs. Beat the eggs till very light and thick, (omitting the whites of two,) and then mix in, gradually, the mushrooms; stirring the whole very hard. Put three ounces of fresh butter into a hot omelet-pan, or a *small* frying-pan; place it over the fire, and stir the butter as it melts. When it has boiled hard, put in the omelet mixture, and as it fries, stir it till it begins to set. Do not turn the omelet; but brown the top by holding close above it a red-hot shovel. When done, drain off the butter; fold over or double the omelet; and serve it up immediately, on a hot dish.

In gathering mushrooms, those that are fit to eat may be known by their being of a pale pearl colour, or of a grayish white, instead of what is called a dead white; and the under side of the flap or head (if good) is of a light pink, or a pinkish salmon colour. The best mushrooms grow on uplands, or in high open fields where the air is pure and good, and they should be gathered early in the morning before the dew is off. All that are found in low swampy ground, or in the woods, or under large trees are poisonous.

SCOLLOPED TOMATOES.—Take fine large tomatoes, perfectly ripe. Scald them to loosen the skins, and then peel them. Cover the bottom of a deep dish thickly with grated bread-crumbs, adding a few bits of fresh butter. Then put in a layer of tomatoes, seasoned slightly with a little salt and cayenne, and some powdered mace or nutmeg. Cover them with another layer of bread-crumbs and butter. Then another layer of seasoned tomatoes; and proceed thus till the dish is full, finishing at the top with bread-crumbs. Set the dish into a moderate oven, and bake it near three hours. Tomatoes require long cooking, otherwise they will have a raw taste, that to most persons is unpleasant.

FRENCH SPINACH.—Having picked them from the stalks, wash the leaves carefully in two or three cold waters, till they are quite free from grit. Put the spinach into a sauce-pan of hot water, in which a very small portion of salt has been boiled. There must be sufficient water to allow the spinach to float. Stir it frequent-ly, that all the leaves may be equally done. Let it boil for a quarter of an hour. Then take it out, lay it in a sieve, and drain it well; pressing it thoroughly with your hands. Next chop it as fine as possible. For a large dish of spinach, put two ounc-es of butter into a stew-pan; dredge in a table-spoonful of flour and four or five table-spoonfuls of rich cream, mixed with a tea-spoonful of powdered loaf-sugar. Mix all well, and when they have come to a boil, add, gradually, the spinach. Stew it about ten minutes, (stirring it frequently,) till the superfluous moisture is all ab-sorbed. Then serve it up very hot, garnishing it all round with leaves of puff-paste, that have been handsomely formed with a tin cutter, and are fresh from the oven.

STEWED SPINACH.—Pick the spinach very clean, and wash it through two or three waters. Then drain it, and put it into a sauce-pan, with only the water that remains about it after the washing. Add a very little salt and pepper, and let it stew for twenty minutes, or till it is quite tender; turning it often, and pressing it down with a broad wooden spoon or flat ladle. When done, drain it through a sieve, pressing out all the moisture, till you get it as dry as you can. Then put it on a flat dish, and chop or mince it well. Set it again over the fire; add to it some bits of butter dredged with flour, and some beaten yolk of egg. Let it simmer five minutes or more, and when it comes to a boil, take it off. Have ready some thin slices of buttered toast, cut into triangular or three-cornered pieces, without any crust. Lay them in regular order round a flat dish, and heap the spinach evenly upon them, smoothing the surface with the back of a spoon, and scoring it across in diamonds.

ASPARAGUS LOAVES.—Having scraped the stalks of three bundles of fine, large asparagus, (laying it, as you proceed, in a pan of cold water,) tie it up again in bunches, put them into a pot with a great deal of boiling water, and a little salt, and boil them about twenty minutes, or till quite tender. Then take out the aspar-agus, and drain it. Cut off the green tops of two-thirds of the asparagus, and on the remainder leave about two inches of the white stalk; this remaining asparagus must be kept warm. Put the tops into a stew-pan with a pint of cream, or rich milk, sufficient to cover them well; adding three table-spoonfuls of fresh butter, rolled in flour, half a grated nutmeg, and the well-beaten yolks of three eggs. Set the stew-pan over hot coals, and stir the mixture till it comes to a boil. Then immediately remove it. Have ready some tall fresh rolls or penny loaves; cut the tops carefully off, in a nice circular or oval piece, and then scoop out the inside of the rolls, and fill them with the stewed asparagus while it is hot. Make small holes very nicely in the tops or lids. Fit the lids again on the rolls, and stick in the holes (of which you must make as many as you can) the remaining asparagus, that has had the bit of stalk left on for this purpose. Send them to table warm, as side-dishes.

ASPARAGUS OMELET.—Take two bunches of the largest and finest aspara-gus. Put it into a pot of boiling water, with a tea-spoonful of salt, and boil it about twenty-five minutes, or till perfectly tender. Then drain it, and chop small all the green part. Beat four eggs very light, and add to them a wine-glass of cream. Mix the chopped asparagus thoroughly with the egg and cream, adding a salt-spoon of salt, and a very little cayenne. Melt a large slice of fresh butter in a frying-pan over the fire; and when it has boiled, and the bubbling has ceased, put in the mixture, and fry it till light and firm. Then slip it from the frying-pan to a hot dish, and fold it over.

For a soft omelet, put the mixture into a skillet, with a piece of fresh butter. Let it stew slowly for ten minutes. Lay a thin slice of buttered toast in the bottom of a hot dish, and cut the toast into small squares, but let them remain close together. With a spoon heap the soft omelet upon the toast, and serve it up.

Any omelet mixture may be kept soft by stewing instead of frying it, and it will be found far more wholesome.

STEWED PEAS.—Take young, tender green peas, and put into a stew-pan, with sufficient fresh butter to keep them from burning, but no water. Season them with a little black pepper, and a very little salt. Set them over a moderate fire, and stir them about till the butter is well mixed through them. Let them simmer till quite soft and slightly broken; taking off the lid occasionally, and giving them a stir up from the bottom. If you find them becoming too dry, add some more butter. When done, drain off what superfluous butter may be about the peas, and send them to table hot. They will be found excellent.

To the taste of many persons, they will be improved by a lump or two of loaf-sugar put in with the butter; and also by a few sprigs of mint, to be removed before the peas go to table.

Lima beans may be stewed in butter, as above: also, asparagus tops, cut off from the white stalk.

FRENCH PEAS.—The peas should be young, freshly gathered, and shelled immediately before they are cooked. Boil them in water slightly salted, till they are perfectly tender. Then put them into a sieve, and drain them as dry as possible. To each quart of peas allow an ounce and a half of the best fresh butter; a large tea-spoonful of flour; and six table-spoonfuls or a tea-cup of rich cream; with a small tea-spoonful of powdered sugar. Put the butter into a stew-pan; place it over the fire; and when it comes to a boil, stir in the flour, making it quite smooth, and free from lumps. Having mixed the sugar with the cream, add it, gradually, to the butter and flour; and when it boils hard stir in the peas, and let them stew till they are all hot through. While stewing, stir them occasionally to prevent their burning. If the pan is small it is better to shake it over the fire.

LETTUCE PEAS.—Having washed four lettuces, and stripped off the outside leaves, take their hearts, and (having chopped them well) put them into a stew-pan with two quarts of young green peas, freshly shelled; a lump or two of loaf-sugar; and three or four leaves of green mint minced as finely as possible. Then put in a slice of cold ham, and a quarter of a pound of butter divided into four bits and rolled in flour; and two table-spoonfuls of water. Add a little black pepper, and let the whole stew for about twenty-five minutes, or till the peas are thoroughly done. Then take out the ham, and add to the stew half a pint of cream. Let it continue stewing five minutes longer. Then send it to table.

PLAIN LETTUCE PEAS.—Cover the bottom and sides of a stew-pan with large fresh leaves taken from lettuces. Have ready the peas, which should be young and green. To each quart of shelled peas allow two table-spoonfuls of fresh butter, and a lump of loaf sugar. Add a very little pepper and salt, and a sprig of green mint. Cover the pan closely, and let it stew for half an hour, or till the peas are thoroughly done. Then take them out from the lettuce leaves, and send only the peas to table.

TO STEW CARROTS.—Half-boil the carrots; then scrape them nicely, and cut them into thick slices. Put them into a stew-pan with as much milk as will barely cover them, a very little salt and pepper, and a sprig or two of chopped parsley. Simmer them till they are perfectly tender, but not broken. When nearly done, add a piece of fresh butter rolled in flour. Send them to table hot. Carrots require long cooking.

Parsnips and salsify may be stewed in the above manner, substituting a little chopped celery for the parsley.

STEWED BEANS, (*French way.*)—Take fresh young green beans, and string them. Do not split them; but merely cut them in half. It destroys the flavour of string-beans to divide them into small pieces. If very young, do not even cut them in half, but merely string them and leave them whole. Have by you a pan of cold water to drop the beans in, as you proceed. Then, having washed and drained them, put them into a stew-pan of boiling water, and let them boil twenty minutes or more, till they are all tender. Then drain them well. Afterwards melt two ounces of butter in a stew-pan, and then stir smoothly into it a tea-spoonful of flour, adding a little powdered mace and a salt-spoon of salt. When it comes to a boil, add a tea-cup of rich cream. Then put in the beans, and stir or shake them over the fire till they are all thoroughly heated. A moment before you take them from the fire, stir in the beaten yolks of two eggs, and send them hot to table.

For this dish, you must have beans enough to absorb nearly all the liquid. They must on no account float about in it, as it is intended for a seasoning, not a gravy.

Stewed beans will be improved by adding a small piece of cold ham, to be removed before they go to table. If ham is used, omit any salt in the seasoning, as the ham will make it quite salt enough.

TO STEW COLD POTATOES.—Take cold potatoes, (either white or sweet ones,) and cut them into round or circular slices. Have ready some nice gravy of roast beef, veal, or fresh pork, that has been left from the preceding day, and well skimmed. Care should every day be taken to save whatever gravy is left of roast meat, skimming off *all* the fat from the surface, and putting away the gravy in a covered vessel set in a cool place. The gravy of cold mutton or lamb is so like tallow that it is unfit to use in any sort of cookery, and should always be consigned to the crock of soap-fat.

Season the sliced potatoes slightly with pepper, and putting them into a skillet with the cold gravy among them, stew them in that only, without a drop of water. Let them stew but a quarter of an hour. They are nice at breakfast, done in this manner; sweet potatoes especially.

TO IMPROVE OLD POTATOES.—In the spring when the potatoes of the preceding autumn have become old, and deteriorated in quality, they will be greatly improved if, previous to boiling, a piece about the size of a shilling or a twelve-cent-piece, is cut off from each end; like "topping and tailing" them. Afterwards boil these potatoes with the skins on, and see that they are thoroughly done. *Old* potatoes require very long boiling, and are unfit to eat if hard in the centre, being then extremely indigestible. Their specks and blemishes make them so unsightly when sent to table whole, that it is best when sufficiently boiled, to peel and mash them. Mash them with milk or cream, if you cannot obtain good fresh butter. Salt butter will spoil their flavour instead of improving it, and all bad butter (whether salt or fresh) is unwholesome, as well as unpalatable, and should never be used for any purpose.

SYDNEY SMITH'S SALAD-DRESSING.—Have ready two well-boiled potatoes, peeled and rubbed through a sieve; they will give peculiar smoothness to the mixture. Also, a very small portion of raw onion, not more than a *quarter* of a tea-spoonful, (as the presence of the onion is to be scarcely hinted,) and the pounded yolks of two hard-boiled eggs. Mix these ingredients on a deep plate with two small tea-spoonfuls of salt; one of made mustard; three table-spoonfuls of olive oil; and one table-spoonful of vinegar. Add, lastly, a tea-spoonful of essence of anchovy; mash, and mix the whole together (using a boxwood spoon) and see that all the articles are thoroughly amalgamated. Having cut up a sufficiency of lettuce, (that has been well washed in cold water, and drained,) add to it the dressing immediately before dinner, mixing the lettuce through it with a boxwood fork.

This salad dressing was invented by the Rev. Sydney Smith, whose genius as a writer and a wit is well-known on both sides the Atlantic. If *exactly* followed, it will be found very fine on trial; no peculiar flavour predominating, but excellent as a whole. The above directions are taken from a manuscript receipt given by Mr. Smith to an American gentleman then in London.

In preparing this, or any other salad-dressing, take care not to use that excessively pungent and deleterious combination of drugs which is now so frequently imposed upon the public, as *the best white wine vinegar*. In reality, it has no vinous material about it, and it may be known by its violent and disagreeable sharpness, which overpowers and destroys the taste (and also the substance) of whatever it is mixed with. And it is also very unwholesome. Its colour is always very pale, and it is nearly as clear as water. No one should buy or use it. The first quality of *real* cider vinegar is good for all purposes.

The above receipt may be tried for lobster-dressing.

LETTUCE CHICKEN SALAD.—Having skinned a pair of cold fowls, remove the fat, and carve them as if for eating, cut all the flesh entirely from the bones, and either mince it or divide it into small shreds. Mix with it a little smoked tongue or cold ham, grated rather than chopped. Have ready one or two fine fresh lettuces, picked, washed, drained, and cut small. Put the cut lettuce on a dish, (spreading it evenly,) or into a large bowl, and place upon it the minced chicken in a close heap in the centre. For the dressing, mix together the following ingredients, in the proportion of the yolks of four eggs well beaten; a tea-spoonful of powdered white sugar; a salt-spoon of cayenne; (no salt if you have ham or tongue with the chicken;) two tea-spoonfuls of made mustard; two table-spoonfuls of vinegar, and four table-spoonfuls of salad oil. Stir this mixture well: put it into a small sauce-pan, set it over the fire, and let it boil three minutes, (not more,) stirring it all the time. Then set it to cool. When quite cold, cover with it thickly the heap of chicken in the centre of the salad. To ornament it, have ready half a dozen or more hard-boiled eggs, which after the shell is peeled off, must be thrown directly into a pan of cold water to prevent their turning blue. Cut each egg (white and yolk together) lengthways into four long pieces of equal size and shape; lay the pieces upon the salad all round the heap of chicken, and close to it; placing them so as to follow each other round in a slanting direction, something in the form of a circular wreath of leaves. Have ready, also, some very red cold beet, cut into small cones or points all of equal size; arrange them in a circle upon the lettuce, outside of the circle of cut egg. To be decorated in this manner, the salad should be placed in a dish rather than a bowl. In helping it, give each person a portion of every thing, and they will mix them together on their plates.

This salad should be prepared immediately before dinner or supper, as standing long will injure it. The colder it is the better.

ITALIAN CHICKEN SALAD.—Make a dressing in the proportion of the yolks of three hard-boiled eggs, mashed or pounded fine; a salt-spoon of salt; and the same quantity of mustard, and of cayenne; and a salt-spoon of powdered white sugar; four table-spoonfuls of salad-oil; and two table-spoonfuls of vinegar, (tarragon vinegar will be best.) Simmer this dressing over the fire, but do not let it come to a boil. Stir it all the time. Take a sufficiency of the white meat of cold fowls, and pull or cut it into flakes. Pile it in the middle of a dish, and pour the salad-dressing over it. Have ready two fine fresh lettuces that have been laid in cold water. Strip off the outside leaves; cut up the best part of the lettuces, and arrange it evenly in a ridge, or circular heap all round the pile of chicken in the centre. On the top of the ridge of lettuce, place the whites of the eggs, cut into rings and laid round so as to form a chain. Of course, a portion of the lettuce is to be helped with the chicken.

A lobster salad may be made as above; also a salad of minced prawns or crabs.

Persons who have no dislike to a very slight flavour of garlic, will find this chicken-salad improved, by a clove of garlic being lightly rubbed over the dish while empty.

In dressing and helping every sort of salad, use a boxwood spoon and fork.

TARRAGON SAUCE.—Take a large handful of tarragon leaves, stripped from the stalks: put them into a small sauce-pan with half a pint of boiling water, and four blades of mace. Cover the sauce-pan, and let it stew slowly till the liquid is reduced to one half, and the flavour of the tarragon is well drawn out. Then strain it; and put the liquid into a clean sauce-pan. Mix together a table-spoonful of flour, and six ounces of butter, and when it has been well-stirred, and beaten smoothly, stir it into the tarragon water. Place the sauce-pan over the fire, and watch it close-ly. When it has simmered well, and is just beginning to boil, take it off immediately and transfer it to a sauce-boat. Eat it with any sort of boiled meat or poultry, or with boiled fish. The tarragon will give it a fine flavour.

You may add to the tarragon, while stewing, a small white onion cut in slices.

This sauce may be coloured a fine green, by pounding in a mortar a sufficient quantity of young parsley or spinach. Then take some of the juice, and add it to the liquid after you have strained it from the tarragon leaves, and before you put in the butter.

Tarragon is an herb well worth cultivating. It grows from a slip or root, and is easily raised. The leaves are fit to gather in July and August. They impart a fine and peculiar flavour to sauces, soups, and salad; and are indispensable in making French mustard. Tarragon may be kept a year or more by drying it in bunches. Also by filling a bottle half with tarragon leaves, and half with good vinegar.

FINE LEMON PICKLE.—Take some fresh ripe lemons, and (having first rolled each one under your hand upon the table) cut them into quarters, and remove all the seeds. Put the pieces of lemon, with all the juice, into a stone jar. Have ready a sufficient quantity of excellent vinegar to cover the lemon well; the vinegar being boiled with a clove or two of garlic; some blades of mace; a broken up nutmeg; whole pepper, (the white or peeled pepper-corns will be best;) some cayenne or bird-pepper; and a very little salt. The proportion of these ingredients may be according to your taste, but the seasoning should be high, yet not so as to overpower the lemon-flavour. Having boiled the vinegar, with all these articles, about ten minutes, pour the whole boiling hot upon the lemon in the jar, and immediately cover it closely. Let the jar stand three weeks in the chimney-corner, stirring it frequently, and setting it occasionally in the oven after the baking is done. Then roll a sheet of blotting paper into a cone, pinning up the side, and folding the cone so as to close up the pointed end. Have ready some small clean black bottles. Set the paper cone into the mouth of the bottle, and through it filter the liquid. Seal the corks. This will be found an excellent sauce for fish, or any sort of white meat; and will keep for years.

PEACH PICKLES.—Stir two pounds of white sugar into two quarts of the best cider vinegar. Boil it ten minutes, skimming it well. Have ready some large fully-ripe peaches; rub them with a clean flannel to take off the down, and stick four cloves into each. Put them into glass or white-ware jars, (rather more than half-full,) and pour on them the vinegar boiling hot. Cover them closely, set them in a cool place, and let them rest for a week. Then pour off the liquid, and give it another boiling. Afterwards pour it again on the peaches; cover them closely, corking the jars, and tying leather over each, and put them away till wanted for use.

Instead of cloves you may stick the peaches with blades of mace, six blades to each peach.

Apricots may be pickled as above. Morella cherries also, using mace instead of cloves.

If you find a coat of mould on the top of a jar of pickles, remove it carefully, and do not throw away the pickles, as they may still be quite good beneath.

CUCUMBER CATCHUP.—For a small quantity, take twelve fine full-grown cucumbers, and lay them an hour in cold water. Then pare them, and grate them down into a deep dish. Grate also six small onions, and mix them with the grated cucumber. Season the mixture to your taste, with pepper, salt, and vinegar; making it of the consistence of rich marmalade or jam. When thoroughly incorporated, transfer it to a glass jar, cover it closely, tying down over the top a piece of bladder, so as to make it perfectly air-tight.

It will be found very nice (when fresh cucumbers are not in season) to eat with beef or mutton, and if properly made and tightly covered will keep well. It should be grated very fine, and the vinegar must be of excellent quality — real cider vinegar.

ONION CUSTARD.—Peel and slice some mild onions, (ten or twelve, in proportion to their size,) and fry them in fresh butter; draining them well when you take them up. Then mince them as fine as possible. Beat four eggs very light, and stir them gradually into a pint of milk, in turn with the minced onions. Season the whole with plenty of grated nutmeg, and stir it very hard. Then put it into a deep, white dish, and bake it about a quarter of an hour. Send it to table as a side dish to be eaten with meat or poultry. It is a French preparation of onions, and will be found very fine.

MEATS, ETC.

STEWED LAMB.—Take a fine quarter of lamb, and for a large dish, cut the whole of it into steaks; for a small dish, cut up the loin only; or slice only the leg. Remove the skin, and all the fat. Place at the bottom of a large stew-pot a fresh lettuce split into long quarters. Having seasoned the steaks with a little salt and cayenne, and some powdered nutmeg and mace, lay them upon the lettuce, pour on just sufficient water to cover the whole, and let it stew gently for an hour, skimming it occasionally. Then put in a quart or two of young green peas, (in proportion to the quantity of meat,) a sprig of fresh green mint, a lump of loaf-sugar, and some bits of fresh butter. Let it cook slowly about half an hour longer, or till the peas are all soft and well-done. In sending it to table, place the meat upon the lettuce, and the peas round it.

Cold ham sliced, and stewed in this manner, will be found excellent. The ham having been already cooked, half an hour will be sufficient to stew it with the lettuce, and another half-hour after the peas are in.

LAMB CUTLETS, (*a French dish.*)—Cut a loin of lamb into chops. Remove all the fat, trim them nicely, scrape the bone, and see that it is the same length in all the cutlets. Lay them in a deep dish, and cover them with salad oil. Let them steep in the oil for an hour. Mix together a sufficiency of finely grated bread-crumbs, and a little minced parsley, seasoned with a very little pepper and salt, and some grated nutmeg. Having drained the cutlets from the oil, cover them with the mixture, and broil them over a bed of hot, live coals, on a previously heated gridiron, the bars of which have been rubbed with chalk. The cutlets must be thoroughly cooked. When half done, turn them carefully. You may bake them in a dutch-oven, instead of broiling them. Have ready some boiled potatoes, mashed smooth and stiff with cream or butter. Heap the mashed potatoes high on a heated dish, and make it into the form of a dome or bee-hive. Smooth it over with the back of a spoon, and place the lamb cutlets all round it, so that they stand up and lean against it, with the broad end of each cutlet downward. In the top of the dome of potatoes, stick a handsome bunch of curled parsley.

FILLET OF MUTTON.—Cut a fillet or round from a leg of mutton; remove all the fat from the outside, and take out the bone. Beat it well on all sides with a meat-beetle or a rolling-pin, to make it more tender, and rub it slightly all over with a very little pepper and salt. Have ready a stuffing made of finely-minced onions, bread-crumbs, and butter; seasoned with a little salt, pepper, and nutmeg, and well-mixed. Fill, with some of this stuffing, the place of the bone. Make deep incisions or cuts all over the surface of the meat, and fill them closely with the same stuffing. Bind a tape round the meat to keep it in shape. Put it into a stew-pan, with just water enough to cover it, and let it stew slowly and steadily during four, five, or six hours, in proportion to its size; skimming it frequently. When done, serve it up with its own gravy.

Tomato sauce is an excellent accompaniment to stewed mutton.

A thick piece of a round of fresh beef will be found very good, stuffed and stewed in the above manner. It will require much longer stewing than the mutton.

STEWED MUTTON CUTLETS.—Having removed all the fat and the bone, beat the cutlets to make them tender, and season them with pepper, salt, and nutmeg. Put them into a circular tin kettle, with some bits of fresh butter that have been rolled in flour. Set the kettle (closely covered) upon a trivet inside of a flat-bottomed pot or stew-pan. Pour boiling water all round, but not so as to come up to the top of the inner kettle. Set the pot over a slow fire, and let the stew simmer for two hours. Then lift up the meat, and put under it a lettuce cut in four; and three cucumbers, pared, split, and quartered; two onions sliced; and four young turnips cut small. Add a few blades of mace, a salt-spoon of salt, and a little more butter rolled in flour. Set it again in boiling water, taking care that the water does not reach the top of the inner kettle, the lid of which must be kept very tight. Let it boil slowly, or rather simmer, two hours longer. Then dish it, placing the meat upon the vegetables, and laying all round a ridge of green peas that have been boiled in the usual way.

The bone (nicely trimmed and scraped) may be left in each cutlet; in which case, when dishing them, stand them up in a circle, with the ends of the bones leaning against each other at the top, somewhat as we see poles placed in circles for lima-bean vines.

VEAL LOAF.—Take a cold fillet of veal, and (omitting the fat and skin) mince the meat as fine as possible. Mix with it a quarter of a pound of the fattest part of a cold ham, also chopped small. Add a tea-cupful of grated bread-crumbs; a grated nutmeg; half a dozen blades of mace powdered; the grated yellow rind of a lemon; and two beaten eggs. Season with a salt-spoon of salt, and half a salt-spoon of cayenne. Mix the whole well together, and make it into the form of a loaf. Then glaze it over with beaten yolk of egg; and strew the surface evenly, all over, with bread raspings, or with pounded cracker. Set the dish into a dutch-oven, and bake it half an hour, or till hot all through. Have ready a gravy made of the trimmings of the veal, stewed in some of the gravy that was left when the fillet was roasted the day before. When sufficiently cooked, take out the meat, and thicken the gravy with beaten yolk of egg, stirred in about three minutes before you take it from the fire.

Send the veal loaf to table in a deep dish, with the gravy poured round it.

Chicken loaf, or turkey loaf, may be made in this manner.

STEWED CALF'S HEAD.—Take a fine, large calf's head; empty it; wash it clean, and boil it till it is quite tender, in just water enough to cover it. Then carefully take out the bones, without spoiling the appearance of the head. Season it with a little salt and cayenne, and a grated nutmeg. Pour over it the liquor in which it has been boiled, adding a jill of vinegar, and two table-spoonfuls of capers, or of green nasturtian-seeds, that have been pickled. Let it stew very slowly for half an hour. Have ready some force-meat balls made of minced veal-suet, grated bread-crumbs, grated lemon-peel, and shred sweet-marjoram,—adding beaten yolk of egg to bind the other ingredients together. Put in the force-meat balls, and stew it slowly a quarter of an hour longer, adding some bits of butter rolled in flour to enrich the gravy. Send it to table hot.

CORNED FILLET OF VEAL.—Take a large fillet of veal, and make deep incisions or cuts all over it with a sharp knife, and insert a slip of the fat into each, pressing it down well to keep it in. Mix a table-spoonful of powdered saltpetre with half a pound of fine salt, and rub the meat all over with it. Make a brine of salt and water strong enough to swim an egg on its surface, adding a lump of salt-petre about the size of a walnut. Put the veal into the brine, (of which there must be enough to more than cover it,) and let it remain ten days; turning it every day. Then take it out, wash off the brine, and boil the veal till thoroughly done and tender all through. It is best to eat it cold, and sliced thin.

FRENCH WAY OF DRESSING A SHOULDER OF VEAL.—Cut the veal into nice square pieces or mouthfuls, and parboil them. Put the bone and trimmings into another pot, and stew them slowly a long time, in a very little water, to make the gravy. Then put the meat into the dish in which it is to go to table, and season it with a very little salt and cayenne pepper, the yellow rind of a large lemon grated, and some powdered mace and nutmeg. Add some bits of fresh butter rolled in flour, or some cold dripping of roast veal. Strain the gravy and pour it in. Set it in a hot dutch-oven, and bake it brown. When nearly done, add two glasses of white wine, and serve it up hot.

Any piece of veal may be cooked in this way.

EXCELLENT MINCED VEAL.—Take three or four pounds of the lean only of a fillet or loin of veal, and mince it very finely, adding a slice or two of cold ham, minced also. Add three or four small young onions, chopped small, a tea-spoonful of sweet-marjoram leaves rubbed from the stalks, the yellow rind of a small lemon grated, and a tea-spoonful of mixed mace and nutmeg powdered. Mix all well together, and dredge it with a little flour. Put it into a stew-pan, with sufficient gravy of cold roast veal to moisten it, and a large table-spoonful or more of fresh butter. Stir it well, and let it stew till thoroughly done. If the veal has been previously cooked, a quarter of an hour will be sufficient. It will be much improved by adding a pint or more of small button mushrooms, cut from the stems, and then put in whole. Also, by stirring in two table-spoonfuls of cream about five minutes before it is taken from the fire.

MINCED TURKEY OR CHICKEN.—Take a cold turkey, or one or two cold fowls; remove all the skin, and cut the flesh from the bones. Then mince it fine, with two or three thin slices of cold smoked tongue, and from half a pint to a pint of button mushrooms well chopped. Add some mace and nutmeg, and put the whole into a stew-pan, with a piece of fresh butter rolled in flour, and sufficient cream to moisten it well. Let it stew ten minutes. Then serve it up in a deep dish.

Instead of mushrooms, you may mix two or three dozen oysters, chopped, and seasoned with pepper and powdered mace.

VEAL WITH OYSTERS.—Take two fine cutlets of about a pound each. Divide them into several pieces, cut thin. Put them into a frying-pan, with boiling lard, and let them fry awhile. When the veal is about half done, add to it a quart of large, fine oysters,—their liquor thickened with a few grated bread-crumbs, and seasoned with mace and nutmeg powdered. Continue the frying till the veal and oysters are thoroughly done. Send it to table in a covered dish.

TERRAPIN VEAL.—Take some cold roast veal (the fillet or the loin) and cut it into *very small* mouthfuls. Put into a skillet or stew-pan. Have ready a dressing made of six or seven hard-boiled eggs minced fine; a small tea-spoonful of made mustard; a salt-spoonful of salt; and the same of cayenne pepper; a large tea-cup-full (half a pint) of cream, and two glasses of sherry or Madeira wine. The dressing must be thoroughly mixed. Pour it over the veal, and then give the whole a hard stir. Cover it, and let it stew over the fire for ten minutes. Then transfer it to a deep dish, and send it to table hot.

Cold roast duck or fowl may be drest as above. Also venison.

VEAL OLIVES.—Take some cold fillet of veal and cold ham, and cut them into thin square slices of the same size and shape, trimming the edges evenly. Lay a slice of veal on every slice of ham, and spread some beaten yolk of egg over the veal. Have ready a thin force-meat, made of grated bread-crumbs, sweet-marjo-ram rubbed fine, fresh butter, and grated lemon-peel, seasoned with nutmeg and a little cayenne pepper. Spread this over the veal, and then roll up each slice tightly with the ham. Tie them round securely with coarse thread or fine twine; run a bird-spit through them, and roast them well. For sauce, simmer in a small sauce-pan, some cold veal gravy with two spoonfuls of cream, and some mushroom catchup.

VEAL RISSOLES.—Take as much fine wheat bread as will weigh one pound, after all the crust is cut off. Slice it; put it into a pan and pour over it as much rich milk as will soak it thoroughly. After it has soaked a quarter of an hour, lay it in a sieve and press it dry. Mince as finely as possible a pound of veal cutlet with six ounces of veal suet; then mix in gradually the bread; adding a salt-spoonful of salt, a slight sprinkling of cayenne, and a small tea-spoonful of powdered mace and nutmeg mixed; also the yellow rind of a lemon grated. Beat two eggs, and moisten the mixture with them. Then divide it into equal portions, and with a little flour on your hands roll it into oval balls rather smaller than an egg. Strew over them some dry bread-crumbs; then fry them in lard or fresh butter—drain them well, and send them to table hot. For gravy (which should be commenced before the rissoles) put some bits and trimmings of veal into a small sauce-pan, with as much water as will cover them; a very little pepper and salt; and three or four blades of mace. Cover the sauce-pan closely, and let the meat stew till all the strength is extracted; skimming it well. Then strain it; return the liquid to the sauce-pan; add a bit of butter rolled in flour; and squeeze in the juice of a lemon. Give it a boil up; and then, at the last, stir in the beaten yolk of an egg. Serve up this gravy in a sauce-boat, to eat with the rissoles.

Instead of stewing meat for the purpose you may make this gravy with the drippings of roast veal saved from the day before. You have then only to melt it over the fire; adding the seasoning; and giving it one boil.

Similar rissoles may be made of minced chicken or turkey.

SWEETBREAD CROQUETTES.—Having trimmed some sweetbreads nicely, and removed the gristle, parboil them, and then mince them very fine. Add grated bread, and season with a *very little* salt and pepper; some powdered mace and nutmeg; and some grated lemon-rind. Moisten the whole with cream, and make them up into small cones or sugar-loaves; forming and smoothing them nicely. Have ready some beaten egg, mixed with grated bread-crumbs. Dip into it each croquette, and fry them slowly in fresh butter. Serve them hot; standing up on the dish, and with a sprig of parsley in the top of each.

Sweetbreads should never be used unless perfectly fresh. They spoil very rapidly. As soon as they are brought from market they should be split open, and laid in cold water. Never attempt to keep sweetbreads till next day, except in cold weather.

Similar croquettes may be made of cold boiled chicken; or cold roast veal; or of oysters, minced raw, and seasoned and mixed as above.

FRICASSEED SWEETBREADS.—Take half a dozen sweetbreads; clean them thoroughly, and lay them for an hour or two in a pan of water, having first removed the strings and gristle. Then put them into a stew-pan with as much rich milk or cream as will cover them well, and a very little salt. Stew them slowly, till tender throughout, and thoroughly done, saving the liquid. Then take them up; cover them; and set them near the fire to keep warm. Prepare a quarter of a pound of fresh butter, divided into four pieces, and rolled in flour. Put the butter into the milk in which the sweetbreads were boiled, and add a few sprigs of parsley cut small; five or six blades of mace; half a nutmeg grated; and a very little cayenne pepper. Have ready the yolks of three eggs well-beaten. Return the sweetbreads to the gravy; let it just come to a boil; and then stir in the beaten egg *immediately before* you take the fricassee from the fire, otherwise it will curdle. Serve it up in a deep dish with a cover.

Chickens, cut up, may be fricasseed in this manner.

TOMATO SWEETBREADS.—Cut up a quarter of a peck (or more) of fine ripe tomatoes; set them over the fire, and let them stew with nothing but their own juice till they go entirely to pieces. Then press them through a sieve, to clear the liquid from the seeds and skins. Have ready four or five sweetbreads that have been trimmed nicely, cleared from the gristle, and laid open to soak in warm water. Put them into a stew-pan with the tomato-juice, seasoned with a little salt and cayenne. Add two or three table-spoonfuls of butter rolled in flour. Set the sauce-pan over the fire, and stew the sweetbreads in the tomato-juice till they are thoroughly done. A few minutes before you take them off, stir in two beaten yolks of eggs. Serve up the sweetbreads in a deep dish, with the tomato poured over them.

SWEETBREADS AND CAULIFLOWERS.—Take four large sweetbreads, and two fine cauliflowers. Split open the sweetbreads and remove the gristle. Soak them awhile in lukewarm water. Then put them into a sauce-pan of boiling water, and let them boil ten minutes over the fire. Afterwards, lay them in a pan of very cold water. The parboiling will render them white; and putting them directly from the hot water into the cold will give them firmness. Having washed and drained the cauliflowers, quarter them, and lay them in a broad stew-pan with the sweetbreads upon them, seasoned with a very little cayenne, two or three blades of mace, and some nutmeg. Add as much water as will cover them; put on closely the lid of the pan; and let the whole stew for about an hour. Then take a quarter of a pound of fresh butter, and roll it in a table-spoonful of flour. Add it to the stew with a tea-cupfull of rich milk or cream; and give it one boil up—not more, or the milk may curdle. Serve it hot in a deep dish; the sweetbreads in the middle with the gravy poured over them, and the quartered cauliflowers laid handsomely round. This stew will be found delicious.

Broccoli may be thus stewed with sweetbreads.

STEWED SWEETBREADS WITH OYSTERS.—Take four fine sweetbreads; cut them open; extract the gristle, and lay them in warm water till all the blood is soaked out. Then transfer them to another vessel, and scald them with boiling water, to render them white and firm. Cover them closely, and let them boil ten minutes in the hot water. Then throw them directly into a pan of cold water. Take them out when quite cold; drain them; and put them into a stew-pan with the liquor of three dozen large fine oysters seasoned with half a grated nutmeg, or more; and eight or ten blades of mace. Add two ounces of fresh butter, mixed very smoothly with a tea-spoonful of flour. Cover the pan; and let them stew gently for half an hour or more. Then put in the oysters, and let them stew with the sweetbreads a little more than five minutes. Lastly stir in a jill (two wine-glasses) of cream, immediately before you take the stew from the fire. Sent it to table in a deep dish with a slice of buttered toast at the bottom.

CLAM SWEETBREADS may be stewed exactly as above, only that clams must be substituted for oysters; the clams being cut up very small, and put in at the *beginning* along with the liquor, &c. The flavour they impart to the stew is by many persons considered superior to that of oysters.

In stewing sweetbreads you may either divide them into halves or quarters.

When cooked with oysters or clams they require no salt.

Sweetbreads should be large, fine, of a delicate colour, and *perfectly fresh*; otherwise they are unfit to eat. They spoil sooner than any part of the calf.

SWEETBREAD OMELET.—For an omelet of six or seven eggs, take two fine sweetbreads. Split them; take out the gristle; and soak them in two lukewarm waters, to extract all the blood. Then put them into very hot water; boil them ten minutes; take them out; set them away to cool; and afterwards mince them small, and season them with a very little salt and cayenne pepper, and some grated nutmeg. Beat the eggs (omitting the whites of two) till very light. Then mix in the chopped sweetbreads. Put three ounces or more of fresh butter into a small frying-pan, and place it over the fire. Stir the butter with a spoon, as it melts; and when it comes to a boil, put in the mixture, stirring it awhile after it is all in. Fry it a rich brown. Heat the plate or dish in which you turn it out of the pan. An omelet should never be turned while frying. The top may be well browned by holding about it a sala-mander or a red-hot shovel.

If you wish it very thick have *three* sweetbreads.

While frying the omelet, lift the edge occasionally by slipping a knife-blade under it, that the butter may get well beneath.

If the omelets are cooked too much they will become tough, and leather-like. Many persons prefer having them sent to table as *soft omelets*, before they have set, or taken the form of a cake. In this case, serve up the omelet in a deep dish, and help it with a spoon.

A ROUND OF BEEF STEWED BROWN. — Take a round of fresh beef; the larg-er it is the more tender it will be: a small round is always, comparatively, hard and tough. Remove the fat; with a sharp knife make deep cuts or incisions all over the meat, and stuff into them a seasoning of finely minced onions, mixed with pow-dered mace, nutmeg, and a little pepper and salt. Then go all over the meat with the drippings or cold gravy of roast beef, and dredge it slightly with flour. Have ready an iron dutch-oven and its lid, well heated by standing up both lid and oven before the fire. Then put the meat into the oven, cover it, and let it brown on all sides. Have ready, cut into small pieces, two turnips; four carrots; four oyster plants or salsify; three stalks of celery; two small onions; and two large tomatoes, or a large table-spoonful of tomato catchup. After the meat is browned, raise it up, and place the vegetables underneath it, and pour on three half-pints of water, or more if the round is very large. Let it cook slowly in the oven, with a regular fire, for several hours, till it is entirely done all through; taking care to keep it closely covered. After the meat is taken out, place it on a large hot dish, with the vegeta-bles round it. Cover it, and keep it hot while you thicken the gravy with a small tea-spoonful of flour, and the beaten yolk of an egg. Simmer this gravy a few min-utes, then put it into a sauce-boat, and serve it up with the meat.

What is left will be very good stewed over again the next day, with fresh vege-tables; letting the meat cook no longer than till the vegetables are sufficiently done. Observe this rule with all stews, soups, hashes, &c., when cooked the second time.

STEWED BEEF STEAKS. — Take beef steaks from the sirloin. Cut them thin; remove the fat and bone, and trim them nicely. Beat them well with a beetle or a rolling-pin. Season them slightly with pepper and salt, and spread them over some finely minced onions, or some chopped mushrooms. Lay among them some bits of fresh butter rolled in flour. Put them into a stew-pan with a very close cover, and without any water. Set the pan not on the fire, but before it or beside it, (turning it round frequently,) and let them stew slowly for two or three hours, or till they are thoroughly done. Then serve them up in their own gravy.

A BEEF STEAK POT-PIE. — Remove the fat and bone from two pounds or more of fine, tender beef steaks, and cut them into small pieces. Season them slightly with a very little salt and pepper; put them into a pot with a piece of fresh butter rolled in flour, and just water enough to cover them. Let them stew slowly (skimming them as soon as the water comes to a boil) for an hour. Boil in another pot some white potatoes, (a dozen small or eight large ones,) cut into quarters. While the steak is stewing, make a paste of finely minced beef-suet and flour, in the proportion of a pound and a half of suet to three pounds of flour. For a large pot-pie, you should have more than the above quantity of paste; the paste being always considered the best part of the pie, and much liked by those who eat it at all. Having rubbed the minced suet into the pan of flour, add a very little salt, and as little water as will suffice to make it into a lump of dough. Beat the dough hard on both sides with the rolling-pin, to assist in making it light and flaky. Divide the dough into two portions; roll out one sheet thicker than the other. Line the sides of a clean iron pot about half-way or two-thirds up with the thin paste. Then, having poured a little of the gravy into the bottom of the pot, put in a layer of the half-stewed beef; then a layer of the thick paste, cut into long squares. Then a layer of the quartered potatoes; then meat; then paste; then potatoes, and so on till the whole is in. Pour on the remainder of the gravy, and add also a pint of warm water. Cover the whole with a sheet of thin paste for a top crust, which must not fit closely round the edge, as there must be room for the gravy to boil up over it. Then place the pot over a moderate fire, and boil it for an hour and a half. Send it to table on a large dish,—the meat, and potatoes, and soft crust in the middle, and the hard crust cut into pieces and laid round. Serve up the gravy in a boat.

This pie will be much improved by a few fresh mushrooms, cut from the stalks, peeled, and put in when the stewed meat is transferred to the pie-pot.

A pot-pie of fowls or rabbits may be made as above.

If you prefer butter to suet for making the paste, allow half a pound of fresh butter to each pound of flour. Cut up the butter into the pan of flour, rub it fine with your hands, wet it with as little water as possible, beat and roll it out as above.

BEEF STEAKS WITH MUSHROOMS.—Take four pounds of the best sirloin steaks, cut thin. Season them with black pepper, and a very little salt. Put four table-spoonfuls of butter into a frying-pan, and set it over the fire. When it is quite hot, put in the steaks and let them brown. Have ready a quart of mushrooms, stemmed and skinned, and moistened with a pint of water, seasoned with a little pepper and salt, and thickened slightly with a good dredging of flour. Pour it over the steaks in the frying-pan, and then let them cook till thoroughly done.

Venison steaks will be found excellent dressed in this manner, but the venison must be fresh.

MINCED BEEF.—Take the lean of some cold roast beef. Chop it very fine, adding a small minced onion; and season it with pepper and salt. Put it into a stew-pan, with some of the gravy that has been left from the day before, and let it stew for a quarter of an hour. Then put it (two-thirds full) into a deep dish. Fill up the dish with mashed potatoes, heaped high in the centre, smoothed on the surface, and browned with a salamander or a red-hot shovel.

Cold roast mutton or lamb may be minced as above, adding some sweet-marjoram to the seasoning, and filling up the dish with mashed turnips instead of potatoes.

Also, cold roast pork; flavouring the seasoning with a little chopped sage. Cover the top with sweet potatoe, boiled and mashed, or with apple-sauce, that has been stewed as thick as possible.

TO STEW COLD CORNED BEEF.—Cut about four pounds of lean from a cold round of beef, that tastes but little of the salt. Lay it in a stew-pan, with a quarter of a peck of tomatoes quartered, and the same quantity of ochras sliced; also, two small onions peeled and sliced, and two ounces of fresh butter rolled in flour. Add a tea-spoonful of whole pepper-corns, (*no salt,*) and four or five blades of mace. Place it over a steady but moderate fire. Cover it closely, and let it stew three or four hours. The vegetables should be entirely dissolved. Serve it up hot.

This is an excellent way of using up the remains of a cold round of beef at the season of tomatoes and ochras, particularly when the meat has been rather under-boiled the first day of cooking it.

A few pounds of the lean of a *fresh* round of beef, will be still better cooked in this manner, increasing the quantity of ochras and tomatoes, and stewing it six hours.

Cold fillet of veal is very good stewed with tomatoes, ochras, and an onion or two. Also, the thick or upper part of a cold leg of mutton; or of pork, either fresh or corned.

TO STEW SMOKED BEEF.—The dried beef, for this purpose, must be fresh and of the very best quality. Cut it (or rather shave it) into very thin, small slices, with as little fat as possible. Put the beef into a skillet, and fill up with boiling water. Cover it, and let it soak or steep till the water is cold. Then drain off that water, and pour on some more, but merely enough to cover the chipped beef, which you may season with a little pepper. Set it over the fire, and (keeping on the cover) let it stew for a quarter of an hour. Then roll a few bits of butter in a little flour, and add it to the beef, with the yolk of one or two beaten eggs. Let it stew five minutes longer. Take it up on a hot dish, and send it to the breakfast or tea-table.

Cold ham may be sliced thin, and stewed in the same manner. Dried venison also.

FRENCH BEEF.—Take a circular piece from the round, (having removed the bone,) and trim it nicely from the fat, skin, &c. Then lard it all over with long slips of fat pork or bacon. The place from whence the bone was taken must be filled with a force-meat, made of minced suet; grated bread-crumbs; sweet-marjoram rubbed fine; and grated lemon-peel; add a little salt and pepper, and mix in the beaten yolk of an egg to bind together the other ingredients. Tie a twine or tape closely round the outside of the beef, to keep it compact, and in shape. Put it into a broad earthen jar with a cover; or into an iron bake-oven. Add some whole pepper; a large onion stuck over with a dozen cloves; a bunch of sweet herbs; three bay-leaves; a quarter of a pound of butter, divided into small bits, (each piece rolled in flour,) and half a pint of claret, or port-wine. Bake or stew it thus in its own liquor, for five, six, or seven hours, (in proportion to its size,) for it must be thoroughly done, quite tender, and brown all through the inside. Serve it up hot with the gravy round it. It is also very good when cold.

A fillet of veal may be cooked in this manner. Also a fillet of fresh pork, cut from the upper part of a hind leg; or a fillet of fresh venison.

BEEF OLIVES.—Take the lean of some cold roast beef; cut it into slices about half an inch thick, and four inches square. They must all be of the same size and shape. Trim the edges nicely. Make a force-meat of grated bread-crumbs, finely-chopped beef-suet; minced onion; grated nutmeg or powdered mace; sweet-marjoram leaves rubbed fine; a *very little* salt and pepper; and some beaten yolk of egg. Having mixed all thoroughly together, spread very thickly a portion of the force-meat upon each slice of the cold beef. Then roll them up, and tie every one securely round with coarse thread or fine twine. Have ready some roast-beef gravy left from the day before, or make a fresh gravy by boiling, or rather stewing the beef bones with as little water as possible. When the gravy is ready, strain it into a clean stew-pan; put in the beef olives; cover the pan, and let them stew slowly for half an hour. Serve them up with their gravy. Remove the strings before the olives go to table.

Veal olives may be made in the above manner, with a cold roast fillet of veal, and veal gravy.

A PLAIN STEW.—Cut steaks from a sirloin or a tender round of beef, omitting the fat and bone. Season them with pepper and a little salt. Put them into a pot, and to three pounds of meat allow a quart of water. When it has simmered for an hour, and been well skimmed, mix among it a dozen potatoes, and half a dozen turnips, all pared and quartered; and (if you like them) two onions sliced thin. If the stew appears too dry, pour in a little *boiling* water from a kettle. Let it stew slowly with the vegetables another hour, or till the whole is perfectly tender. Serve it up with the vegetables round it on a large dish.

Beef stewed with parsnips only is very good.

Lamb or veal cutlets may be stewed in this manner.

A fillet or round of fresh pork is excellent stewed with sweet potatoes, which must be scraped or pared, and split in half.

BEEF'S TONGUE STEWED.—Take a fresh beef's tongue of the largest size. Remove the little bones, skin, &c., from about the root, and trim it nicely. Take a table-spoonful each of salt, pepper, and powdered cloves, and mix them all together. Rub the tongue well all over with this seasoning. Lay it in a deep earthen pan, cover it with the best cider vinegar, and let it stand three days, turning it frequently, and keeping it closely covered. Then (having wiped off all the seasoning) put the tongue into a stew-pot, and add half a pint of water—not more—and stew it slowly till quite done. Have ready some force-meat balls, made with minced veal, mixed with the ingredients usual in force-meat. Put in the balls about twenty minutes before you take up the tongue. When it is thoroughly done, and tender all through, peel it, and send it to table with the force-meat balls round it.

BAKED TONGUE.—Take a large smoked tongue, put it into warm water and soak it all day. Change the water in the evening, and then let it remain in soak all night. Before you cook it, trim the root handsomely. Make a coarse paste or dough, merely of flour and water, as it is not to be eaten. Roll it out thin, and enclose the tongue in it. Put it into an oven, and bake it slowly. It will require four hours or more. When you think it is done, break a little of the paste just over the thickest part, and try it by sticking a fork through it. If not perfectly tender, let it bake a while longer. When quite done, remove the paste, and either serve up the tongue, or set it away to get cold. This is the best way of cooking a tongue to be eaten cold. If to be eaten warm, send it to table surrounded with mashed potatoes, and the root concealed with parsley sprigs. The best way to carve a tongue, is to cut it across in round slices, beginning at the middle. If cut lengthways the flavour will be impaired. Nevertheless, if you have two tongues, and wish to make a large handsome-looking dish of them, (having first removed the root,) split one lengthways, and lay the two halves spread open and near together on a bed of mashed potatoes; and cut the other tongue into circular slices. Arrange these slices in a handsome form or pattern all round the split tongue that occupies the centre of the mashed potatoe; and decorate the whole with sprigs of double parsley. If the tongues are cold, instead of mashed potatoe, lay them on a bed of salad-dressed lettuce, cut or chopped very small; or on chopped celery, dressed as lettuce.

FILLET OF PORK.—Cut a fillet or round, handsomely and evenly, from a fine leg of fresh pork. Remove the bone. Make a stuffing or force-meat of grated bread-crumbs; butter; a tea-spoonful of sweet-marjoram or tarragon leaves; and sage leaves enough to make a small table-spoonful, when minced or rubbed fine; all well mixed, and slightly seasoned with pepper and salt. Add some beaten yolk of egg to bind the whole together; then stuff it closely into the hole from whence the bone was taken. Score the skin of the pork in circles to go all round the fillet. These circles should be very close together, or not quite half an inch apart. Rub into them, slightly, a little powdered sage. Put it on the spit, and roast it well, till it is thoroughly done throughout; as pork, if the least underdone, is not fit to eat. Place it for the first hour not very close to the fire, that the meat may get well heated all through, before the skin begins to harden so as to prevent the heat from penetrating sufficiently. Then set it as near the fire as it can be placed without danger of scorching. Keep it roasting steadily with a bright, good, regular fire, for two or three hours, or longer still if it is a large fillet. It may require near four hours. Baste it at the beginning with sweet oil (which will make the skin very crisp) or with lard. Afterwards, baste it with its own gravy. When done, skim the fat from the gravy, and then dredge in a little flour to thicken it. Send the pork to table with the gravy in a boat; and a small tureen of apple-sauce, made very thick, flavoured with lemon, and sweetened well.

A fillet of pork is excellent stewed slowly in a very little water, having in the same stew-pot some sweet potatoes, peeled, split, and cut into long pieces. If stewed, put *no sage* in the stuffing; and remove the skin of the pork. This is an excellent family dish in the autumn.

ITALIAN PORK.—Take a nice leg of fresh pork; rub it well with fine salt, and let it lie in the salt for a week or ten days. When you wish to cook it, put the pork into a large pot with just sufficient water to cover it; and let it simmer, slowly, during four hours; skimming it well. Then take it out, and lay it on a large dish.

Pour the water from the pot into an earthen pan; skim it, and let it cool while you are skinning the pork. Then put into the pot, a pint of good cider vinegar, mixed with half a pound of brown sugar, and a pint of the water in which the pork has been boiled, and from which all the fat has been carefully skimmed off. Put in the pork with the upper side towards the bottom of the pot. Set it again over the fire, (which must first be increased,) and heat the inside of the pot-lid by standing it upright against the front of the fire. Then cover the pot closely, and let the pork stew for an hour and a half longer; basting it frequently with the liquid around it, and keeping the pot-lid as hot as possible that the meat may be well browned. When done, the pork will have somewhat the appearance of being coated with molasses. Serve up the gravy with it. What is left of the meat may be sliced cold for breakfast or luncheon.

You may stew with it when the pork is put into the pot a second time, some large chesnuts, previously boiled and peeled. Or, instead of chesnuts, sweet potatoes, scraped, split, and cut into small pieces.

PORK OLIVES.—Cut slices from a fillet or leg of cold fresh pork. Make a force-meat in the usual manner, only substituting for sweet herbs some sage-leaves chopped fine. When the slices are covered with the force-meat, and rolled up and tied round, stew them slowly either in cold gravy left of the pork, or in fresh lard. Drain them well before they go to table. Serve them up on a bed of mashed turnips or potatoes, or of mashed sweet potatoes, if in season.

PIGS' FEET FRIED.—Pigs' feet are frequently used for jelly, instead of calves' feet. They are very good for this purpose, but a larger number is required (from eight to ten or twelve) to make the jelly sufficiently firm. After they have been boiled for jelly, extract the bones, and put the meat into a deep dish; cover it with some good cider-vinegar, seasoned with sugar and a little salt and cayenne. Then cover the dish, and set it away for the night. Next morning, take out the meat, and having drained it well from the vinegar, put it into a frying-pan in which some lard has just come to a boil, and fry it for a breakfast dish.

CONNECTICUT SAUSAGE-MEAT.—To fifteen pounds of the lean of fresh pork, allow five pounds of the fat. Having removed the skin, sinews, and gristle, chop both the fat and lean as fine as possible, and mix them well together. Rub to a powder sufficient sage-leaves to make four ounces when done. Mix the sage with three ounces of fine salt, two ounces of brown sugar, an ounce of powdered black pepper, and a quarter of an ounce of cayenne. Add this seasoning to the chopped pork, and mix it thoroughly. Pack the sausage-meat down, hard and closely, into stone jars, which must be kept in a cool place, and well covered. When wanted for use, make some of it into small, flat cakes, dredge them with flour, and fry them well. The fat that exudes from the sausage-cakes, while frying, will be sufficient to cook them in.

A FINE VENISON PIE.—Cut steaks from a loin, or haunch of venison, which should be as freshly killed as you can get it. The strange prejudice in favour of hard, black-looking venison, that has been kept till the juices are all dried up, is fast subsiding; the preference is now given to that which has been newly killed, whenever it can be obtained. Those who have eaten venison fresh from the woods, will never again be able to relish it in the state in which it is brought to the Atlantic cities.

Having removed the bones, and seasoned it with a little salt and pepper, put the venison into a pot, with barely as much water as will cover it, and let it stew till perfectly tender, skimming it occasionally. Then take it out, and set it to cool, saving the gravy in a bowl. Make a light paste, in the proportion of three quarters of a pound of fresh butter to a pound and a half of flour. Divide the paste into two portions, and roll it out rather thick. Butter a deep dish, and line it with one of the sheets of paste. Then put in the venison. Season the gravy with a glass of *very good* wine, either red or white, a few blades of mace, and a powdered nutmeg. Stir into it the crumbled yolks of some hard-boiled eggs. Pour the gravy over the meat, and put on the other sheet of paste as the lid of the pie. Notch it handsomely round the edges, and bake it well. If a steady heat is kept up, it will be done in an hour. Send it to table hot.

Instead of wine, you may put into the gravy a glass of currant-jelly.

Any sort of game may be made into a pie, in the above manner.

A VERY PLAIN VENISON PIE. — Cut from the bone some good pieces of fresh venison; season them a little with salt and pepper, and put them into a pot, with plenty of sliced potatoes, (either white or sweet,) and barely as much water as will cover the whole. Set it over the fire, and let it stew slowly, till the meat is tender, and the potatoes also. Make a paste of flour shortened with cold gravy, or drippings saved from roast venison. The fat must be removed from the surface of the cold gravy, of which you may allow half a pint to each pound of flour. Mix half the shortening with the flour, using a broad knife or a spoon for the purpose, and adding gradually sufficient cold water to make it into a stiff dough. Beat the lump of dough well on all sides, with the rolling-pin. Then take it out of the pan, roll it into a thick sheet, and spread evenly over it with a knife the remainder of the drippings. Flour it, fold it up, beat it with the rolling-pin, let it rest a short time, and then roll it out again. Divide it into two sheets; grease a pie-dish, and line the bottom and sides with one sheet. Put in the venison and potatoes, with a portion of the gravy. Lay on the other sheet of paste, as a lid, and crimp the edges. Set the pie into the oven, and bake it brown. Eat it either hot or cold.

If you have no cold venison drippings, use drippings of cold roast-beef; or an equal mixture of lard and butter.

A beef-pie may be made as above.

Mutton-pies are not recommended; as mutton cooked in a pie is entirely too strong. The fat or drippings of mutton should *never* be used in any sort of cooking, as it tastes exactly like tallow, which it really is.

The above quantity of paste is only sufficient for a small pie. Paste for meat-pies should be made very thick.

An excellent pot-pie may be made with venison and potatoes previously stewed together. Boiled paste is always best when shortened with minced suet.

Beef-suet is superior to any other.

A VENISON PUDDING.—Take nice steaks of *fresh* venison; season them slightly with salt and pepper; put them into a pot, with a piece of fresh butter, and stew them in barely sufficient water to keep them from scorching. When they are quite tender, take them, up; cut all the meat from the bones, and set it to cool. Save the gravy, and when cold carefully remove all the fat from the surface. Prepare a paste, in the proportion of three quarters of a pound of beef-suet, finely minced, to two pounds of flour. Rub the suet thoroughly into the flour, adding a small salt-spoon of salt, and sufficient cold water to moisten it into a stiff dough. Beat the lump of dough, on all sides, with the rolling-pin, to increase the lightness of the paste. Roll it out thick; put the venison into it; and pour on enough of the gravy to wet the meat all through. Then close over the paste, so as to form a large dumpling, with the venison in the middle. Have ready a thick pudding-cloth, that has been dipped in boiling water, shaken out, dredged with flour, and spread open in a broad pan. Place the pudding in the cloth, tie it firmly, leaving room for the pudding to swell; and, to prevent the water getting in, stop up the tying-place with a bit of coarse dough. Lay an old plate at the bottom of a large pot of boiling water; put in the pudding, and keep it boiling steadily for an hour or more, turning it several times. When done, dip it into cold water, untie the cloth, and turn out the pudding. Send it to table hot.

A beef-steak pudding may be made as above.

You may make the crust of fresh butter, instead of suet; allowing a pound of butter to two pounds, or two quarts of flour.

VENISON CHESNUT PUDDING.—Take some steaks of fresh-killed venison; season them slightly with pepper and salt. Have ready a sufficient quantity of large chesnuts, boiled and peeled. Make a crust of flour and suet, in the proportion of three quarters of a pound of finely minced suet to two pounds of flour. Roll it out thick, in two pieces, and place on one piece the venison and chesnuts, in alternate layers. Pour on a little water. Cover it with the other piece of paste, uniting it closely round the edges. Put it into a strong pudding-cloth; tie it tightly, and plaster the tying-place with a lump of flour and water. Put the pudding into a pot of boiling water, and boil it four hours.

For the chesnuts, you may substitute cold, boiled sweet potatoes, cut into round, thick slices.

This is an excellent pudding in a venison country; but the meat must be very fresh and juicy. The paste may be made with butter.

FRENCH STEW OF RABBITS.—Having cut up the rabbits, lay the pieces in cold water, to soak out the blood. Then wash them through another water. Season them with a little pepper, some powdered mace and nutmeg, and the yellow rind of a lemon grated. Put them into a jar, or a wide-mouthed pitcher, adding some chopped celery, sweet-marjoram, and tarragon leaves. Intersperse them with a few small thin slices of cold ham or smoked tongue, and add a tea-cup full of water and two glasses of white wine. Cover the jar very closely, so that none of the flavour may escape with the steam; set it over the fire in a large kettle of cold water, and let it stew slowly two hours. When nearly done, add some pieces of butter rolled in flour.

Hares may be stewed in the same manner; also, fresh venison.

For the wine, you may substitute two wine-glasses of rich cream.

TONGUE TOAST.—Take a cold smoked tongue that has been well boiled; and grate it with a coarse grater, or mince it fine. Mix it with cream, and beaten yolk of egg; and give it a simmer over the fire. Having first cut off all the crust, toast very nicely some slices of bread; and then butter them rather slightly. Lay them in a flat dish that has been heated before the fire; and cover each slice of toast thickly with the tongue-mixture, spread on hot; and send them to table covered. This is a nice breakfast or supper dish.

For tongue, you may substitute cold ham finely minced.

BISCUIT SANDWICHES.—Split some light *soft* milk biscuits (or small French rolls) and butter them. Cover the lower half thickly with grated ham, or smoked tongue; pressing it down upon the butter. Then put on the upper half or lid; pressing that on, to make it stick. Pile the biscuits handsomely in a pyramid upon a flat dish, and place among them, at regular distances, green sprigs of pepper-grass, corn-salad, water-cresses, or curled parsley, allowing four or six to each biscuit. Put in the sprigs between the upper and lower halves of the biscuits, so that they may stick out at the edges.

To make more space for the grated ham, you may scoop out a little of the inside of the upper-half of each milk biscuit or roll. They should be fresh, of that day's baking.

This is a nice supper-dish.

POTTED HAM.—Take some cold ham, slice it, and mince it small, fat and lean together. Then pound it in a mortar; seasoning it as you proceed with cayenne pepper, powdered mace, and powdered nutmeg. Then fill with it a large deep pan, and set it in an oven for half an hour. Afterwards pack it down hard in a stone jar, and fill up the jar with lard. Cover it closely, and paste down a thick paper over the jar. If sufficiently seasoned, it will keep well in winter; and is convenient for sandwiches, or on the tea-table. A jar of this will be found useful to travellers in remote places.

A FRENCH HAM PIE.—Having soaked and boiled a small ham, and taken out the bone, trim the ham nicely so as to make it a good shape; and of the bone and trimmings make a rich gravy, by stewing them in a sauce-pan with a little water; carefully skimming off the fat. Make a sufficient quantity of force-meat, out of cold roast chicken or veal, minced suet, grated bread-crumbs, butter, pepper, chopped sweet-marjoram or tarragon; and grated lemon-peel, adding the lemon-juice, and some beaten egg. Mix the ingredients thoroughly. You may add some chopped oysters.

Having made a standing crust, allowing to two pounds of flour half a pound of butter, and a pound of minced suet, wetted to a paste with boiling water, put in the ham, (moistening it with the gravy,) and fill in all the vacancies with the force-meat, having a layer of force-meat at the bottom and top. Then put on the lid, pinching the edges together so as to close them well. Brush the paste all over with beaten yolk of egg; then put on the ornamental flowers and leaves that have been cut out of the dough. Bake it three or four hours. It may be eaten warm, but is generally preferred cold. It keeps well, if carefully secluded from the air.

TONGUE PIE is made as above; only substituting a smoked tongue for the ham. The tongue must be nicely trimmed and peeled, and the root minced fine, and mixed with the veal or chicken force-meat.

Either of these pies may be made and baked in deep dishes, and with paste made in the usual way of butter and flour, wetted with a little cold water.

HAM TOAST.—Grate a sufficiency of the lean of cold ham. Mix some beaten yolk of egg with a little cream, and thicken it with the grated ham. Then put the mixture into a sauce-pan over the fire, and let it simmer awhile. Have ready some slices of bread nicely toasted (all the crust being pared off) and well buttered. Spread it over thickly with the ham mixture, and send it to table warm.

POULTRY, GAME, ETC.

CHICKENS STEWED WHOLE.—Having trussed a pair of fine fat young fowls or chickens, (with the liver under one wing, and the gizzard under the other,) fill the inside with large oysters, secured from falling out, by fastening tape round the bodies of the fowls. Put them into a tin butter-kettle with a close cover. Set the kettle into a larger pot or sauce-pan of boiling water, (which must not reach quite to the top of the kettle,) and place it over the fire. Keep it boiling till the fowls are well done, which they should be in about an hour after they begin to simmer. Occasionally take off the lid to remove the scum; and be sure to put it on again closely. As the water in the outside pot boils away, replenish it with more *hot* water from a tea-kettle that is kept boiling hard. When the fowls are stewed quite tender, remove them from the fire; take from them all the gravy that is about them, and put it into a small sauce-pan, covering closely the kettle in which they were stewed, and leaving the fowls in it to keep warm. Then add to the gravy two table-spoonfuls of butter rolled in flour; two table-spoonfuls of chopped oysters; the yolks of three hard-boiled eggs minced fine; half a grated nutmeg; four blades of mace; and a small tea-cup of cream. Boil this gravy about five minutes. Put the fowls on a dish, and send them to table, accompanied by the gravy in a sauce-boat. This is an excellent way of cooking chickens.

FOWL AND OYSTERS.—Take a fine fat young fowl, and having trussed it for boiling, fill the body and crop with oysters, seasoned with a few blades of mace; tying it round with twine to keep them in. Put the fowl into a tall strait-sided jar, and cover it closely. Then place the jar in a kettle of water; set it over the fire, and let it boil at least an hour and a half after the water has come to a hard boil. When it is done, take out the fowl, and keep it hot while you prepare the gravy, of which you will find a quantity in the jar. Transfer this gravy to a sauce-pan; enrich it with the beaten yolks of two eggs, mixed with three table-spoonfuls of cream; and add a large table-spoonful of fresh butter rolled in flour. If you cannot get cream, you must have a double portion of butter. Set this sauce over the fire; stirring it well; and when it comes to a boil, add twenty oysters chopped small. In five minutes take it off; put it into a sauce-boat, and serve it up with the fowl, which cooked in this manner will be found excellent.

Clams may be substituted for oysters; but they should be removed from the fowl before it is sent to table. Their flavour being drawn out into the gravy, the clams themselves will be found tough, tasteless, and not proper to be eaten.

FRENCH CHICKEN PIE.—Parboil a pair of full-grown, but fat and tender chickens. Then take the giblets, and put them into a small sauce-pan with as much of the water in which the chickens were parboiled as will cover them well, and stew them for gravy; add a bunch of sweet herbs and a few blades of mace. When the chickens are cold, dissect them as if for carving. Line a deep dish with thick puff-paste, and put in the pieces of chicken. Take a nice thin slice of cold ham, or two slices of smoked tongue, and pound them one at a time in a marble mortar, pounding also the livers of the chickens, and the yolks of half a dozen hard-boiled eggs. Make this force-meat into balls, and intersperse them among the pieces of chicken. Add some bits of fresh butter rolled in flour, and then (having removed the giblets) pour on the gravy. Cover the pie with a lid of puff-paste, rolled out thick; and notch the edges handsomely; placing a knot or ornament of paste on the centre of the top. Set it directly into a well-heated oven, and bake it brown. It should be eaten warm.

This pie will be greatly improved by a pint of mushrooms, cut into pieces. Also by a small tea-cup of cream.

Any pie of poultry, pigeons, or game may be made in this manner.

CHICKEN GUMBO.—Cut up a young fowl as if for a fricassee. Put into a stew-pan a large table-spoonful of fresh butter, mixed with a tea-spoonful of flour, and an onion finely minced. Brown them over the fire, and then add a quart of water, and the pieces of chicken, with a large quarter of a peck of ochras, (first sliced thin, and then chopped,) and a salt-spoon of salt. Cover the pan, and let the whole stew together till the ochras are entirely dissolved, and the fowl thoroughly done. If it is a very young chicken, do not put it in at first; as half an hour will be sufficient to cook it. Serve it up hot in a deep dish.

A cold fowl may be used for this purpose.

You may add to the ochras an equal quantity of tomatoes cut small. If you use tomatoes, no water will be necessary, as their juice will supply a sufficient liquid.

TOMATO CHICKEN.—Take four small chickens or two large ones, and cut them up as for carving. Put them into a stew-pan, with one or two large slices of cold boiled ham cut into little bits; eight or ten large tomatoes; an onion sliced; a bunch of pot-herbs, (cut up;) a small green pepper, (the seeds and veins first extracted;) half a dozen blades of mace; a table-spoonful of lard, or of fresh butter rolled in flour; and two pounded crackers, or a handful of grated bread-crumbs. Add a tumbler or half a pint of water. Cover the sauce-pan closely with a cloth beneath the lid; set it on hot coals, or over a moderate fire; and let it stew slowly till the chickens are thoroughly done, and the tomatoes entirely dissolved. Turn it out into a deep dish.

Rabbits may be stewed in this manner. Also, veal steaks, cut thin and small.

TURKEY AND CHICKEN PATTIES.—Take the white part of some cold turkey or chicken, and mince it very fine. Mince also some cold boiled ham or smoked tongue, and then mix the turkey and ham together. Add the yolks of some hard-boiled eggs, grated or minced; a very little cayenne; and some powdered mace and nutmeg. Moisten the whole with cream or fresh butter. Have ready some puff-paste shells, that have been baked empty in patty-pans. Place them on a large dish, and fill them with the mixture.

Cold fillet of veal minced, and mixed with chopped ham, and grated yolk of egg, and seasoned as above, will make very good patties.

CHICKEN RICE PUDDING.—Parboil a fine fowl, and cut it up. Boil, till soft and dry, a pint of rice; and while warm, mix with it a large table-spoonful of fresh butter. Beat four eggs very light; and then mix them, gradually, with the rice. Spread a coating of the rice, &c., over the bottom and sides of a deep dish. Place on it the pieces of the parboiled fowl, with a little of the liquid in which it was boiled—seasoned with powdered mace and nutmeg. Add some bits of fresh butter rolled in flour, and a little cream. Cover the dish closely with the remainder of the rice; set the pudding immediately into the oven and bake it brown.

Cold chicken or turkey cooked the day before may be used for this purpose. The pudding may be improved by the addition of a few very thin, small slices of cold ham or smoked tongue.

RICE CROQUETTES.—Boil half a pound of rice till it becomes quite soft and dry. Then mix with it two table-spoonfuls of rich (but not strong) grated cheese, a small tea-spoonful of powdered mace, and sufficient fresh butter to moisten it. Mince very fine six table-spoonfuls of the white part of cold chicken or turkey, the soft parts of six large oysters, and a sprig or two of tarragon or parsley; add a grated nutmeg, and the yellow rind of a lemon. Mix the whole well, moistening it with cream or white wine. Take of the prepared rice a portion about the size of an egg, flatten it, and put into the centre a dessert-spoonful of the mixture; close the rice round it as you would the paste round a dumpling-apple. Then form it into the shape of an egg. Brush it over with some beaten yolk of egg, and then dredge it with pounded crackers. In this way make up the whole into oval balls. Have ready, in a sauce-pan over the fire, a pound of boiling lard. Into this throw the croquettes, two at a time, so as to brown them. Let them brown for a few minutes; then take them out with a perforated skimmer. Drain them from the lard, and serve them up hot, garnished with curled parsley.

COLUMBUS EGGS.—Take twelve hard-boiled eggs. Peel off the shells, and cut the eggs into equal halves; cutting off also a little piece from each of the ends to enable them to stand alone, in the form of cups. Chop the yolks, and with them mix cold ham or smoked tongue, minced as finely as possible. Moisten the mixture with cream, (or a little fresh butter,) and season it with powdered mace or nutmeg. Fill with it the cups or empty whites of the eggs, (being careful not to break them;) pressing the mixture down, and smoothing it nicely. Arrange them on a dish; putting two halves close together, and standing them upright, so as to look like whole eggs.

WHITE FRICASSEE.—Cut a pair of chickens into pieces, as for carving; and wash them through two or three waters. Then lay them in a large pan, sprinkle them slightly with salt, and fill up the pan with boiling water. Cover it, and let the chickens stand for half an hour. Then put them immediately into a stew-pan; adding a few blades of mace, and a few whole pepper-corns, and a handful of celery, split thin and chopped finely; also, a small white onion sliced. Pour on cold milk and water (mixed in equal portions) sufficient to cover the chickens well. Cover the stew-pan, set it over the fire, and let it stew till the chickens are thoroughly done, and quite tender. While the chickens are stewing, prepare, in a smaller sauce-pan, a gravy or sauce made as follows:—Mix two tea-spoonfuls of flour with as much cold water as will make it like a batter, and stir it till quite smooth and free from lumps. Then add to it, gradually, half a pint of boiling milk. Next put in a quarter of a pound of fresh butter, cut into small pieces. Set it over hot coals, and stir it till it comes to a boil, and the butter is well melted and mixed throughout. Then take it off the fire, and, while it is hot, stir in a glass of madeira or sherry, and four table-spoonfuls of rich cream, and some grated nutmeg. Lastly, take the chickens out of the stew-pan, and pour off all the liquor, &c. Return the chicken to the stew-pan, and pour over it, hot, the above-mentioned gravy. Cover the pan closely, and let it stand in a hot place, or in a kettle of boiling water for ten minutes. Then send it to table in a covered dish.

To the taste of many persons, this fricassee will be improved by adding to the chicken, while stewing, some small, thin slices of cold boiled ham.

Rabbits or veal may be fricasseed in the above manner.

BROWN FRICASSEE.—Half roast a pair of ducks. Then cut them apart, as for carving. If they are wild-ducks, parboil them with a large carrot (cut to pieces) inside of each, to draw out the fishy or sedgy taste. Having thrown away the carrot, cut the ducks into pieces, as for carving. Put them into a clean stew-pan, and season them with pepper and salt. Mix in a deep dish a very small onion minced fine, a table-spoonful of minced or powdered tarragon-leaves, (for which you may substitute sage and sweet-marjoram, if you cannot procure tarragon,) and two or three large tomatoes, scalded, peeled, and quartered, or two large table-spoonfuls of thick tomato catchup. Put in, also, two table-spoonfuls of fresh butter rolled in grated bread-crumbs, and a glass of port wine, claret, or brandy, with a small tea-spoonful of powdered mace. Cover the pieces of duck with this mixture, and then add barely as much water as will keep the whole from burning. Cover the pan closely, and let the fricassee stew slowly for an hour, or till the duck, &c., are thoroughly done.

Venison or lamb cutlets may be fricasseed in this manner. Likewise, tame fat pigeons, which must previously be split in two. This, also, is a very nice way of dressing hares or rabbits.

STEWED WILD DUCKS.—Having rubbed them slightly with salt, and parboiled them for about twenty minutes with a large carrot (cut to pieces) in each, to take off the sedgy or fishy taste, remove the carrots, cut up the ducks, and put them into a stew-pan with just sufficient water to cover them, and some bits of butter rolled slightly in flour. Cover the pan closely; and let the ducks stew for a quarter of an hour or more. Have ready a mixture in the proportion of a wine-glass of sherry or madeira; the grated yellow rind and the juice of a large lemon or orange, and one large table-spoonful of powdered loaf-sugar. Pour this over the ducks, and let them stew in it about five minutes longer. Then serve them up in a deep dish with the gravy about them. Eat the stewed duck on hot plates with heaters under them.

Cold roast duck that has been under-done is very fine stewed as above. Venison also, and wild geese.

TO ROAST CANVAS-BACK DUCKS.—Having trussed the ducks, put into each a thick piece of soft bread that has been soaked in port wine. Place them before a quick fire and roast them from three quarters to an hour. Before they go to table, squeeze over each the juice of a lemon or orange; and serve them up very hot with their own gravy about them. Eat them with currant jelly. Have ready also a gravy made by stewing slowly in a sauce-pan the giblets of the ducks in butter rolled in flour and as little water as possible. Serve up this additional gravy in a boat.

CANVAS-BACK DUCKS DRESSED PLAIN.—Truss the ducks without washing; but wipe them inside and out with a clean dry cloth. Roast them before a rather quick fire for half an hour. Then send them to table hot, upon a large dish placed on a heater. There must also be heaters under each plate, and currant jelly on both sides of the table, to mix with the gravy, on your plate; claret or port wine also, for those who prefer it as an improvement to the gravy.

TO STEW CANVAS-BACK DUCKS.—Put the giblets into a sauce-pan with the yellow rind of a lemon pared thin, a very little water, and a piece of butter rolled in flour, and a very little salt and cayenne. Let them stew gently to make a gravy; keeping the sauce-pan covered. In the mean time, half roast the ducks, saving the gravy that falls from them. Then cut them up; put them into a large stew-pan, with the gravy (having first skimmed off the fat) and merely water enough to keep them from burning. Set the pan over a moderate fire, and let them stew gently till done. Towards the last (having removed the giblets) pour over the ducks the gravy from the small sauce-pan, and stir in a large glass of port wine, and a glass of currant jelly. Send them to table as hot as possible.

Any ducks may be stewed as above. The common wild-ducks, teal, &c., should always be parboiled with a large carrot in the body to extract the fishy or sedgy taste. On tasting this carrot before it is thrown away, it will be found to have imbibed strongly that disagreeable flavour.

PARTRIDGES IN PEARS.—Cut off the necks of the partridges close to the breast. Truss them very tight and round, and rub over them a little salt and cayenne pepper mixed. Cut off one of the legs, and leave the other on. Make a rich paste of flour, butter, and beaten yolk of egg, with as little water as possible. Roll it out thin and evenly, and put a portion of it nicely round each partridge, pressing it on closely with your hand, and forming it into the shape of a large pear. Leave one leg sticking out at the top to resemble the stem. Set them in a pan; and bake them in a dutch oven. In the mean time, make in a small sauce-pan, a rich brown gravy of the livers, and other trimmings of the partridges, and some drippings of roast veal or roasted poultry. It will be better still if you reserve one or two small partridges to cut up, and stew for the gravy. Season it with a little salt and cayenne. When it has boiled long enough to be very thick and rich, take it off, strain it, and put the liquid into a clean sauce-pan. Add the juice of a large orange or lemon, made very sweet with powdered white sugar. Set it over the fire; and when it comes to a boil, stir in the beaten yolks of two eggs. Let it boil two or three minutes longer; then take it off, and keep it hot till the partridges and their paste are thoroughly well-baked. When done, stand up the partridges in a deep dish, and serve up the gravy in a sauce-boat. Ornament the partridge-pears by sticking some orange or lemon leaves into the end that represents the stalk. This is a nice and handsome side dish, of French origin.

Pigeons and quails may be dressed in this manner.

SALMI OF PARTRIDGES, (*French dish.*)—Having covered two large or four small partridges with very thin slices of fat cold ham, secured with twine, roast them; but see that they are not too much done. Remove the ham, skin the partridges, cut them into pieces, and let them get quite cold. Partridges that have been roasted the preceding day are good for this purpose. Cut off all the meat from the bones, season it with a little cayenne, and put it into a stew-pan. Mix together three table-spoonfuls of sweet oil; a glass of excellent wine (either red or white) and the grated peel and juice of a lemon. Pour this gravy over the partridges, and let them stew in it during ten minutes; the add the beaten yolk of an egg, and stew it about three or four minutes longer. All the time it is stewing, continue to shake or move the pan over the fire. Serve it up hot.

A NICE WAY OF COOKING GAME.—Pheasants, partridges, quails, grouse, plovers, &c., are excellent stuffed with chesnuts: boiled, peeled, and mashed or pounded. Cover the birds with very thin slices of cold ham; then enclose them in vine-leaves tied on securely so as to keep in the gravy. Lay them in a deep dish, and bake them in a close oven that has nothing else in it, (for instance an iron dutch oven,) that the game may imbibe no other flavour. When done, remove the ham and the vine leaves, and dish the birds with the gravy that is about them.

Pheasants are unfit to eat after the first snow, as they then, for want of other food, are apt to feed on wild laurel berries, which give their flesh a disagreeably bitter taste, and are said to have sometimes produced deleterious effects on persons who have eaten it.

BIRDS WITH MUSHROOMS.—Take two dozen reed-birds, (or other nice small birds,) and truss them as if for roasting. Put into each a button-mushroom; of which you should have a heaping pint after the stalks are all removed. Put the birds, and the remaining mushrooms into a stew-pan. Season them with a very little salt and pepper, and add either a quarter of a pound of fresh butter (divided into four, and slightly rolled in flour) or a pint of rich cream. If cream is not plenty, you may use half butter and half cream, well mixed together. Cover the stew-pan closely, and set it over a moderate fire, to stew gently till the birds and mushrooms are thoroughly done and tender all through. Do not open the lid to stir the stew; but give the pan, occasionally, a hard shake. Have ready on a dish a thin slice of buttered toast with the crust all cut off. When done, lay the birds on the toast with the mushrooms all round.

If you cannot get button-mushrooms, divide large ones into quarters.

Plovers are very nice stewed with mushrooms.

BIRDS IN A GROVE, (*French dish.*)—Having roasted some reed-birds, larks, plovers, or any other small birds, such as are usually eaten, mash some potatoes with butter or cream. Spread the mashed potatoe thickly over the bottom, sides, and edges of a deep dish. Nick or crimp the border of potatoe that goes round the edge; or scollop it with a tin cutter. You may, if you choose, brown it by holding over it a salamander, or a red-hot shovel. Then lay the roasted birds in the middle of the dish, and stick round them and among them, very thickly a sufficient number of sprigs of curled or double parsley.

THATCHED HOUSE PIE, (*French dish.*)—Rub the inside of a deep dish with two ounces of fresh butter, and spread over it two ounces of vermicelli. Then line the dish with puff-paste. Have ready some birds seasoned with powdered nutmeg and a very little salt and pepper. Place them with their breasts downward. They will be much improved by putting into each a mushroom or an oyster chopped fine. Lay them on the paste. Add some gravy of roast veal, (cold gravy saved from veal roasted the preceding day will do very well,) and cover the pie with a lid of puff-paste. Bake it in a moderate oven, and when done, turn it out *carefully* upon a flat dish, and send it to table. The vermicelli which was originally at the bottom, will now be at the top, covering the paste like thatch upon a roof. Trim off the edges so as to look nicely. You may, if you choose, use a larger quantity of vermicelli. The yellow sort will be best for this purpose.

RICE PIE.—Pick clean a quart of rice, and wash it well through two or three waters. Tie it in a cloth, put it into a pot of boiling water, and boil it till perfectly soft. Then drain and press it till as dry as possible, and mix with it two ounces of fresh butter, and two table-spoonfuls of mild grated cheese. Take a small tin butter-kettle; wet the inside, put in the rice, and stand it in a cool place till quite cold. Then turn it carefully out of the kettle, (of which it will retain the form,) rub it over with the beaten yolk of an egg, and set it in an oven till lightly browned. Cut out from the top of the mass of rice an oval lid, about two inches from the edge, so as to leave a flat rim or border all round. Then excavate the mould of rice; leaving a standing crust all round and at the bottom, about two inches thick. Have ready some hot stewed oysters or birds, or brown or white fricassee. Fill up the pie with it—adding the gravy. Lay on the lid, and decorate it with sprigs of green curled parsley, stuck in all round the crack where the lid is put on.

This pie may be filled with curried chickens.

A RAISED FRENCH PIE.—These pies have standing crust or walls, and may be filled with game or poultry, previously boned, seasoned, and stewed. They are generally made very large, and in winter will keep a week or two if closely covered. They are frequently sent a considerable distance, as Christmas presents; well packed in a close tin box.

To make the paste for a large pie:—Sift three pounds of flour into a pan, and make a hole in the centre. Cut up a pound of fresh butter, and two pounds of beef-suet, finely chopped. Put them into a clean pot, with as much boiling water as will cover them. Set them over the fire; and when the butter and suet are entirely dissolved, stir the whole with a spoon, and pour it into the hole in the middle of the flour; mix it with a spoon into a stiff paste, till it becomes cold enough for you to knead with your hands into a lump of dough. Sprinkle some flour on your paste-board, and on your hands; make the dough into the form of a cone or sug-ar-loaf, and with your hands smooth and flatten the sides of it. Then squeeze or press down the point of the cone; straighten the sides; and flatten the top, so as to give it the shape of a hat crown. Next, cut off from the top a thick, round slice, and lay it aside for the lid, and another slice for the ornaments. With one hand make a hollow in the large mass of dough, and with the other shape out and smooth the sides, leaving enough for a crust at the bottom. In this manner, hollow it into the shape of a straight-sided pan, leaving the wall or crust so thick that it will stand alone. Then fill it with the bones of the poultry or game, and some crusts of bread to keep it in shape. The portion of dough reserved for the lid must then be moulded on the inverted bottom of a deep plate, previously buttered. The lid may be a little larger than the top of the pie. The paste reserved for the ornaments should be rolled out, and cut with tin cutters into the form of leaves and flowers, or vine-leaves and grapes. These should be carefully placed in a wreath round the middle of the standing crust of the pie. A smaller wreath may be laid like a border round the lid, at the top of which place a large flower of paste, to look like a handle by which to lift it. Before you put on the ornaments, have ready the beaten yolks of two eggs; and dipping in a clean brush, glaze with it the whole outside of the pie, including the lid. Then stick on the decorations. Put the pie into a moderate oven, and bake it brown. The lid must be baked separately. When both are done, remove the bones, &c., from the inside of the pie, and fill it with the ingredients prepared, which must be previously stewed in their own gravy, with the addition of some bits of butter rolled in flour. Put on the lid, and cement the edges by glaz-ing them with a little beaten egg. These pies are usually made with slices of ham or smoked tongue at the bottom; then partridges, pheasants, moor-fowl, and other large game, all boned; and the spaces between filled up with force-meat, or with mushrooms stewed and chopped. They may be made with venison, wild turkeys, or wild ducks. Whatever is put into these pies must have no bone about it, and should be well seasoned.

The ingredients may be put into the pie, and the lid laid on at once,—pinching the edges together. In this case, it must bake three or four hours, in proportion to its size.

PIGEONS WITH HAM.—Take fine fat tame pigeons. For stuffing, boil some chesnuts till quite soft; and having peeled them, mash or pound them smooth. Mix with them a little fat of cold ham, finely minced and pounded. For chesnuts, may be substituted boiled sweet potatoe, mashed with butter. Fill the pigeons with the stuffing, having first slightly peppered their insides. Cover them with very thin slices of cold ham, (fat and lean together,) and wrap them in fresh vine-leaves, tied round with twine. Put them on a spit, and roast them three quarters of an hour. When done, carefully remove the strings, and serve up the pigeons, still wrapped in the ham and vine-leaves. They will be found very nice.

Partridges and quails may be drest in this manner.

Wild pigeons are so seldom fat, and have so little meat upon their bones, that except for soups and gravies, they are scarcely worth buying. In places where they abound, they may be turned to good account by catching them in nets; clipping their wings; and keeping them in an enclosure till they are fattened by feeding them well with corn, or Indian meal moistened with water. When managed thus, they will be found quite equal, if not superior, to tame pigeons.

A GIBLET PIE.—Clean, very nicely, the giblets of two geese or four ducks. Put them into a stew-pan, with a sliced onion; a bunch of tarragon, or sweet-marjoram and sage; half a dozen pepper-corns; and four or five blades of mace. Add a very little water; cover the pan closely, and let them stew till the giblets are tender. Then take them out, and save all the gravy; having strained it from the seasoning articles. Make a rich paste, and roll it out into two sheets. With one sheet cover the bottom and sides of a deep dish. Put in the giblets,—mixing among them a few cold boiled potatoes sliced, the chopped yolks of some hard-boiled eggs, and some bits of butter rolled in flour. Pour the gravy over the giblets, &c. Cover the pie with the other sheet of paste, and notch the edges. Bake it brown, and send it to table hot.

A pigeon pie may be made in a similar manner: also, a rabbit pie.

MOOR-FOWL OR GROUSE PUDDING.—Having skinned the moor-fowls, cut them up as for carving, and season them slightly with salt and pepper. Have ready a sufficient quantity of paste, made in the proportion of a pound of fresh butter to two pounds of sifted flour. Roll it out thick, and line with it a pudding mould, which must first be buttered; reserving sufficient paste for the lid. Then put in the pieces of moor-fowl, and place between each layer a layer of small mushrooms, or of fresh oysters cut small. Next pour in a little water, (about half a pint,) and add a piece of fresh butter rolled in flour. Then cover it with the remaining paste, pressing it down very closely round the edge. Dip a strong clean cloth into boiling water, dredge it with flour, and tie it tightly over the mould or pudding-basin. Put it into a pot of boiling water, and boil it three hours or more, according to its size.

A similar pudding may be made of pheasants, partridges, or quails; and is a delicious way of cooking game of any sort: rabbits, also, are very nice, cut up and put into a crust for boiling.

A BONED TURKEY.—For this purpose you must have a fine, large, tender turkey; and after it is drawn, and washed, and wiped dry, lay it on a clean table, and take a very sharp knife, with a narrow blade and point. Begin at the neck; then go round to the shoulders and wings, and carefully separate the flesh from the bone, scraping it down as you proceed. Next loosen the flesh from the breast, and back, and body; and then from the thighs. It requires care and patience to do it nicely, and to avoid tearing or breaking the skin. The knife should always penetrate quite to the bone; scraping loose the flesh rather than cutting it. When all the flesh has been completely loosened, take the turkey by the neck, give it a pull, and the whole skeleton will come out entire from the flesh, as easily as you draw your hand out of a glove. The flesh will then fall down, a flat and shapeless mass. With a small needle and thread, carefully sew up any holes that have accidentally been torn in the skin.

Have ready a large quantity of stuffing, made as follows:—Take three sixpenny loaves of stale bread; grate the crumb; and put the crusts in water to soak. When quite soft, break them up small into the pan of grated bread-crumbs, and mix in a pound of fresh butter, cut into little pieces. Take two large bunches of sweet-marjoram; the same of sweet-basil; and one bunch of parsley. Mince the parsley very fine, and rub to a powder the leaves of the marjoram and basil. You should have two large, heaping table-spoonfuls of each. Chop, also, two very small onions or shalots, and mix them with the herbs. Pound to powder a quarter of an ounce of mace; a quarter of an ounce of cloves; and two large nutmegs. Mix the spices together, and add a tea-spoonful of salt and a tea-spoonful of ground black pepper. Then mix the herbs, spice, &c., thoroughly into the bread-crumbs; and add, by degrees, four beaten eggs to bind the whole together.

Take up a handful of this filling; squeeze it hard, and proceed to stuff the turkey with it,—beginning at the wings; next do the body; and then the thighs. Stuff it very hard, and as you proceed, form the turkey into its natural shape, by filling out, properly, the wings, breast, body, &c. When all the stuffing is in, sew up the body, and skewer the turkey into the usual shape in which they are trussed; so that, if skilfully done, it will look almost as if it had not been boned. Tie it round with tape, and bake it three hours or more; basting it occasionally with fresh butter. Make a gravy of the giblets, chopped, and stewed slowly in a little water. When done, add to it the gravy that is in the dish about the turkey, (having first skimmed off the fat,) and enrich it with a glass of white wine, and two beaten yolks of eggs, stirred in just before you take it from the fire.

If the turkey is to be eaten cold at the supper-table, drop table-spoonfuls of currant or cranberry jelly all over it at small distances, and in the dish round it.

A very handsome way of serving it up cold is, after making a sufficiency of nice clear calves'-foot jelly, (seasoned, as usual, with wine, lemon, cinnamon, &c.,) to lay the turkey in the dish in which it is to go to table, and setting it under the jelly-bag, let the jelly drip upon it, so as to form a transparent coating all over it; smoothing the jelly evenly with the back of a spoon, as it congeals on the turkey. Apple jelly may be substituted.

Large fowls may be boned and stuffed in the above manner: also a young roasting pig.

PUDDINGS, ETC.

COLUMBIAN PUDDING.—Tie up closely in a bit of very thin white muslin, a vanilla bean cut into pieces; and a broken-up stick of cinnamon. Put this bag with its contents into half a pint of rich milk, and boil it a long time till very highly flavoured. Then take out the bag; set the milk near the fire to keep warm in the pan in which it was boiled, covering it closely. Slice thin a pound of almond sponge-cake, and lay it in a deep dish. Pour over it a quart of rich cream, with which you must mix the vanilla-flavoured milk, and leave the cake to dissolve in it. Blanch, in scalding water, two ounces of shelled bitter almonds or peach-kernels; and pound them (one at a time) to a smooth paste in a marble mortar; pouring on each a few drops of rose-water or peach-water to prevent their oiling. When the almonds are done, set them away in a cold place till wanted. Beat eight eggs till very light and thick; and having stirred together, hard, the dissolved cake and the cream, add them, gradually, to the mixture in turn with the almond, and half a pound of powdered loaf sugar, a little at a time of each. Butter a deep dish, and put in the mixture. Set the pudding into a brisk oven and bake it well. Have ready a star nicely cut out of a large piece of candied citron, a number of small stars all of equal size, as many as there are states in the Union: and a sufficiency of rays or long strips also cut out of citron. The rays should be wide at the bottom and run to a point at the top. As soon as the pudding comes out of the oven, while it is smoking, arrange these decorations. Put the large star in the centre, then the rays so that they will diverge from it, widening off towards the edge of the pudding. Near the edge place the small stars in a circle.

Preserved citron-melon will be still better for this purpose than the dry candied citron.

This is a very fine pudding; suitable for a dinner party, or a Fourth of July dinner.

A MARIETTA PUDDING.—Take a teacup-full of loaf-sugar broken up. On some of the largest lumps rub off the yellow rind of a large lemon. Then put all the sugar into a pint of rich cream; when the sugar is melted, set it over the fire, and when it comes to a boil, pour it hot over half a pound of fresh savoy biscuits or lady-fingers, (maccaroons will be still better,) laid in a deep dish. Cover the dish, and when the cakes are quite dissolved, stir the cream well among them. Beat eight eggs very light; and when the mixture is quite cold, stir the beaten eggs gradually into it. Add, by degrees, four peels of candied citron, cut into slips, and dredged with flour to prevent their sinking to the bottom. Put the mixture into a deep dish, and bake it. When done, sift sugar over the top. It may be eaten warm or cold. Send to table with it a sauce, made of fresh butter and white sugar, beaten together till very light, and flavoured with the juice of the lemon, whose rind was rubbed on the lumps of sugar, and also with some grated nutmeg.

Instead of citron you may put into this pudding a pound of Zante currants, (picked, washed, dried, and floured,) stirred gradually in at the last.

AN ORLEANS PUDDING.—Half fill a deep dish with almond sponge-cake sliced thin, or with sliced lady-cake. Grate the yellow rind of a lemon, and mix it among the cake; adding also the juice of the lemon, and sufficient white wine to moisten the cake, so that after standing awhile it can be easily mashed. For wine you may substitute brandy; or wine and brandy mixed. Beat six eggs very light, and stir them gradually into a pint of cream or rich milk; adding four table-spoon-fuls of powdered white sugar, and half a nutmeg grated. Mix the eggs, &c., by degrees, with the dissolved cake; stirring it very hard. The dish should be full. Set it into the oven, and bake it brown. When cold, have ready a meringue, made of beaten white of egg thickened with powdered loaf-sugar, and flavoured with lem-on-juice or rose-water. Spread this evenly over the top of the pudding, putting one layer of the meringue over another till it is very thick. Then set it for a few minutes into the oven to brown slightly on the top.

Any very nice baked pudding will be improved by covering the surface with a meringue.

HANOVER PUDDING.—Cut up half a pound of fresh butter in half a pint of milk. Set them over the fire till the butter is soft enough to mix thoroughly with the milk. Then take it off, and let it stand till lukewarm. Have ready four well-beaten eggs. Stir them hard into the butter and milk. Then add very gradually a pound of sifted flour. Last stir in two large table-spoonfuls of strong fresh yeast. Beat the whole very hard. Cover the pan, and let it stand near the fire for three hours or till the mixture is quite light. Have ready half a pound of Zante currants, picked, washed, and dried; or half a pound of fine raisins, seeded and cut in half. Dredge the fruit thickly with flour to prevent its sinking. Then mix it, gradually, into the pudding with two large table-spoonfuls of sugar, and a tea-spoonful of powdered cinnamon; and a salt-spoon of sal-eratus, or small tea-spoonful of bi-carbonate of soda, dissolved in a very little lukewarm water. Stir the whole very hard. Transfer it to a deep tin pan, well-buttered, and bake it thoroughly. Before it goes to table, turn it out on a dish, and serve it up warm with any sort of nice sweet sauce.

TURKISH RICE PUDDING.—Pick and wash half a pound of rice. Prepare also half a pound of Zante currants, which must be carefully picked clean, washed through two waters, drained well, and then spread out to dry on a flat dish before the fire. Put the rice into a sauce-pan, with a quart of rich milk. Having dredged the currants with flour, stir them a few at a time into the rice and milk. Then add four ounces of broken up loaf-sugar, on which you have rubbed off the yellow rind of a large ripe lemon or orange, and squeezed the juice. Stir in two ounces of fresh butter divided into bits. When the rice is well swollen and quite soft, take it from the fire, and mix with it gradually eight well-beaten yolks of eggs. Transfer it to a deep china dish, and put it into an oven for half an hour. Then sift powdered sugar thickly over the top, and brown it by holding above it a red-hot shovel or salamander. Serve it up warm.

This pudding may be made with ground rice, or rice flour.

CREAM COCOA-NUT PUDDING.—Take two cocoa-nuts of large size. Break them up, and pare off the brown skin from the pieces. Then grate them very fine. Stir together a quarter of a pound of the best fresh butter, and a quarter of a pound of finely-powdered loaf-sugar, till perfectly light. Beat six eggs till very thick and smooth: afterwards mix them, gradually, with a pint of rich cream. Add this mixture, by degrees, to the beaten butter and sugar, in turn with the grated cocoa-nut; a little at a time of each, stirring very well as you proceed. Then give the whole a hard stirring. Put the mixture into a deep white dish and bake it well. Send it to table *cold*, with loaf-sugar sifted over the top.

You may season the mixture by stirring in, at the last, a tea-spoonful of mixed nutmeg and cinnamon finely powdered. And you may add a table-spoonful of rose-brandy.

This pudding may be baked in puff-paste in two deep plates, with a broad border of paste round the edge, handsomely notched. Or it may be done without any paste *beneath* the mixture; but merely a paste border round the edge of the dish, which last is the better way. Paste at the bottom of these soft pudding-mixtures is usually tough and clammy, from the almost impossibility of getting it thoroughly done; and therefore it is best omitted, as is now generally the case. If there is no paste under it, the pudding should be baked in the dish in which it is to go to table. Unless the oven is so hot as to burn the pudding, no dish will be injured by baking. No pie or pudding should be sent to table in any thing inferior to white-ware.

PINE-APPLE PUDDING.—Take half a pound of grated pine-apple; half a pound of powdered white sugar, and a quarter of a pound of fresh butter. Put the sugar into a deep pan, cut up the butter among it, and stir them together till very light. Then add, by degrees, the grated pine-apple. Grate a small two-penny sponge-cake, and mix it with a large tea-cup of rich cream, and grate into it a small nutmeg, or half a large one. Add this to the pine-apple mixture in the pan. Beat six eggs very light, and stir them in gradually a little at a time. Stir the whole very hard, after all the ingredients are put together. Butter a deep dish, put in the mixture, and bake it well.

If your dish has a broad rim, lay round the edge a border of puff-paste, cut into leaves resembling a wreath.

AN ALMOND RICE PUDDING.—Blanch, in boiling water, three ounces of shelled bitter almonds, afterwards throwing them into cold water. Pound them, one at a time, in a mortar, till they become a smooth paste; adding frequently, as you pound them, a few drops of rose-water, to make them white and light, and to prevent their oiling. Take a quart of rich, unskimmed milk, and stir into it, gradually, three large, heaping table-spoonfuls of ground rice flour, alternately with the pounded almonds, and four heaping table-spoonfuls of powdered loaf-sugar. Set the mixture over the fire, and boil and stir it till very thick. Then put it into a deep dish, and set it away to cool. When cold, have ready the whites of two eggs beaten to a stiff froth, and thickened with powdered sugar, that has been melted in rose-water. Cover with this the surface of the pudding. Set it in an oven just long enough to be slightly coloured of a light brown. Send it to table cold.

BOILED ALMOND PUDDING.—Blanch, in boiling water, a quarter of a pound of shelled sweet almonds, and two ounces of shelled bitter almonds. Throw them into a pan of cold water, as you blanch them. Afterwards pound them, one at a time, in a mortar; adding to them, as you proceed, the beaten whites of two or three eggs, a little at a time. They must be pounded till they become a smooth paste; mixing together the sweet and the bitter almonds, and removing them, as you go on, from the mortar to a plate. Then set them in a cool place. Boil slowly a quart of cream, or rich, unskimmed milk, with half a dozen blades of mace, whole; and half a nutmeg, powdered. It may simmer half an hour, and when it comes to a boil, take it off, remove the mace, and set the milk to cool. Beat eight eggs very light, (omitting the whites of three,) and then add to them a heaped table-spoonful of flour. Stir the beaten eggs and the pounded almonds, alternately, into the pan of milk, (after it has become quite cold,) add a table-spoonful of orange-flower or rose-water, and stir the whole very hard. Have ready, over the fire, a pot of boiling water. Dip into it a thick pudding-cloth, shake it out, spread it open in a large empty pan, dredge it well with flour, and pour the pudding-mixture into it. Tie it very closely, leaving sufficient space for the pudding to swell, and plug the tying-place with a small lump of flour-and-water dough. Lay an old plate in the bottom of the pot of boiling water. Put in the pudding, and turn it over in a quarter of an hour. Boil it very fast for an hour, or more, after it has commenced boiling; replenishing the pot from a kettle of *boiling* water. When the pudding is done, dip it a moment into cold water; then turn it out on a dish. Send it to table immediately, with a sauce of sweetened cream, flavoured with rose or orange-flower water.

BISCUIT PUDDINGS.—Grate some stale milk-biscuits, till you have six heaping table-spoonfuls of fine crumbs. Then sift them through a coarse sieve. Beat six eggs very light, and stir them into a pint of cream, or rich, unskimmed milk, alternately with the biscuit crumbs, a little of each at a time. Beat the mixture very hard, and then butter some large breakfast-cups, such as hold near half a pint. Nearly fill them with the batter. Set them immediately into a brisk oven, and bake them half an hour, or more. This quantity will make five puddings. Serve them up hot in the cups, and eat them with wine-sauce, or with sauce of butter and sugar, stirred to a cream, and flavoured with nutmeg and lemon.

MARMALADE PUDDINGS.—Make the above mixture, and, when they are baked, turn the puddings out of the cups, make a slit or opening in the side of each, and fill up the inside or cavity of each pudding with any sort of nice marmalade or jam; taking care to fill them well. Then close the slit with your fingers. They may be eaten warm or cold, and require no other sauce than sweetened cream.

AN EXCELLENT CORN-MEAL PUDDING.—Boil a quart of rich milk, and pour it scalding hot into a large pan. Stir in, gradually, a quart of sifted Indian meal, and a quarter of a pound of fresh butter; adding the grated yellow rind of a lemon or orange. Squeeze the juice upon a quarter of a pound of brown sugar, and stir that in also. Add a large tea-spoonful of powdered cinnamon. Have ready a pound of raisins, seeded, and cut in half, and dredged thickly with wheat flour, to prevent their sinking. Beat six eggs very light, and stir them gradually into the mixture. Lastly, stir in the raisins, a few at a time, and stir the whole very hard. Have ready a large pot of boiling water; dip into it a square pudding-cloth, shake it out, and dredge it with flour. Spread out the cloth in a deep, empty pan, and pour into it the pudding-mixture. Tie it firmly, leaving room for the pudding to swell. Put it into the pot of hot water, and boil it four hours, or five; turning it several times, while boiling; and replenishing the water, as it boils away, with water kept hot, for the purpose, in a kettle. When done, take out the pudding from the pot; dip it, for a minute into cold water, before you untie the cloth; then turn it out into a dish, and send it to table. It should not be taken out of the pot till a minute or two before it is wanted.

Eat it with wine-sauce; or with butter, white sugar nutmeg, and lemon or orange-juice, beaten together to a light cream.

What is left, may be tied again in a cloth, and boiled for an hour, next day.

Instead of butter, you may use a quarter of a pound of beef-suet, minced as fine as possible.

PEACH INDIAN PUDDING.—Wash a pint, or more, of dried peaches; then drain them well; spread them on a large dish, and set them in the sun, or near the fire, till all the water that remains about them is entirely exhaled. Boil a quart of rich milk; mix it, while hot, with a pint of West India molasses, and then set it away to cool. Chop, very fine, a quarter of a pound of beef-suet, (veal-suet will do,) and stir it gradually into the milk, a little at a time. Beat six eggs very light, and stir them, by degrees, into the mixture, in turn with as much yellow Indian meal (sifted) as will make a moderately thick batter. Having dredged the peaches thickly with wheat flour, to prevent their sinking, add them, one at a time, to the mixture, stirring it well; and, lastly, stir in a table-spoonful of ground ginger, or a tea-spoonful of powdered cinnamon. Dip a thick, square pudding-cloth into boiling water, then shake it out, spread it open in a large pan, dredge it with flour, and pour in the pudding-mixture. Tie it fast; leaving room for it to swell; and plaster the tying-place with a bit of dough, made of flour and water. Put the pudding into a large pot of boiling water, with an old plate laid at the bottom, and boil it from four to five or six hours, filling up the pot, as it boils away, with hot water from a tea-kettle, and turning the pudding frequently. When done, dip it in cold water, lay it in a pan, and turn it out of the cloth. Eat it with butter and sugar, beaten to a cream, and seasoned with powdered nutmeg.

If there is not time to boil the pudding several hours, on the day you want it for dinner, prepare it the day before; boil it then all the afternoon, and boil it again the following day. Indian puddings can scarcely be boiled too long. They will be the better, indeed, for eight hours' boiling.

A FINE INDIAN PUDDING.—Take a pound of raisins, and cut them in half, having first removed the seeds. Then spread them on a large dish, and dredge them thickly with fine wheat flour, turning them about, that both sides may be well floured. Boil a quart of rich milk, and when it has come to a boil, take it off the fire, and set it to cool. Transfer the half of this milk (one pint) to another pan, and, while it is still warm, stir into it a quarter of a pound of butter, cut into bits; a quarter of a pound of brown sugar, (or else a half pint of West India molasses,) mixed with the grated yellow rind of a large lemon or orange, and also the juice. Add a large tea-spoonful of powdered cinnamon and nutmeg, mixed, and a glass of brandy. Beat eight eggs very light; and, when it is quite cold, stir the eggs, gradually, into the other pint of milk. Then mix the ingredients of both pans together; adding eight large table-spoonfuls of Indian meal, or enough to make a thick batter. Lastly, mix in the floured raisins, a few at a time, stirring the whole very hard. Have ready, over the fire, a large pot of boiling water. Dip a square pudding-cloth into it; shake it out; spread it open over the inside of an empty pan, and dredge it with flour; pour the batter into it, and tie it firmly; leaving room for the pudding to swell. Plaster a small lump of flour-and-water dough upon the crevice of the tying-place, to assist in keeping out the water, which, if it gets in, will render the pudding heavy. Put it into the pot of hot water, and boil it steadily for four, five, or six hours, turning it frequently in the water. It can scarcely be boiled too long. Keep at the fire a kettle of *hot* water, to replenish the pudding-pot, as it boils away. Do not take up the pudding, till immediately before it is to go to table. Dip it into cold water, and then turn it out of the cloth upon a dish. Eat it with wine-sauce, or with butter, sugar, and nutmeg. If enough of the pudding is left, it may, next day, be tied in a cloth, and re-boiled for an hour.

RASPBERRY PUDDING.—Fill a deep dish with a quart of ripe raspberries, well mixed with four or five large table-spoonfuls of powdered sugar. As you put in the raspberries mash them slightly with the back of a spoon. Beat six eggs as light as possible, and mix them with a pint of cream or rich unskimmed milk, and four more spoonfuls of sugar, adding some grated nutmeg. Pour this over the raspberries. Set the dish immediately into a moderate oven, and bake the pudding about half an hour. When done, set the dish on ice, or where it will become quite cold before it goes to table.

A similar pudding may be made with ripe currants, picked from the stalks; or with ripe cherries stoned.

A pine-apple pudding made in this way is excellent. There must be as much pine-apple as will measure a quart, after it is pared, sliced, and grated fine. Sweeten it well with loaf-sugar.

A COTTAGE PUDDING.—Take ripe currants, and having stripped them from the stalks, measure as many as will make a heaping quart. Cover the bottom of a deep dish with slices of bread, slightly buttered, and with the crust cut off. Put a thick layer of currants on the bread; and then a layer of sugar. Then other layers of bread, currants, and sugar, till the dish is full; finishing at the top with very thin slices of bread. Set it into the oven, and bake it half an hour. Serve it either warm or cold; and eat it with sweetened cream.

Instead of currants you may take cherries, (first stoning them all,) raspberries, ripe blackberries, or barberries, plums, (first extracting the stones,) stewed cranberries, or stewed gooseberries. If the fruit is previously stewed, the pudding will require but ten minutes' baking. When it is sent to table have sugar at hand in case it should not be sweet enough.

RIPE CURRANT PUDDING.—Take two quarts of fine ripe currants, strip them from the stalks, and mix with them a quarter of a pound of sugar. Make a paste of a pound and a half of sifted flour, and three-quarters of a pound of the best fresh butter. Cut up half a pound of the butter into the pan of flour, and rub the butter into the flour with your hands till it is thoroughly mixed all through. Mix with it barely as much cold water as will make it into a stiff dough. If you use too much water the paste will be tough. Beat the lumps of dough on both sides with the rolling-pin. Then transfer it to your paste-board; roll it out into a thin sheet, and spread over it with a knife another quarter of a pound of butter. Then flour it, fold it up, and beat it again with the rolling-pin. Afterwards roll it out thicker. Put the currants into it, and close the paste over the top in the manner of a large dumpling. Boil it in a cloth in the usual manner. It will require two hours or more. Eat it with sugar.

You may make the paste of minced suet instead of butter.

CHERRY PUDDING may be made as above, first stoning the cherries, which should be ripe and red, and made very sweet with sugar.

GOOSEBERRY PUDDING.—Take a quart or more of full-grown green goose-berries. Pick off the tops and tails, and as you do so, lay the gooseberries in a pan. Then pour on sufficient boiling water to scald them thoroughly, cover the pan, and let the gooseberries stand till they grow cold. Next put them into a sieve and drain off the water. While the gooseberries are cooling, prepare a paste for them. Take six ounces of fresh beef-suet; weighed after you have trimmed it, and removed the strings. Mince it as finely as possible. Sift a pound of flour into a pan, and rub the minced suet into it; adding half a pint of cold water, or barely enough to make it into a dough, and a small salt-spoon of salt. Beat the lump of dough on all sides with the rolling-pin; this will add to its lightness. Then transfer it to your paste-board, and roll it out very evenly into a circular sheet. When the gooseberries are cold, mix with them half a pound of the best brown sugar, and lay them in a heap in the middle of the sheet of paste. Close the paste over them in the manner of a large dumpling. Have ready a pot of boiling water. Dip your pudding cloth into it; shake it out; spread it open in a broad pan; and dredge it with flour. Then lay the pudding in it, and tie the cloth very firmly, but leaving room for the pudding to swell. Stop up the crevice at the tying-place with a small lump of stiff dough made of flour and water. Put the pudding into the pot, (which should be boiling hard at the time,) having placed an old plate at the bottom as a preventive to the pudding sticking there, and scorching. After it has been in fifteen minutes, turn it with a fork. If the water boils away replenish it with more hot water from a kettle. Boil the pudding three hours or more. Then take it up, dip it into cold water and turn it out into a dish. Send it to table hot, and eat it with additional sugar. If too much sugar is put in with the gooseberries at first, and boiled with them, it will render them tough. It is best to depend chiefly on sweetening them at table.

A similar pudding may be made of currants either green or ripe. They will not require scalding. The paste may be of fresh butter instead of suet.

A RAISIN PUDDING.—Stone a pound of large fine fresh raisins, and cut them in half. If using the sultana, or seedless raisins, you may leave them whole. Spread the raisins on a large flat dish; and mix with them the yellow rind of a large fresh lemon, or orange. This rind must be pared off as thin as possible, and cut into very small slips. Dredge the raisins and peel thickly with flour to prevent their sinking or clodding, tumbling them about with your hands that they may be well floured all over. Mix the juice of the lemon or orange with five or six large table-spoonfuls of sugar heaped up. Mince, as finely as possible, half a pound of beef-suet. Beat six eggs very light, and then stir into them, gradually, the suet and the sugar, in turn with six heaped table-spoonfuls of sifted flour. Then add by degrees the fruit and a powdered nutmeg. Lastly, stir in gradually a pint of rich milk. Stir the whole very hard. Scald a large square pudding-cloth; shake it out; spread it open in a deep pan; dredge it with flour; put in the pudding-mixture, and tie the cloth firmly. It should be little more than three-quarters full, that the pudding may have room to swell. Mix with flour and water a small lump of stiff dough, and plaster it on the tying-place to prevent the water getting inside. Have ready a pot full of boiling water; and put in the pudding, having laid an old plate at the bottom of the pot, to keep it from burning if it should sink. Turn the pudding several times while boiling. It should boil hard at least four hours, (five will not be too long,) and if the water boils away so as not entirely to cover the whole of the bag it must be replenished from a boiling kettle. Take up the pudding immediately before it is to go to table. Dip it in cold water for an instant, then turn it out of the cloth into a dish, and serve it up hot. Eat it with wine-sauce; or with butter and sugar beaten to a cream.

MINCE PUDDING.—Take a pound and a half of mince-meat, and sift three-quarters of a pound of flour. Beat six eggs very light, and stir into them, alternately, the mince-meat and the flour, a little at a time of each. Stir the whole very hard. Have ready a pudding-cloth dipped into a pot of boiling water, then shook out, and dredged with flour. Spread out the cloth in a large pan, and pour into it the pudding. Tie it tightly, leaving room for the pudding to swell; and stop up the tying-place with a small bit of dough made of flour and water. Put it immediately into a large pot of boiling water, having an old plate at the bottom to keep the pudding from scorching. Boil it steadily five or six hours, turning it in the pot every hour. As the water boils away, replenish it from a kettle of water that is kept boiling hard. Do not turn out the pudding till immediately before it is sent to table. Eat it with wine-sauce.

This pudding is excellent. The mince-meat is the same that is prepared for mince-pies.

A TEMPERANCE PLUM PUDDING.—Take a pound of the best raisins, and cut them in half, after removing the seeds. Or use sultana raisins that have no seeds. Pick, and wash clean, a pound of currants, and dry them before the fire, spread out on a large flat dish. Cut into slips half a pound of citron. Then mix together, on the same dish, the currants, the raisins, and the citron, and dredge them thickly with flour to prevent their sinking or clodding in the pudding; tumbling them about with your hands till they are all over well-covered with the flour.

Mince very fine a pound of beef-suet. Mix a pint of West India molasses with a pint of rich milk. Sift into a pan a pound of flour. In another pan beat eight eggs very light. Stir the beaten eggs, gradually, into the mixed molasses and milk; alternately with the flour, and half a pound of sugar, (which should previously be crushed smooth by roiling it with a rolling-pin,) a little at a time of each. Then add, by degrees, the fruit and the suet, a little of each alternately. Beat and stir the whole very hard, till all the ingredients are thoroughly mixed. Take a large clean square cloth of coarse strong linen, dip it in boiling water, shake it, spread it out in a large pan, and dredge it with flour to prevent the pudding from sticking to it when boiled. Then pour the pudding-mixture into the cloth; leave room for it to swell, and tie it firmly, plastering up the tying-place with a bit of coarse dough made of flour and water. Have ready a large pot *full* of water, and boiling hard. Put in the pudding, and boil it well from six to eight hours. Less than six will not be sufficient, and eight hours will not be too long. Turn it several times while boiling, and keep at hand a kettle of *hot* water to replenish the pot as it boils away. Do not take it up till immediately before it is wanted on the table. Then dip it for a moment into cold water, untie the cloth, and turn out the pudding. Serve it up with a sauce-boat of sweetened cream, seasoned with nutmeg; or with butter and sugar beaten together till light and white, and flavoured with lemon. What is left of the pudding may be tied up in a cloth and boiled again next day for an hour or more. It will be equally as nice as on the first day. This is a much better way of re-cooking than to slice and fry it.

This pudding may be made with sifted yellow Indian meal, instead of wheat flour.

MARROW PUDDING.—Grate a quarter of a pound of sponge-cake, and mix with it a quarter of a pound of beef-marrow, finely minced. Add the grated peel and the juice of a large lemon or orange; half a grated nutmeg; and four table-spoonfuls of sugar. Stone half a pound of very good fresh raisins, cut them in half, and dredge them well with flour. Beat four eggs very light, and stir them gradually into half a pint of cream or rich milk. Mix it, by degrees, with the other ingredients. Lastly add the raisins, a few at a time; and stir the whole very hard. Butter a deep dish; put in the mixture; bake it an hour or more, and send it to table warm, with slips of candied citron stuck all over the top, so as to stand upright. For sauce have white wine, mixed with sugar and lemon juice.

This pudding may be boiled in a cloth. It will require three hours' boiling.

TRANSPARENT PUDDING.—Warm half a pound of fresh butter, but do not allow it to melt. Mix with it half a pound of powdered loaf-sugar, and stir them together till they are perfectly light. Add a small nutmeg grated, or half a large one. Beat eight eggs as light as possible; and stir them gradually into the butter and sugar. Finish with sufficient extract of roses to give it a fine flavour. Stir the whole very hard; butter a deep dish, put in the mixture, and bake it half an hour. Serve it up cold.

You may bake this pudding in puff-paste.

TAPIOCA PUDDING.—Put four large table-spoonfuls of tapioca into a quart of milk, and let it stand all night. In the morning put half a pint of milk into a small sauce-pan, and boil in it a large stick of cinnamon broken up, and a handful of bitter almonds or peach-kernels broken small. Keep it covered and boil it slowly, till highly flavoured with the cinnamon and almond, which must then be strained out, and the milk mixed with that which has the tapioca in it. Put it into a tin vessel or one lined with porcelain, and boil it till it becomes very thick with the dissolved tapioca; stirring it frequently down to the bottom. Add a piece of fresh butter as large as an egg; a quarter of a pound of sugar, and four well-beaten eggs stirred in gradually; a table-spoonful of brandy; and a grated nutmeg. Stir the whole well together, put it into a deep dish, and bake it an hour.

Instead of boiling bitter almonds with the cinnamon in the extra half pint of milk, you may boil the cinnamon only. And when you are afterwards finishing the whole mixture, stir in a table-spoonful of peach-water at the last.

Tapioca is to be bought at the grocer's, and also at the druggist's.

EXCELLENT GROUND RICE PUDDING.—Take half a pint from a quart of rich milk, and boil in it a large handful of bitter almonds or peach kernels, blanched and broken up; also half a dozen blades of mace, keeping the sauce-pan closely covered. When the milk is highly flavoured and reduced to one half the quantity, take it off and strain it. Stir, gradually, into the remaining pint and a half of milk, five heaping table-spoonfuls of ground rice; set it over the fire in a sauce-pan, and let it come to a boil. Then take it off, and while it is warm, mix in gradually a quarter of a pound of fresh butter and a quarter of a pound of white sugar. Afterwards, beat eight eggs as light as possible, and stir them, gradually, into the mixture. Add some grated nutmeg. Stir the whole very hard; put it into a deep dish; and set it immediately into the oven. Keep it baking steadily for an hour. It should then be done. It may be eaten either warm or cold.

To ornament it, have ready some sweet almonds blanched whole, and then split in half. Place six of them on the centre of the pudding, so as to form a star. Lay others in lines like rays diverging from the star, and place the remainder in a circle near the edge of the pudding.

Any pudding may be ornamented as above.

A SOUFFLÉ PUDDING.—Take eight rusks, or soft sugar-biscuits, or plain buns. Lay them in a large deep dish, and pour on a pint of milk, sufficient to soak them thoroughly. Cover the dish, and let them stand, undisturbed, for about an hour and a half before dinner. In the mean time, boil half a pint of milk in a small sauce-pan with a handful of bitter-almonds or peach-kernels, broken small; or a small bunch of fresh peach-leaves, with two large sticks of cinnamon broken up. Boil this milk slowly, (keeping it covered,) and when it tastes strongly of the flavouring articles, strain it, and set it away to cool. When cold, mix it into another pint of milk, and stir in a quarter of a pound of powdered loaf-sugar. Beat eight eggs very light, and add them gradually to the milk, so as to make a rich custard. After dinner has commenced, beat and stir the soaked rusk very hard till it becomes a smooth mass, and then, by degrees, add to it the custard. Stir the whole till thoroughly amalgamated. Set the dish into a brisk oven, and bake the pudding rather more than ten minutes. The yeast, &c., in the rusk will cause it to puff up very light. When done, send it to table warm, with white sugar sifted over it. You may serve up with it as sauce, sweetened thick cream flavoured with rose-water, and grated nutmeg. Or powdered loaf-sugar and fresh butter stirred together in equal portions, and seasoned with lemon and nutmeg.

Another way in making a soufflé pudding, instead of boiling the flavouring in a separate half pint of milk, is, after making the custard of cold milk, sugar, and eggs, to stir into it a wine-glass of peach-water, rose-water, or orange-flower water; or else two table-spoonfuls of Oliver's extract of vanilla. Or you may flavour it with the yellow rind of a large lemon rubbed off upon some lumps of the sugar before it is powdered.

A CHARLOTTE PUDDING.—Have ready a sufficiency of dried peaches that have been stewed very soft, and flavoured, while stewing, with the yellow rind of one or two oranges, pared very thin and cut into small slips. The stewed peaches must be mashed very smooth. Take a deep dish, and cover the inside with a layer of brown sugar mixed with powdered cinnamon or nutmeg. Upon this put a layer of thin slices of bread and butter with all the crust pared off; turning the buttered side downward. Next put on a thick layer of the stewed peaches. Then more sugar and spice; then more bread and butter, and then another layer of peach. Proceed thus till the dish is full; and cover the top slightly with grated bread-crumbs. Put it into a moderate oven; and bake it brown.

It may be eaten either warm or cold.

Instead of peaches, you may make this pudding of stewed apple flavoured with lemon; or with stewed goose-berries made very sweet with brown sugar. If you use goose-berries, the spice should be nutmeg, not cinnamon.

A NOVICE'S PUDDING.—Beat to a stiff froth the whites only of eight eggs. Then beat into them half a pound of powdered white sugar—a tea-spoonful at a time. Stir into a pint of rich cream or unskimmed milk a wine-glass of rose-water, or a table-spoonful of extract of roses. You may substitute two table-spoonfuls of extract of vanilla; or two of peach water. Stir the beaten egg and sugar into the milk, alternately with four ounces of sifted flour, a spoonful at a time. Beat the whole very hard; put it into a deep dish, well-buttered, and set it immediately into a rather quick oven, and bake it well. Serve it up warm; and eat it with butter and white sugar beaten to a cream, and flavoured in the same manner as the pudding.

This pudding will be found very white and delicate. It is peculiarly excellent made with melted ice-cream that has been left.

CHOCOLATE PUDDING.—Have the best and strongest American chocolate or cocoa. Baker's prepared cocoa will be found excellent for all chocolate purposes; better indeed than any thing else, as it is pure, and without any adulteration of animal fat, being also very strong, and communicating a high flavour. Of this, scrape down, very fine, two ounces or more. Add to it a tea-spoonful of mixed spice, namely, powdered nutmeg and cinnamon. Put it into a very clean sauce-pan, and pour on a quart of rich milk, stirring it well. Set it over the fire, or on hot coals; cover it; and let it come to a boil. Then remove the lid; stir up the chocolate from the bottom, and press out all lumps. Then return it to the fire, and when thoroughly dissolved and very smooth, it is done. Next stir in, gradually, while the chocolate is still boiling-hot, a quarter of a pound or more of powdered loaf-sugar. If you use such white sugar as is bought ready powdered, you must have near half a pound, as that sugar has very little strength, being now adulterated with ground starch. When the chocolate is well sweetened, set it away to cool. Beat eight eggs very light, and pour them through a strainer into the pan of chocolate, when it is quite cold. Stir the whole very hard. Then put it into the oven, and bake it well. Try it when you think it done, with the twig from a broom. If on putting the twig into the middle of the pudding, and sticking it quite down to the bottom, the twig comes out clean, and with nothing clammy adhering to it, the pudding is then sufficiently baked. It should be eaten cold. Sift white sugar thickly over it before it goes to table. It will be found very nice.

This pudding will bake best by sitting the pan in a dutch oven half-filled with boiling water.

MACCARONI PUDDING.—Boil a quarter of a pound of maccaroni in a pint of rich unskimmed milk, with a handful of blanched bitter almonds or peach-kernels, and two sticks of cinnamon broken into pieces. It must boil till the maccaroni is soft, and dissolving. Then remove the bitter almonds and the cinnamon; stir in, while it is hot, a quarter of a pound of fresh butter, a quarter of a pound of powdered sugar, and half a pint of rich cream. Mix all well, and beat it hard. Then beat four eggs till very thick and light, and stir them gradually into the mixture after it has cooled. Add a grated nutmeg, and a table-spoonful of brandy. Butter a deep dish; put in the mixture; set it directly into the oven, and bake it.

Vermicelli pudding may be made as above. Also a ground rice pudding.

A LADY'S PUDDING.—Rub off on lumps of loaf sugar the yellow rind of one large lemon, or two small ones. Then crush that sugar, and add more to it till you have four heaped table-spoonfuls. Beat to a stiff froth the whites only of four eggs. Then gradually add the sugar (a little at a time) to the beaten white of egg. Have ready in a pan, a pint of cream or rich unskimmed milk. Stir into it by degrees the mixture of white of egg and sugar, alternately with four heaped table-spoonfuls or four ounces of sifted flour. When the whole is mixed, stir it long and hard; and then transfer it to a deep dish, the inside of which must be slightly buttered. Bake it from half an hour to three quarters; and when done sift powdered sugar over the top. Send it to table warm, with a sauce of equal quantities of fresh butter and powdered white sugar stirred together to a light cream, and flavoured with lemon-juice and grated nutmeg.

This pudding will be found very delicate. For a large one, take the whites of eight eggs, the rind of two large lemons, half a pound of sugar, a quart of cream or rich milk, and eight heaped table-spoonfuls of flour.

BOILED LEMON PUDDING.—Grate very fine as many bread-crumbs as will weigh half a pound. Take half a pound of broken up loaf-sugar, and on some of the lumps rub off the yellow rind of two large lemons, or three small ones, having first rolled the lemons under your hand upon a table to increase the juice. Then powder finely all the sugar, including the lumps on which the lemon-rind has been rubbed. Cut up in a deep pan a quarter of a pound of fresh butter. Add to it half the powdered sugar, and stir them hard together till very light and thick. Beat six eggs till as light as possible; and then (having stirred in two table-spoonfuls of sifted flour) add them gradually to the beaten butter and sugar, in turn with the bread crumbs, a little at a time of each. Squeeze the juice of the lemons through a strainer, and mix it with the remaining sugar. Then add that sugar, gradually, to the other ingredients, and stir the whole very hard. Have ready a pudding-cloth dipped in boiling water, shaken out, spread open over a pan, and then dredged with flour. Put in the pudding-mixture, and tie it firmly, leaving room for it to swell, and not forgetting to stop up the little aperture at the tying-place with a bit of flour-and-water dough. Put the pudding into a large pot of boiling water, and keep it boiling steadily for two hours or more, turning it several times in the pot. Serve it up hot, accompanied by a cold sauce of equal portions of powdered white sugar and fresh butter, beaten together to a cream, and flavoured with lemon-juice and nutmeg.

You may boil it in a pudding-mould, with a hole or cavity in the centre. After turning it out on the dish, fill up the hole with the above-mentioned sauce, heaping high in the middle. For this purpose the sauce should be made rather stiff, allowing more sugar and less butter.

A boiled orange pudding may be made in the same manner.

POTATOE-FLOUR PUDDING.—Boil a quart of rich milk; and while boiling, stir in gradually a quarter of a pound of potatoe-flour well pulverized; add a quarter of a pound of sugar, three ounces of butter, and a tea-spoonful of powdered nutmeg and cinnamon. When it has thoroughly boiled, set it to cool. When cold, stir in, by degrees, four eggs well beaten. Put it into a deep dish, and bake it half an hour. Send it to table cold with white sugar sifted over the top.

GREEN CUSTARD.—Pound in a marble or white-ware mortar a sufficient quantity of fresh spinach, till you have extracted as much green juice as will half fill a half-pint tumbler, or two common-sized wine-glasses. Mix this quantity of spinach juice with a quart of rich unskimmed milk, and a quarter of a pound of loaf-sugar, broken very small. Flavour it with a wine-glass of peach water, or with the yellow rind of two large lemons grated off on some of the largest lumps of the sugar. Or, for the flavouring, you may use a vanilla bean, or a handful of bitter almonds or peach-kernels, boiled a long time in half a pint of milk, which must then be strained, and mixed with the other milk. Beat very light eight eggs, or the yolks only of sixteen; mix them with the milk, &c., (having first strained the beaten eggs,) and having stirred the whole very hard, pour it into a white-ware pitcher, and set it into a pot rather more than half-full of boiling water. Place it on a stove or a bed of hot coals on the hearth, and stir it to the bottom, and watch it continually till it has almost come to a boil. When very near boiling, take it off the fire immediately; for if it *quite* boils, it will curdle. Set it away to get cold. When lukewarm it will be an improvement to stir into it two table-spoonfuls or more of rose-water. Cover the bottom of a large glass-bowl or a deep dish, with slices of sponge-cake or Naples biscuit. Then put on green sweetmeats, such as preserved goose-berries, green gages, green grapes, or green citron melon. When the custard is quite cold pour it on, and fill up the bowl with it. If made as above, this will be found both delicious and ornamental for a dessert, or supper table.

It may be served up in glass cups; putting into the bottom of each cup a portion of sponge-cake, then a portion of green sweetmeats, and then filling up with the green custard after it has become cold.

Pistachio-nuts pounded in a mortar will give a fine green colour.

RED CUSTARD—May be made according to the foregoing receipt, only colouring it red by adding a teacup-full of milk, in which has been steeped a small thin muslin bag filled with alkanet. Instead of *green* sweet-meats, use preserved cherries, strawberries, or raspberries.

Alkanet is to be bought at the druggists, is very cheap, perfectly innoxious, and is now much used for colouring confectionary. The colour it imparts is more beautiful than any other red.

You may obtain a good red colouring by pounding boiled beets in a mortar. Pounded beet-leaves will also furnish a juice for colouring red.

GELATINE CUSTARD.—Soak half an ounce of gelatine for three or four hours in a pan of cold water. Have ready a quart of milk. Boil in half a pint of it a bunch of peach-leaves, or a handful of bitter almonds broken up; also, a stick of cinnamon broken in pieces. When it is highly flavoured, strain this milk into the pan that contains the rest. Beat four eggs very light, and mix them gradually with the milk, adding, by degrees, the gelatine, (well drained,) and four heaping table-spoonfuls of sugar. Set it over a slow fire and boil it, stirring it frequently. As soon as the gelatine is entirely dissolved, and thoroughly mixed, the custard will be done. Transfer it to a deep dish or to cups, and set it on ice or in a cold place till wanted.

INDIAN PUFFS.—Boil a quart of milk; and when it has come to a boil, stir into it, gradually, eight large table-spoonfuls of Indian meal; four large table-spoonfuls of powdered sugar; and a grated nutmeg. Stir it hard; letting it boil a quarter of an hour after all the Indian meal is in. Then take it up, and set it to cool. While cooling, beat eight eggs as light as possible, and stir them, gradually, into the batter when it is quite cold. Butter some large tea-cups; nearly fill them with the mixture; set them into a moderate oven; and bake them well. Send them to table warm, and eat them with butter and molasses; or with butter, sugar, lemon-juice, and nutmeg stirred to a cream. They must be turned out of the cups.

SWEETMEAT DUMPLINGS.—Make a paste of half a pound of fresh butter, or finely minced suet, and a pound of flour, moistened with a very little cold water. Beat the lump of paste on all sides with a rolling-pin. Then roll it out into a sheet, and divide it into equal portions. Lay on the middle of each two halves (laid on each other) of preserved peaches, or quinces, or large preserved plums. Then close the paste round the sweetmeat, so as to form a dumpling. Have ready a pot of boiling water. Throw the dumplings into it, tied up in little cloths, and let them boil twenty-five minutes or half an hour. Try one first, to see if they are done. When quite done, take them up, dip them in cold water, turn them out of the cloths, and send the dumplings to table immediately. Eat them with sugar only, or with sweetened cream.

These dumplings may be made with jam or marmalade, formed into a heap or lump, and laid in the centre of each piece of paste.

ALTONA FRITTERS.—Pare some fine pippin or bell-flower apples that are quite ripe, and of the largest size. Then extract the cores with a tin apple-corer, so as to leave the hole in the centre smooth and even. Spread the sliced apples on a large flat dish, and squeeze on each slice some lemon-juice. Then sprinkle them thickly with powdered white sugar. Prepare a batter, made in the proportion of eight eggs to a quart of rich milk, and a pint and a half of sifted flour. Having beaten the eggs till very light and thick, add them gradually to the milk in turn with the flour, a little at a time of each, and stir the whole very hard. Have ready, over hot coals, a skillet with a plentiful portion of the best fresh butter, melted and boiling hard. Dip the slices of apple twice into the batter, and then put them into the skillet of butter; as many at a time as it will contain without danger of running into each other as they spread. While they are frying, keep shaking the skillet about, holding it by the handle. They will puff up very light, and must be done of a bright brown. Take them out with a perforated skimmer, that will drain off the butter. Have ready some powdered sugar, flavoured with nutmeg or cinnamon. Roll the fritters in this, and send them to table hot. This is a German preparation of fritters, and will be found excellent on trial. They may be made of large peaches instead of apples; paring the peaches, and cutting them in two, having removed the stones. Allow half a peach (well sugared) to each fritter.

You may fry these fritters in lard, but they will not be so nice as if done in fresh butter.

WASHINGTON FRITTERS.—Boil four large potatoes; peel them; and, when cold, grate them as fine as possible. Mix well together two large table-spoonfuls of cream, two table-spoonfuls of sweet white wine, half a grated nutmeg, two table-spoonfuls of powdered sugar, and the juice of a lemon. Beat eight eggs very light, (omitting the whites of two,) and then mix them gradually with the cream, wine, &c., alternately with the grated potatoe, a little at a time of each. Beat the whole together at least a quarter of an hour after all the ingredients are mixed. Have ready, in a frying-pan over the fire, a large quantity of boiling lard; and when the bubbling has subsided, put in spoonfuls of the batter, so as to make well-formed fritters. Fry them a light brown, and take them up with a perforated skimmer, so as to drain them from the lard. Lay them on a hot dish, and send them immediately to table. Serve up with them, in a boat, a sauce made in the proportion of two glasses of white wine, the juice of two lemons, and a table-spoonful of peach-water, or a glass of rose-water. Make the sauce very sweet with powdered white sugar, and grate nutmeg into it.

These fritters may be made with boiled sweet potatoes, grated when cold.

WINE FRITTERS.—Beat six eggs till very thick and smooth; and when they are quite light, beat into them, gradually, six table-spoonfuls of sweet malaga or muscadel wine, and six table-spoonfuls of powdered white sugar. Have ready a sufficient number of large fresh milk biscuits, split in two, soaked in a bowl of sweet wine about five minutes, and drained on a sieve. Put some fresh lard into a frying-pan, and when it boils, and has been skimmed, dip each piece of the split biscuit into the batter of wine, eggs, and sugar, and fry them a light brown. When done, take them up with a perforated skimmer, and drain them well from the lard. Strew powdered white sugar over them.

SWEETMEAT FRITTERS.—Having boiled a large beet till it is tender all through, and scraped off the outside, cut the beet into pieces, and pound them in a marble mortar till you have extracted the juice. Then stir into a quart of milk enough of the beet-juice to give it a deep red colour. Beat seven eggs till very smooth and light, and stir them gradually into the milk; alternately with a pint and a half of sifted flour. The red colour will look paler after the egg is mixed with the milk. If you find it too pale, add more beet-juice. Have ready some boiling lard in a frying-pan over the fire; and when it has ceased to bubble, and the surface has become smooth, put in the mixture by spoonfuls, so as to form round or oval cakes of an equal size, and fry them a light brown. If you find the batter too thin, stir in a very little more flour. As the fritters are done, take them out, on a perforated skimmer, draining the lard back into the frying-pan. Dredge the fritters thickly with powdered sugar, and lay on each some preserved peach, plum, or other sweetmeat. You may heap on every one a table-spoonful or more of marmalade. Send them to table hot.

GREEN FRITTERS.—Are made as above; but coloured with the juice of spinach, extracted by pounding in a mortar.

BREAD FRITTERS.—Pick, wash, and dry half a pound of Zante currants, and having spread them out on a flat dish, dredge them well with flour. Grate some bread into a pan, till you have a pint of crumbs. Pour over the grated bread a pint of boiling milk, into which you have stirred, as soon as taken from the fire, a piece of fresh butter, the size of an egg. Cover the pan, and let it stand an hour. Then beat it hard, and add nutmeg, and a quarter of a pound of powdered white sugar, stirred in gradually, and two table-spoonfuls of the best brandy. Beat six eggs till very light, and then stir them, by degrees, into the mixture. Lastly, add the currants, a few at a time; and beat the whole very hard. It should be a thick batter. If you find it too thin, add a little flour. Have ready over the fire a hot frying-pan with boiling lard. Put in the batter in large spoonfuls, (so as not to touch,) and fry the fritters a light brown. Drain them on a perforated skimmer, or an inverted sieve placed in a deep pan, and send them to table hot. Eat them with wine, and powdered sugar.

Instead of currants, you may use sultana raisins, cut in half and well floured.

INDIAN FRITTERS.—Having beaten eight eggs very light, stir them gradually into a quart of rich milk, in turn with twelve large table-spoonfuls of yellow Indian meal, adding a salt-spoon of salt. When all is in, stir the whole very hard. Have ready over a clear fire, in a pot or a large frying-pan, a pound of fresh lard, boiling fast. Drop the batter into it, a ladleful at a time. If you find the batter too thin, stir into it a little more Indian meal. As the lard boils away, replenish it with more. As fast as they are done, take out each fritter with a perforated skimmer;

through the holes of which let the lard drip back into the pot. The fritters must all be well drained. Send them to table hot, and eat them with wine and sugar, or with molasses.

In cooking these fritters, you may drop in three or four, one immediately after another; and they will not run, if the lard is boiling fast, and the batter thick enough, and made with the proper number of eggs.

VERY FINE MINCE-MEAT.—Boil two beef's tongues, (perfectly fresh,) and, when cold, skin and mince them; including the fat about the roots. Mince, also, one pound of beef-suet, and mix it with the chopped tongues. Add four nutmegs powdered; two ounces of powdered cinnamon; and an ounce of powdered mace, with a table-spoonful of powdered cloves. Pick clean, wash, and dry three pounds of Zante currants. Seed and chop three pounds of the *best* raisins. Mix the fruit with the other ingredients, adding a pound of citron sliced, and the grated yellow rind, and the juice of three large lemons or oranges. Sweeten the mixture with two pounds of sugar, and moisten it with a quart of excellent brandy, and a quart of sherry or Madeira wine. Having thoroughly mixed the whole, pack it down, hard, into small stone jars, covering them closely, and pasting strong white paper over the lids. Do not add the apples till you take out the mince-meat for use, as it keeps better without them. Then take a sufficient number of pippins or bell-flowers, pare, core and chop them, and mix them with the mince-meat, allowing three large apples to a pint of mince-meat. Their freshness will improve the flavour.

It is best to make mince-meat two or three times during the winter; as it will not continue very good longer than five or six weeks. Whenever you take any out of the jars, put some additional brandy to the remainder.

For mince-meat, and all other purposes, use none but the *best* raisins. What are called *cooking* raisins, (like *cooking* butter and *cooking* wine,) injure instead of improving the articles with which they are mixed. All things of bad quality are unwholesome as well as unpalatable. It is better to do without mince-pies, plum-puddings and plum-cakes, than to spoil them with hard, dried up, indigestible raisins; to say nothing of the trouble of stoning and stemming them, when they are nearly all seeds and stems.

TEMPERANCE MINCE-MEAT.—Take three pounds of the lean of a round of fresh beef, that has been boiled the day before. It must be thoroughly boiled, and very tender. Mince it, as finely as possible, with a chopping-knife; and add to it two pounds of beef-suet, cleared from the skin and filaments, and minced very small. Mix the suet and the lean beef well together; and add a pound of brown sugar. Pick, wash, and dry before the fire, two pounds of Zante currants. Seed and chop two pounds of the best raisins. Sultana raisins have no seeds, and are therefore the most convenient for all cookery purposes. Grate the yellow rind of three large lemons or oranges into a saucer, and squeeze upon it their juice, through a strainer. Mix this with the currants and raisins. Prepare a heaped-up table-spoonful of powdered cinnamon; the same quantity of powdered ginger; a heaped tea-spoonful of powdered nutmeg; the same of powdered cloves; and the same of powdered mace. Mix all these spices into a quart of the best *West India* molasses. Then mix well together the meat and the fruit; and wet the whole with the spiced molasses; of which you must have enough to make the mixture very moist, but not too thin. If you want the mince-meat for immediate use, add to it four pounds of minced apple. The apples for this purpose should be pippins or bell-flowers, pared, cored, quartered, and chopped fine. Add, also, half a pound of citron, not minced, but cut into long slips.

If you intend the mince-meat for keeping, do not add the apple and citron until you are about to make the pies, as it will keep better without them. Mix all the other articles thoroughly, and pack down the mince-meat, hard, in small stone jars. Lay upon the top of it, a round of thin white paper, dipped in molasses, and cut exactly to fit the inside circumference of the jar. Secure the jars closely with flat, tight-fitting corks, and then with a lid; and paste paper down over the top on the outside.

West India molasses will be found a good substitute for the wine and brandy generally used to moisten mince-meat.

TRANSPARENT PASTE.—Take twelve ounces (or a pint and a half) of the best fresh butter. Wash and squeeze it through several cold waters, and press out whatever milk may remain about it. Then set it over the fire to soften all through; but do not allow it to melt, so as to become liquid or oily. Beat two eggs till very light and smooth; and when the butter is cool, stir the eggs into it, adding, very gradually, a pound of sifted flour that has been dried before the fire. Mix the whole into a lump of soft dough, and beat it well on all sides with the rolling-pin. Then transfer it to a paste-board, and roll it out thin. As quickly as possible butter some tart-pans, and line them with the paste; then brush it lightly with a little cold water, and sift on, thickly, some powdered sugar. They must be baked empty. Set them immediately in a rather brisk oven, and bake them a light brown. When cool, turn them out, and fill them with marmalade, jam, or any very nice sweetmeats. If properly made and baked, this paste looks very handsome. It may be baked in large patty-pans the size of soup-plates.

LIGHT PASTE.—Sift into a pan three quarters of a pound of flour, and another quarter on a plate. Beat the whites of two eggs to a stiff froth, and mix them with a wine-glass or more of cold water. With this wet the flour to a stiff paste; and when it is formed into a lump, beat it on all sides with the rolling-pin. Then lay it on the paste-board, and roll it out into a thin sheet. Use the extra quarter of flour for sprinkling and rolling. Have ready three quarters of a pound of the best fresh butter, divided into three portions. Cover the sheet with one portion of the butter, placed all over it in bits of equal size, and laid on at equal distances. Then sprinkle on a little flour; fold up the sheet of paste; flour it slightly when folded; roll it out again; and put on in the same manner another portion of the butter; then flour it slightly; fold it up; roll it out again; and add the third division of butter. Then fold it, flour it, and give it a hard final rolling, always moving the rolling-pin *from* you instead of *towards* you. The paste will then be ready for any nice purpose.

ORANGE TARTS.—Take six or seven fine large sweet oranges; roll them under your hand on a table to increase the juice, and then squeeze them through a strainer over half a pound or more of powdered loaf-sugar. Mix the orange-juice and the sugar thoroughly together. Use *none* of the peel. Break twelve eggs into a large shallow pan, and beat them till thick and smooth. Then stir in, gradually, the orange-juice and sugar. Have ready a sufficiency of the best puff-paste, roll it out thin, and line some patty-pans with it, having first buttered them inside. Then fill them with the orange-mixture, and set them immediately into a rather brisk oven. Bake the tarts a light brown; and when done, set them to cool. When quite cold, take them out of the patty-pans, put them on a large dish, and grate sugar over their tops.

Lemon tarts may be made in a similar manner, but they require double the quantity of sugar.

For baking tarts it is well to use (instead of tin patty-pans) small deep plates of china or white-ware, with broad flat edges, like little soup-plates. You can then have all round the edge a rim of paste ornamentally notched. In notching the edge of a tart, (this must, of course, be done before it goes into the oven,) use a sharp knife. Make the cuts at equal distances about an inch broad, so as to form squares. Turn upwards one square, and leave the next one down; and so on all round the edge. This is the *chevaux-de-frize* pattern. For the shell-pattern, having notched the edge of the paste into squares, turn up one half of *every* square, giving the corner a fold down. The paste should always be thickest round the rim or edge.

All tarts are best the day they are baked; but they should never be sent to table warm.

A VERY FINE CHARLOTTE RUSSE.—Boil a vanilla bean and a few blades of mace in half a pint of rich milk till it is highly flavoured. Then take out the bean; wipe it; and put it away for another time, and remove the mace also. Mix the flavoured milk with a large half-pint of cream. Beat four or five eggs till very light and thick; strain them, and add them gradually to the cream, (when it is entirely cold,) to make a rich custard. Set this custard over the fire, (stirring it all the time,) and before it comes to a hard boil, take it off, and set it on ice. Have ready, in another sauce-pan, an ounce of the best Russia isinglass boiled to a thick jelly in a half pint of water. When the custard and isinglass are both cold, (but not hard,) mix them well together, and add four table-spoonfuls of powdered loaf-sugar. Then take half a pound of loaf-sugar in lumps, and rub on them the yellow rind of two lemons. Mix together the strained juice of the lemons, and two glasses of sherry or madeira, and a glass of brandy; pour it upon the sugar; and when the sugar is entirely dissolved, mix it with a quart of rich cream, and whip it with rods or a whisk to a stiff froth. Take off the froth as it stiffens, and add it gradually to the custard, stirring it very hard, at the time; and also after the whole is mixed. Then set it on ice.

Cover the bottom of a handsome china dish or a glass bowl, with sliced almond sponge-cake cut to fit. Then place round the sides slices of the cake all of the same shape and size, making them wrap a little over each other. Pour in the mixture. Cover the top with a layer of cake cut very thin. Have ready an icing made in the usual manner of beaten white of egg and powdered loaf-sugar; and flavoured with rose or lemon. Spread it thickly and evenly over the surface of the top, smoothing it with a broad knife dipped in cold water. Then set it on ice till wanted. This Charlotte Russe is not to be turned out of the dish. It may be made in two dishes.

Instead of vanilla, you may flavour the custard with a handful of peach-leaves, or of broken up bitter almonds, boiled in the first half-pint of milk, and two large sticks of cinnamon broken in pieces.

When the icing on the top has about half-dried, you may ornament it by sticking on ripe strawberries of equal size in circles, stars, or any fanciful figures. Or it may be decorated with white grapes, each grape standing on end, if oval or long shaped.

ANOTHER CHARLOTTE RUSSE.—Take a large circular or oval lady cake, and with a sharp knife cut out nicely the inside, leaving the sides and bottom standing, (about half an inch thick,) in the form of a mould. Make a rich boiled custard, allowing eight eggs to a quart of unskimmed milk, half a pint of which has been previously flavoured by boiling in it half a dozen blades of mace with a vanilla bean, or a handful of shelled bitter almonds or peach-kernels blanched and broken up. Strain this flavoured milk and add it to the other. Then beat the eggs very light and stir them gradually into the milk. Set it over hot coals, stirring it all the time, but take it off before it comes to a boil, or it will curdle. Have ready an ounce of isinglass boiled to a jelly in a little water. When the custard and the isinglass are both cold (not hard) mix them well together and add sufficient powdered loaf-sugar to make it very sweet. Take a quart of rich cream that has been seasoned with extract of roses, and whip it to a stiff froth. Take off the froth as it stiffens, and add it gradually to the custard, stirring it very hard after it is all in to prevent its separating. Fill with the mixture the scooped-out sponge cake. Then cover the whole with an icing made in the usual way of white of egg and sugar, flavoured with rose or lemon. Then set it on ice till wanted.

AN ITALIAN CHARLOTTE.—Take a pint of rich cream; set it on ice, and beat and stir it till it becomes a solid froth. Then boil a vanilla bean in half a pint of rich milk till it is highly flavoured. Strain the milk, and when cold mix with it six ounces of loaf-sugar and the beaten yolks of four eggs, and set it over the fire, or rather on a bed of hot coals. Boil it ten minutes, stirring it frequently. When it comes to a boil, add half a pint of clear firm jelly-stock that has been made of calves' feet, or else an ounce of isinglass that has been melted in barely as much boiling water as will cover it. Stir the mixture well, and let it remain five minutes over the fire. Then take it off, and place it on ice, stirring it till it begins to thicken. When it is about the consistence of very thick gruel, add the whipped cream. Have ready an almond sponge cake, baked in the form of a circular loaf. With a sharp knife cut out the inside of this cake carefully and smoothly; leaving the sides and bottom together, so as to form a mould not quite an inch thick. Fill this up to the top with the Charlotte mixture; and placing a large plate beneath it, set it on ice to congeal. In the mean time, prepare a meringue or icing of beaten white of egg, thickened with powdered loaf-sugar, and flavoured with extract of orange-flowers. Cover the top and sides of the Charlotte with this icing; spread on evenly, and smoothed with a knife dipped in cold water. Ornament it with coloured sugar-jelly rings, handsomely arranged, or any other nice bonbons.

A FRENCH CHARLOTTE.—Lay in a deep dish or pan half a pound of bitter almond maccaroons (chocolate maccaroons will be still better) and pour on sufficient white wine to cover them well, and let them stand till entirely dissolved. Whip to a stiff froth a pint of rich cream, sweetened with sugar and flavoured with rose or lemon. Have ready a large circular almond sponge cake with the inside cut out, so as to leave the sides and bottom standing in the form of a mould, not quite an inch thick. Ornament the edge with a handsome border of icing. In the bottom of this mould put the dissolved maccaroons; over them a layer of thick jelly, made of some very nice fruit; and fill up with the whipped cream, heaping it high in the centre.

This is a very fine Charlotte, and is easily made, no cooking being required, after the materials are collected.

A SWEET OMELET.—Break small in an earthen pan six maccaroons made with bitter almonds, and mix with them a dozen orange-blossoms pounded to a paste. If the orange-flowers are not quite blown, the fragrance and flavour will be finer. If more convenient, substitute for the blossoms a large wine-glass of orange-flower water. Add six ounces of powdered loaf-sugar, and mix all well together. Separate the whites from the yolks of six eggs. Beat the yolks in a broad earthen pan till very light and smooth, and add to them, gradually, the other ingredients. Have ready the whites beaten to a stiff froth, and stir them in at the last, a little at a time. Put four ounces of fresh butter into an omelet pan (or a small, clean, short-handled frying-pan, tinned or enamelled inside.) Set it over hot coals, and when the butter is all melted put in the omelet-batter; which some one should continue to beat till the last minute. When the omelet has become hot and has begun to colour, transfer it to a well-buttered dish. Place it instantly in a rather brisk oven and bake it from five to ten minutes, till it is a light-yellowish brown, and puffed up high. Sift powdered sugar over it as quickly as possible, and carry it immediately to the dinner-table; handing it round rapidly for every one to take a piece, as it falls very soon.

These omelets are served up at dinner-parties immediately on the removal of the meats.

They must be made, cooked, served up, and eaten with great celerity. Therefore it is not usual to commence mixing a sweet or soufflée omelet, till after the company has set down to dinner.

If exactly followed, this receipt will be found excellent.

SUNDERLANDS OR JELLY PUFFS.—Take a broad pan, and put into it a pint of rich milk, and half a pound of the best fresh butter. Cut up the butter in the milk, and, if in cold weather, set it in a warm place, on the stove, or on the hearth near the fire, till the butter is quite soft; but do not allow it to melt or oil; it must be merely warmed so as to soften. Then take it off, and with a knife stir the butter well through the milk till thoroughly mixed. Have ready half a pound of fine flour sifted into a deep dish. In a broad pan beat eight eggs, with a whisk, till they are very thick and light. Then stir the beaten egg into the pan of milk and butter, in turn with the sifted flour, a little at a time of each. Stir the whole very hard, and then put the mixture into buttered tea-cups, filling them only two-thirds. Set them *immediately* into a brisk oven, and bake them twenty minutes or more, till they are well browned, and puffed up very light. Then take them from the oven, and with a knife open a slit in the side of each puff, and carefully put in, with a spoon, sufficient fruit jelly or marmalade to fill up the whole inside or cavity. Afterwards close the slit, and press it together with your fingers. As you fill them, lay each on a large dish; and before they go to table, sift powdered white sugar over them. Eat them cold. If properly made they will be found delicious.

Instead of jelly or marmalade, you may fill the Sunderlands with a rich boiled custard, flavoured with vanilla or bitter almonds; and made with yolk of egg, omitting the whites.

Or the filling may be of thick cream, made very sweet with loaf sugar, and flavoured with rose or peach water, or with orange-flower water, or with white wine.

RHUBARB CUPS.—Take twenty stalks of green rhubarb; cut them, and boil them in a quart of water. When it comes to a hard boil, take it from the fire; strain off the water; drain the rhubarb as dry as possible, and then mash it, and make it very sweet with brown sugar. Have ready half a pint of rice, that has been boiled in a quart of water, till soft and dry. Mix the rhubarb and the rice well together; beating them hard. Then mould it in cups slightly buttered, and set them on ice, or in a very cold place. Just before dinner, turn them out on a large dish. Serve up with them, in a bowl, cream and sugar, into which a nutmeg has been grated; or else a sauce made of equal portions of fresh butter and powdered white sugar, beaten together till very light, and flavoured with powdered cinnamon, or nutmeg, and oil of lemon or lemon-juice.

SPANISH BLANC-MANGE.—Weigh half a pound of broken-up loaf-sugar of the best quality. On one of the pieces rub off the yellow rind of a large lemon. Then powder all the sugar, and mix with it a pint of rich cream, the juice of the lemon, and half a pint (not less) of madeira or sherry. Stir the mixture very hard, till all the articles are thoroughly amalgamated. Then stir in, gradually, a second pint of cream.

Put into a small sauce-pan an ounce of the best isinglass, with one jill (or two common-sized wine-glass-fulls) of cold water. Set the pan over hot coals, and boil it till the isinglass is completely dissolved, and not the smallest lump remaining. Frequently, while boiling, stir it down to the bottom; taking care not to let it scorch. When the melted isinglass has become lukewarm, stir it, gradually, into the mixture of other ingredients; and then give the whole a hard stirring. Have ready two or three white-ware moulds, that have just been dipped and rinsed in cold water. Fill them with the mixture, and set them immediately on ice, and in about two hours (or perhaps more) the blanc-mange will be congealed. Do not remove it from the ice till *perfectly* firm. Dip the moulds for a moment in lukewarm water; then turn out the cream on glass dishes.

This will be found a delicious article for a dessert, or an evening party, provided the receipt is *exactly* followed. We highly recommend it, and *know* that if fairly tried, precisely according to the above directions, there can be no failure. It is superior to any of the usual preparations of blanc-mange. The wine (which must be of excellent quality) gives it a delicate and beautiful colour, and a fine flavour.

VANILLA BLANC-MANGE.—Chip fine an ounce of the best isinglass, and put it into a small sauce-pan, with a jill of cold water, and boil it till entirely dissolved. In another sauce-pan boil half a pint of rich milk and a vanilla bean. Boil it, (with the lid on,) till the flavour of the vanilla is well extracted. Whip a quart of rich cream to a stiff froth. Separate the whites and yolks of four eggs. Beat the whites till they stand alone. Then, in another pan, beat the yolks, and when they are very light and smooth, add to them, gradually, a quarter of a pound of powdered loaf-sugar, beaten in very hard. Then (having strained out the bean) mix with the cream the milk in which it was boiled. Then beat in, by degrees, the yolk of egg and sugar; then the white of egg; and, lastly, the melted isinglass. When all the ingredients are united, beat and stir the whole very hard. Rinse your moulds in cold water. Then put in the mixture, and set it on ice, for two hours or more, to congeal. When quite firm, (and just before it is wanted,) dip each mould down, into a pan of lukewarm water, (taking care that the water does not reach the top,) and turn out the blanc-mange on glass or china dishes. Keep it on ice, till the minute before it is served up. It will be found very fine.

MACCAROON BLANC-MANGE.—Chip small an ounce of the best Russia isinglass; put it into a small sauce-pan; pour on it a jill of cold water; and boil it till the isinglass is entirely melted, stirring and skimming it well. Then strain it; cover it; and set it away. Have ready a quart of cream, or very rich milk, boiling hot. Crush half a pound or more of *bitter*-almond maccaroons; mix them well with the boiling cream; cover the vessel, and let it stand (stirring it occasionally) till the maccaroons are all dissolved. Next add the lukewarm isinglass; stir the whole very hard, and then transfer it to blanc-mange moulds, that have been slightly rubbed on the inside with a little sweet oil. Set it on ice, (or in a very cold place,) and stir it occasionally till it begins to congeal; then let it rest. When quite firm all through, loosen it in the moulds, by slipping a knife beneath the edge of the blanc-mange, and warm a clean cloth, and lay it a minute over the top. This will render it easy to turn out. Or you may loosen the blanc-mange by setting the mould in a pan of lukewarm water. Turn it out into a glass dish. Lay on the top of the blanc-mange a sufficient number of whole maccaroons, handsomely arranged in a large star, or in a circle, and place another circle on the dish, round the bottom.

CHOCOLATE BLANC-MANGE.—The day before you want the blanc-mange, take four calves' feet, (singed but not skinned,) or eight or ten pigs' feet. Boil them slowly, (with frequent skimming,) in four quarts of water, till all the meat drops from the bones. Then strain the liquid, through a sieve, into a broad tin pan, cover it, and set it away in a cold, dry place. Next day it should be a solid cake of clear jelly. Then scrape off all the fat and sediment; cut the jelly into small bits; and put it into a porcelain kettle or preserving pan, and melt it over the fire. Have ready six ounces, or more, of cocoa or chocolate, that has been scraped fine, and melted, over the fire, in a pint of boiling cream, with six ounces of powdered loaf-sugar. When the chocolate, cream, and sugar have boiled together five minutes after coming to a boil, mix them with the melted jelly, and let the whole come to a boil again; and then boil them together five minutes more, stirring it occasionally. Next put it into moulds that have set all night in cold water. Do not wipe the moulds, but leave them damp. Stir their contents well; and when the blanc-mange is thickening, so that it is hard to stir, set the moulds on ice, or place them in the cellar, in pans of cold water. When the blanc-mange has quite congealed, and is very firm, turn it out of the moulds, first setting them in lukewarm water, and serve it up on china dishes.

Instead of calves' or pigs' feet, you may substitute an ounce of the best Russia isinglass, or an ounce and a half of the common sort. The isinglass must be previously dissolved, by boiling it in as much water as will cover it, taking care not to let it burn. It must be melted quite smooth. Mix it, while warm, with the chocolate, cream, and sugar.

COFFEE BLANC-MANGE may be made as above, substituting, for the chocolate, six ounces of the best coffee, freshly roasted and ground, and boiled in a pint of rich, unskimmed milk; or of cream, into which there has been stirred an ounce or an ounce and a half of isinglass, previously melted by boiling in water; and, also, six ounces of powdered sugar. Boil all together, and then strain the liquid into moulds, and set them on ice.

GELATINE BLANC-MANGE.—From two quarts of rich milk take a pint, and put the pint into a small saucepan, with the yellow rinds of three lemons, pared thin, and half a beaten nutmeg. For the lemon-rind, you may substitute a handful of bitter almonds or peach-kernels, broken up; or else a vanilla bean. Having boiled the pint of milk long and slowly, till it tastes strongly of the flavouring articles, (keeping it closely covered,) strain it, and mix it, in a larger sauce-pan, with the other three pints of milk. Add an ounce and a half of gelatine, (that has first been soaked in cold water,) and a quarter of a pound of fine loaf-sugar. Set it over the fire, and continue to boil and stir it five minutes after it has come to a boil. Then strain it, and transfer it to blanc-mange moulds, first wetting the inside of each mould with cold water. Place the moulds on ice, or in a very cold place, till the blanc-mange has thoroughly congealed. Then turn it out on dishes.

CAKE SYLLABUB.—Half fill a glass bowl with thin slices of sponge-cake or almond-cake. Pour on sufficient white wine to dissolve the cake. Then rub off, on pieces of loaf-sugar, the yellow rind of two lemons, and dissolve the sugar in a pint of rich cream. Squeeze the juice of the lemons on some powdered loaf-sugar, and add it, gradually, to the cream. Whip or mill the cream to a stiff froth; and then pile it on the dissolved cake in the glass bowl. It should be heaped high above the edge of the bowl. You may ornament the top of the syllabub with a circle of real roses or other flowers,—a large one in the centre, and smaller ones placed round in a ring.

ORANGE FLUMMERY.—Begin the day before, by boiling four large calves' feet or eight small ones in three quarts of water. The best feet for this purpose are those that are scalded and scraped, but not skinned. After they have boiled slowly about five hours, put in the yellow rind of four large oranges, pared very thin and cut small, and several sticks of cinnamon broken up; and, if you choose, a dozen bitter almonds or peach-kernels slightly pounded. Then let it boil an hour longer, till the meat all drops from the bones, and is reduced to shreds, and till the liquid is little more than a quart. Strain it through a sieve over a broad white pan, and set it in a cold place till next morning, when it ought to be a solid cake. Scrape off all the fat and sediment carefully; otherwise it will not be clear when melted. Cut the cake into pieces; put it into a porcelain kettle, with half a pound of double-refined loaf-sugar, broken up, and melt it over the fire, adding, when it has entirely dissolved, the juice of six large oranges. Next stir in, gradually, the yolks of six eggs well-beaten, and continue stirring till it has boiled ten minutes. Then take it off the fire, transfer it to a broad pan, and set it on ice or in cold water. Continue stirring till it is quite cold but not set. Wet some moulds with cold water, put the mixture into them, and set it in a cold place or on ice to congeal. When perfectly firm, wrap a cloth dipped in warm water round the moulds, and turn it out on glass dishes.

Lemon flummery may be made in the same manner.

VANILLA FLUMMERY.—Take two quarts of rich milk. Put a pint of it into a clean sauce-pan, and boil in it a vanilla bean, (keeping it closely covered,) till the milk is highly flavoured. Then strain it into a pan, and stir into it, gradually, half a pound of ground rice flour, mixing it smoothly and free from lumps, till it becomes a thick batter. If you find it too stiff, thin it with a little milk. Put the rest of the milk (about three pints) into a larger sauce-pan, and set it over the fire. When it comes to a boil, stir in, gradually, the rice-flour-batter, alternately with a quarter of a pound of powdered loaf-sugar. Let it continue boiling five minutes after all the batter has been put in. Then take it off, and stir in two table-spoonfuls of rose-water. Wet some moulds with cold water; put in the flummery and set it on ice or in a very cold place to congeal. When quite firm, set the moulds for an instant into a pan of lukewarm water.

Have ready a rich boiled custard, flavoured by boiling in the milk the same vanilla bean that was previously used for the flummery. The custard should be made in the proportion of a pint of milk to four eggs, and four table-spoonfuls of sugar. Stir it all the time it is over the fire, and take it off just as it begins to boil hard. When it is quite cold, send it to table in a glass pitcher or bowl to eat with the flummery.

Rice flummery may be flavoured by boiling in the first pint of milk a stick of cinnamon and a handful of bitter almonds or peach-kernels all broken up.

The custard should then be flavoured also with cinnamon and bitter almonds boiled in the custard milk.

Flummery may be coloured green by boiling in the last milk, spinach juice extracted by pounding in a mortar some raw spinach, or some pistachio nuts.

To colour it red, mix with the milk the juice of a beet that has been boiled, scraped, cut up and pounded. Or boil in the milk a very small muslin bag with alkanet tied up in it.

MERINGUED APPLES.—Pare and core (with a tin apple-corer) some fine large pippin apples, but do not quarter or slice them. Wash them separately in cold water, and then with the water still remaining about the surface of the apples, stand them up in a deep baking-dish, but do not place them so near each other as to touch. Pour into the bottom of the dish just water enough to prevent their burning, set them into a close oven, and bake them till they are perfectly tender all through, but not to break; as they must on no account lose their shape. When done, take them out; remove them to a flat china dish; and set them immediately to cool, clearing off any juice that may be about them. When quite cold, fill up the hole from whence the cores were extracted with thick marmalade or fruit jelly. Have ready a meringue or icing made of beaten white of egg, thickened with finely powdered loaf-sugar and flavoured with lemon-juice, or extract of roses. In making a meringue the usual proportion is the whites of four eggs to a pound of powdered sugar. The white of egg must first be whisked to a stiff firm froth, and the sugar then beaten into it, gradually, a spoonful at a time; the flavouring being added at the last. When the apples are quite cold cover them all over with the meringue, put on in table-spoonfuls, beginning at the top of each apple and then spreading it down evenly with a broad-bladed knife dipped frequently into a bowl of cold water. The meringue must be put on very smoothly and of equal thickness all over. Then dredge the surface with finely powdered loaf-sugar sifted in from a very small sieve. Set them into a rather cool oven, and as soon as the meringue is hardened, take them out.

Fine large free-stone peaches may be meringued in this manner. To extract the stones of peaches loosen them carefully all round with a sharp, narrow-pointed knife. You may then easily thrust them out, without breaking the peaches, which for this purpose should not be over-ripe.

CHOCOLATE CREAM.—Scrape down a quarter of a pound of the best chocolate, or of Baker's prepared cocoa. Put it into a marble mortar. Pour on by degrees as much boiling water as will dissolve it, and beat it well for about a quarter of an hour. Then sweeten it with four table-spoonfuls of powdered loaf-sugar. Add, gradually, a pint and a half of rich cream. Mill it with a chocolate mill, or a little tin churn; or beat it hard with rods. As the froth rises, take it off and lay it on the inverted bottom of a sieve that is placed in a deep pan. When done, take the liquid that has drained through the sieve, and put a portion of it in the bottom of each glass. Then fill the glasses with the froth, heaping it high on the top, and set it in a cool dry place till wanted.

ANOTHER WAY.—Boil a vanilla bean in half a pint of milk till the flavour is well-extracted. Then take out the bean, wipe it dry, and put it away. It may be used a second time for a slight vanilla flavouring. Scrape down a quarter of a pound of excellent chocolate, or of Baker's prepared cocoa, and mix with it the vanilla-milk. Put it into a chocolate pot or a sauce-pan, and pour on it a pint and a half of rich milk. Set it over the fire, or on a bed of hot coals, and boil it slowly; stirring it till the chocolate is entirely dissolved and thoroughly incorporated with the milk. Beat six eggs very light, and stir them, gradually, into the mixture; continuing to stir, lest it should curdle. When the egg is all in, and it begins to boil up, take it off, and when cool enough transfer it to glasses, or to a bowl.

PISTACHIO CREAM.—Take half a pound of pistachio nuts. Throw them into scalding water, and peel off the skins. Put the nuts (not more than two at a time) into a marble mortar, and pound them to a smooth paste, adding frequently, as you proceed, a few drops of rose-water. Sweeten a quart of cream with half a pound of powdered loaf-sugar, and stir into it, gradually, the pistachio paste. Set the mixture over the fire; and let it just come to a boil. Then take it out; stir in two table-spoonfuls of rose-water or peach-water, and set on ice to cool. Either serve it up liquid in a glass bowl, or put it into a freezer, and freeze it as ice-cream. If you freeze it, you must substitute for the rose-water or peach-water, a table-spoonful of extract of roses, or the same quantity of extract of bitter almonds. The process of freezing diminishes the strength of every sort of flavouring; and of sweetening also.

If you serve it up as frozen, stick it all over with slips of pistachio nut, peeled and sliced.

ALMOND CREAM.—Take a pound of shelled sweet almonds, and two ounces or more of shelled bitter almonds, or peach-kernels. Blanch them in scalding water, throwing them as you proceed into a bowl of cold water. Then pound them (one at a time) in a mortar, till each becomes a smooth paste; pouring in, as you proceed, a little rose-water to make the almonds white and light, and transferring the paste to a plate as you go on. Then when they are all done, mix the almonds with a quart of rich cream, and a quarter of a pound of powdered loaf-sugar. Add half a dozen blades of mace; put the mixture into a porcelain kettle, and boil it, slowly, stirring it frequently down to the bottom. Having given it one boil up, remove it from the fire, take out the mace, and when it has cooled a little, put the cream into glass cups, grating nutmeg over each. Serve it up quite cold. You may ornament each cup of this cream with white of egg, beaten to a stiff froth, and heaped on the top.

COCOA-NUT CREAM may be made as above; substituting for the almonds a pound of cocoa-nut grated finely. When it has boiled, and is taken from the fire, stir into the cream a wine-glass of rose-water.

A similar cream may be made with pounded pistachio nuts.

Pecan nuts, blanched and pounded, (adding occasionally a little cold water to take off the oiliness,) may be boiled as above, with cream, sugar, and spice.

All these creams may be frozen, and served up as ice-cream.

VANILLA CREAM.—Boil a vanilla bean in half a pint of rich milk, till the milk is highly flavoured with the vanilla. Then (having taken out the bean) strain the milk into a pint of thick cream. Beat the yolks of five eggs till very light, and then mix gradually with the beaten egg a quarter of a pound of powdered loaf-sugar, beating it in very hard. Set the cream over hot coals, and add to it by degrees the egg and sugar. Stir it continually till it is on the point of coming to a boil. It must be very thick and smooth. Cover the bottom and sides of a glass bowl or dish, with three quarters of a pound of lady-cake, cut into nice even slices. Pour on the mixture, and then set the bowl on ice or snow till wanted.

For lady-cake, you may substitute finger-biscuit, or slices of almond sponge-cake.

You may ornament the bowl by beating to a stiff froth the whites of two or three of the eggs, and heaping it on the top.

ICED JELLY.—Make calves' feet jelly in the usual way. Then put it into a freezer, and freeze it as you would ice-cream. Serve it up in a glass bowl or in jelly-glasses. You cannot mould it this way; but the taste of jelly when broken up is much more lively than when moulded; also it sparkles and looks handsomer.

CURRANT ICE.—Pick a sufficiency of ripe currants from their stems. Then squeeze the currants through a linen bag, and to each quart of the juice allow a pound of powdered loaf-sugar. Mix them together, and when the sugar is thoroughly melted, put it into a freezer, and freeze it in the manner of ice-cream. Serve it up in glass bowls. It will be found delicious in warm weather.

PLUM-WATER ICE.—Take some fine ripe plums. Wash them; cut them in half, and stone them. Crack the stones, and take out the kernels. Weigh the plums, and to every pound allow a pound and a half of loaf-sugar, and the white of an egg beaten to a stiff froth. Mix, in a preserving kettle, the white of egg with the sugar, which should be finely powdered; and allow to each pound and a half of sugar, half a pint of water. Having stirred it well, set on the fire, (but not till all the sugar is melted,) add the plum-kernels, and boil and skim it. When the scum ceases to rise, take the syrup off the fire, pour it into a white-ware vessel, and remove the kernels. While you are boiling the sugar, put the plums into another vessel and boil them by themselves to draw out the juice. Then put them into a linen bag, and squeeze all the juice into a deep pan or pitcher placed beneath. Afterwards mix the plum-juice with the syrup; stirring them thoroughly together; and put it into a freezer. Freeze it well, and when done, serve it in a glass bowl, and eat it in saucers.

DAMSON-WATER ICE may be made as above; except that you boil the damsons whole and make no use of the kernels. When the damsons have all burst open, put them into a linen bag; squeeze it well, mix the juice with the syrup which you have previously prepared, and freeze it. The juice of damsons is much thicker and richer than that of plums; but it requires still more sugar.

CHERRY-WATER ICE is made nearly as above; except that the cherries must be stoned, but not boiled. Put them raw into the bag, and squeeze them. The cherries should be of the best and most juicy red sort, and thoroughly ripe.

STRAWBERRY ICE is made of ripe strawberries put into a linen bag, and the juice squeezed out. Then measure it, and to each pint of juice allow half a pound of powdered loaf-sugar. Having mixed thoroughly the juice and the sugar, put it into a freezer and freeze it. In this manner ices (without cream) may be made of currant and raspberry juice, mixed raw with sugar.

GOOSEBERRY-WATER ICE.—Having stewed the gooseberries, squeeze out the juice through a linen bag. To every pint, allow a pound of loaf-sugar. Mix it well, and freeze it.

PEACH ICE-CREAM.—Take fine soft free-stone peaches, perfectly ripe. Pare them, and remove the stones. Crack about half the stones, and extract the kernels, which must be blanched by putting them into a bowl, and pouring on boiling water to loosen the skins. Then break them up, or pound them slightly; put them into a little sauce-pan, and boil the kernels in a small quantity of rich milk, till it is highly flavoured with them; keeping the sauce-pan covered. Strain out the kernels, and set the milk to cool. Cut up the peaches in a large, broad, shallow pan, or a flat dish, and chop them very small. Mix with the chopped peaches sufficient powdered loaf-sugar to make them very sweet, and then mash them to a smooth jam with a silver spoon. Measure the peach jam; and to each quart allow a pint of cream, and a pint of rich unskimmed milk. Mix the whole well together, and put it into the freezer; adding when the mixture is about half-frozen, the milk in which you boiled the kernels, and which will greatly improve the peach-flavour. When well frozen, turn out the cream and serve it in a glass bowl. If you wish to have it in a shape, transfer it to a mould, and give it a second freezing. Before you turn it out, wash the outside of the mould all over with cold water, or wrap a wet cloth round it. Then open it, and the ice-cream will come out easily.

Apricot ice-cream may be made as above.

CHOCOLATE ICE-CREAM.—Scrape down half a pound of the best chocolate or of Baker's prepared cocoa. Put it into a sauce-pan, and pour on it a pint of boiling milk. Stir, and mix it well, and smoothly. Then set it over the fire, and let it come to a boil. Mix together in a pan, a quarter of a pound of powdered loaf-sugar, and a pint of rich cream. In another pan beat very light the yolks of nine eggs. Afterwards gradually stir the beaten egg into the cream and sugar, and then put the mixture into a sauce-pan; stir in, by degrees, the chocolate; set it over the fire, and simmer it till it is just ready to come to a boil. Strain it through a sieve, transfer it to a freezer, and freeze it in the usual manner of ice-cream.

BISCUIT ICE-CREAM.—Take some pieces of broken loaf-sugar, and rub off on them the yellow rind of four lemons. Then pulverize the sugar and mix it with half a pound of loaf-sugar already powdered. Have ready eight small Naples biscuits or sponge-cakes, grated fine; stir them, in turn with the sugar, into a quart of cream. Give the whole one boil up. Then put it into a freezer, and freeze it in the usual manner. Afterwards transfer it to a pyramid mould, and freeze it a second time.

Similar ice-cream may be made with maccaroons broken small and dissolved in the cream, from whence half a pint must be previously taken and boiled with a handful of broken up bitter almonds. Afterwards strain this, and mix it with the rest.

FLAVOURED CURDS AND WHEY.—To turn two quarts of milk, take a piece of dried rennet about the size of the palm of your hand; wash it well through several cold waters to get the salt entirely off, and then wipe it dry. Put it into a small bowl, and pour on it half a tumbler (a quarter of a pint) of lukewarm water. The water must on no account be hot, as to scald rennet weakens it and diminishes its power of converting milk into curd. Cover the bowl; and let it stand to infuse at least four hours. A longer time will do no harm; therefore, if you intend making the curd early in the day, you may put the rennet in soak over night. For lemon-flavouring—to two quarts of milk allow two lemons, using only the *yellow* rind or surface of the skin, and grating it as finely as possible. Reserve the juice of the lemons for some other purpose. Mix the grated rind with the rennet-water, first removing the piece of rennet that has been soaking in it. Have ready in a large china or glass bowl two quarts of rich milk, and stir into it the rennet-water and lemon-rind. Cover the bowl, and set it in a moderately warm place till the curd has become a firm, smooth, unbroken mass, and the whey looks clear and greenish. Then set the bowl on ice, and keep it there till wanted for the table. Accompany it with a small pitcher of rich cream, and a little bowl of powdered loaf-sugar and nutmeg. Send it round on saucers. It is a delicious article for summer dessert, or for a summer tea-table.

To flavour curds and whey with vanilla—boil a vanilla bean slowly in half a pint of milk, keeping the saucepan closely covered. When the milk is highly flavoured with the vanilla, strain it; and when cold, mix it with the milk you intend for the curds. Afterwards add the rennet-water. Or you may use instead of the bean, extract of vanilla, allowing four table-spoonfuls to two quarts of milk. Oliver's extract of vanilla is of excellent quality, and may be obtained in small bottles at most of the drug stores in Philadelphia.

To give curds and whey a peach-flavour—stir into the milk some peach-water, as soon as you have added the rennet-water; allowing two table-spoonfuls of the peach-water to each quart of milk. If you have no peach-water, take a handful of peach-kernels, (saved from the stones,) pound them, and boil them slowly in half a pint of milk till it tastes strongly of them. Then strain the milk, and when cold, mix it with the rest, and add the rennet-water. A handful of *fresh* peach-leaves boiled long and slowly in a small portion of milk will produce a similar flavour.

For a rose taste, stir into two quarts of milk a tea-spoonful of extract of roses; or more if it is not very strong; or add four table-spoonfuls of rose-water.

Curds and whey that has *not* been previously flavoured, should be sent to table with a small pitcher containing white wine, loaf-sugar, and powdered nutmeg.

RENNETS.—Milk turned into a curd with wine, is by no means so good as that which is done with rennet-water alone. The curd and whey do not separate so completely: the curd is less firm, and the whey less clear; the latter being thick and white, instead of thin and greenish as it ought to be. Neither is it so light and wholesome as when turned with rennet.

Rennets of the best quality can be had at all seasons in Philadelphia market; particularly in the lower part, called the Jersey market. They are sold at twelve, eighteen, or twenty-five cents, according to their size, and will keep a year or two; but have most strength when fresh. You may prepare excellent rennets yourself at a very trifling expense, by previously bespeaking them of a veal butcher; a rennet being the stomach of a calf. Its form is a bag. As soon as you get the rennet, empty out all its contents, and wipe it very clean, inside and out; then rinse it with cold water; but do not wash it much, as washing will weaken its power of turning milk into curd. When you have made it quite clean, lay the rennet in a broad pan, strew it over on both sides with plenty of fine salt; cover it, and let it rest five days. When you take it out of the pan, do not wipe or wash it, for it must be stretched and dried with the salt on. For this purpose hold it open like a bag, and slip within it a long, thick, smooth rod, bent into the form of a large loop; wide at the top, and so narrow at the bottom as to meet together. Stretch the rennet tightly and smoothly over this bent rod, on which it will be double, and when you have brought the two ends of the rod together at the bottom, and tied them fast, the form will somewhat resemble that of a boy's kite. Hang it up in a dry place, and cut out a bit as you want it. A piece about two inches square will turn one quart of milk, a piece of four inches two quarts. Having first washed off all the salt in several cold waters, and wiped the bit of rennet dry; pour on it sufficient *lukewarm* water to cover it well. Let it stand several hours; then pour the rennet-water into the milk you intend for the curd, and set it in a warm place. When the curd is entirely formed, set the vessel on ice.

Rennet may be used with good effect before it has *quite* dried.

HINTS ON CALVES' FOOT JELLY. — In making calves' foot jelly, if you intend it for moulds, put in two or three pieces of isinglass when you are boiling the in-gredients. If you wish it a deep rich colour, put into the bottom of the straining-bag a large tea-spoonful of *brown* sugar, before you pour in the jelly. After all the jelly has run through the bag, (which must on no account be squeezed,) let it, gradually, become perfectly cold before you remove it to a colder place to congeal.

SWEETMEATS, ETC.

AMERICAN CITRON.—Pare a sufficient number of citron-melons, and cut each melon into four thick quarters. Weigh them, and put them over-night into a tureen, or a large white-ware pan or basin. Prepare some very weak brine, allowing a table-spoonful of salt to a quart of water, for every pound of citron. Pour the salt and water over the citron; cover it, and let it stand all night to draw out the sliminess. Prepare some alum-water, allowing to each quart of water a bit of alum about the size of a grain of Indian corn. In the morning, drain the citron from the brine, and wash every piece separately in the alum-water, which will green and clear it. After it has lain half an hour in the alum-water, drain the citron, and put it into a porcelain preserving-kettle, allowing to every four pounds of the citron a large half pint of clear fresh water. There must be water enough to cover the citron, and keep it from burning. Add to every four pounds, the yellow rind of a large lemon, grated, or pared off very thin, and cut into shreds. Set the kettle over a clear fire, and boil it slowly, till the citron is tender enough to be easily pierced through with a large needle. If it seems to be boiling dry, add a little more cold water. When all are quite tender, take out each piece separately with a fork. Spread them out on a large dish. Then strain and measure the liquid; and to each pint allow a pound of the best double-refined *loaf-sugar*; not the sugar that is sold ready-powdered, as that is so adulterated with ground starch, that it has little or no strength, and sweetmeats made with it are sure to spoil, unless four times the usual quantity is put in.

Having broken up the loaf-sugar, add it to the liquid in the preserving-kettle, and let it boil (skimming it well) till it becomes a thick, rich, jelly-like syrup. It will most probably be boiled sufficiently in about half an hour. Next put in the pieces of citron, one at a time, and boil them ten minutes, or more, in the syrup, till it has thoroughly penetrated them. Afterwards take out the citron; spread it on a dish to cool; and transfer the syrup to a large pitcher. When cold, put the citron into glass jars, and pour the syrup over it. Cover the tops with white paper, dipped in brandy, and tie closely over each another covering of bladder, that has been previously soaked in water. The covers of lacquered tin, that belong to glass jars, seldom fit perfectly tight, and are not to be trusted without another covering over them.

This will be found a very fine sweetmeat. To dry it, in imitation of foreign citron, select some of the finest pieces; spread them on a dish; and set them for three days in the hot sun, turning each piece several times a-day. Then make a hole near the end of each piece; run a twine string through them, and hang them on lines, across an open, sunny window. When sufficiently dry, put them into tight jars, or boxes, and keep them to use, as citron, in cakes or mince-pies.

Preserved citron may be candied, (after it has lain five or six months in the syrup,) by taking out the pieces, spreading them on a dish, and boiling the syrup again, till it is as thick as possible. It may require some additional sugar. Then pour it on the citron; and when it has grown cold, and has dried on the pieces, put them into a jar.

When giving the citron its first boiling, in the lemon-peel and water, you may add, to every four pounds of citron, half an ounce of root-ginger, (if green and tender, it will be better,) or else a few pieces of preserved ginger.

To increase the lemon-flavour, rub off, upon some lumps of sugar, (before you make the syrup,) the yellow rind of two or three other lemons.

PRESERVED CITRON-MELONS.—Take some fine citron-melons; pare, core, and cut them into slices. Then weigh them; and, to every six pounds of melon, allow six pounds of the best double-refined loaf-sugar; and the juice and yellow rind (pared off very thin) of four large, fresh lemons; also, half a pound of race-ginger.

Put the slices of melon into a preserving-kettle, and boil them half an hour, or more, till they look *quite* clear, and are so tender that a broom-twig will pierce through them. Then drain them; lay them in a broad pan of cold water; cover them; and let them stand all night. In the morning, tie the race-ginger in a thin muslin cloth, and boil it in three pints of clear spring or pump-water, till the water is highly flavoured. Then take out the bag of ginger. Having broken up the sugar, put it into a clean preserving-kettle, and pour the ginger-water over it. When the sugar is all melted, set it over the fire; put in the yellow peel of the lemons; and boil and skim it till no more scum rises. Then remove the lemon-peel; put in the sliced citrons, and the juice of the lemons; and boil them in the syrup till all the slices are quite transparent, and so soft that a straw will go through them; but do not allow them to break. When quite done, put the slices (while still warm) into wide-mouthed glass or white-ware jars; and gently pour on the syrup. Lay inside of each jar, upon the top of the syrup, a double white tissue-paper, cut exactly to fit the surface. Put on the lids of the jars, and paste thick paper over them.

This will be found a delicious sweetmeat; equal to any imported from the West Indies, and far less expensive. We recommend it highly. Citron-melons are brought to Philadelphia market in the month of August.

AN EASY WAY OF PRESERVING PINE-APPLES.—Take pine-apples, as ripe as you can possibly get them; pare them, and cut them into thin, circular slices. Weigh them, and to each pound of pine-apple allow a pound of the best double-refined loaf-sugar. Place a layer of the pine-apple slices in the bottom of a large, deep dish, or white-ware pan, and sprinkle it thickly with a layer of the sugar, which must first be powdered. Then put another layer of the pine-apple, and sugar it well; and so on, till the dish is full; finishing with a layer of sugar on the top. Cover the dish, and let it stand all night. In the morning remove the slices of pine-apple to a tureen. Pour the syrup into a porcelain preserving-kettle, and boil and skim it at least half an hour. Do not remove it from the fire, till the scum has entirely ceased to rise. Then pour the syrup, *boiling hot*, over the slices of pine-apple in the tureen. Cover it, and let it stand till cold. Then transfer the sliced pine-apple and the syrup to wide-mouthed glass jars, or to large tumblers. Cover them well, pasting down thick white paper over the top.

FINE PINE-APPLE MARMALADE.—Take the largest, ripest, and most perfect pine-apples. Pare them, and cut out whatever blemishes you may find. Weigh each pine-apple, balancing the other scale with an equal weight of the best double-refined sugar, finely powdered, *at home*. The white sugar, that is sold ready-powdered, is generally so adulterated with finely pulverized starch, as to have very little strength or sweetness, and is, therefore, unfit for sweetmeats, as, when made with it, they will not keep. Grate the pine-apples on a large dish; using a large, coarse grater, and omitting the hard core that goes down the centre of each. Put the grated pine-apple and the sugar into a preserving-kettle, mixing them thoroughly. Set it over a moderate and very clear fire, and boil and skim it well, stirring it after skimming. After the scum has ceased to appear, stir the marmalade frequently till it is done, which will generally be in an hour, or an hour and a half after it has come to a boil. But if it is not smooth, clear, and bright, in that time, continue the boiling till it is. Put it, warm, into tumblers, or broad-mouthed glass jars. Lay inside the top of each, doubled white tissue-paper, cut exactly to fit, and press it down lightly with your finger, round the edge, so as to cover smoothly the surface of the marmalade. Then paste strong white paper over the top of each glass, and set them in a cool, dry place.

This is a very delicious preparation of pine-apple.

THE BEST WAY OF PRESERVING PINE-APPLES.—Take six large, fine, ripe pine-apples. Make them very clean, but do not pare off the rind, or cut off the leaves. Put them, whole, into a very large and very clean pot or kettle. Fill it up with cold water, and boil the pine-apples till they are so tender that you can penetrate them all through with a twig from a broom. Then take them out and drain them. When cool enough to handle without inconvenience, remove the leaves, and pare off the rind. The rind and leaves being left on, while boiling, will *keep in* the flavour of the fruit. Cut the pine-apples into round slices, about half an inch thick, extracting the core from the centre, so as to leave a round hole in the middle of every slice. Weigh them; and to each pound allow a pound of double-refined loaf-sugar, broken up and powdered. Cover the bottom of a large dish, or dishes, with a layer of the sugar. On this, place a layer of pine-apple slices; then a layer of sugar; then one of pine-apple; and so till the pine-apple slices are all covered; finishing with a layer of sugar. Let them stand twenty-four hours. Then drain the slices from the syrup, and lay them in wide jars. Put the syrup into a clean preserving-kettle, and boil and skim it till the scum ceases to rise. Then pour it hot upon the pine-apple. While still warm, cover the jars closely, and paste paper over them. They will be found very fine.

QUINCES may be preserved in a similar manner; first boiling them whole, with the skin on; then peeling them, and extracting the cores; then slicing the quinces into round, thin pieces, and letting them stand twenty-four hours in layers of sugar. Boil the syrup, and pour it over the quinces, after they are in the jars.

Save the parings and cores, and also some of the water in which the quinces were boiled. Weigh the boiled cores and parings, and to each pound allow a half-pint of the quince-water. Set them over the fire, in a clean kettle, and boil them, till dissolved as much as possible. Then strain them through a linen bag. To each pint of juice allow a pound of loaf-sugar, powdered. Having washed the kettle, put in the sugar; pour on it the quince-liquor; and boil it till it becomes a jelly. Try it, by holding a spoonful in the open air, and, if all is right, it will congeal very soon.

FINE ORANGE MARMALADE.—Quarter some large, ripe oranges, and remove the rind, the seeds, and the strings, or filaments; taking care, as you do so, to save all the juice. Put the pulp and juice into a porcelain sauce-pan, and mix with it an equal quantity of strained honey. If not sweet enough, add some powdered loaf-sugar. Boil them together slowly, stirring it frequently. Try if it is done, by taking out a spoonful, and placing it in the cold air. If, in cooling, it becomes a very thick marmalade, it is sufficiently boiled. Put it into wide-mouth glass jars, and cover it closely; first, with a double white tissue-paper, cut exactly to fit the surface of the marmalade, and then with thick white paper, pasted down, carefully, over the top of the jar. A cover of bladder, soaked in water, and put on wet, that it may contract in drying, is still better.

APPLE MARMALADE.—Break up four pounds of fine loaf-sugar. Put it into a preserving-kettle, and pour on a quart of clear, cold water. When the sugar has melted, stir it; set the kettle over the fire, and let it boil for a quarter of an hour after it has come to a boil; skimming it well. Have ready some fine, ripe pippin or bell-flower apples, pared, cored and sliced. There must be apple enough to weigh four pounds, when cut up. Put it into the syrup, adding the grated rinds of four large lemons. Let it simmer, stirring it well, till the apple is all dissolved, and forming a smooth mass. Then add the juice of the lemons; boil it fast; and continue boiling and stirring, till it becomes a very thick marmalade. It will generally require *simmering* an hour and a half, and *boiling fast* half an hour, or more. When it is done, put it, warm, into deep white-ware jars; cover it closely, and paste paper over the top, or tie a piece of bladder closely; and put it away in a dry, cool place. If you want any for immediate use, put some into a handsome mould, and, when cold and firm, turn it out on a glass dish; first dipping the mould in warm water.

FINE ORANGE JELLY.—Take four large calves' feet, that have been singed, but not skinned. Boil them in a gallon of clear, soft water, till the liquid is reduced to one quart, and all the meat has dropped from the bones. Strain it into a pan, cover it, and let it stand till next morning. It should then be a firm cake. Take a knife, and carefully remove all the fat from the top of the cake, and all the sediment from the bottom, and press some clean, soft, blotting-paper (or white paper) upon it, to clear it from all remains of greasiness. Then cut the cake of jelly into slices, and put it into a preserving-kettle. Add to it a pound and a half of loaf-sugar, broken up, a pint and a half of strained orange-juice, and the yellow rinds of four oranges, pared thin, and cut in pieces. Beat, slightly, the whites of six eggs, and add them to the mixture, with three of their shells, crushed small. Set the kettle over a clear fire, and stir till you see indications of the scum begin to rise. Then cease stirring, immediately, or the jelly will be cloudy. After it has come to a boil, simmer it ten minutes. Then take it off the fire. Let it stand about five minutes, and then pour the whole into a jelly-bag; place a white pan beneath, for the jelly to drip into. Take care not to squeeze the bag, or the clearness of the jelly will be irrecoverably destroyed. If it is not clear, on first running through, empty the bag, wash it clean, and return the jelly to it, and let it drip again. Repeat this, if necessary, till it is quite bright and transparent. When it has congealed, and become firm, put it into a glass bowl, and break it up. If you wish it in moulds, put it into them, of course, while it is liquid; but not till it is quite clear.

It will be clear much sooner, and with certainty, if you add two or three blades of isinglass, when it first begins to boil.

The oranges should be ripe, high-coloured, and rolled under the hand, to increase the juice.

EXCELLENT CURRANT-JELLY.—The currants should be quite ripe, but not *over*-ripe. Having picked them from the stems, put the fruit into a large stone jar, or pitcher, and tie closely over the top a very thick paper, (for instance, sugar-loaf paper, or coarse brown.) Set the jar into a kettle of boiling water, the water not quite reaching the top of the jar; and let the currants remain over a moderate fire an hour after they have begun to boil. Then pour them into a linen bag, and let the juice drip into a vessel beneath. Do not squeeze the bag, or the jelly will not be clear. When the juice has ceased to drip, measure it; and to each quart allow a pound of the best double-refined loaf-sugar, broken up. Crush the sugar small, by rolling it on a clean paste-board, with a rolling-pin. Put the juice (*without the sugar*) into a preserving-kettle, and let it just come to a boil. Then take it off; and, while it is very hot, immediately stir into it the sugar, a handful at a time, using a wooden spoon to stir it with. If the sugar is of the best sort, it will require no skimming, and will have no sediment. Therefore, as nothing of it will be lost or wasted, it is more economical than sugar of inferior quality. Put the jelly immediately into tumblers, or white jars, and cover it at once; first, with double white tissue-paper, cut to fit exactly the inside of the top; and then with writing-paper, cut larger, so as to turn downward, round the outside of the top. Paste the paper firmly on, and set the jelly away in a dry, cool place. Notch the edge of the paper, with scissors.

White currant-jelly may be made as above. It will be a clear, bright, amber colour.

Raspberry, strawberry, grape, gooseberry, and cranberry-jelly, can be made in this manner. For the gooseberry, allow a pound and a half of sugar to every pint of juice; for the cranberry, a pound and a half, also.

FINE BLACK CURRANT-JELLY.—Make black currant-jelly according to the above receipt; except that when you have stemmed the black currants, and put them into the jar, to boil, you must add a little water; allowing a small half-pint of water to each quart of the stemmed currants. The juice of black currants is so very thick, that, if undiluted, the jelly would be tough and ropy.

FOUR FRUIT JELLY.—Take equal quantities of ripe strawberries, raspberries, currants, and red cherries. All should be fully ripe, and the cherries must be stoned, taking care to save the juice that comes from them in stoning. Add it, afterwards, to the rest. Mix the fruit together, and put it in a linen bag. Squeeze it well into a tureen placed beneath. When it has ceased to drip, measure the juice; and to every pint, allow a pound and two ounces of the best double-refined loaf-sugar, finely powdered. Mix together the juice and the sugar. Put them into a porcelain preserving-kettle; set it over the fire, and let it boil half an hour—skimming it frequently. Try the jelly by dipping out a spoonful, and holding it in the open air. If it congeals readily, it is sufficiently done. Put the jelly warm into tumblers or other wide-topped glasses. Cover it with double-tissue paper, which must be white, and cut exactly to fit the surface of the jelly. Lay it nicely and smoothly inside the top of the glass, pressing it down with your fingers all round the edge. Then paste white paper over the top, and a little way down the sides of the glass, notching it round with scissors to make it fit the better.

Set away the jelly in a cool dry closet.

BARBERRY JAM.—Take barberries that are perfectly ripe. Pick them from the stems; and to each quart of berries, allow three-quarters of a pound of clean rich brown sugar. Mash the barberries, and put them with all their juice into a preserving-kettle, mixing with them the sugar, and stirring it well in. Boil and skim till the scum ceases to rise, and the jam has become a thick mass, which it will not be in less than an hour. Put it warm into stone or glass jars. Cover them immediately and paste down paper over their tops. It is a cheap and good sweetmeat for family use, either on the tea-table or in tarts.

Barberries in bunches may be put loosely into jars, and sufficient cold molasses poured in to fill up the vessels, which must be kept tightly covered. Frost grapes, also, can be kept in this homely manner.

DAMSON JAM.—Fill a stone jar with fine ripe damsons that have been washed in cold water but not dried. Cover it, set it in an open kettle with water which must not quite reach the neck of the jar, and place it over a hot fire. Let the water boil round the jar, till the stones of the damsons are all loose, and falling out from the pulp. Then transfer the damsons and their juice, to a broad pan, and carefully pick out all the stones. Next mash the pulp with a broad flat wooden ladle, or with a potatoe-masher, till it is all smooth and of an even consistence throughout. Then measure it; and to every quart of the pulp allow a pound and a half, or three large closely-packed pints of the best brown sugar. Stir the sugar and pulp well together, till it becomes a thick jam. Put the jam into a clean preserving-kettle, and boil it slowly an hour or more, skimming it well. When done, put it into broad flat stone jars, pressing it down, and smoothing the surface with the back of a large spoon. Cover the jars closely, and put them away in a cool dry place. If more convenient, you can put the jam into tumblers, pasting thick white paper closely over each. If properly made it will be so firm that you may cut it down in slices like cheese.

Plum jam may be made as above; but damsons are better for this purpose, and also for jelly, as the juice is much thicker and richer than that of plums.

It is an old-fashioned error to use unripe fruit for any sort of sweet-meat. When the fruit is thoroughly ripe it has more flavour, is far more wholesome, and keeps better.

AN EXCELLENT WAY OF PRESERVING STRAWBERRIES.—Select the largest and finest strawberries. Having hulled them, or removed the green tops, weigh the strawberries; and allow to each pound a pound of the best double-refined loaf-sugar, finely powdered. Divide the sugar into two equal portions. Put a layer of strawberries into the bottom of a preserving-kettle, and cover them with a layer of sugar; then a layer of strawberries; then a layer of sugar; until half the sugar is in. Next set the kettle over a moderate fire, and let it boil slowly, till all the sugar is melted. Then put in, gradually, the remainder of the sugar; and after it is all in, let it boil hard for five minutes, taking off the scum with a silver spoon; but there will be little or no scum if the sugar is of the very best quality. Afterwards remove the kettle from the fire, and take out the strawberries, one at a time, in a tea-spoon. Spread out the strawberries on large flat dishes, so as not to touch each other, and set them immediately in a cold place or on ice. Hang the kettle again on the fire and give the syrup one boil up; skimming it, if necessary. Place a fine strainer over the top of a mug or pitcher, and pour the syrup through it. Then put the strawberries into glass jars or tumblers; pour into each an equal portion of the syrup. Lay at the top a round piece of white paper dipped in brandy. Close the jars tightly, and paste paper over them.

Raspberries may be preserved as above. Also large ripe gooseberries. To each pound of gooseberries allow a pound and a half of sugar.

VERY FINE PRESERVED PEACHES.—Take fine ripe free-stone peaches; pare them; cut them in half and remove the stones. Have ready a sufficiency of the best double-refined loaf-sugar, finely powdered. Weigh the sugar and the peaches together, putting the sugar into one scale and the peaches into the other, and balancing them evenly. Put the peaches into a large pan or tureen, and strew among them one-half of the sugar. Cover them, and let them stand in a cool place till next morning. Then take all the juice from them, and put it into a porcelain preserving-kettle with the remainder of the sugar. Set it over a moderate fire, and boil and skim it. When it is boiling well, and the scum has ceased to rise, put in the peaches and boil them till they are perfectly clear, but not till they break; carefully skimming them. Boil with them a handful of fresh clean peach-leaves tied in a bunch. When quite clear take the peaches out of the syrup, and put them on a flat sloping dish to drain into a deep dish placed below it. Take this syrup that has drained from the peaches, put it to the syrup in the kettle, and give it one more boil up. Then throw away the leaves. Lay the peaches flat in small glass jars. Pour an equal portion of the hot syrup into each jar, and put on the top a table-spoonful of the best white brandy. Cork the jars, and paste down paper closely over the mouth of each.

COMMON PEACH JAM.—Take good ripe free-stone peaches, pare them, and cut them into small pieces, seeing that none are blemished in the least. Cover the bottom of a stone jar with a *thick* layer of powdered sugar, (very good brown sugar will do when strict economy is expedient,) then put in a layer of the cut peaches, (without any cooking;) then another of sugar; then one of peaches, and so on till the jar is filled; packing the contents down as closely as possible. The top layer must be of sugar, spread on thickly. Cover the jar immediately, and paste paper down closely over the cover. This jam will be found very good for children; and for family use when fresh peaches are not to be had. It may be put into plain pies, or spread over the paste of a rolled-up pudding. If the peaches are free from decay-spots, and the sugar in sufficient abundance, the jam will keep many months; always excluding the air from the jar.

TO PRESERVE GREEN GAGES.—Take gages that are perfectly ripe. Weigh them; and to each pound of fruit allow a pound of the best double-refined loaf-sugar, broken up. Put a layer of grape-leaves in the bottom and round the sides of your preserving-kettle. Then put in the gages, interspersing them thickly with vine-leaves, and covering them with a thick layer. Pour in just enough of water to keep them from burning. Set the kettle over the fire, cover it, and let it simmer slowly till the gages are well greened. Then take them out, and spread them on a large dish to cool. Afterwards prick them in several places with a needle. Having washed the kettle clean, put the sugar into it with a very little water,—about half a pint to each pound of sugar. Set it over the fire, and boil and skim it till no more scum rises. Then put in the gages, and boil them half an hour. When done, and cold, put them into glass jars, and pour the syrup over them. Paste paper closely down over the lids of the jars.

FINE BRANDY PEACHES.—Take large ripe free-stone peaches: the white ones are best for this purpose. Having rubbed off the wool with a clean flannel, put the peaches whole into boiling water, just to scald, but not to boil them. Having remained in about five minutes, take them out, and put them into cold water for an hour or more. After which, drain them in a sieve, and wipe them dry. While the peaches are cooling, prepare a syrup for them; allowing two pounds of the best double-refined loaf-sugar, and the white of two eggs, and a pint of water, to two dozen large peaches. Having broken up the sugar, put it into a preserving kettle. Beat the white of egg to a stiff froth, and stir it into the water. Then pour the water on the sugar, and let it dissolve before you set the kettle over the fire; stirring it several times. Boil and skim it well. When it is nearly up to the top, throw in a small tea-cup of cold water. When it rises again, take it off the fire, and let it stand close to it for a quarter of an hour; then skim it well, and pour it carefully into a pitcher, taking care not to disturb any sediment that may remain at the bottom of the preserving kettle. Put the peaches into wide-mouthed glass jars, and pour into every jar an equal portion of the syrup. Then fill up the jars with the best white brandy. Cork them tightly, and paste paper closely over the tops; or tie on each a piece of bladder, that has first been soaked to make it contract and fit the closer when dry.

EXCELLENT BRANDY PEACHES.—Take fine large free-stone peaches, quite ripe, but not too soft. Put them into a pan containing a weak solution of sal-eratus and water; and let them lie in it till you find, upon trial, that the wool can be easily rubbed off with a coarse clean towel. Weigh them; and to each pound of peaches allow a pound of broken-up loaf-sugar,—the best double-refined. Then crush the sugar by rolling it with a rolling-pin. Have ready some large glass jars, with lacquered tin covers. Put a layer of sugar into the bottom of each jar; then a layer of peaches; then sugar; then peaches; and so on till the jar is very nearly full,—the upper layer being of sugar. Then pour in some of the best white brandy till the jars are filled quite to the top. Cover them closely, and set them into a large flat-bottomed kettle of cold water. The water must be a little below the tops of the jars. Place the kettle over a moderate fire, and keep the peach-jars boiling in it half an hour after they have come to a boil. Then set them away in your sweetmeat closet.

As the lids of glass jars seldom fit tightly, put beneath each lid a round of thick, soft white paper, and cover the top of the outside with a piece of bladder tied down.

BRANDY PEARS may be done as above. It is customary to leave the stems on. Rub off, upon some lumps of the sugar before crushing it, the yellow rind of several fresh lemons, and squeeze the lemon-juice among the crushed sugar. Allow the rind and juice of one large lemon to a small jar of pears. In whatever way pears are cooked, they should always be flavoured with lemon; otherwise they will be insipidly sweet.

To colour them a fine red, tie up a little cochineal, or some well-picked alkanet, in a very thin muslin or bobbinet bag, and boil it with the pears. When done, take out the bag.

BRANDY PEACHES THE FRENCH WAY.—Put large white peaches (a few at a time) into scalding lye. Let them rest for a minute or two, till the skin loosens so that it can be easily peeled off. Next put the peaches into cold water, and let them remain till you have hot water ready to scald them. After scalding, put into a large, broad preserving kettle as many peaches as will lie side by side in the bottom. Pour on as much cold water as will rather more than cover them; set the kettle over a clear fire; and let them boil till they are soft enough to be easily dented when pressed by your finger. Take them out; place them with the stem end downward, on an inverted sieve set on a large dish. Then put some more peaches into the kettle; add more cold water; boil them; and put them to drain afterwards. Repeat this till all your peaches have had a boil. Spread them on large dishes, and let them stand all night in a cold place. Mix together some of the best white brandy and the best loaf-sugar, powdered fine,—allowing a pound of sugar to every pint of brandy. Stir it well while the sugar is dissolving; and when melted, set it also in a cold place, and let it stand all night. In the morning, put the peaches into glass jars, which should be all of the same size, and fill them up with the brandy syrup; allowing an equal portion to each jar. Cover the jars closely, and paste white paper over their tops.

BRANDY GREEN GAGES.—Take the largest and finest green gages, quite ripe. Prick every one with a needle in several places. Spread fresh grape-leaves over the bottom, and round the sides of a preserving kettle. Put in a layer of green gages and a layer of grape-vine leaves, alternately, adding to each layer a bit of alum but little larger than a grain of indian corn. Cover the last layer of fruit thickly with vine-leaves; fill up the kettle with cold water, and place it over a moderate fire. Simmer the fruit slowly, but do not let it break. When the gages are hot all through, take them out, and throw them into *cold* water. Afterwards weight them; and to every pound of fruit, allow a pound of the best double-refined loaf-sugar, powdered. Remove the vine-leaves from the preserving-kettle, and put into it the sugar, with barely sufficient water to keep it from burning. Stir the sugar well with the water till it is dissolved, adding to every three pounds the beaten white of an egg. Place the kettle over the fire, and boil and skim till very clear, and the scum ceases to rise. Then take it off, measure it, and to every pint of syrup allow a large half-pint of the best and clearest brandy. Mix the syrup and brandy together. Having well drained the green gages from the cold water, put them (two-thirds full) into glass jars. Fill the jars up to the top with the liquor, poured on warm. Cover them closely, pasting paper over the lids, and set them in a dry, cool closet.

If the gages are not green enough with the first simmering, get fresh vine-leaves, and simmer them again very slowly, hanging the kettle high.

Instead of vine-leaves, you may green any preserves by boiling them with layers of the green husks that surround the ears of young indian corn.

BRANDY GRAPES.—For this purpose the grapes should be in large close bunches, and quite ripe. Remove every grape that is the least shrivelled, or in any way defective. With a needle prick each grape in three places. Have ready a sufficiency of double-refined loaf-sugar, powdered and sifted. Put some of the sugar into the bottom of your jars. Then put in a bunch of grapes, and cover it thickly with sugar. Then another bunch; then more sugar, and so on till the jar is nearly full; finishing with a layer of sugar. Then fill up to the top with the best white brandy. Cover the jars as closely as possible, and set them away. They must not go over the fire. The grapes should be of the best quality, either white or purple.

ICED GRAPES.—Take large close bunches of fine ripe thin-skinned grapes, and remove any that are imperfect. Tie a string in a loop to the top of the stem. Strain into a deep dish a sufficient quantity of white of egg. Dip the bunches of grapes into it, immersing them thoroughly. Then drain them, and roll them about in a flat dish of finely-powdered loaf-sugar till they are completely coated with it, using your fingers to spread the sugar into the hollows between the grapes. Hang up the bunches by the strings till the icing is entirely dry. They should be dried in a warm place. Send them to the supper-table at a party, on glass dishes.

Ripe currants may be iced as above. Raspberries, strawberries, ripe gooseberries, plums and cherries, may be thus dipped in white of egg, and rolled in sugar.

AMERICAN PRUNES.—Take the largest and finest purple plums, (oval or long-shaped if you can get them.) They must be quite ripe. Spread them separately on flat dishes, and set them in a large oven, directly after the bread, pies, &c., have been taken out. Let the plums stay in till the oven is cool; taking them out and turning them over two or three times. If you bake every day, put in the plums as before, till they are sufficiently dry. Otherwise; set the dishes in a balcony, or on the roof of an out-house, or in some place where they will be exposed to the hot sun. It will be well to cover them with thin gauze, to keep off wasps, flies, &c. Continue to set them every day in the sun till they are well dried, and look like prunes. Then pack them down in jars or boxes; laying orange or lemon-leaves among them.

TO STEW DRIED PEACHES.—Dried peaches can be used for no purpose without first being thoroughly stewed. They should be soaked for some hours before cooking. Take a sufficient quantity, and put them over night into a pan, (having first picked out all that are defective,) and wash them well through two cold waters. Drain them, lay them in a clean pan, and fill it up with scalding water. Cover them closely, and let them stand all night. In the morning pour off the water, leaving just enough of it about the peaches to keep them from burning when stewed, and transfer them to a clean earthen pipkin or a sauce-pan. Set them over a moderate fire, or on a bed of hot coals, (renewing the live coals when necessary,) and let them stew till thoroughly done, and quite soft, so that every piece can be mashed to a jam. While stewing, stir them up frequently from the bottom, mashing them with the back of the spoon against the sides of the pipkin. Keep them well covered, except when you are stirring. When quite done, transfer them to a deep dish, and mix with them, while they are smoking hot, a large portion of brown sugar, so as to make them very sweet. Set them away to cool. They will then be ready to use for pies, puddings, or as sauce to roast meat.

DRIED APPLES should be soaked and stewed as above. They will be much improved by stewing with them some thin slips of the yellow rind of lemon or orange; or by the addition of a few cloves.

Sugar should always be added after the fruit is done stewing, and while still hot. If put in at first, it renders the fruit hard and tough; besides that much of the sweetness is wasted in evaporation.

BREAKFAST AND TEA CAKES.

INDIANA BATTER CAKES.—Sift into a pan three large pints of yellow corn-meal; and add a large table-spoonful of fresh lard; or of nice drippings of roast beef, well cleared from fat. Add a small tea-spoonful of sal-eratus, or a large one of soda, dissolved in a little warm water. Next make the whole into a soft dough, with a pint of cold water. Afterwards thin it to the consistence of a moderate batter, by adding, gradually, not quite a pint and a half of warm water. When it is all mixed, continue to stir it well for half an hour. Have ready a griddle heated over the fire, and bake the batter in the manner of buckwheat-cakes; send them to table hot, and eat them with butter or molasses.

These cakes are very light and good, and convenient to make; as they require neither eggs, milk, nor yeast. They may either be baked as soon as mixed, or they may stand for an hour or more.

KENTUCKY BATTER CAKES.—Sift a quart of yellow indian meal into a large pan; mix with it two large table-spoonfuls of wheat flour, and a salt-spoonful of salt. Warm a pint and a half of rich milk in a small sauce-pan, but do not let it come to a boil. When it begins to simmer, take it off the fire, and put into it two pieces of fresh butter, each about the size of a hen's egg. Stir the butter into the warm milk till it melts, and is well mixed. Then stir in the meal, gradually, and set the mixture to cool. Beat four eggs, very light, and add them, by degrees, to the mixture, stirring the whole very hard. If you find it too thin, add a little more corn-meal. Have ready a griddle heated over the fire, and bake the batter on it, in the manner of buckwheat-cakes. Send them to table hot, and eat them with butter, to which you may add molasses or honey.

RYE BATTER-CAKES.—Beat two eggs very light. Mix them, gradually, with a quart of lukewarm milk, and sufficient rye-meal to make a batter about as thick as for buckwheat-cakes. Then stir in a large table-spoonful of the best brewer's yeast; or twice that quantity, if the yeast is home-made. Cover it, and set it to rise in a warm place. If too thin, add more rye-meal. When quite light, and covered on the surface with bubbles, bake it on a griddle, in the manner of buckwheat cakes. Butter them, and eat them warm, at breakfast or tea.

If you cannot obtain good yeast, and wish to have the cakes ready with as much expedition as possible, you may use patent yeast-powders, according to the directions that accompany them. In this case, the cakes must be baked in half an hour after the powders are mixed into the batter.

Yeast-powders, put in at the last, are an improvement to all sorts of batter-cakes that have been previously raised with good *real* yeast; also to cakes made light by eggs. But to depend *entirely* on the powders, without either real yeast, or eggs, is not well; as the cakes, though *eatable*, are generally too tough and leathery to be wholesome. In cities, fresh yeast, from the brewers, can be obtained every day, at a very trifling cost, during the brewing season; which is usually from October till April. At other seasons, it can be procured from the bakers, or made at home; and should always be used in preference to depending solely on yeast-powders. Though they improve the lightness of batter, for which real yeast or beaten eggs have already been used, they will not, of themselves alone, give it a wholesome degree of either lightness or crispness. Too much dependence on yeast-powders is one reason that the buckwheat-cakes of the present day are so inferior to those of former times, when they were always made with real yeast.

Indian batter-cakes may be made as above.

HARLEM CAKES.—Sift into a pan three pints of flour. Warm, in a sauce-pan, a pint of milk, and cut up in it half a pound of fresh butter. When the butter is soft enough to mix with the milk, stir them well together, and remove the sauce-pan from the fire. Beat three eggs, very light, and mix them with the milk and butter, after they have cooled. Then make a hole in the middle of the flour, and pour in the mixture, and two large table-spoonfuls of strong fresh yeast. With a spoon, mix the flour into the liquid, till the whole is thoroughly incorporated. Then cover the pan with a thick woollen cloth, and set it near the fire, to rise. It should be light in about five hours; perhaps sooner. When quite light, mix in a tea-spoonful of soda, dissolved in a very little warm water; divide the dough into long oval cakes, or rolls; knead each separately. Sprinkle an iron baking-pan with flour; put in the cakes; cover the pan, and let it stand half an hour before baking. Bake the cakes in a moderate oven. Eat them fresh, with butter. They are excellent tea cakes. Of course, they must be mixed in the forenoon.

BREAD MUFFINS.—Take four thick slices of *baker's bread*, and cut off all the crust. Lay them in a pan, and pour boiling water over them; but barely enough to soak them well. Cover the bread, and after it has stood an hour, drain off the water, and stir the soaked bread till it is a smooth mass; then mix in two table-spoonfuls of sifted flour, and a half-pint of milk. Having beaten two eggs very light, stir them, gradually, into the mixture. Grease some muffin-rings; set them on a hot griddle, and pour into each a portion of the mixture. Bake them brown; send them to table hot; pull them open with your fingers, and spread on butter. They will be found an excellent sort of muffin; very light and nice.

SWEET POTATOE PONE.—Stir together, till very light and white, three quarters of a pound of fresh butter, and three quarters of a pound of powdered white sugar, adding two table-spoonfuls of ginger. Grate a pound and a half of sweet potatoe. Beat eight eggs, very light, and stir them, gradually, into the butter and sugar, in turn with the grated sweet potatoe. Dissolve a tea-spoonful of sal-eratus or soda, in a gill of sour milk, and stir it in at the last, beating the whole very hard. Butter the inside of a tin pan. Put in the mixture, and bake it four hours, or more. It should be eaten fresh.

RICE BREAD.—To a pint of well-boiled rice, add half a pint of wheat-flour, mixing them well together. Take six eggs, and beat the whites and yolks separately. Having beaten the whites to a stiff froth, mix them, gradually, with a pint of rich milk, and two large table-spoonfuls of fresh butter, softened at the fire. Mix, by degrees, the yolks of the eggs with the rice and flour. Then add the white-of-egg mixture, a little at a time. Stir the whole very hard. Put it into a buttered tin pan, with straight or upright sides. Set it in a moderate oven, and bake it an hour or more. Then turn it out of the pan, put it on a dish, and send it warm to the breakfast-table, and eat it with butter.

This cake may be baked, by setting the pan that contains it, into an iron dutch-oven, placed over hot coals. Heat the lid of the oven on the inside, by standing it up, before the fire, while the rice-bread is preparing, and, after you put it on, keep the lid covered with hot coals.

Rice-bread may be made of ground rice-flour, instead of whole rice.

RICE-FLOUR BREAD.—Sift into a pan a pint and a half of rice-flour, and a pint and a half of fine wheat-flour. Add two large table-spoonfuls of fresh butter, or lard; and mix in a pint and a half of milk. Beat four eggs, very light, and then stir them, gradually, into the mixture. When the whole has been well-mixed, add, at the last, a small tea-spoonful of soda, or sal-eratus, dissolved in as much warm water as will cover it. Put the whole into a buttered tin pan; set it, immediately, into a quick oven, and bake it well. It is best when eaten fresh. Slice and butter it.

RICE-FLOUR BATTER-CAKES.—Melt a quarter of a pound of fresh butter, or lard, in a quart of milk; but be careful not to let it begin to boil. Divide the milk equally, by putting it into two pans. Beat three eggs, very light, and stir them into one half of the milk, with the addition of a large table-spoonful of wheat-flour. Stir in as much ground rice-flour as will make a thick batter. Then put in a *small* tea-cupful of strong, fresh yeast, and thin the batter with the remainder of the milk. Cover it, and set it to rise. When it has risen high, and is covered with bubbles, bake it on a griddle, in the manner of buckwheat-cakes. Send them to table hot, and butter them.

Similar cakes may be made with indian-meal, instead of rice-flour.

LONG ROLLS.—Sift three quarts of flour into a large pan, and mix with it a tea-spoonful of salt. Warm half a pint of water, but do not let it become hot. Mix with it six table-spoonfuls of strong, fresh yeast. Make a deep hole in the middle of the pan of flour. Pour in the liquid, and, with a spoon, work into it the flour, round the edge of the hole; proceeding gradually till you have all the flour mixed in, so as to form a batter. Stir it well, for two or three minutes. Then strew the top all over with a handful of dry flour. Cover the dough with a thick, double cloth, and set it in a warm place, to rise. When it is quite light, and the surface cracked all over, mix in three table-spoonfuls (not more) of lard, or fresh butter. Knead it long and hard, and make it into long, oval-shaped rolls, making, with a knife, a cleft in the top of each. Sprinkle some square baking-pans with flour; lay the rolls in them, at equal distances; cover them, as before; and set them in a warm place, for half an hour. In the meantime, have the oven ready; put in the rolls, and bake them brown.

Their lightness may be improved by mixing in (while kneading the dough, previous to forming it into cakes) a heaping tea-spoonful of soda, or sal-eratus, dissolved in as much warm water as will cover it.

In cold weather, you may mix these rolls with milk, instead of water; but in summer the milk may turn sour, and spoil the dough. This, however, may be corrected, by adding the soda, or sal-eratus; always a good remedy for sour dough or batter.

POTATOE ROLLS.—Take fine large potatoes. Boil, peel, and mash them. Then rub the mashed potatoe through a sieve. To each potatoe allow a pint of sifted flour; a table-spoonful of strong fresh yeast; a jill of milk-warm water; a salt-spoon of salt; the yolk of an egg; and a bit of fresh butter about the size of a large hickory-nut. Mix together in a large broad pan the flour, the mashed potatoe, and the salt. Make a hole in the centre of the mixture, and pour into it the yeast mixed with the warm water. Sprinkle a little flour over the top, and mix in a little from round the sides of the hole. Cover it with a clean towel, and over that a flannel, and set it near the fire to rise. When the dough is quite light, and cracked all over the surface, knead in the butter and also the yolks of eggs, having previously beaten them well, and add a small tea-spoonful of soda dissolved in a little warm water. Then divide the dough into equal parts, make it into long-shaped rolls, and lay them in a tin or iron pan sprinkled with flour. Cover them, and again set them to rise in a warm place. When perfectly light, (which should be in about an hour,) set the pan into the oven, and bake the rolls brown. They are best when quite fresh. Pull them open with your fingers, and eat them with butter.

CAKES, ETC.

TO BEAT EGGS.—In making cakes it is of the utmost importance that the eggs should be properly and sufficiently beaten; otherwise the cakes will most certainly be deficient in the peculiar lightness characterizing those that are made by good confectioners. Home-made cakes, if good in other respects, are too frequently (even when not absolutely heavy or streaked) hard, solid and tough. This often proceeds from too large a portion of flour, and too small an allowance of butter and eggs. The richest cake that can be made (provided it is light and well baked) is less unwholesome than what are called plain cakes, if they are solid or leathery. Cakes cannot be crisp and light without a due proportion of the articles that are to make them so; and even then, the ingredients must be thoroughly stirred or beaten; and of course thoroughly baked afterwards.

Persons who do not know the right way, complain much of the fatigue of beating eggs, and therefore leave off too soon. There will be no fatigue, if they are beaten with the proper stroke, and with *wooden* rods, and in a shallow, flat-bottomed *earthen* pan. The coldness of a tin pan retards the lightness of the eggs. For the same reason do not use a metal egg-beater. In beating them do not move your elbow, but keep it close to your side. Move only your hand at the wrist, and let the stroke be quick, short, and horizontal; putting the egg-beater always down to the bottom of the pan, which should therefore be shallow. Do not leave off as soon as you have got the eggs into a foam; they are then only *beginning* to be light. But persist till after the foaming has ceased, and the bubbles have all disappeared. Continue till the surface is smooth as a mirror, and the beaten egg as thick as a rich boiled custard; for till then it will not be really light. It is seldom necessary to beat the whites and yolks separately, if they are afterwards to be put together. The article will be quite as light, when cooked, if the whites and yolks are beaten together, and there will then be no danger of their going in streaks when baked. The justly-celebrated Mrs. Goodfellow, of Philadelphia, always taught her pupils to beat the whites and yolks together, even for sponge-cake; and lighter than hers no sponge-cake could possibly be.

When white of egg is to be used without any yolk, (as for lady-cake, maccaroons, meringues, icing, &c.,) it should be beaten till it stands alone on the rods; not falling when held up.

Hickory rods for egg-beating are to be had at the wooden-ware shops, or at the turner's. For stirring butter and sugar together, nothing is equal to a wooden spaddle. It should be about a foot long, and flattened at the end like that of a mush-stick, only broader. Spoons are very tedious and inconvenient either for beating eggs or stirring butter and sugar, and do not produce the proper lightness.

BOSTON CAKE.—Put a pound of powdered white sugar into a deep pan, and cut up in it a pound of fresh butter. Stir the butter and sugar together till perfectly light. Then add a powdered nutmeg, a table-spoonful of powdered mace and cinnamon mixed together, and a large wine-glass of excellent brandy. If the brandy is of bad quality it will give the cake a disagreeable taste. If very good, it will highly improve the flavour, and also add to the lightness of the cake. Sift into a pan a pound of flour. In another pan beat six eggs till very thick and smooth. Stir them gradually into the butter and sugar, alternately with the flour, and a pint of rich milk or cream, a little of each at a time. Have ready a level tea-spoonful (not heaped) of pearlash, or sal-eratus, (or a full tea-spoonful of bi-carbonate of soda,) dissolved in as much warm water as will cover it. Add this at the last, and then give the whole a very hard stirring. Butter a large square pan. Put in the mixture. Set it immediately into the oven, and bake it thoroughly. It requires very long baking. A thick square Boston cake will scarcely be done in less than three hours. At the end of the first hour, increase the heat of the oven, and also at the second. When cool, sift powdered sugar over it, and cut it into squares.

If properly made, and well-baked, (following exactly the above directions,) this cake will be found excellent, and will seem fresh longer than any other; the milk keeping it soft.

Milk turned sour is very good for Boston cake; as by stirring the dissolved pearlash or soda into the milk, the acidity will be entirely removed, and the alkali rendered more effective in increasing the lightness of the cake. Still great care will be necessary in baking it.

The best confectioners make this cake every day without any failure.

ALBANY CAKE.—Sift three pounds of flour into a pan. Stir together a pound of fresh butter, and a pound of brown sugar. Mix together a pint of West India molasses, and half a pint of rich milk. Have ready a pound and a half of raisins, seeded, cut in two, and well dredged with flour to prevent their sinking. Beat five eggs very light, and mix them gradually with the milk and molasses, adding a glass of brandy, and a table-spoonful of cinnamon powdered. Add the mixture gradually to the beaten butter and sugar, alternately with the flour, a little at a time of each. Next stir in a small teacup-full of strong fresh yeast. Then sprinkle in the raisins. Lastly, stir in a very small tea-spoonful of bi-carbonate of soda, or a still smaller portion of sal-eratus, dissolved in as much lukewarm water as will cover it. Stir the whole mixture long and hard. Cover it, and set it in a warm place to rise. When quite light, butter a deep tin pan, put in the mixture, and bake it in a loaf. It will require very long and steady baking.

Like all others that have yeast in them, this cake is best when fresh.

AUSTRIAN CAKE.—Take a thick straight-sided pound cake about the circumference of a large dinner-plate, and cut it horizontally into slices, the whole breadth of the cake, and rather more than half an inch thick. Spread each slice, thickly and smoothly, with marmalade of peach, raspberry, strawberry, or orange. The marmalade may be all the same, or of a different sort on each slice. Lay the slices, nicely, and evenly, one upon another, taking care that none of the marmalade oozes down from between the edges. Then make a thick icing of white of egg and powdered loaf-sugar, and flavour it with rose or orange-flower water. Heap a large portion of it on the centre of the cake, and with a broad knife (dipped frequently in cold water) spread it smoothly all over the top and sides. Then set it away to harden. You may ornament it by putting icing into a small syringe and pressing it out into the form of a centre-piece and border of flowers. To do this requires practice, taste, and ingenuity.

When the cake is to be eaten, cut it down into triangular pieces; each including a portion of the different layers of marmalade.

Instead of marmalade you may use for this cake, fresh strawberries, mashed smoothly and sweetened with white sugar.

MADISON CAKE.—Pick clean two pounds of sultana raisins, (those that have no seeds,) and cut them in half. If you cannot procure the sultana, use the bloom or muscatel raisins, removing all the seeds. When the raisins are cut in two, dredge them *thickly* on all sides with flour, to prevent their sinking or clodding in the cake while baking. Sift into a pan a pound and three quarters (*not more*) of flour. Cut up a pound of fresh butter into a deep pan. Mix with it a pound of white lump-sugar finely powdered; and stir them together till they become a thick, white, cream. Have ready a tea-spoonful of powdered nutmeg, and a table-spoonful of powdered cinnamon, and mix these spices, gradually, with the butter and sugar. Beat fourteen eggs (*not fewer*) till very light and thick. Then stir them, gradually, into the beaten butter and sugar, alternately with the flour and a pint of rich milk, (sour milk will be best.) Add at the last a very small tea-spoonful of pearlash, or of bi-carbonate of soda, dissolved in a large wine-glass of brandy. Give the whole a hard stirring, and then put it immediately into a deep circular tin pan, the sides and bottom of which have been first well greased with fresh butter. Set it directly into a well-heated oven, and let it bake from five to six hours, according to its size. It requires long and steady baking. When cool, cover it (top and sides) with a thick icing, made in the usual way of beaten white of egg and sugar, and flavoured with rose-water or lemon.

If the above directions are closely followed this will be found a very fine cake, and it will keep soft and fresh a week if the air is carefully excluded from it.

It will be still better, if in addition to the two pounds of raisins, you mix in two pounds of Zante currants, picked, washed, dried before the fire, and then well floured. Half a pound of citron cut into slips and floured, may also be added.

STRAWBERRY CAKES.—Sift a small quart of flour into a pan, and cut up among it half a pound of the best fresh butter; or mix in a pint of butter if it is soft enough to measure in that manner. Rub with your hands the butter into the flour, till the whole is crumbled fine. Beat three eggs very light; and then mix with them three table-spoonfuls of powdered loaf-sugar. Wet the flour and butter with the beaten egg and sugar, so as to form a dough. If you find it too stiff, add a very little cold water. Knead the dough till it quits your hands, and leaves them clean. Spread some flour on your paste-board, and roll out the dough into a rather thick sheet. Cut it into round cakes with the edge of a tumbler, or something similar; dipping the cutter frequently into flour to prevent its sticking. Butter some large square iron pans or baking sheets. Lay the cakes in, not too close to each other. Set them in a brisk oven, and bake them light brown. Have ready a sufficient quantity of ripe strawberries, mashed and made very sweet with powdered white sugar. Reserve some of your finest strawberries whole. When the cakes are cool, split them, place them on flat dishes, and cover the bottom piece of each with mashed strawberry, put on *thickly*. Then lay on the top pieces, pressing them down. Have ready some icing, and spread it thickly over the top and down the sides of each cake, so as to enclose both the upper and lower pieces. Before the icing has quite dried, ornament the top of every cake with the whole strawberries, a large one in the centre, and the smaller ones placed round in a close circle.

These are delicious and beautiful cakes if properly made. The strawberries, not being cooked, will retain all their natural flavour. Instead of strawberries you may use raspberries. The large white or buff-coloured raspberry is the finest, if to be eaten uncooked.

PEACH CAKES.—Pick clean and wash a quart of dried peaches, and let them stew all night in as much clear water as will cover them. In the morning, drain off most of the water, leaving only as much of it about the peaches as will suffice to prevent them from burning after they are set over the fire. It will be best to have them soaked in the vessel in which you intend to stew them. Keep them covered while stewing, except when you take off the lid to stir them up from the bottom. When they are all quite soft, and can be mashed into a smooth jam or marmalade, mix in half a pound of brown sugar, and set the peaches to cool. In the mean time, soften a quarter of a pound of the best fresh butter in half a pint of warm milk, heated on the stove, but not allowed to come to a simmer. Sift a pound of flour into a pan; pour in the warm milk and butter (first stirring them well together) and a wine-glass of strong, fresh yeast. Mix the whole into a dough. Cover it, and set it in a warm place to rise. When quite light and cracked all over the surface, flour your paste-board, put the dough upon it; mix in a small tea-spoonful of sub-carbonate of soda, and knead it well; set it again in a warm place for half an hour. Then divide the dough into equal portions, and make it up into round cakes about the size in circumference of the top of a tumbler. Knead each cake. Then roll them out into a thin sheet. Have ready the peach jam, mashed very smooth, and with a portion of it cover thickly the half of each cake. Fold over the other half, so as to enclose the peach jam in the form of a half-moon. Bring the two edges closely together and crimp them neatly. Lay the cakes in buttered square pans, and bake them brown. When done grate sugar over the top. These cakes are nice for children, being very light, if properly made and baked. They are by no means rich, and are good substitutes for tarts.

Similar cakes may be made with stewed apple, flavoured with lemon and sweetened. Or with raspberries, or any other convenient fruit stewed to a jam.

SMALL LEMON CAKES.—Break up a pound of fine loaf-sugar, and on some of the lumps rub off all the yellow rind of four lemons. Then powder all the sugar. Beat to a stiff froth the whites of three eggs. Mix the sugar, gradually (a tea-spoonful at a time) with the beaten white of egg, so as to make a paste, stirring it very hard. Spread some white paper (cut exactly to fit) on the bottom of a square shallow baking-pan. Place equal portions of the paste at regular distances on this paper, making them into round heaps, and smoothing their surfaces with the back of a spoon or a broad-bladed knife, dipped frequently in cold water. Put the cakes into a moderate oven and bake them a light brown. When cool take them off the paper.

You may make orange cakes in this manner.

Strawberry cakes may be made as above, mixing the juice of ripe strawberries with the sugar. Raspberry cakes also.

FINE HONEY CAKE.—Mix a quart of strained honey with half a pound of powdered white sugar, and half a pound of fresh butter, and the juice of two oranges or lemons. Warm these ingredients slightly, just enough to soften the butter. Then stir the mixture very hard, adding a grated nutmeg. Mix in, gradually, two pounds (or less) of sifted flour. Make it into a dough, just stiff enough to roll out easily. Beat it well all over with a rolling-pin. Then roll it out into a large sheet, half an inch thick; cut it into round cakes with the top of a tumbler, (dipped frequently in flour,) lay them in shallow tin pans, (slightly buttered,) and bake them well.

CHOCOLATE CAKE.—Scrape down three ounces of the best and purest chocolate, or prepared cocoa. Cut up, into a deep pan, three-quarters of a pound of fresh butter; add to it a pound of powdered loaf-sugar; and stir the butter and sugar together till very light and white. Have ready fourteen ounces (two ounces *less* than a pound) of sifted flour; a powdered nutmeg; and a tea-spoonful of powdered cinnamon—mixed together. Beat the whites of ten eggs till they stand alone; then the yolks till they are very thick and smooth. Then mix the yolks and whites gradually together, beating very hard when they are all mixed. Add the eggs, by degrees, to the beaten butter and sugar, in turn with the flour and the scraped chocolate,—a little at a time of each; also the spice. Stir the whole very hard. Put the mixture into a buttered tin pan with straight sides, and bake it at least four hours. If nothing is to be baked afterwards, let it remain in till the oven becomes cool. When cold, ice it.

LEMON PUFFS.—Take a pound of the best loaf-sugar, and powder it. Grate upon lumps of the same sugar the yellow rind of four large ripe lemons; having first rolled each lemon under your hand, upon a table, to increase the juice. Then powder these pieces of sugar also, and add them to the rest. Strain the juice of the lemons over the sugar, mixing it well in. Have ready in a saucer some extra powdered sugar. Beat to a stiff froth the whites of four eggs, and then gradually and thoroughly beat into it the lemon and sugar, till the mixture is very thick and smooth. If too thin, add more sugar; if too thick, more beaten white of egg. Take a sheet of nice white paper, and lay it smoothly in a square tin pan; having first cut it to fit exactly. Put on it, at equal distances, a round spot of thinly-spread powdered loaf-sugar, about the size of a half-dollar or a little larger. Upon each spot place with a spoon a pile of the mixture; smoothing it with a knife dipped in water, and making the surface even. Sift over each a little powdered sugar. Set the pan in a quick oven, and bake the puffs of a light brown. A few minutes' baking will suffice. They should rise very high. When cool, loosen them carefully from the paper by inserting a broad knife beneath. Then spread them out on a large flat dish, and keep them in a dry, cool place till wanted.

ORANGE PUFFS may be made in the same manner, omitting the rind, and using the juice only of *five* oranges; unless they are all of a very large size, and then four may suffice. Very nice puffs can be made with the juice of strawberries, raspberries, currants, or cherries; mixed, as above, with beaten white of egg and sugar.

ROSE MERINGUES.—Beat to a stiff froth the whites of six eggs, and then beat in by degrees, a spoonful at a time, a pound or more of finely-powdered loaf-sugar, till it is of the consistence of very thick icing or meringue. Have ready a sufficient quantity of freshly-gathered rosebuds, about half grown. Having removed the stalks and green leaves, take as many of the buds as will weigh three ounces. With a pair of sharp scissors clip or mince them as small as possible into the pan of meringue; stirring them in with a spoon. Then stir the whole very hard. Have ready some sheets of white paper, laid on baking tins. Drop the meringues on it, in heaps all of the same size, and not too close together. Smooth them with the back of a spoon or broad knife, dipped in cold water. Set them in a moderate cool oven, and bake them about twenty minutes. Take out one and try it, and if not thoroughly done, continue them longer in the oven.

To heighten the red colour, add to the white of egg, before you beat it, a very little water, in which has been steeped a thin muslin bag of alkanet-root; or you may colour it with a little cochineal powder.

Orange-blossom meringues may be made as above.

WHIPPED CREAM MERINGUES.—Take the whites of eight eggs, and beat them to a stiff froth, that will stand alone. Then beat into them, gradually, a tea-spoonful at a time, two pounds or more of finely-powdered loaf-sugar; continuing to add sugar till the mixture is very thick, and finishing with a little lemon-juice or extract of rose. Have ready some sheets of white paper, laid on a baking-board, and with a spoon drop the mixture on it in long oval heaps, about four inches in length. Smooth and shape them with a broad-bladed knife, dipped occasionally in cold water. The baking-board used for this purpose should be an inch thick, and must have a slip of iron beneath each end to elevate it from the floor of the oven, so that it may not scorch, nor the bottoms of the meringues be baked too hard. This baking-board must not be of pine wood, as a pine board will communicate a disagreeable taste of turpentine. The oven must be moderate. Bake the meringues of a light brown. When done, take them off the paper by slipping a knife nicely beneath the bottom of each. Then push back or scoop out carefully a portion of the inside of each meringue, taking care not to break them. Have ready some nice whipped cream, made in the following proportion:—Take a quarter of a pound of broken-up loaf-sugar, and on some of the lumps rub off the yellow rind of two large lemons. Powder the sugar, and then mix with it the juice of the lemons, and grate in some nutmeg. Mix the sugar with a half-pint of sweet white wine. Put into a pan a pint of rich cream, and whip it with rods or a wooden whisk, or mill it with a chocolate mill, till it is a stiff froth. Then mix in, gradually, the other ingredients; continuing to whip it hard a while after they are all in. As you proceed, lay the froth on an inverted sieve, with a dish underneath to catch the droppings; which droppings must afterwards be whipped, and added to the rest. Fill the inside of each meringue with a portion of the whipped cream. Then put two together, so as to form one long oval cake, joining them nicely, so as to unite the flat parts that were next the paper, leaving the inside filled with the whipped cream. Set them again in the oven for a few minutes. They must be done with great care and nicety, so as not to break. Each meringue should be about the usual length of a middle finger. In dropping them on the paper, take care to shape the oval ends handsomely and smoothly. They should look like very long kisses.

CREAM TARTS.—Put into a tea-cup a large table-spoonful of arrow-root flour. Pour on it a very little cold milk, and mix it very smooth with a spoon; seeing that it is entirely free from lumps. Boil, in a sauce-pan, a quart of cream or rich unskimmed milk, with the yellow rind of a large lemon or orange, pared thin, or cut into slips; or use for flavouring a handful of bitter almonds or peach kernels, blanched and broken up; or, what is still better, a vanilla bean. The milk must boil slowly (keeping it closely covered) till it is highly flavoured. Then strain out the lemon-peel or other flavouring, and set away the milk to cool. Beat the yolks of eight eggs till very thick and smooth, and stir them gradually into the milk, alternately with four heaped table-spoonfuls of powdered loaf-sugar. Add some grated nutmeg. Put the whole into a sauce-pan, and place it on hot coals or on the stove, and continue to stir it till it begins to boil. Then remove it immediately, lest it should curdle, and keep stirring it till it begins to cool. Afterwards set it in a cold place.

Sift into a pan a pound and a half of flour; mix in a quarter of a pound of white sugar; cut up in it half a pound of fresh butter, and rub it well into the flour and sugar. Beat two eggs very light, and with them wet the flour, &c., to a dough, adding a very small level tea-spoonful of soda, dissolved in a very little cold water. Mix the paste well till it becomes a lump of dough. Then beat it on all sides with the rolling-pin. Transfer it to the paste-board, and roll it out thin. Divide it equally into *square* pieces. Put thickly on each piece a portion of the cream or custard mixture, and fold over it the four corners of the paste, so that they approach each other in the centre. Dredge each tart with powdered loaf-sugar. Set them into the oven, and let them bake of a light brown. They are best when fresh, but not warm; and will be found delicious.

The custard may be coloured green by boiling pistachio nuts in the milk, with the flavouring.

ICE-CREAM CAKES.—Stir together, till very light, a quarter of a pound of powdered sugar and a quarter of a pound of fresh butter. Beat six eggs very light, and stir into them half a pint of rich milk. Add, gradually, the eggs and milk to the butter and sugar, alternately with a half pound of sifted flour. Add a glass of sweet wine, and some grated nutmeg. When all the ingredients are mixed, stir the batter very hard. Then put it into small, deep pans, or cups, that have been well-buttered, filling them about two-thirds with the batter. Set them, immediately, into a brisk oven, and bake them brown. When done, remove them from the cups, and place them, to cool, on an inverted sieve. When quite cold, make a slit or incision in the side of each cake. If very light, and properly baked, they will be hollow in the middle. Fill up this cavity with ice-cream, carefully put in with a spoon, and then close the slit, with your fingers, to prevent the cream running out. Spread them on a large dish. Either send them to table immediately, before the ice-cream melts, or keep them on ice till wanted.

LEMON OR ORANGE KISSES.—Take three large, ripe lemons, or oranges, and rub off the yellow rind, upon some pieces belonging to a pound of fine loaf-sugar. Then powder all the pound of sugar, and squeeze among the sugar (through a strainer) the juice of the lemons or oranges; mixing it well in. Beat the whites of four eggs to a stiff froth, that will stand alone. Then beat in, very hard, the sugar, &c., a tea-spoonful at a time. Lay a sheet of white paper on a board. Drop the mixture on it, in oval piles, smoothing them with a broad-bladed knife, dipped frequently in cold water. Set them in a moderate oven, and when they are coloured a light brown, take them out, slip a knife carefully under each, to remove them from the papers, and place two bottoms together, so as to give them the form of an egg. If you use oranges, scoop out a small hollow in the bottom of each half-kiss, as soon as they are baked, and fill the cavity with orange-pulp, sweetened. Then join the two halves together.

Instead of lemon or orange, they may be finely flavoured, by mixing with the powdered sugar a sufficient quantity of extract of vanilla.

CHOCOLATE MACCAROONS.—Blanch half a pound of shelled sweet almonds, by scalding them with boiling water, till the skin peels off easily. Then throw them into a bowl of cold water, and let them stand awhile. Take them out and wipe them, separately. Afterwards set them in a warm place, to dry thoroughly. Put them, one at a time, into a marble mortar, and pound them to a smooth paste; moistening them, as you proceed, with a few drops of rose-water, to prevent their oiling. When you have pounded one or two, take them out of the mortar, with a tea-spoon, and put them into a deep plate, beside you, and continue removing the almonds to the plate, till they are all done. Scrape down, as fine as possible, half a pound of the best chocolate, or of Baker's prepared cocoa, and mix it, thoroughly, with the pounded almonds. Then set the plate in a cool place. Put the whites of eight eggs into a shallow pan, and beat them to a stiff froth, that will stand alone. Have ready a pound and a half of finely-powdered loaf-sugar. Stir it, hard, into the beaten white-of-egg, a spoonful at a time. Then stir in, gradually, the mixture of almond and chocolate; and beat the whole very hard. Drop the mixture, in equal portions, upon thin white paper, laid on square tin pans, smoothing them, with a spoon, into round cakes, about the size of a half-dollar. Dredge the top of each, lightly, with powdered sugar. Set them into a quick oven, and bake them a light brown. When done, take them off the paper.

For the first experiment, in making these maccaroons, it may be well to try a smaller quantity. For instance, a quarter of a pound of shelled almonds; a quarter of a pound of chocolate; four eggs; and three-quarters of a pound of sugar.

LEMON MACCAROONS.—Take four large ripe lemons, and rub off the yellow surface of the rind, upon a lump of sugar. Then powder that sugar, and add to it not quite a pound of loaf-sugar, already powdered. Break four eggs into a shallow pan, and beat them till very thick and light. Then add the juice of the lemons, squeezed through a strainer, and a tea-spoonful of powdered nutmeg and cinnamon, and stir in the sugar, a little at a time, alternately with three large heaped-up table-spoonfuls of sifted flour. A little more flour may, probably, be found necessary. Mix the whole, thoroughly, so as to form a soft paste. Have ready some shallow, square baking-pans, or sheets of iron, the bottoms covered with white paper, laid smoothly in. Moisten your hands with water, and then take up portions of the mixture, and roll them into balls, about the size of a large plum, laying them, as you proceed, upon the paper, but rather more than an inch apart. Lastly, with the blade of a knife, dipped in water, smooth the surface of each. Set them into a moderate oven, and bake them brown. Try one, when you think they are done. If not sufficiently baked, let them remain longer in the oven. As soon as they are cold, loosen them from the paper, by slipping under them a broad-bladed knife. Orange maccaroons may be made in this manner, using the grated rind of two oranges only, but the juice of four. To make vanilla maccaroons, boil, in a covered vessel, a vanilla bean, with as much milk as will barely cover it. When the milk is strongly flavoured with the vanilla, strain it, and, when cold, add it to the beaten egg. Then stir in, gradually, the sugar, spice, and flour, and proceed as above.

GROUND-NUT MACCAROONS.—Take a sufficiency of ground-nuts, that have been roasted in an iron pot, over the fire; remove the shells; and weigh a pound of the nuts. Put them into a pan of cold water, and wash off the skins. Have ready some beaten white of egg. Pound the ground-nuts, (two or three at a time,) in a marble mortar, adding, frequently, a little cold water, to prevent their oiling. They must be pounded to a smooth, light paste; and, as you proceed, remove the paste to a saucer or a plate. Beat, to a stiff froth, the whites of four eggs, and then beat into it, gradually, a pound of powdered loaf-sugar, and a large tea-spoonful of powdered mace and nutmeg mixed. Then stir in, by degrees, the pounded ground-nuts, till the mixture becomes very thick. Flour your hands, and roll, between them, portions of the mixture, forming each portion into a little ball. Lay sheets of white paper on flat baking-tins, and place on them the maccaroons, at equal distances, flattening them all a little, so as to press down the balls into cakes. Then sift powdered sugar over each. Place them in a brisk oven, with more heat at the top than in the bottom. Bake them about ten minutes.

Almond maccaroons may be made as above, mixing one-quarter of a pound of shelled bitter almonds with three-quarters of shelled sweet almonds. For almond maccaroons, instead of flouring your hands, you may dip them in cold water; and when the maccaroons are formed on the papers, go slightly over every one, with your fingers wet with cold water.

Maccaroons may be made, also, of grated cocoa-nut, mixed with beaten white of egg and powdered sugar.

WEST INDIA COCOA-NUT CAKE.—Cut up and peel some pieces of a very ripe cocoa-nut. Lay the pieces for awhile in cold water. Then take them out; wipe them very dry; and grate, very finely, as much as, when grated, will weigh half a pound. Powder half a pound of the best loaf-sugar. Beat eight eggs, till very light, thick, and smooth. Then stir the grated cocoa-nut and the powdered sugar, alternately, into the pan of beaten egg, a little at a time of each; adding a handful of sifted flour, a powdered nutmeg, and a glass of sweet wine. Stir the whole very hard. Butter a square tin pan. Put in the mixture, set it immediately into a quick oven, and bake it well; seeing that the heat is well kept up all the time. When cool, cut it into squares. Have ready a thick icing, made of powdered sugar and white of egg, flavoured with rose-water, or extract of roses. Ice each square of the cake, all over the top and sides.

You may bake it in a loaf, in a deep, circular pan. Ice the whole surface, and ornament it.

For a large cake, baked in a loaf, allow a pound of grated cocoa-nut; a pound of sugar; sixteen eggs; two handfuls of flour; two nutmegs, and two glasses of wine. It will require very long baking.

RICE-FLOUR POUND-CAKE.—Weigh a pound of broken up loaf-sugar of the best quality. Upon some of the largest lumps rub off the yellow rind of three large ripe lemons that have been previously rolled under your hand, on a table, to increase the juice. Then powder finely all the pound of sugar. Cut up into a deep pan a pound of the best fresh butter; mix with it the powdered sugar, and stir them together, with a wooden spaddle, till perfectly light. Squeeze the juice of the lemons through a strainer into a bowl, mix with it half a grated nutmeg, and add it to the butter and sugar. Sift a pound (or a quart) of rice-flour into a pan, and in another shallow pan beat twelve eggs till they are smooth and thick. Then stir the beaten egg and the rice-flour, alternately, into the butter and sugar, a little at a time of each. Having stirred the whole long and hard, put the mixture into a buttered tin pan that has straight or upright sides; set it immediately into a well-heated oven, and bake it thoroughly. It will require four or five hours, in proportion to its thickness. When done, it will shrink a little from the sides of the pan; and a twig from a corn-broom, or a wooden skewer plunged down to the bottom of the cake, will come out dry and clean. When cool, ice it; adding a little rose-water or lemon-juice to the icing. Heap the icing first on the centre of the top, and then with a broad-bladed knife, (dipped occasionally into a bowl of cold water,) spread it evenly all over the surface of the cake.

Instead of lemons, you may use for flavouring this cake, the yellow rind of *two* oranges grated on the sugar, and the juice of *three* mixed with the spice. Orange-rind being stronger and more powerful in taste than that of lemon, a smaller quantity of it will suffice.

You may bake the above mixture in little tins, like queen-cakes; taking care to grease them with *fresh* butter.

This mixture will make a nice pudding; using only *half* a pound of rice-flour, but the above quantities of all the other ingredients. Bake it in china or handsome white-ware, as it must go to table in the dish it is baked in.

RICE SPONGE-CAKE.—Put twelve eggs into a scale, and balance them in the other scale with their weight in broken loaf-sugar. Take out four of the eggs, remove the sugar, and balance the remaining eight eggs with an equal quantity of rice-flour. Rub off on some lumps of the sugar, the yellow rind of three fine large ripe lemons. Then powder all the sugar. Break the eggs, one at a time, into a saucer, and put all the whites into a pitcher, and all the yolks into a broad shallow earthen pan. Having poured the whites of egg from the pitcher through a strainer into a rather shallow pan, beat them till so stiff that they stand alone. Then add the powdered sugar, gradually, to the white of egg, and beat it in well. In the other pan, beat the yolks till very smooth and thick. Then mix them, gradually, a little at a time, with the white of egg and sugar. Lastly, stir in, by degrees, the rice-flour, adding it lightly, and stirring it slowly and gently round till the surface is covered with bubbles. Transfer it directly to a butter tin pan; set it *immediately* into a brisk oven; and bake it an hour and a half or more, according to its thickness. Ice it when cool; flavouring the icing-with lemon or rose. This cake will be best the day it is baked.

In every sort of sponge-cake, Naples-biscuit, lady-fingers, and in all cakes made without butter, it is important to know that though the egg and sugar is to be beaten very hard, the flour, which must *always* go in at the last, must be stirred in very slowly and lightly, holding the whisk or stirring-rods perpendicularly or upright in your hand; and moving it gently round and round on the surface of the batter without allowing it to go down deeply. If the flour is stirred in *hard and fast,* the cake will certainly be tough, leathery, and unwholesome. Sponge-cake when cut should look coarse-grained and rough.

SWEET POTATOE CAKE.—Half-boil some fine sweet potatoes; peel them; and when cold, grate as much as will weigh half a pound. If boiled long enough to become soft, they will render the cake heavy. Stir together in a deep pan, half a pound of fresh butter, and half a pound of powdered loaf-sugar, till quite light and creamy. Then add a tea-spoonful of powdered mace, nutmeg, and cinnamon, all mixed together; and the juice and grated rind of two large lemons or oranges. Beat in a shallow pan six eggs till very smooth and thick; and stir them into the pan of butter and sugar in turn with the grated sweet-potatoe, a little of each at a time. Then stir the whole very hard. Butter a deep tin pan with straight sides. Put in the mixture, and bake it well. If you want more cake than the above quantity, double the proportions of *each* ingredient; but bake the mixture in two pans, rather than in one. Ice it when cold, adding a little lemon or orange-juice to the icing. In spreading the icing, begin by heaping it on the centre of the cake, and then gradually bringing it all over the top and sides, dipping the knife, frequently, into a bowl of cold water.

CHOCOLATE PUFFS.—Beat very stiff the whites of two eggs, and then beat in, gradually, half a pound of powdered loaf-sugar. Scrape down very fine, an ounce and a half of the best chocolate, (prepared cocoa is better still,) and dredge it with flour to prevent its oiling; mixing the flour well among it. Then add it, gradually, to the mixture of white of egg and sugar, and stir the whole very hard. Cover the bottom of a square tin pan with a sheet of fine white paper, cut to fit exactly. Place upon it thin spots of powdered loaf-sugar about the size of a half-dollar. Pile a portion of the mixture on each spot, smoothing it with the back of a spoon or a broad knife, dipped in cold water. Sift white sugar over the top of each. Set the pan into a brisk oven, and bake them a few minutes. When cold, loosen them from the paper with a broad knife.

COCOA-NUT PUFFS.—Break up a large ripe cocoa-nut. Pare the pieces, and lay them awhile in cold water. Then wipe them dry, and grate them as finely as possible. Lay the grated cocoa-nut in well-formed heaps on a large handsome dish. It will require no cooking. The heaps should be about the circumference of a dollar, and must not touch each other. Flatten them down in the middle, so as to make a hollow in the centre of each heap; and upon this pile some very nice sweetmeat. Make an excellent whipped cream, well sweetened and flavoured with lemon and wine, and beat it to a stiff froth. Pile some of this cream high upon each cake over the sweetmeats. If on a supper-table you may arrange them in circles round a glass stand.

PALMER CAKES.—Sift a pound of flour into a pan, and rub into it half a pound of butter, and a quarter of a pound of powdered loaf-sugar. Add a tea-spoonful of mixed spice, powdered cinnamon, nutmeg, and mace. Wet the mixture with two well-beaten eggs; the juice of a large lemon or orange; and sufficient rose-water to make it into a dough just stiff enough to roll out easily. Sprinkle a little flour on the paste-board; lay the lump of dough upon it, roll it out rather thin, and cut it into round cakes with the edge of a tumbler dipped every time in flour to prevent stickiness. Lay the cakes in buttered square pans. Set them in a rather brisk oven, and bake them brown.

LIGHT SEED CAKE.—Sift into a pan a pound and a half of flour; cut up in it a pound of fresh butter, and rub it well into the flour with your hands. Mix in six table-spoonfuls of strong fresh yeast; add gradually as much warm milk as will make it a soft dough, and knead it well. Cover it with a double cloth and set it in a warm place to rise. When quite light, and cracked all over the surface, mix in, alternately, a quarter of a pound of powdered white sugar, and a quarter of a pound of carraway seeds, a little of each at a time. Knead the dough well a second time, adding a small tea-spoonful of soda dissolved in a very little warm water. Cover it and set it to rise again. It will probably require now but half an hour. Transfer it to a circular tin pan, slightly buttered, and bake it in a loaf. It is best when eaten fresh, but not warm. It may be baked in a square pan, and cut into square pieces when cool.

CARRAWAY CAKE.—Sift half a pound of rice flour into a dish. In a deep pan cut up half a pound of fresh butter, and mix with it half a pound of powdered loaf-sugar. Having warmed them slightly, stir together the butter and sugar till very light and creamy. Break five eggs, and beat them in a shallow pan till thick and smooth. Then stir them, gradually, into the pan of beaten sugar and butter, alternately with the flour; a little of each at a time. Add, by degrees, a tea-spoonful of powdered cinnamon and nutmeg mixed; a wine-glass of rose water or of rose-brandy, and half an ounce or more of carraway seeds thrown in a few at a time, stirring hard all the while. Butter a square iron pan; put in the mixture; set it in a rather brisk oven, and bake it well. When done, sift powdered sugar over it;

and when cool, cut it into long squares.

WONDERS.—Cut up half a pound of fresh butter into a pound of sifted flour, and rub them well together with your hands. Mix in three-quarters of a pound of white sugar, and a large tea-spoonful of cinnamon. Add a glass of good white wine, and a glass of rose-water. Beat six eggs very light, and mix them gradually with the above ingredients, so as to form a dough. If you find the dough too soft, add by degrees a little more flour. Roll out the dough into a thick sheet, and cut it into long slips with a jagging-iron. Then form each strip into the figure 8. Have ready over the fire a pot of boiling lard. Throw the cakes into it, a few at a time, and let them cook till they are well browned all over. Then take them out, with a perforated skimmer, draining back into the pot the lard that is about them. As you take them out lay them on a flat dish, the bottom of which is strewed with powdered sugar. They will keep a week, but like most other cakes are best the day they are baked.

SOFT CRULLERS.—Sift three quarters of a pound of flour, and powder half a pound of loaf-sugar. Heat a pint of water in a round-bottomed sauce-pan, and when quite warm, mix the flour with it gradually. Set half a pound of fresh butter over the fire in a small vessel; and when it begins to melt, stir it gradually into the flour and water. Then add by degrees the powdered sugar, and half a grated nutmeg. Take the sauce-pan off the fire, and beat the contents, with a wooden spaddle or spatula, till they are thoroughly mixed. Then beat six eggs very light, and stir them gradually into the mixture. Beat the whole very hard, till it becomes a thick batter. Flour a paste-board very well, and lay out the batter upon it in rings, (the best way is to pass it through a screw funnel.) Have ready, on the fire, a pot of boiling lard of the very best quality. Put in the crullers, removing them from the board by carefully taking them up, one at a time, on a broad-bladed knife. Boil but a few at a time. They must be of a fine brown. Lift them out on a perforated skimmer, draining the lard from them back into the pot. Lay them on a large dish, and sift powdered white sugar over them.

Soft crullers cannot be made in warm weather.

NOTIONS.—Put into a sauce-pan a pint of milk, and two table-spoonfuls of fresh butter. Set it over the fire, and when the butter begins to melt, stir it well through the milk. As soon as it comes to a boil, begin to stir in a pint of sifted flour, a little at a time; making the mixture very smooth, and pressing out all the lumps. Let it continue to boil five minutes after the flour is all in. Then pour it into a deep pan, and set it to cool. In another pan beat six eggs very light. When it is nearly cool, stir the beaten egg into the mixture, a little at a time; stirring the whole very hard, till it is as light as possible.

Have ready, over the fire, a pot with a pound or more of fresh lard melting in it. When the lard comes to a boil, take up portions of the batter in a large spoon, or a small ladle, and drop them into the boiling lard, so as to form separate balls. When they are well browned, take them out with a perforated skimmer, draining the lard from them back into the pot. Lay them on a flat dish, and when all are done, sift over them a mixture of powdered sugar and powdered cinnamon or nutmeg. They should be eaten quite fresh.

CROSS-BUNS.—Pick clean a pound and a half of Zante currants; wash, drain, and dry them; spreading them on a large flat dish, placed in a slanting position near the fire or in the sun. When they are perfectly dry, dredge them thickly with flour to prevent their sinking or clodding in the cakes. Sift into a deep pan two pounds of fine flour, and mix thoroughly with it a table-spoonful of powdered cinnamon, (or of mixed nutmeg and cinnamon,) and half a pound of powdered white sugar. Cut up half a pound of the best fresh butter in half a pint of rich milk. Warm it till the butter is quite soft, but not till it melts. While warm, stir into the milk and butter two wine-glasses (or a jill) of strong fresh yeast. Make a hole in the centre of the pan of flour; pour in the mixed liquid; then, with a spoon or a broad knife, mix the flour gradually in; beginning round the edge of the hole. Proceed thus till you have the entire mass of ingredients thoroughly incorporated; stirring it hard as you go on. Cover the pan with a clean flannel or a thick towel, and set it in a warm place near the fire to rise. When it has risen well, and the surface of the dough is cracked all over, mix in a small tea-spoonful of soda, dissolved; flour your pasteboard; divide the dough into equal portions, and mixing in the currants, knead it into round cakes about the size of a small saucer. Place them on a large flat dish, cover them, and set them again in a warm place for about half an hour. Then butter some square tin or iron baking-pans; transfer the buns to them; and brush each bun lightly over with a glazing of beaten white of eggs, sweetened with a little sugar. Then, with the back of a knife, mark each bun with a cross, deeply indented in the dough, and extending entirely from one edge to another. Let the oven be quite ready; set in it the buns; and bake them of a deep brown colour. In England, and in other parts of Europe, it is customary to have hot cross-buns at breakfast on the morning of Good Friday. They are very good cakes at any time; but are best when fresh.

TO ICE A LARGE CAKE.—It requires practice to ice cakes smoothly. It is a good rule to allow a *large* quarter of a pound of powdered loaf-sugar to the white of every egg. The whites of four eggs and a pound of sugar will ice a large cake. Having strained the white of egg into a broad, shallow pan, beat it to a stiff froth with hickory rods or a large silver fork. It must be beaten till it stands alone. Have ready the powdered sugar in a bowl beside you; add it, gradually, to the beaten white of egg, a tea-spoonful at a time, and beat it very hard. Perhaps some additional sugar may be required to make the icing sufficiently thick. Flavour it by beating in at the last a few drops of oil of lemon, or a spoonful of fresh lemon or orange-juice, or a few drops of extract of vanilla, or extract of roses. Lemon-juice will make it more adhesive, so that it will stick on better. Turn bottom-upwards the empty pan in which the cake was baked, and place this pan on a large flat dish, or an old server. Dredge the cake all over with flour, to take off the greasiness of the outside, which greasiness may otherwise prevent the icing from sticking well. Then wipe off the flour with a clean towel. Take up the icing with a spoon, and begin by heaping a large quantity of it on the middle of the top of the cake. Then, with a broad-bladed knife, spread it down evenly and smoothly, till the top and sides are all covered with it of an equal thickness. Have beside you a bowl of cold water, into which dip the knife-blade, occasionally, as you go on spreading and smoothing the icing. Put it into a warm place to harden. When nearly dry, have ready sufficient icing to ornament or flower the cake. This must be done by means of a small syringe. By working and moving this syringe skilfully, the icing will fall from it so as to form borders, beadings, wreaths, and centre-pieces, according to your taste. If you cannot procure a syringe, a substitute may be formed by rolling or folding a piece of thick, smooth writing paper into a conical or sugar-loaf form. At the large end of this cone leave paper enough to turn down all round, so as to prevent the side opening, and the icing escaping. The pointed end must be neatly cut off with scissors, leaving a small round hole, through which the icing is to be pressed out when ornamenting the cake. The hole must be cut perfectly even; otherwise the icing will come out crooked and unmanageable. These paper cones, in skilful hands, may succeed tolerably; but they must be continually renewed, and are far less convenient than a syringe, which can be bought at a small cost, and is always ready for use. Where much icing is to be done, it is well to have a set of syringes with the points of different patterns.

To decorate cakes with ornamental icing, requires practice, skill, and taste. A person that has a good knowledge of drawing can generally do it very handsomely.

To colour it of a beautiful pink, tie up a little alkanet in a thin muslin bag, and let it infuse in the icing after it is made, squeezing the bag occasionally. When sufficiently coloured, take out the bag, and give the icing a hard stirring or beating before you put it on. Cover the cake all over with the pink icing, and then have ready some white icing for the border and other ornaments,—to be put on with the syringe.

Icing may be made stiffer and more adhesive by mixing with it, gradually, a small portion of dissolved gum tragacanth. This solution is prepared by melting gum tragacanth in *boiling* water, (if wanted for immediate use,) having first picked the gum quite clean. The proportion is half an ounce of the gum to half a pint of water. It is slow in dissolving. To keep it from spoiling, add to the gum (before the water) a few drops of strong oil of lemon, or oil of cinnamon.

FRENCH ICING FOR CAKES.—Dissolve some fine white gum arabic (finely powdered) in rose-water. The proportion should be, as much of the gum-arabic powder as will lie on a ten-cent piece to a tea-spoonful of rose-water. Beat some white of egg to a stiff froth that will stand alone. Stir in, gradually, sufficient double-refined powdered loaf-sugar to make it very thick, (a good proportion is four ounces of sugar to the white of one egg,) add to this quantity a tea-spoonful of the rose-water with the gum arabic dissolved in it, and beat the whole very hard. Instead of rose-water you may dissolve the gum in fresh lemon-juice. Previous to icing the cake, dredge it with flour, and in a few minutes wipe it off with a clean towel. This, by removing the greasiness of the outside, will make the icing stick on the better. Heap the icing first on the middle of the top of the cake; then with a broad-bladed knife spread it evenly all over the surface. Dip the knife frequently in a bowl of cold water as you proceed, and smooth the icing well. If not thick enough, wait till it dries, and then add a second coat.

ALMOND ICING.—Take half a pound of shelled sweet almonds, and three ounces of shelled bitter almonds. Put them, a few at a time, into a large bowl, and pour on boiling water to loosen the skins. As you peel them, throw the almonds into a bowl of cold water. When they are all blanched, pound them one at a time in a marble mortar, adding frequently a few drops of rose-water to prevent their oiling. They must be pounded to a smooth paste without the smallest particles of lumps. As you pound the almonds, remove this paste with a tea-spoon to a deep plate. Beat the whites of four eggs to a stiff froth. Then, gradually beat in a pound of the best double-refined sugar. Lastly, add, by degrees, the almond paste, a little at a time, and beat the whole very hard. If too thick, thin it with lemon-juice.

APPLE CAKE.—Make a nice light paste with the proportion of three quarters of a pound of fresh butter to a pound and a quarter of sifted flour. Roll it out into a large round sheet. Have ready a sufficiency of fine juicy apples, pared, cored, and sliced thin; mixed with one or two sliced quinces; and half a pound, or more, of the best raisins, seeded and cut in half. Make the mixture very sweet with brown sugar; and add some grated nutmeg; and a wine-glass, or more, of rose-water; or else the juice and grated yellow rind of one or two lemons. Mix all thoroughly, and put it on the sheet of paste; which must then be closed over the heap of mixture so as to form a very large dumpling. Put it into a small dutch-oven, and set it over hot coals, having previously heated the oven-lid by standing it upright before the fire. Then lay on the lid, with hot coals spread over it. Have ready a sufficient quantity of butter, brown sugar, and powdered cinnamon, stirred together till very light. Spread a portion of it on the bottom of the oven. While the cake is baking, remove the oven-lid frequently, and baste the cake with this mixture, which will form a sort of thick brown crust, covering it all over. It should bake from two to three hours; or longer if it is large. When thoroughly done, turn it out on a dish. It should be eaten fresh, the day it is baked; either warm or cold.

This is a German cake, and will be found very good.

CINNAMON CAKES.—Make a paste as above, and roll it out thin into a square sheet. Have ready a mixture of brown sugar; fresh butter; and a large portion of ground cinnamon; all stirred together till very light. Spread this mixture thickly over the sheet of paste; then roll it up, as you would a rolled up marmalade pudding. After it is rolled up, cut it down into pieces or cakes of equal size, and press them rather flat. Have ready over the fire a skillet or frying-pan with plenty of fresh butter boiling hard. Put in some of the cakes and fry them brown. As fast as they are done, take them out on a perforated skimmer; drain off the butter, and lay them on a hot dish. Then put in more cakes, till all are fried. They should be eaten warm, first sifting powdered white sugar over them.

These cakes, also, are German. They may be conveniently prepared when you are making pies, as the same paste will do for both.

GINGER POUND CAKE.—Cut up in a pan three quarters of a pound of butter; mix with it a pint of West India molasses, and a tea-cup of brown sugar. If in winter, set it over the fire till the butter has become soft enough to mix easily with the molasses and sugar. Then take it off, and stir them well together. Sift into a pan a pound of flour. In another pan, beat five eggs very light. Add gradually the beaten eggs and the flour, to the mixture of butter, sugar, and molasses, with two large table-spoonfuls of ground ginger, and a heaped tea-spoonful of powdered cinnamon. Then stir in a glass of brandy, and lastly a small tea-spoonful of sal-eratus or sub-carbonate of soda melted in a very little milk. Stir the whole very hard. Transfer the mixture to a buttered tin-pan, and bake it in a moderate oven from two to three hours, in proportion to its thickness.

This cake will be much improved by the addition of a pound of sultana or seedless raisins, well dredged with flour to prevent their sinking, and stirred in, gradually, at the last.

You may add also the yellow rind of a lemon or orange grated fine.

FLEMINGTON GINGERBREAD.—Stir together till quite light, a quarter of a pound of fresh butter, and a quarter of a pound of brown sugar. Then mix in half a pint of West India molasses. Sift rather less than a pint and a half of flour. Beat four eggs till very light, and stir them gradually into the mixture, alternately with the sifted flour. Add a heaping table-spoonful of ginger, and a tea-spoonful of powdered cinnamon. Stir all well. Dissolve a level tea-spoonful of soda or pearlash in as much warm water as will melt it; then stir it in at the last. Put the mixture into a buttered tin-pan, (either square or round,) set it *immediately* into the oven, which must be brisk but not too hot; and bake it well. When you think it done, probe it to the bottom with a knife or a broom-twig, stuck down into the centre; and do not take the cake from the oven unless the knife comes out clean and dry. It requires long baking.

GINGER CRACKERS.—Mix together in a deep pan, a pint of West India molasses; half a pound of butter; and a quarter of a pound of brown sugar; two large table-spoonfuls of ginger; a tea-spoonful of powdered cinnamon; a small tea-spoonful of pearlash or soda, dissolved in a little warm water; and sufficient sifted flour to make a dough just stiff enough to roll out conveniently. Let the whole be well incorporated into a large lump. Knead it till it leaves your hands clean; then beat it hard with a rolling-pin, which will make it crisp when baked. Divide the dough, and roll it out into sheets half an inch thick. Cut it into cakes with a tin cutter about the usual size of a cracker-biscuit, or with the edge of a teacup dipped frequently into flour to prevent its sticking. Lay the cakes at regular distances in square pans slightly buttered. Set them directly into a moderately brisk oven, and bake them well, first pricking them with a fork.

Ginger crackers are excellent on a sea voyage. If made exactly as above they will keep many weeks.

In greasing all cake-pans use only the best fresh butter: otherwise the outside of a thick cake will taste disagreeably, and the whole of a thin cake will have an unpleasant flavour.

SEA-VOYAGE GINGERBREAD.—Sift two pounds of flour into a pan, and cut up in it a pound and a quarter of fresh butter; rub the butter well into the flour, and then mix in a pint of West India molasses and a pound of the best brown sugar. Beat eight eggs till very light. Stir into the beaten egg two glasses or a jill of brandy.

Add also to the egg a teacup-full of ground ginger, and a table-spoonful of powdered cinnamon, with a tea-spoonful of soda melted in a little warm water. Wet the flour, &c., with this mixture till it becomes a soft dough. Sprinkle a little flour on your paste-board, and with a broad knife spread portions of the mixture thickly and smoothly upon it. The thickness must be equal all through; therefore spread it carefully and evenly, as the dough will be too soft to roll out. Then with the edge of a tumbler dipped in flour, cut it out into round cakes. Have ready square pans, slightly buttered; lay the cakes in them sufficiently far apart to prevent their running into each other when baked. Set the pans into a brisk oven, and bake the cakes well, seeing that they do not burn.

You may cut them out small with the lid of a cannister (or something similar) the usual size of gingerbread nuts.

These cakes will keep during a long voyage, and are frequently carried to sea. Many persons find highly-spiced gingerbread a preventive to sea-sickness.

SPICED GINGERBREAD.—Sift into a deep pan a pound and a half of flour, and cut up in it half a pound of the best fresh butter. Rub them together, with your hands, till thoroughly incorporated. Then add half a pound of brown sugar, crushed fine with the rolling-pin; a table-spoonful of mixed spice, consisting of equal quantities of powdered cloves, mace, and cinnamon. Also, a table-spoonful of ground ginger, and two table-spoonfuls of carraway seeds. Mix the whole together, and wet it with a pint of West India molasses. Dissolve a small tea-spoonful of pearlash or soda in a very little warm water. Mix it into the other ingredients. Spread some flour on your paste-board, take the dough out of the pan, flour your hands, and knead the dough till it ceases entirely to be sticky. Roll it out into a very thick square sheet; cut it into long straight slips; twist every two slips together, rounding off the ends nicely. Lay them (not too closely) in buttered square pans, and bake them well. As gingerbread burns easily, take care not to have the oven too hot. Instead of forming it into twisted strips, you may cut the sheet of gingerbread-dough into round cakes with the edge of a tumbler, which, as you proceed, must be frequently dipped in flour.

CARRAWAY GINGERBREAD.—Cut up half a pound of fresh butter in a pint of West India molasses and warm them together slightly, till the butter is quite soft. Then stir them well, and add, gradually, a pound of good brown sugar, a table-spoonful of powdered cinnamon, and two heaped table-spoonfuls of ground ginger, or three, if the ginger is not very strong. Sift two pounds or two quarts of flour. Beat four eggs till very thick and light, and stir them, gradually, into the mixture, in turn with the flour, and five or six large table-spoonfuls of carraway seeds, a little at a time. Dissolve a very small tea-spoonful of pearlash or soda in as much lukewarm water as will cover it. Then stir it in at the last. Stir all very hard. Transfer it to a buttered tin pan with straight sides, and bake it in a loaf in a moderate oven. It will require a great deal of baking.

MOLASSES GINGERBREAD.—Mix together a quart of West India molasses, and a pint of milk. Cut up in them a pound of fresh butter. Set the pan on a stove, or in a warm place till the butter becomes soft enough to stir and mix well into the molasses and milk. They must be merely warmed but not made hot. Then stir in a small teacup of ginger, and a table-spoonful of powdered cinnamon. Add, gradually, a little at a time, three pounds of sifted flour. The whole should be a thick batter. Lastly, stir in a large tea-spoonful of soda, or a smaller one of pearlash or sal-eratus, dissolved in a very little lukewarm water. Bake the mixture either in little tins, or in a large loaf. If the latter, it will require very long baking; as long as a black-cake.

MOLASSES CAKE.—Cut up a quarter of a pound of fresh butter into a pint of West India molasses. Warm it just sufficiently to soften the butter, and make it mix easily. Stir it well into the molasses, and add a table-spoonful of powdered cinnamon. Beat three eggs very light, and stir them, gradually, into the mixture, in turn with barely enough of sifted flour (not more than a pint and a half) to make it about as thick as pound-cake batter. Add, at the last, a small or level tea-spoonful of pearlash, or a full one of soda, dissolved in a very little warm water. Butter some small tin cake-pans, or patty-pans, put in the mixture, and set them immediately into the oven, which must not be too hot, as all cakes made with molasses are peculiarly liable to scorch on the outside.

SUGAR CAKE.—Sift two pounds of flour into a pan, and cut up in it a pound of fresh butter. Rub with your hands the butter into the flour till it is thoroughly mixed. Then rub in a pound of sugar, and a grated nutmeg. Wet the whole with half a pint of rich milk (or a jill of rose-water, and a jill of milk) mixed with a well-beaten egg. Add, at the last, a very small tea-spoonful of pearlash or soda, dissolved in a little vinegar or warm water. Roll out the dough thick, and beat it well on both sides with the rolling-pin. Then roll it thin, and cut it into square cakes, notching the edges with a knife. Put them into a shallow pan slightly buttered, (taking care not to place them too near, lest they run into each other,) and bake them a light brown.

You may mix into the dough two table-spoonfuls of carraway seeds.

MOLASSES BREAD CAKE.—On a bread-making day, when the wheat-bread has risen perfectly light and is cracked on the surface, take as much of the dough as will fill a quart bowl, and place it in a broad pan. Cut up a quarter of a pound of fresh butter, and set it over the fire to warm and soften, but do not let it melt to an oil. When quite soft, mix with it half a pint of West India molasses, a small table-spoonful of powdered cinnamon, and the finely-grated yellow rind of a large orange or lemon; adding also the juice. Have ready three eggs, well beaten, and add them gradually to the mixture. It must form a lump of soft dough; but not too thin to knead with your hands. Knead it well on the paste-board for a quarter of an hour. Butter some tin pans; put an equal portion of the dough into each; cover them; and set them in a warm but not a hot place for a quarter of an hour before baking. Then bake the cakes well. Instead of small pans you may bake the whole of the dough in one large one. This cake should be eaten the day it is baked; fresh but not warm. All *sweet* cakes in which yeast is an ingredient are best and most wholesome when fresh, as the next day they become hard, dry, and comparatively heavy.

BREAD MUFFINS.—Take some bread dough that has risen as light as possible, and knead into it some well-beaten egg in the proportion of two eggs to about a pound of dough. Then mix in a tea-spoonful of soda that has been dissolved in a very little lukewarm water. Let the dough stand in a warm place for a quarter of an hour. Then bake it in muffin-rings. You can thus, with very little trouble, have muffins for tea whenever you bake bread in the afternoon.

TO FRESHEN CAKES.—Cakes when stale may be much improved, if about an hour before they are wanted for tea, you enclose them in a circular *wooden* box with a tight-fitting lid, and place it on the marble hearth before a good coal fire; but not so close as to be in danger of scorching the box, which must be turned round, occasionally, so as to receive the heat equally on all sides. A tin or stone-ware box will not answer at all for this purpose, being too cold. If you burn wood-fires, set the box with the cake into a plate-warmer, or place it on a tall skillet, so as to be out of the way of coals or ashes falling on it, should the sticks break on the fire.

DOMESTIC LIQUORS, ETC.

GOOSEBERRY CHAMPAGNE.—Take large, fine gooseberries, that are full-grown, but not yet beginning to turn red; and pick off their tops and tails. Then weigh the fruit, and allow a gallon of clear, soft water to every three pounds of gooseberries. Put them into a large, clean tub; pour on a little of the water; pound and mash them, thoroughly, with a wooden beetle; add the remainder of the water, and give the whole a hard stirring. Cover the tub with a cloth, and let it stand four days; stirring it frequently and thoroughly, to the bottom. Then strain the liquid, through a coarse linen cloth, into another vessel; and to each gallon of liquid add four pounds of fine loaf-sugar; and to every five gallons a quart of the best and clearest French brandy. Mix the whole well together; and put it into a clean cask, that will just hold it, as it should be filled full. Place the cask on its side, in a cool, dry part of the cellar; and lay the bung loosely on the top. Secure the cask firmly in its place, so that it cannot, by any chance, be shaken or moved; as the least disturbance will injure the wine. Let it work for a fortnight, or more; till the fermentation is quite over, and the hissing has ceased. Then bottle it; driving in the corks tightly. Lay the bottles on their sides. In six months, it will be fit for drinking, and will be found as brisk as real champagne.

GREEN CURRANT WINE.—The currants must be full-grown, but not yet beginning to redden. Strip them from the stems; weigh them; and to every three pounds allow a gallon of soft water. Mash them well, and proceed exactly as in the receipt for gooseberry champagne; except that you may use the best light-coloured brown sugar, instead of loaf. Instead of bottling it, as soon as it has done fermenting, you may, whenever the hissing is over, put in the bung tightly; and let the wine remain in the cask. In six months, it will be fit for drinking.

PEACH WINE.—Take eight pounds of ripe, juicy, free-stone peaches, of the best kind. Slice them into two gallons of soft water; and add five pounds of loaf-sugar, broken small. Crack all the stones; extract the kernels; break them up; and lay them in the bottom of a clean tub. Put the peaches, with the dissolved sugar, into a kettle; and boil and skim it, until the scum ceases to rise. Then strain it, through a large sieve, into the tub that has the kernels in the bottom. Stir all well together, and cover it closely till it grows quite cool. Then put in a large slice of toasted bread, covered all over with strong, fresh yeast. Leave it to ferment; and, when the fermentation is over, strain it into a keg, and add a bottle of muscadel or sweet malaga wine. Let it stand six months. Then draw off a little in a glass, and, if it is not quite clear, take out a pint of the wine; mix with it an ounce of powdered gum-arabic; dissolve it in a slow heat; and then add an ounce of powdered chalk. When they are dissolved, return the pint of wine to the keg, stirring it in, lightly, with a stick; but taking care not to let the stick go down to the bottom, lest it should disturb the lees, or sediment. Let it stand three days longer, and then bottle it. It will be fit for use in another six months.

Apricot wine may be made in the same manner.

DOMESTIC FRONTINIAC.—Put into a large kettle, twelve pounds of broken-up loaf-sugar; and pour on it six gallons of clear, soft water, and let the sugar dissolve. Take seven pounds of the best raisins, and chop them small, having first removed the seeds. Mix the raisins with the dissolved sugar; set the kettle over the fire, and let it boil for an hour, skimming it well. Have ready half a peck of full-blown elder-blossoms, gathered just before they are ready to fall from the branches. Take the kettle from the fire; pour the liquor into a clean tub; and as soon as it has cooled, (so as to be merely lukewarm,) stir in the elder-flowers. Cover it closely. Next day, add six large table-spoonfuls of lemon-syrup, and four of strong, fresh yeast. After the wine has fermented two days, strain it into a clean cask; and, after it has stood two months, bottle it. Next summer, it will be in fine order for drinking, and will be found a delicious wine; very similar to the real Frontiniac.

MORELLA WINE.—Take a sufficiency of large, fine morella cherries. They must all be perfectly ripe, and free from blemish. Extract the stones; carefully saving all the juice. Return it to the cherries; put them into a clean tub; and let them stand, in a cold place, undisturbed, till next morning. Then mash and press them through a cullender, or sieve, or put them into a thin linen bag, and squeeze out all the juice; then measure it. To every quart of juice, allow a large half-pound of fine loaf-sugar, and mix them well together, in a clean cask. Crack the stones; tie them up in a thin bag; and suspend the bag in the cask, in the midst of the liquor. Leave it to ferment; and, when the fermentation ceases, stop it closely. Let it stand four months, leaving the bag of cherry-stones in the cask. Then bottle it, and in three months it will be fit to drink.

DOMESTIC TOKAY.—Take fine grapes, that are all *perfectly* ripe; pick them carefully from the stalks, omitting all that are blemished; put them into a large hair sieve, placed over a large, deep pan, or a clean tub. Mash the grapes, with your hand, squeezing and pressing out all the juice. To every quart of juice, allow a pound of sultana raisins, chopped small, or of bloom raisins, seeded and chopped. Let the grape-juice and raisins stand twelve days; stirring it twice or three times every day. Then strain the liquor into a cask; but do not stop it closely till after three days. Let it stand eight months; then bottle it. If it is not clear, take out a pint of the wine; mix with it half an ounce of isinglass, shaved fine, or an ounce of powdered gum-arabic. Set it in a warm place, and, when dissolved, add an ounce of fine chalk. This will be sufficient to fine a barrel of wine. Stir it lightly into the rest. Let it stand three or four days, and then bottle it.

BLACKBERRY WINE.—The blackberries must all be full ripe, and without blemish. Measure them; and to every quart of fruit allow a quart of clear, soft water. Boil the water by itself. Put the blackberries into a clean tub, and mash them with a wooden beetle, or a mallet. When the water has boiled, pour it on the blackberries, and let it stand, till next morning, in a cool place, stirring it occasionally.

Then press out all the juice, measure it, and to every quart of liquid allow half a pound of sugar. Put the sugar into a cask, and strain the liquid upon it, through a linen bag. Stir it frequently, till the sugar is thoroughly dissolved. Let the cask remain unstopped, till the liquor has done working. Then add half an ounce of isinglass, or an ounce of gum-arabic, dissolved in a little hot water. You may substitute, for the isinglass, or gum-arabic, the beaten whites of four eggs. Keep it open till next day. Then bung it. It may be bottled in two months.

Raspberry wine may be made as above.

Black currant wine, also.

ROSOLIS.—Put four pounds of the best loaf-sugar into a large porcelain kettle; and pour on it three quarts of water. When it has melted, set it over the fire, and boil and skim it, till the scum ceases to rise. Then add the whites of three eggs, whisked to a froth; and put in the shells also, broken small. Let it again come to a boil. Then take it off the fire; and, when it is only lukewarm, throw in a quart of fresh rose-leaves, stirring them well through the liquid. Cover the vessel, and let it stand till next day, till the fragrance of the roses is extracted. Then remove the first rose-leaves, with a skimmer, and put into it a second, and afterwards, a third supply. When the syrup has a fine rose-flavour, strain it through a linen bag. If not perfectly clear, filter it through blotting-paper, pinned inside the bottom of a sieve. Then add half a pint of spirits of wine, that has been coloured red, by infusing in it some alkanet root, tied up in a thin muslin bag. Bottle the mixture; and it will be a delicate liqueur. Instead of rose-leaves, you may flavour it immediately, by stirring in a large portion of extract of roses.

This liqueur can be made very conveniently, where there is a garden abounding in roses.

HIPPOCRAS.—Put into a jar a quart of the best port wine. Beat, separately, in a mortar, a quarter of an ounce of cinnamon, two nutmegs, twelve blades of mace, and a tea-spoonful of coriander seeds. Then mix them all together; and put them into the wine. Add the yellow rind of four large lemons, pared thin, and their juice, mixed with half a pound of powdered loaf-sugar. Cover the vessel closely, and let it infuse a week, or more. Then strain the liquid through a linen bag, and bottle it.

PERSICOT.—Blanch, in scalding water, a pound and a half of bitter almonds, and pound them in a mortar, till they are broken very small. Then put them into two quarts of the best French white brandy. Let them remain twenty-four hours in the brandy; shaking the mixture frequently. Boil one quart of rich milk; and, when it has boiled, take it off the fire, and mix with it two pounds of white sugar-candy, pounded fine. Then mix the whole together, almonds, brandy, milk, and sugar-candy; and let it stand for a week or two, or till very highly flavoured; shaking or stirring it frequently. Afterwards strain it through a linen bag, and bottle it. Drink it from small liqueur-glasses, with a bit of ice in each.

NECTAR.—Take a pound of the best raisins, seeded and chopped; four lemons, sliced thin, and the yellow rind pared off from two other lemons; and two pounds of powdered loaf-sugar. Put into a porcelain preserving-kettle two gallons of water. Set it over the fire, and boil it half an hour. Then, while the water is boiling hard, put in the raisins, lemons, and sugar; and continue the boiling for ten minutes. Pour the mixture into a vessel with a close cover, and let it stand four days; stirring it twice a-day. Then strain it through a linen bag, and bottle it. It will be fit for use in a fortnight. Drink it from wine-glasses, with a small bit of ice in each.

MINT JULEP.—Put into the bottom of a tumbler, about a dozen sprigs of young and tender mint. Upon them place a large tea-spoonful of fine white sugar; and then pour on peach-brandy, so as to reach nearly one-third the height of the tumbler. Fill up with ice, pounded fine; and lay on the top a thin slice of pine-apple, cut across into four pieces. As an ornament, stick into the centre a handsome cluster of mint-sprigs, so as to rise far above the edge of the tumbler. It will be the better for standing awhile, in a vessel of finely-broken ice.

VANILLA SYRUP.—Put four or five vanilla beans into a very small, clean sauce-pan, with half a pint of boiling water. Set it over the fire, (closely covered,) and boil it, till the flavour of the vanilla is thoroughly extracted, and the water tastes of it very strongly. Then take out the vanilla, and strain the liquid. Break up three pounds of the best double-refined loaf-sugar, and put it into a preserving-kettle, with a quart of hot water. When thoroughly melted, set it on the fire, and boil and skim it well; till the whole is reduced to nearly a quart. Then stir in the vanilla liquid, and let it boil five or six minutes longer. After taking it from the fire, pour it into a pitcher, till it is cool enough to transfer to small bottles. Then cork it tightly, and seal the corks.

It will be found excellent for flavouring custards, creams, &c., or to mix with ice-water, for a summer beverage.

The extract will be stronger if the vanilla beans are split and cut into pieces before boiling, and tied up in a very thin muslin bag.

ORANGE MILK.—Take two dozen large ripe oranges. Cut them in two; remove the seeds; and squeeze the juice into a very large and clean *stone* jar. Never use earthen-ware, to hold any thing acid, as the lead glazing may produce the most deleterious effects. Have ready four pounds of the finest loaf-sugar, dissolved in a gallon of the best rum or brandy. Pour it into the jar that contains the orange-juice; stir the mixture well; and add the yellow rind of the oranges, cut into little slips. Cover the jar, and let it stand four days; stirring it frequently. Then take a gallon of new, unskimmed milk, (the morning's milk of that day,) boil it, and, when it has come to a hard boil, pour it, hot, into the mixture. Cover it closely, and let it stand till it gets quite cold. Then strain it into another vessel, through a linen jelly-bag. Bottle it immediately, and seal the corks. It improves by keeping, and will continue good for many years.

To use it, mix a sufficient quantity, in a tumbler, with ice-water; or take it, undiluted, in a small cordial glass.

ORANGE SYRUP.—Take large fine ripe oranges, with smooth thin rinds, and roll each orange under your hand upon the table to increase the juice. Set a very clean sieve upon a large bowl, and cut the oranges over it; first halving them, and then notching each half to let out as much juice as possible when squeezing them.

Press them with all your strength in a wooden squeezer, letting the juice drain through the sieve into the bowl. To each pint of juice allow a pound and a half (a quart and a pint) of the best double-refined loaf-sugar broken up. Put the sugar into a preserving-kettle; pour the juice upon it; cover it, and let it stand till all the sugar is quite soft, and can be easily mixed with the juice. Next set the kettle over a moderate fire that has no blaze or smoke, and boil it slowly; skimming it carefully till the scum ceases to rise. Then take it off, remove the syrup from the kettle, and when it is milk-warm, put it into very clean bottles, (new ones will be best,) cork them tightly, and seal the corks. Keep it in a dry, cool place. It is very fine for flavouring cakes, puddings, sweet sauces, &c. Or for mixing with ice-water as a pleasant beverage. Also for ice-cream or water-ice, when oranges are not to be had. Or for mixing with powdered sugar to make the confection called orange-drops. Some persons, to increase the strength of orange syrup, add the yellow rind of the oranges grated on lumps of the sugar. This will do very well if the syrup is to be used up soon. But by long keeping, the peel will give it a very disagreeable taste and odour, resembling turpentine; unfitting it for all purposes.

Lemon syrup may be made as above. To *this* the addition of the yellow rind of the lemons grated on sugar will be an improvement; as lemon rind never acquires a turpentine taste.

IMITATION LEMON SYRUP.—Break up twelve pounds of the best double-refined loaf-sugar. Put it into a preserving-kettle, and pour on it a gallon of very clear soft water. When it has dissolved set it over a moderate fire, and boil and skim it till the scum ceases to rise. Then take it off, and stir in immediately, while the syrup is hot, six large tea-spoonfuls of the best oil of lemon, and a quarter of an ounce of tartaric acid. When cold, bottle the liquid, and cork it tightly. The bottles for this purpose should either be quite new, or such as have been used before for lemon syrup. Mixed with ice-water it is a wholesome and refreshing beverage, and if you stir into a half tumbler of the mixture a half tea-spoonful, or more, of carbonate of soda, it will foam up, and be just like the soda-water you buy in the shops at six cents per glass.

The above is the lemon syrup generally used for this purpose by the druggists and confectioners.

CARBONATED SYRUP WATER.—Put into a tumbler lemon, raspberry, strawberry, pine-apple, or any other *acid* syrup, sufficient in quantity to flavour the beverage very highly. Then pour in *very cold ice-water* till the glass is half full. Add *half* a tea-spoonful of bi-carbonate of soda, (to be obtained at the druggists',) and stir it well in with a tea-spoon. It will foam up to the top immediately, and must be drank during the effervescence.

By keeping the syrup, and the carbonate of soda in the house, and mixing them as above with ice-water, you can at any time have a glass of this very pleasant drink; precisely similar to that which you get at the shops. The cost will be infinitely less.

FINE RASPBERRY CORDIAL.—Fill a large stone jar with ripe raspberries. Cover the jar closely, and let it stand in a corner of the hearth near the fire, or on the top of a stove, till the fruit is heated so as to break. Then put the raspberries into a linen bag, and squeeze the juice into a pan beneath. Measure the juice, and to every quart allow a pound of loaf-sugar, broken very small. Do not use the white sugar that is sold ready-powdered; it is generally so adulterated with pulverized starch, as to be unfit for any thing that is to be set away for keeping. Put the juice and sugar (well mixed) into a preserving-kettle. Give it a boil, and skim it well. When it has come to a boil, and the scum has ceased to appear, take off the kettle; measure the liquid; and pour it carefully into a large vessel; allowing an equal quantity of the best French brandy. Stir it well, and when cold, put it into a demi-john, or a large stone jug, and cork it tightly. Let it stand undisturbed a fortnight; then, if it is not perfectly clear, filter it through blotting-paper pinned inside the bottom of a sieve. Bottle it, and seal the corks. Instead of brandy, you may use the best Jamaica spirits.

Currant or cherry cordial may be made in the above manner: first stoning all the cherries, which should be fully ripe, and of the largest and best kind; either red or black, or a mixture of both. The flavour will be much improved by cracking the stones, and putting them into the demijohn before you pour on the liquid.

Peach cordial, also, may be made as above. The peaches should be fine, ripe, juicy free-stones; cut in pieces, and the stones removed. Afterwards, crack the stones, and put the kernels (broken up) into the bottom of the demijohn, to infuse with the liquid.

FINE RASPBERRY VINEGAR.—Put a sufficient quantity of ripe raspberries into a large wooden or stone vessel, and pour on as much of the best *genuine* white wine vinegar as will cover them well. Cover the vessel, and let it stand undisturbed during twenty-four hours; or longer, if the juice is not entirely extracted; when it is, the raspberries will look whitish and shrunk. You must, on no account, bruise or stir them. Then strain the whole liquid through a large hair sieve placed over a broad stone pan. Let the juice run through of itself, without any mashing or squeezing. The least pressing will cause the liquid, when finished, to look cloudy and dull. Have ready, in another vessel, the same quantity of fresh raspberries that you put in at first; and pour the strained liquid over them. Cover it, and let it again stand undisturbed for twenty-four hours or more. Then again pass it through a sieve, without any squeezing. A third time pour the liquid over the original quantity of fresh raspberries in another vessel, and let it stand untouched during twenty-four hours. Afterwards measure the liquid, and to every pint allow a pound of the best double-refined loaf-sugar, broken small. Put the whole into a large preserving-kettle, and boil and skim it about twenty minutes. Then pour it into a clean stone vessel, and set it to cool. Cover it, and let it stand all night. Next day, transfer it to bottles, which must be perfectly dry and clean. Cork them closely, and seal the corks. It will keep for years if made exactly according to the above directions.

To use it as a beverage, put a large wine-glass of the raspberry vinegar into a tumbler, and fill it up with ice-water. Mixed with hot water, and drank as warm as possible immediately on going to bed, it is an excellent palliative for a cold; and, by producing a perspiration, will sometimes effect a cure.

FRENCH RASPBERRY VINEGAR.—Take a sufficiency of fine ripe raspberries. Put them into a deep pan, and mash them with a wooden beetle. Then pour them, with all their juice, into a large linen bag, and squeeze and press out the liquid into a vessel beneath. Measure it; and to each quart of the raspberry-juice allow a pound of powdered white sugar, and a pint of the best cider vinegar. First mix together the juice and the vinegar, and give them a boil in a preserving-kettle. When they have boiled well, add gradually the sugar, with a beaten white of egg to every two pounds; and boil and skim it till the scum ceases to rise. When done, put it into clean bottles, and cork them tightly. It is a very pleasant and cooling beverage in warm weather, and for invalids who are feverish. To use it, pour out half a tumbler of raspberry vinegar, and fill it up with ice-water.

It is a good palliative for a cold, mixed with hot water, and taken as hot as possible immediately on going to bed, so as to produce perspiration.

GOOD VINEGAR.—Take five gallons of soft, clear water, two quarts of whisky, two quarts of the best West India molasses, and half a pint of the best fresh yeast. Lay a sheet of white foolscap paper at the bottom of a very clean keg, and pour in the mixture. Place it in the sun the first warm weather at the close of May, or beginning of June. In six weeks it will be fit for use. Put in the bung loosely, and do not stop it tight till the fermentation is over. If you make it in winter, keep it in a place where there is a stove or furnace.

Much of the vinegar that is offered for sale is excessively and disagreeably sharp; overpowering the taste of every thing with which it is combined. This vinegar is deleterious in its effects, and should never be used; it is made entirely of drugs. Oysters and pickled vegetables have been entirely destroyed or eaten up by it in a few hours, so that nothing was left but a whitish liquid. To avoid all risk from the unwholesome vinegar offered for sale, families would do well to make their own. A keg of hard cider kept in a warm kitchen in winter, and exposed to the hot sun in summer, will become excellent vinegar.

COMMON MOLASSES VINEGAR.—Mix together a gallon of West India molasses, and four gallons of lukewarm water. Pour it into a clean five-gallon cask, and place it in the chimney-corner; standing the cask on end, and leaving the bung out. To give it, occasionally, some additional heat, set the cask in the mouth of the oven on baking-days, after the bread is drawn, and let it remain while the oven continues warm. In three months it will be excellent and wholesome vinegar, at a very trifling cost,—only that of the gallon of molasses. When the liquid is sufficiently acid, stop the bung-hole closely, and remove the cask to a cool place. In summer, you may make this vinegar by letting the cask stand three or four months exposed to the hot sun; taking care to cover the bung-hole in damp or rainy weather.

APPLE-WATER.—Take three large, juicy pippin apples; pare, core, and cut them into very thin slices. Put them into a pitcher, (the yellow rind of a lemon, pared thin, will be an improvement,) and pour on a pint of boiling water. Cover the pitcher closely, and let it stand four hours. Then pour the liquid into a glass, and sweeten it with loaf-sugar.

This is a cooling drink in a fever.

TOAST-WATER.—Take *thin* slices of wheat bread, and toast it very brown on both sides, but do not let it burn or blacken. Put the toast into a pitcher that has straining holes at the spout, and pour over it, from a tea-kettle, as much boiling water as you wish to make into drink. The water must be actually boiling at the time. Cover the pitcher, and let it stand till the water is cold. Then pour it off into a decanter. Made in this way, toast-water is very wholesome and refreshing, and is frequently drank at table by persons in health, as well as by invalids.

AN EXCELLENT WAY OF MAKING COFFEE.—For this purpose you should have a percolator, or coffee-pot with strainers inside. The coffee will be much stronger and better, if roasted and ground just before it is put in the pot. There are no coffee-roasters so good as those of sheet-iron, made somewhat in the form of a large long candle-box; standing before the fire on feet; and turned round by a handle, so as to give all the coffee that is inside an equal chance of heat. When about half done, put among the coffee a piece of fresh butter. It should be roasted evenly throughout, of a fine brown colour, and not allowed to blacken or burn. Grind it while warm; and put into the percolator a sufficient quantity of coffee, placing it *between* the two strainers. Then (having stopped up the spout) pour into the upper strainer a due proportion of *cold* water; allowing a quart of water to half a pint or more of ground coffee. Cold water is now found to make a stronger infusion than hot water, as there is less evaporation, and none of the strength of the coffee is carried off in steam. As soon as the water is all in, put on the lid closely, and set away the pot. It is well to put the coffee to infuse over night, if wanted for breakfast; and in the morning, if required for evening. But, when necessary, it may be done in a much shorter time. A little before the coffee is to go to table, lift off the upper half of the percolator, (the part that contains the strainers,) transfer the lid to the lower part; set the pot over the fire, and give it one boil up—not more. As soon as it has come to a boil it is ready for drinking; being already strained, and drawn. It will be found clear, strong, and in all respects superior to that prepared in any other manner. A short boil is sufficient to take off all taste of rawness. Long boiling weakens coffee, and frequently turns it sour.

The above method will, we are confident, be highly approved on trial. Also, it saves the expense of isinglass, white of egg, and other articles generally used in clearing coffee. Percolators for making coffee in this manner, can be obtained of all sizes at the large tin manufactory of Messrs. Williams & Co., 276 Market street, between Seventh and Eighth streets, Philadelphia.

A china or metal coffee-pot should always be scalded twice before coffee is transferred to it, from the vessel in which it has been made.

COCOA.—The cocoa which is put up solid in close packages, and usually sold at a shilling a paper, is far superior to the chocolate that is manufactured into squares or cakes, and which is too frequently adulterated with lard and meal. Baker's prepared cocoa is excellent. When you intend having it for drinking, shave down, or cut fine a sufficient quantity of the cocoa; allowing about half the contents of a paper to a quart of water, if you wish it very strong, and three pints of water for moderate strength. Then put the cocoa into a clean sauce-pan or a tin pot with a spout. Measure the water from a kettle that is boiling hard at the time; and when you have the proper quantity pour it scalding hot on the cocoa. Cover it closely; place it over the fire; and let it boil till it is all dissolved into the same consistence, and quite smooth, and free from the smallest lumps. While boiling, you must several times take off the lid, and with a spoon stir the cocoa down to the bottom. Then transfer it to your chocolate pot, which must be twice scalded with boiling water. Send it to table as hot as possible, adding milk and sugar to the cups when poured out. Eat with it dry toast; *unbuttered* rolls; milk-biscuit; or sponge-cake.

TO KEEP ORANGE-JUICE.—The oranges must be large and ripe. To increase the quantity of juice, roll each orange under your hand on a table, or with your foot upon a clean hearth-stone. Then cut them in half, and score each half with four deep notches, so that when squeezed the juice may run out more freely. Squeeze them through a strainer into a large bowl. To each pint of juice allow a pound of the best loaf-sugar, broken small. Cover the bowl, and let it stand undisturbed all night. In the morning remove all the scum that has risen to the surface, and pour the liquid through a funnel into clean, well-dried pint bottles; into each of which you have previously put a table-spoonful of the best white brandy. Cork each bottle tightly, and tie down a thin wet leather closely over each cork. Keep the bottles in a dry place. You will find this preparation excellent for flavouring, when fresh oranges are not to be had.

Lemon-juice may be kept in the same manner, for flavouring or for punch.

TO PRESERVE LEMON-JUICE FOR A VOYAGE.—Select only the best and freshest lemons. One that is in the least tainted will spoil the whole. Roll every lemon under your hand upon a table to increase the juice. Then squeeze them well through a strainer. To every quart of juice add an ounce of cream of tartar. Let it stand three days, (stirring it frequently,) and then filter it through thin muslin pinned tightly on the bottom of a sieve. Put it into pint-bottles; filling up the neck of each bottle with a little of the best olive oil. The corks must be put in very tightly, and then sealed. When you open a bottle, avoid shaking it; and carefully pour off the olive oil that is on the top of the lemon-juice.

FINE MEAD.—Beat to a strong froth the whites of three eggs, and mix them with six gallons of water; sixteen quarts of strained honey; and the yellow rind of two dozen large lemons, pared very thin. Boil all together, during three-quarters of an hour; skimming it well. Then put it into a tub; and when lukewarm, add three table-spoonfuls of the best fresh yeast. Cover it, and leave it to ferment. When it has done working, transfer it to a barrel, with the lemon-peel in the bottom. Let it stand six months. Then bottle it.

TO KEEP CIDER SWEET.—When barreling the cider, put into each barrel or keg a jill (eight large table-spoonfuls) of white mustard-seed. This will retard its becoming hard or sour.

TO MAKE BOTTLED CIDER VERY BRISK.—When you are bottling the cider, put a large raisin into the bottom of each bottle before you pour in the cider. Then cork it tightly.

In bottling spruce or molasses beer put in also a raisin.

TO KEEP ORANGES AND LEMONS.—Take a sufficiency of fine sand, and make it very dry by exposing it to the heat of the sun or the fire, stirring it frequently. Afterwards let it become quite cold, and then put a quantity of it in a close box or barrel. Bury your oranges (which must all be perfectly good) in this sand; placing them so as not to touch each other, and with the stem-end downwards. At the top put a thick layer of sand quite two inches deep. Cover the box closely, and keep it in a cool place.

TO KEEP GRAPES.—See that there are no imperfect grapes on any of the bunches. They must not be too ripe. Put in the bottom of a keg a layer of bran that has been dried in the sun, or in an oven, and afterwards become quite cold. Upon the bran, place a layer of grapes with bran between the bunches so that they may not touch each other. Proceed thus with alternate layers of bran and grapes till the keg is full; seeing that the last is a thick layer of bran. Then close the keg, nailing on the head so that no air can penetrate.

Grapes may also be packed in fine wood-ashes that has been well sifted.

TO KEEP APPLES.—Wipe every apple dry with a cloth, and see that no blemished ones are left among them. Have ready a very dry tight barrel, and cover the bottom with dry pebbles. These will attract the damp of the apples. Then put in the fruit; head up the barrel; and plaster the seams with mortar, taking care to have a thick rim of mortar all round the top. Let the barrel remain undisturbed in the same place till you want the apples for use. Pippins, bell-flowers, or other apples of the best sorts, may be kept in this way till July.

TO KEEP CARROTS, PARSNIPS, BEETS, AND SWEET POTATOES.—These should all be housed before the first frost. Range them side by side, and bury them in dry sand; a bed of sand at the bottom; another between each layer of the vegetables, and a thick sand covering for the whole. When wanted for use, begin at one end, and draw them out in regular order, and not out of the middle till you come to it.

TO KEEP FRESH BUTTER FOR FRYING, STEWING, &c.—Take several pounds of the *very best* fresh butter. Cut it up in a large tin sauce-pan, or in any clean cooking vessel lined with tin. Set it over the fire, and boil and skim it during half an hour. Then pour it off, carefully, through a funnel into a stone jar, and cover it closely with a bladder or leather tied down over the lid. The butter having thus been separated from the salt and sediment, (which will be found remaining at the bottom of the boiling-vessel,) if kept closely covered and set in a cool place, will continue good for a year, and be found excellent for frying, and stewing, and other culinary purposes. Prepare it thus in May or June, and you may use it in winter, if living in a place where fresh butter is not to be obtained in cold weather. Try it.

AN EASY WAY OF MAKING BUTTER IN WINTER.—The following will be found an excellent method of making butter in cold weather for family use. We recommend its trial. Take, in the morning, the unskimmed milk of the preceding evening, (after it has stood all night in a *tin* pan,) and set it over a furnace of hot coals, or in a stove; being careful not to disturb the cream that has risen to the surface. Let it remain over the fire till it simmers, and begins to bubble round the edges; but on no account let it come to a boil. Then take the pan carefully off, (without disturbing the cream) and carry it to a cool place, but not where it is cold enough to freeze. In the evening, take a spoon, and loosen the cream round the sides of the pan. If very rich it will be almost a solid cake. Slip off the sheet of cream into another and larger pan; letting as little milk go with it as possible. Cover it, and set it away. Repeat the process for several days, till you have thus collected a sufficiency of clotted cream to fill the pan. Then scald a wooden ladle, and beat the cream hard with it during ten minutes. You will then have excellent butter. Take it out of the pan; lay it on a flat dish; and with the ladle, squeeze and press it hard, till all the butter-milk is entirely extracted and drained off. Then wash the butter in cold water, and work a very little salt into it. Set it away in a cool place for three hours. Then squeeze and press it again; also washing it a second time in cold water. Make it up into pats, and keep it in a cool place.

The unskimmed morning's milk, of course, may also be used for this purpose, after it has stood twelve hours. The simmering over the fire adds greatly to the quantity of cream, by throwing all the oily part of the milk to the surface; but if allowed to boil, this oleaginous matter will again descend, and mix with the rest, so as not to be separated.

This is the usual method of making winter butter in the south of England; and it is very customary in the British provinces of America. Try it.

COCHINEAL COLOURING.—Take an ounce of cochineal, and pound it to a fine powder. Put it into an earthen or porcelain vessel, that is quite clean, and entirely free from grease. Add a small salt-spoonful of potash, or soda, and pour in a pint of clear, soft water. Set it over the fire; and, when it has come to a boil, add a quarter of an ounce of cream of tartar, with a quarter of an ounce of powdered alum; and let it boil ten minutes. Then, while it is boiling hot, stir in three ounces of powdered loaf-sugar. Bottle it, when cold, and keep it closely corked. You can then have it always at hand, as a fine red colouring for icings, blanc-mange, creams, jellies, and other sweetmeats.

COLOURING FOR CHEESE.—An ounce of real Spanish arnotta will colour fifty pounds of cheese. Tie up the arnotta, in a thin linen rag, and put it, over-night, into half a pint of warm water. In the morning, put the arnotta-water into the tub of milk, along with the infusion of rennet, indispensable in making cheese. For a deeper tint, dip the bag into the milk, and squeeze it as long as any colour runs out.

ALKANET COLOURING.—Alkanet is now much used for giving a beautiful red colour to confectionary. It is much cheaper than cochineal, and more easily prepared. It has no peculiar taste, and no unwholesome properties. You can purchase it at any druggist's, and at a trifling cost. It comes in small, dark-red chips. Before using it, pick it clean, and see that there is none of the dust or powder remaining about it. Tie up some of the alkanet chips, in a bit of very thin, clean muslin, like a small bag, and let it infuse with the mixture you wish to colour. It either may, or may not be boiled.

FINE RED OIL FOR LAMPS.—Infuse, for two or three hours, (or till the colour is well communicated,) a muslin bag of alkanet chips, in the clearest and best winter-strained lamp-oil. Then remove the bag of alkanet, (which may be used again for the same purpose,) and put the oil into clear glass lamps. It will be coloured of a beautiful red. According to the quantity of alkanet, or the length of time it remains steeping in the oil, you may have it of different tints, from light pink to deep crimson. Oil thus coloured is beautiful for illuminations; ball-rooms; or dispersed among the shrubbery, at a garden entertainment. The price of alkanet does not exceed six cents per ounce; and an ounce will do a great deal of colouring.

COLOURED WATER.—Slice a fresh red cabbage, and pour boiling water upon it. Cover it, and let it stand till cold. Then strain off the water, and put a portion of the infusion into three glasses. Pour into one glass a little alum-water; into the second, a little dissolved potash; and into the third, a few drops of muriatic acid. The liquid in the first glass will be turned of a purple colour, by the alum-water; that in the second will be changed to a green, by the solution of potash; and the third will assume a fine crimson, from the muriatic acid. This water is used by druggists, for the coloured jars in their shop-windows.

PERFUMERY, REMEDIES, ETC.

MACASSAR OIL.—This popular and pleasant unguent for the hair can (*as we know*) be prepared at home, so as to equal, in efficacy and appearance, any that is for sale in the shops; and at less than one-third the expense. Take half an ounce of chippings of alkanet root, which may be bought at a druggist's, for a few cents. Divide this quantity into two portions, and having cleared away any dust that may be about the alkanet, put each portion of the chips into a separate bit of new bob-binet, or very clear muslin. In tying it, use white thread, or fine white cotton cord; as a coloured string may communicate a dirty tinge to the oil. Put these little bags into a large glass tumbler, or a straight-sided white-ware jar, and pour on half a pint of the best fresh olive oil. Cover the vessel, and leave it undisturbed, for several days, or a week; taking care not to shake or stir it; and do not press or squeeze the bags. Have ready some small, flat-bottomed phials, or one large one, that will hold half a pint. Take out carefully the bags of alkanet, and lay them on a saucer. You will find that they have coloured the oil a bright, beautiful crimson. The bags will serve a second time for the same purpose. Put into the bottom of each phial a small quantity of any pleasant perfume; such as oil of orange-flowers; jessamine; rose; carnation; bergamot; oil of rhodium; oil of ambergris; or oil of cloves, mixed with a little tincture of musk. Then fill up each phial with the coloured oil, poured in through a small funnel; and, corking them tightly, tie a piece of white kid leather over the top.

To use macassar oil, (observing *never to shake the bottle,*) pour a little into a saucer, and, with your finger, rub it through the roots of the hair.

ANTIQUE OIL.—This is a fine oil for the hair. Mix together, in a clean glass vessel, half a pint of oil of sweet almonds, and half a pint of the best olive oil. Then scent it with any sort of perfume.

To give it the colour and odour of roses, infuse, in the mixed oil, a small, thin muslin bag of alkanet chips, and set it in a warm place, till coloured of a beautiful pink. Then remove the bag of alkanet, and perfume the oil with ottar of roses. Put it immediately into a bottle, and cork it well.

For a violet perfume, infuse, in the above quantity of the mixed oils, an ounce of the best orris powder. Let it stand, in a warm place, for a week; then pour the whole into a strainer, press out the liquid, and bottle it.

For an orange perfume, scent the oil with essence of neroli, or orange-flowers.

For jasmine, with extract of jasmine.

For bergamot, with essence of bergamot.

OIL OF CASSIA.—Put into a wide-mouthed glass vessel, an ounce of ground cassia. Heat three ounces of the best oil of cloves; and, while warm, pour it on the cassia. Cover it closely, and let it stand a week. Then press it through a sieve, placed over a bowl. Transfer it to small bottles, and cork them closely. It is a fine perfume. To weaken it, add a little *inodorous* alcohol, which, on inquiring for, you can obtain at the druggists'.

MILLEFLEURS PERFUME.—Mix together an ounce of oil of lavender; an ounce of essence of lemon; an ounce and a quarter of oil of ambergris; and half an ounce of oil of carraway. Add half a pint of alcohol, or spirits of wine, which should be of the inodorous sort. Shake all well together. Let it stand a week, closely corked, in a large bottle. You may then divide it in small bottles.

By mixing this perfume with equal quantities of olive oil, and oil of sweet almonds, instead of alcohol, you will have what is called millefleurs antique oil, which is used to improve the hair of young persons.

FRENCH HUNGARY WATER.—Take two large handfuls of the flowers and young leaves of rosemary; with a handful of lavender-blossoms; half a handful of thyme-blossoms; and half a handful of sage. Mix them well; put them into a large glass jar or bottle, and pour on a quart of inodorous spirits of wine. Then put in, as a colouring, some small bits of alkanet tied in a thin muslin bag. Cork the bottle closely, and shake it about for a while. Let it infuse during a month, exposed to the heat of the sun. Then strain it, and transfer it to smaller bottles.

FINE LAVENDER WATER.—Mix together, in a clean bottle, a pint of inodorous spirit of wine; an ounce of oil of lavender; a tea-spoonful of oil of bergamot; and a table-spoonful of oil of ambergris.

BERGAMOT WATER.—Melt a pound of the best broken-up loaf-sugar in a pint of water; add the yellow rind of six lemons or oranges, pared very thin. Set it over the fire, and boil and skim it till the scum ceases to rise. Then add the juice of the lemons or oranges; having squeezed it through a strainer into a bowl. After stirring in the juice, take the syrup from the fire, remove the pieces of rind, and stir in a tea-spoonful of genuine essence of bergamot. Bottle it, and it will be immediately fit for drinking. Pour some of it into a glass, and add a little ice-water. It will be found very fine.

TO PERFUME SOAP.—Take half a pound or more of the best white soap. Shave it down with a knife. Put the shavings into a clean white-ware jar; cover the top closely, and secure the cover by tying down a cloth over it. Set it into a large kettle or sauce-pan of hot water. The water must not come up near the top of the jar. It is well to place a trivet in the bottom of the kettle for the jar to stand on, so that a portion of the water may go under it. Place the kettle over the fire, or in a hot stove, and keep it boiling hard, till the soap in the jar within is thoroughly dissolved. It must become liquid all through, and have no lumps in it. Stir it well when done; and add, while warm, a sufficient portion of any nice perfume to scent it highly. For instance, oil of bitter almonds; extract of verbena; tincture of musk, or ambergris; oil of rhodium; oil of bergamot, lavender, jessamine, rose, cinnamon, cloves, &c. Having well stirred in the perfume, transfer the melted soap to gallicups, or little square tin-pans, and set it away to cool and harden. Afterwards, take out the cakes of soap, and wrap each cake closely in soft paper. Put them away where the air cannot reach them.

COLUMBIAN SOAP.—Blanch, in scalding water, two ounces of bitter almonds. Beat them in a mortar with an ounce of gum camphor, till completely mixed; putting in, with every almond, a morsel of the camphor. Then beat in an ounce and a quarter of tincture of benjamin, and remove the mixture to a bowl. Afterwards, having shaved down a pound of the best white soap, beat that also in the mortar; mixing with it, gradually, as you proceed, the above ingredients, till the whole is thoroughly incorporated. Divide it into equal portions, and roll it with your hands into the form of balls. This soap will be found very fine.

If you wish to have it in cakes, after you have shaved down the white soap, put it into a clean jar, cover it, and set the jar into a pot of boiling water, placed over the fire. When the soap is melted, remove it from the fire; and when it begins to cool, (but is still liquid,) stir in the other ingredients that have been mixed together as above. Then mould it in little square tin pans, and set it to cool. When quite cold, take it out of the pan, and wrap each cake in paper.

GOOD TOOTH-POWDER.—Procure, at a druggist's, half an ounce of powdered orris-root, half an ounce of prepared chalk finely pulverized, and two or three small lumps of dutch pink. Let them all be mixed in a mortar, and pounded together. The dutch pink is to impart a pale reddish colour. Keep it in a close box.

ANOTHER TOOTH-POWDER.—Mix together, in a mortar, half an ounce of red Peruvian bark, finely powdered; a quarter of an ounce of powdered myrrh; and a quarter of an ounce of prepared chalk.

PARCHMENT GLUE.—Take half a pound of clean parchment cuttings, and boil it in three quarts of soft water till reduced to one pint. Then strain it from the dregs, and boil it again, till of the consistence of strong glue.

LIP GLUE.—Take of isinglass and parchment glue, of each one ounce; sugar-candy and gum tragacanth, each two drachms. Boil them in an ounce of water, till the mixture is of the consistence of thick glue. When cold, roll it between your hands, till you get it into the form of small sticks, like sealing-wax.

By wetting it with your tongue, and rubbing the moistened end of the stick on the edges of the paper that you wish to unite, it will, when dry, form a firm cement. A stick of lip-glue is very convenient to take with you when travelling, in case you should have occasion for some sort of paste.

PERPETUAL PASTE.—Buy, at a druggist's, an ounce of the best gum tragacanth, (sometimes called gum dragon,) and six cents' worth of powdered corrosive sublimate. Pick the gum tragacanth clean, and put it into a wide-mouthed glass or white-ware vessel, that will hold a quart. Add as much corrosive sublimate as will lie on a five-cent piece. Pour on a pint and a half of clear cold, soft water. Cover the vessel, and let it stand till next day. The gum tragacanth will then be much swelled, and nearly to the top of the vessel. Stir it down to the bottom with a stick, as the corrosive sublimate will blacken a metal spoon. Stir it several times during that day; but afterwards, do not stir it at all; leaving it to form a smooth white mass, like a very thick jelly. Then cover it closely, and set it away for use; taking care to keep it out of the way of children, as the corrosive sublimate will render it poisonous if swallowed.

This paste will keep to an indefinite period, if the air is carefully excluded from it, and if it is not transferred to a vessel made of any sort of metal. It forms a strong, colourless, and firm cement for paper, &c.; and when once made, may be kept always at hand; and is most convenient for all sorts of pasting; particularly little things, for which it would seem scarcely worth while to take the trouble of boiling flour-paste. It only spoils when kept in metal, or from long exposure to the air.

We can certify to its superiority over all other paste, having the experience of using it continually. The advantage of its being always ready is an important recommendation. Try it, and you will be induced to keep it constantly in the house.

GUM-ARABIC PASTE.—Take a common-sized tea-cup of cold, soft water, and dissolve in it a large tea-spoonful of the best and cleanest powdered gum-arabic. When the gum is entirely melted, stir in, by degrees, a table-spoonful of fine wheat flour; carefully pressing out all the lumps, and making it as smooth as possible. Keep it closely covered, and in a cool place. If, after a few days, it should appear spotted or mouldy on the top, remove the surface, and the paste beneath will still be fit for use. This is a good cement for artificial flowers, and for ornamental pasteboard work.

CEMENT FOR JARS AND BOTTLES.—According to the quantity of cement required, take one-third bees-wax and two-thirds rosin. Pound the rosin to a fine powder, and then put it, with the bees-wax, into any sauce-pan or skillet suited to the purpose, and set them over the fire to melt. When it becomes thoroughly liquid, take it off the fire, and stir in some finely-powdered brickdust, till the mixture becomes as thick as melted sealing-wax. Then plaster it, warm, round the covers of your preserve or pickle-jars. If you use it for bottles, first cork them tightly, and then dip their tops into the cement. It will dry in a few minutes. This cement is very strong and very cheap, and especially useful for articles that are to be carried to sea.

COVERING FOR CORKS.—The odour of a cologne bottle, or of any other scented liquid, may be prevented from escaping by keeping the cork and the neck of the bottle covered with the finger-end or thumb of an old kid glove, cut off, for the purpose, at a suitable length and breadth, and stretched or drawn down closely and tightly. This is more convenient than the usual kid-leather covers, that must be untied and tied again whenever the bottles are opened.

MILK OF ROSES.—Mix together a pint of rose-water, and an ounce of oil of sweet almonds. Then add ten drops of oil of tartar. Bottle it, and shake it well. It is good for the hands.

EXCELLENT POMATUM.—Melt some beef's marrow on a slow fire, being careful not to let it burn; then strain it several times over, that it may be well purified. When partially cool, beat in some *castor* oil, a table-spoonful at a time. The proportion should be two-thirds of melted marrow to one-third of oil. Perfume it by stirring in, as you proceed, any sort of essential oil that is not too pungent. You may give it a fine red colouring by putting in, after the marrow has melted, some chips of alkanet tied in a very thin muslin bag, letting it remain till the tint is thoroughly infused. Keep it in covered gallicups. A little rubbed every day, or twice or three times a week, with the finger among the roots of the hair, will greatly improve its growth and softness.

AN EXCELLENT WAY OF IMPROVING THE HAIR.—Once in three days take some rich *unskimmed* milk that has been made sour by standing in the sun. Stir it up, so as to mix all through it the cream that has collected on the surface. Wash the hair with this, rubbing it well into the roots. Let it remain on the hair about a quarter of an hour or more. Then wash it off, with a lather of white soap and warm water; rinsing the hair, afterwards, with fresh water, either warm or cold, according to the season. This is an Asiatic process; and if continued every third day, seldom fails to render the hair of young people thick, soft, and glossy.

TO HAVE GOOD HAIR.—The women of Germany have remarkably fine and luxuriant hair. The following is their most usual method of managing it. About once a fortnight, boil for half an hour or more, a large handful of bran in a quart of soft water. Strain it into a basin, and let it cool till it is merely tepid or milk-warm. Rub into it a little white soap; then dip in the corner of a soft linen towel, and wash your head with it, thoroughly; dividing or parting aside the hair all over; so as to reach the roots. Next take the yolk of an egg, (slightly beaten in a saucer,) and with your fingers rub it well into the roots of the hair. Let it rest a few minutes; and then wash it off entirely, with a cloth dipped in pure water; and rinse your hair well, till all the yolk of egg has disappeared from it. Afterwards, wipe and rub it dry with a towel, and comb the hair up from your head, parting it with your fingers. In winter it is best to do all this near the fire.

Have ready some soft pomatum, made of fresh beef-marrow, boiled with a little almond oil or olive oil, stirring it all the time till it is well amalgamated, and as thick as an ointment. When you take it from the fire (and not before) stir into it a little mild perfume; such as rose-water, orange-flower water, extract of roses, oil of carnations, or essence of violets. Put it into gallicups that have lids, and keep it for use; always well-covered. Take a very small quantity of this pomatum, and rub it among your hair on the skin of your head, after it has been washed as above.

At any time you may make your hair curl more easily by rubbing into it some beaten yolk of egg, (washed off, afterwards with clear water,) and then putting on a little pomatum before you pin up your curls. It is well always to go through this process when you resume curls after having worn your hair plain.

All hair should be combed every morning with a fine-toothed comb, to remove the dust which insensibly gets into it during the preceding day, and to keep the skin of the head always clean.

To prevent your bonnet being injured by any oiliness about your hair, baste a piece of white or yellow oiled silk inside of that part of the bonnet where the crown unites with the brim, carrying the silk some distance up into the crown, and some distance down into the brim or front.

Clean your head-brushes by washing them thoroughly with a bit of soft sponge tied on the end of a stick, and dipped into a warm solution of pearlash, prepared by dissolving a large table-spoonful of pearlash in a pint of boiling water. When the bristles have thus been made quite clean, rinse the brushes in hot water; letting them remain in it till it becomes cool, or cold. Afterwards, drain the brushes; wipe them with a clean cloth; and set them upright before the fire to dry.

The most convenient way of cleaning combs is with a strong silk thread, made fast to the handle of a bureau-drawer—in front of which, seat yourself with a towel spread over your lap to catch whatever impurities may fall from the comb. Holding the comb in your left hand, and the thread in your right, pass the thread hard between each of the comb-teeth. Afterwards wash the comb in soap-suds, rinse it in cold water, and dry it with a clean cloth.

SALT OF LEMON OR STAIN POWDER.—This powder, which is erroneously called salt of lemon, is in reality composed simply of equal portions of finely pulverized salt of sorrel and cream of tartar, (for instance an ounce of each,) mixed together in a mortar, and afterwards put into small covered boxes, or gallipots. It will immediately remove ink spots, fruit stains, &c., from the hands or from any articles of *white* linen or muslin; first wetting the place with water (warm water is best) and then with your finger rubbing on the powder, till the stain disappears. Immediately afterwards wash it off with soap-suds. If applied to a *coloured* article that has been inked or stained, the powder in removing the stain will take out the colour. But the colour (particularly if black) may in most cases be restored by rubbing the place with hartshorn; which if very strong should be somewhat diluted with water, or it will leave a tinge of its own. If the hartshorn fails to restore the colour, it is on account of some peculiarity in the dye. It is always worth trying. We have seen a large splash of ink taken out of a carpet by first wetting it with warm water and rubbing on some of the above-mentioned stain powder. The colours were all restored to their former brightness by afterwards applying hartshorn. Next day, the place where the ink had been spilled on the carpet could not be distinguished. We have also known the same experiment tried with perfect success on a mousseline de laine dress on which an ink-stand had been overset.

Ink spots can be removed from *white* clothes by the simple application of a bit of clean tallow picked from the bottom of a mould candle, rubbed on the ink spot, and left sticking there when the article goes into the wash-tub. It will come out of the wash freed from the ink stain.

This stain powder should be kept out of the way of children, as if swallowed it is poisonous.

Fresh lemon-juice mixed with a little salt is excellent for removing stains of ink, iron mould, &c.

TO MAKE GREASE BALLS.—Shave down half a pound of white soap, and mix it with three ounces of fuller's earth, powdered. Then mix together three ounces of ox-gall, and two ounces of spirits of turpentine. With this, moisten the soap and fuller's earth, till you have a stiff paste. Mix it thoroughly, and beat it well. Make it into balls with your hands, and place the balls where they will dry slowly.

To use it, scrape down a sufficiency, and spread it on the grease spot. Let it rest awhile; then brush it off, and scrape and apply some more. A few applications will generally remove the grease.

TO EXTRACT GREASE WITH CAMPHINE OIL.—Grease of the very worst sort (for instance whale oil) may be extracted successfully even from silks, ribbons, and other delicate articles, by means of camphine oil, which can always be procured at the lamp-stores. As this oil is best when fresh, get but a small quantity at a time. Pour some camphine into a clean cup, and dip lightly into it a bit of clean, soft, white rag. With this rub the grease spot. Then take a fresh rag dipped in the camphine, and continue rubbing till the grease is extracted, which will be very soon. You will find the colour of the article uninjured. To remove the turpentine odour of the camphine, rub the place with cologne water or strong spirits of wine, and expose it to the open air. If any of the camphine-scent remains, repeat the cologne. We have known lamp oil removed from white satin by this process.

FINE YELLOW COLOURING FOR WALLS.—Procure from a paint-shop one pound of chrome yellow, and three pounds of whiting. Mix and grind them thoroughly together; and then add a quart of boiling water, and stir it well in. Next boil a quarter of a pound of glue in a quart of water, and when completely dissolved, add it immediately to the mixture, and stir the whole very hard. Thin it with more water till you get it of the desired consistence. It will be a beautiful yellow, approaching to lemon colour.

BLUE WASH FOR WALLS.—Get a pound of blue vitriol from a drug or paint store, and have it powdered very finely in a mortar. Provide also two quarts of lime. Take six cents' worth of glue, and boil it in a quart of soft water till thoroughly dissolved. Put the powdered vitriol into a wooden bucket, and when the glue-water is cold, pour it on the vitriol, and mix and stir it well. When the vitriol is dissolved in the glue-water, stir in by degrees the two quarts of lime. Then try the tint of the mixture by dipping a piece of white paper into it; and when it dries, you can judge if it is the colour you want. It should be a clear light beautiful blue. If you think it too dark, add some more lime. If too pale, stir in a little more of the powdered vitriol. It is well to provide an extra quantity of each of the articles, in case a little more of one or the other should be required on trial of the colour.

TO CLEAN WHITEWASH BRUSHES.—Wash off, with cold water, the lime from the bristles of the brush; and scrub well with a hard scrubbing-brush the part where the bristles are fixed into the wood. This should be done at once, as soon as the whitewashing for that day is finished. It is far better than to let them soak all night.

AN EASY WAY TO MAKE INK.—Take two ounces of the best and most perfect nut-galls, and bruise them to pieces with a hammer. Put them into a large mug, with half an ounce of copperas, and a quarter of an ounce of powdered gum-arabic. Pour on a pint of boiling water. Cover the vessel, and let it stand in a warm place for a week; frequently stirring the contents with a stick. Afterwards leave it one day undisturbed; and then pour off the liquid through a funnel into a bottle; in the bottom of which you have put half a dozen cloves or a spoonful of brandy, either of which will prevent the ink from moulding. Keep the bottle closely corked.

TO USE DURABLE INK.—It is an error (rectified by experience) to wash as soon as possible articles that have been marked with durable ink. On the contrary, they should be kept *without washing* for at least a week. If washed too soon, the soap and water will disturb the ink before it is thoroughly dried in, causing the letters to spread and look rough. Also, it will not be so good a black. Every time, before using it, set the little bottle with the marking liquid in the sun, or before a bright fire; and then stir it up from the bottom. This will increase its blackness. After putting the wash or gum-liquid on the place to be marked, dry it by the fire or in the hot sun, and then iron it smoothly. Do not write the name till next day, and then, as above mentioned, set the marking ink in the sun, and stir it up from the bottom. When the name is written, dry it as soon as possible, and then iron it again.

Durable ink may be extracted by wetting the writing with hot water, and then rubbing on a little sal-ammonia.

After making durable ink, set the marking liquid or lunar caustic preparation for three or four days in the hot sun; otherwise it will not become black.

SUMACH INK.—The milk or gum that exudes from the sumach is a good substitute for durable ink. Break off the stalks that support the leaves. Squeeze them into a cup, and write with the liquid. Expose it to the sun and it will become a fine black.

VERY FINE INK.—Into a large jar or pitcher put half a pound of the best Aleppo galls, broken up with a hammer or flat-iron; but not pounded. Pour on two quarts of soft water, nearly of boiling heat. Cover the vessel; and let it stand on a warm hearth or in the hot sun for a fortnight; stirring it to the bottom twice a day, with a stick. At the end of the fortnight, add two ounces of green copperas; two ounces of logwood chips; two ounces of gum-arabic; half an ounce of alum; and half an ounce of sugar-candy. Let the whole remain in a moderate heat a fortnight longer; stirring it twice a day. Keep the mouth of the vessel covered with paper only, tied down over it. On the last day, do not stir it, but pour the ink through a strainer into another vessel, and then with a funnel transfer it to bottles. Pour a small tea-spoonful or more of brandy into the top of each bottle, if small. To a pint bottle there should be a table-spoonful of brandy. This will preserve the ink from moulding. Cork the bottles well, and seal the corks. Keep them in a place of temperate heat.

In buying Aleppo galls get those that are dark coloured, heavy, and free from holes.

GOOD INK.—Bruise two ounces of Aleppo galls; put them into a pitcher with half an ounce of copperas, and a quarter of an ounce of gum arabic. Pour on a pint of soft water at boiling heat. Cover it, and let it stand a week; stirring it several times a day, except on the last day. Then pour it through a funnel into a bottle that has half a dozen cloves in it. In pouring, see that you do not disturb the sediment at the bottom of the pitcher. Cork the bottle tightly.

TO SOFTEN SPONGES.—A sponge, when first purchased, is frequently hard, stiff, and gritty. To soften it, and dislodge the particles of sea-sand from its crevices, (having first soaked and squeezed it through several cold waters,) put the sponge into a clean tin sauce-pan, set it over the fire, and boil it a quarter of an hour. Then take it out, put it into a bowl of cold water, and squeeze it well. Wash out the sauce-pan, and return the sponge to it, filling up with clean cold water, and boil it another quarter of an hour. Repeat the process, giving it three boils in fresh water; or more than three if you find it still gritty. Take care not to boil it too long, or it will become tender, and drop to pieces. You may bleach it by adding to the water a few drops of oil of vitriol.

The Mediterranean sponges are the best.

After using a sponge, always wash it immediately in clean water, squeeze it out, and put it to dry.

TO REMOVE THE ODOUR FROM A VIAL.—The odour of its last contents may be removed from a vial by filling it with cold water, and letting it stand in any airy place uncorked for three days; changing the water every day.

TO LOOSEN A GLASS STOPPER.—The manner in which apothecaries loosen glass stoppers when there is difficulty in getting them out, is to press the thumb of the right hand very hard against the lower part of the stopper, and then give the stopper a twist the other way, with the thumb and fore-finger of the left hand; keeping the bottle stiff in a steady position.

TO GET A BROKEN CORK OUT OF A BOTTLE.—If in drawing a cork it breaks, and the lower part falls down into the liquid, tie a long loop in a bit of twine, or small cord, and put it in; holding the bottle so as to bring the piece of cork near to the lower part of the neck. Catch it in the loop, so as to hold it stationary. You can then easily extract it with a cork-screw.

TO PURIFY THE ATMOSPHERE OF A ROOM.—Mix, in a cup, some brown sugar, with sufficient water to make it a thick liquid. Put a hot coal on a shovel; pour on the coal a tea-spoonful, or more, of the sugar, and carry it carefully about the room. The smoke will entirely remove any disagreeable odour. If the sugar is thrown dry upon the hot coal, it will blaze up, and burn out immediately, without effecting the desired purpose; but if mixed with a little water, it will not blaze at all, but the vapour arising from it will continue to smoke, till the unpleasant smell is entirely dispelled.

A few sprigs of lavender, laid on hot coals, and carried round the room, on a shovel, is a good remedy for a disagreeable odour.

Chloride of lime, sprinkled on dry, will, *unfailingly*, dispel the effluvia of any ill-scented substance. It is very cheap. A jar of it should be kept in every house; as, for this purpose, there is nothing more effectual.

TO CLEAN JARS.—There is frequently much trouble in cleaning the inside of jars that have contained sweet-meats, pickles, mince-meat, &c., so as entirely to remove all the odour of their former contents, before they can be used for another purpose. If the jars are of stone, fill them up with scalding water, and let them stand awhile. If of white-ware, or glass, the water must be merely warm; for if hot, it will crack them. Then stir in a large tea-spoonful, or more, of pearlash. Whatever of the former contents has remained sticking about, and adhering to the sides and bottom, will immediately disengage itself, and float loose through the water. Afterwards empty the jar, and if any odour lingers about its inside, fill it again with warm water and a spoonful of pearlash, and let it stand, undisturbed, a few hours, or till next day. Then empty it again, and rinse it with cold water. Wash phials in the same manner. Also, the inside of tea, coffee, and chocolate-pots. If you cannot, conveniently, obtain pearlash, the same purpose may be answered, nearly as well, by filling the vessels with strong lye, poured off clear from the wood-ashes. For kegs, buckets, crocks, or other large vessels, lye may always be used.

TO CLEAN LOOKING-GLASSES.—Take a newspaper, or a part of one, according to the size of the glass. Fold it small, and dip it into a basin of clean, cold water. When thoroughly wetted, squeeze it out in your hand, as you would a sponge; and then rub it, hard, all over the face of the glass; taking care that it is not so wet that the moisture will stream down the glass. Also, if any drops get beneath the frame, and behind the glass, they will remain there, in bubbles, and cannot be dislodged, without removing the board at the back. There is no danger of any such accidents, if the newspaper is merely moistened, or damped throughout; without being so wet as to drip. After the glass has been well rubbed, with the damp paper, let it rest a minute. Then go over it with a fresh newspaper, (folded small in your hand,) till it looks clear and bright; which it will, almost immediately. Finish with a fresh piece of newspaper, thoroughly dry.

This method, simple as it is, will be found, on trial, the best and most expeditious way of cleaning mirrors, or any plate-glass; giving a clearness and polish, that cannot be so soon produced by any other process. The inside of window-panes may be cleaned in this manner; the windows having been first washed on the *outside.* Also, the glasses of spectacles, &c. The glass globe of a lamp may thus be cleaned with newspapers.

The efficacy is attributed to the materials used in making the printing-ink.

TO REMOVE DARK STAINS FROM SILVER.—There are many substances that communicate a dark, inky stain to silver spoons, forks, &c.; a stain sometimes so inveterate as to resist all common applications. A certain remedy is, to pour a little sulphuric acid into a saucer; wet with it a soft linen rag; and rub it on the blackened silver, till the stain disappears. Then brighten the article with whiting, finely powdered and sifted, and moistened with spirits of wine. When the whiting has dried on, and rested a quarter of an hour, or more, wipe it off with a silk handkerchief, and polish with a soft buckskin.

TO CLEAN RINGS, BROOCHES, AND OTHER JEWELRY.—Put a little hartshorn into a saucer; dip into it a clean, soft rag, from an old cambric handkerchief. With the rag, go carefully over the jewelry, on both sides. Then dry and polish, with another bit of soft rag; and, finally, with a soft piece of old silk. Precious stones, mosaics and cameos may be cleaned in this manner. To brighten pearls, tear off a small bit of pin-paper, (such as rows of pins are stuck in,) roll it up, and, with the end of the roll, rub each pearl, separately; renewing the paper frequently.

The application of hartshorn, rubbed on with the finger, will generally remove the stain-spots that are sometimes found on new silk, and on new kid gloves. There are few stains, indeed, that may not be obliterated by hartshorn. If too strong, dilute it with a little water. Pour out, into your saucer, but very little hartshorn, at a time, as it evaporates almost immediately.

Reddish stains, on black silk, or worsted, can, almost always, be removed by hartshorn; and the original black colour will immediately re-appear.

TO KEEP SILVER ALWAYS BRIGHT.—Silver, in constant use, should be washed every day in a pan of suds made of good white soap and warm water; drying it with old soft linen cloths. Twice a week, (after this washing,) give it a thorough brightening with finely-powdered whiting, mixed to a thin paste with alcohol; rubbing longer and harder where there are stains. Then wipe this off, and polish with clean soft old linen. Silver is cleaned in this manner at the best hotels.

PLATE POWDER.—Buy, at a druggist's, an ounce of levigated oxide of iron, and four ounces of prepared chalk, finely pulverized. Mix them well together, and put the mixture into small boxes. Rub it, dry, on the silver, and then polish with a clean buckskin; finishing with an old silk handkerchief. This is the composition usually sold as plate powder. Its colour is a reddish brown.

POWDER FOR CLEANING GOLD LACE.—Of burnt roche-alum, powdered as fine as possible, take two ounces and a half. Mix, thoroughly, with it, half an ounce of finely-powdered chalk. Take a small, clean, dry brush; dip it into the mixture, and rub it, carefully, on gold lace, or gold embroidery, that has become tarnished. Finish with a clean piece of new canton flannel. Keep a box or bottle of this mixture, that it may be ready to use on occasion. It is equally good for silver lace, and for jewelry.

TO KEEP BRITANNIA-METAL BRIGHT.—Dip a clean woollen cloth into the best and cleanest lamp oil, and rub it, hard, all over the outside of your Britannia-ware. Then wash it well in strong soap-suds, and afterwards polish with finely-powdered whiting and a buckskin. The inside of Britannia vessels should be washed with warm water, in which a little pearlash has been dissolved. They should then be set, open, to dry in the sun and air. If not kept very nice, this metal will communicate a disagreeable taste. There is so much copper in its composition, that tea-pots or coffee-pots of china, or white-ware, are far preferable to Britannia-metal.

TO CLEAN SILVER EXPEDITIOUSLY.—Put some powdered magnesia into a saucer. Have ready a few bits of new canton flannel. It is well, in cutting out canton flannel, to save the small shavings, or clippings, for this purpose. Dip a bit of the flannel into the magnesia, and with it rub the silver, very hard. It will brighten, immediately, if there are no black stains on it. Finish, by polishing with a clean piece of the flannel, without magnesia.

Dark stains on silver are best removed by rubbing them with flannel, dipped in sulphuric acid. This should be done before any brightening substance is applied.

PASTE FOR CLEANING KNIVES.—Make a mixture, one part emery, and three parts crocus martis, in very fine powder. Mix them to a thick paste, with a little lard or sweet oil. Have your knife-board covered with a thick buff-leather. Spread this paste on your leather, to about the thickness of a quarter-dollar. Rub your knives in it, and it will make them much sharper and brighter, and will wear them out less, than the common method of cleaning with brick-dust, on a bare board.

A GOOD WAY OF CLEANING SILVER.—Mix in a cup or saucer a paste of powdered magnesia, and the best and clearest lamp oil, (whale oil,) and cover with this paste the silver that is to be cleaned. Let it rest a quarter of an hour or more; applying the paste to all the articles you intend cleaning before you begin to remove it from any one of them. Afterwards wipe it off, entirely, with a soft linen rag, and then proceed to polish the plate with a soft buckskin, and some dry magnesia. Finish with a silk handkerchief. The longer you rub, the brighter will be the silver, but you must change frequently to clean parts of the buckskin. If the silver has much chasing or ornamental frost-work, it may be necessary to take a small soft brush to clean out all the hollows and crevices. But, if possible, avoid using a brush, as it wears the silver thin.

Silver may be kept continually bright with very little trouble, by cleaning it three times a-week, or every day, with dry magnesia rubbed on with a bit of clean shaggy canton flannel that has never been washed. Scraps and clippings of woollen flannel should never be used for cleaning plate, as its roughness may scratch it.

Dark stains on silver or gold may be immediately removed (however bad) by the application of a little sulphuric acid poured into a saucer and rubbed on with a soft rag. Then polish with magnesia and canton flannel.

The colour of silver will always be injured by keeping it in a room where there is a coal fire.

The cases of gold or silver watches may be cleaned, as above, with powdered magnesia and canton flannel.

TO TAKE WHITE MARKS FROM MAHOGANY.—If a white mark has been left on a mahogany table by carelessly setting down on it a vessel of hot water, rub the place hard with a rag dipped in lamp oil; and afterwards pour on a little cologne water, or a little alcohol, and rub it dry with a clean rag.

The dish-marks left on a dining-table can of course be taken off in the same manner.

If brandy is spilt on mahogany, and leaves a whitish mark, that mark can be removed by rubbing it hard with a rag dipped in more brandy. Try it.

TO TAKE SPERMACETI OUT OF A HEARTH OR FLOOR.—First scrape off the drops of spermaceti with a knife. Then take a live coal in the tongs and hold it carefully and closely over the place. Afterwards wipe it with a rag, and then wash it with hot soap-suds.

TO REMOVE GREASE FROM A STOVE HEARTH.—When oil or any other grease has been dropped on a stove hearth, immediately cover the place with *very hot* ashes. Afterwhile, clear away the ashes; and if the grease has not quite disappeared, repeat the process.

TO MAKE SHOES OR BOOTS WATER-PROOF.—Melt together, in a pipkin, equal quantities of bees-wax and mutton suet. While liquid, rub it over the leather, including the soles.

TO EXTRACT OIL FROM THE FLOOR OR HEARTH.—Mix together two heaped table-spoonfuls on powdered fuller's earth; one large table-spoonful of potash or pearlash; and one large table-spoonful of soft soap. Add sufficient boiling water to make it into a thick paste. Spread it hot on the oil spot, with a broad flat stick; let it remain an hour or two. Then brush it off, and renew the application. When the grease has disappeared, scrub the place with soap and water.

This mixture is equally good for boards, stone, or marble.

TO TAKE OFF WALL PAPER.—To clear a wall from paper previous to painting or white-washing it, wet the old paper thoroughly with a long-handled brush dipped in a bucket of water, (warm water is best.) Let it rest till the water has penetrated it, and the paper blisters and loosens, so that you can peel it off with your hands. Do not wet too much at a time. If any small bits are found still adhering, wet them afresh, and scrape them off with a strong knife.

TO REMOVE PAINT FROM THE WALL OF A ROOM.—If you intend papering a painted wall, you must first get off the paint, otherwise the paper will not stick. To do this mix in a bucket with warm water a sufficient quantity of pearlash, or potash, so as to make a strong solution. Dip a brush into this, and with it scour off all the paint, finishing with cold water and a flannel.

DUSTING FURNITURE.—If a hand-brush is employed for dusting furniture it should always be followed by a cloth; and the cloth should be so used as to *wipe up* the dust; and not merely flirted about it, so as to drive the particles from one place to another. The cloth in wiping up the dust should hold it *in*, and then be shaken frequently out of a back window. A brush or a bunch of feathers will keep the dust floating about the room; dislodging but not absorbing it; and only removing it from one article to settle it on another. Therefore a cloth is indispensable in *really* freeing the furniture from dust. A yard of sixpenny calico, or of strong unbleached muslin, will make two small dusters or one large one. They should be hemmed or whipped over the edges, that servants may have no pretext for regarding them as mere rags, to be thrown away or torn up when dirty. It is difficult to dust well with a ragged dusting-cloth.

TO TAKE FRUIT STAINS FROM WHITE DOILIES OR NAPKINS.—The use of coloured doilies for wiping the fingers after eating fruit being nearly exploded, and small white napkins being now substituted for that purpose, let them, as soon as taken from table, be thrown *immediately* into a large vessel of clean water. If hot water is at hand it will be better than cold. Leave them to soak during the remainder of the day. Then take them out, put them where they will dry; and you will generally find that the fruit stains have disappeared. If any remain, wet the stains with hot water, and then rub on some lemon-juice, or salt-of-lemon stain-powder; washing it off as soon as it has removed the stain. Cream of tartar will sometimes produce this effect. It is scarcely possible to get a stain out of any sort of linen after it has been previously washed with soap.

TO CLEAR CLOSETS FROM COCKROACHES.—Remove every article from the closet, scrub the shelves with lye, and then whitewash the closet walls. Next take a sufficiency of *black* wadding, and soak it in spirits of turpentine or camphor, or a mixture of both. Then with a fork or the point of a knife, stuff it close and hard into every crevice, crack, and hole, however small. United with the copperas dye of the black wadding, the camphor and turpentine will destroy or expel the cockroaches, so that for a long time you will see no more of them. If they return, repeat the remedy; which of course will be as effective if applied to the crevices about the kitchen walls or floors. Let the closet remain empty for several days. Then place on each shelf a small plate with dry chloride of lime to dissipate the smell of the turpentine.

The preparation of phosphorus called Levy's Exterminator, and which is to be had at the druggists', is very destructive to cockroaches, rats, and mice. Cover with it a slice of bread and butter, then sprinkle on some brown sugar, and lay it in places where these vermin have been seen.

A mixture in the proportion of three table-spoonfuls of meal, and one table-spoonful of red lead, wetted to a thin paste with West India molasses, if laid on old plates, and set about their haunts, is very efficacious in expelling cockroaches.

These remedies are all good; and if used perseveringly and always resumed, as soon as the cockroaches begin to appear again, there will be but little trouble with these detestable insects. Nothing has yet been found that can banish them from a house so effectually as to preclude all danger of their ever returning. But much comfort is gained by even a temporary relief from them.

If an insect gets into the ear it may be destroyed by pouring in a little sweet oil. They have been sometimes enticed out, by applying to the ear a piece of ripe peach or apple.

SMALL COCKROACHES.—Many houses are much infested with small brown cockroaches, which are especially troublesome and disgusting from their disposition to get into bureaus, wardrobes, trunks, and even band-boxes. They will soon depart, if bunches of pennyroyal (as fresh as you can get it, and frequently renewed) are laid in all the places where they have appeared, or are likely to come. Pennyroyal is to be generally bought in market at the very trifling cost of one cent a bunch. At any season it can be had at the druggists', and at the garden stores. Rags dipped in oil of pennyroyal, and laid about their haunts, will frequently expel these cockroaches. But every one that is seen should be immediately killed, and not merely brushed off, to run to another place. There is little difficulty in keeping a house free from cockroaches and all other vermin, if the remedies are applied in time, and with perseverance.

The very bad practice of using old bricks for cellar-walls and back-buildings, is the chief cause of new houses becoming immediately infested with cockroaches, &c. They have in this way been introduced at once into some very elegant mansions in Philadelphia, where old bricks have been used for the cellars; these bricks having originally belonged to old almshouses, long since pulled down. To buy such bricks, however cheap, is a miserable economy.

TO DESTROY CRICKETS.—Mix some powdered arsenic with roasted apple, and put it into the cracks and holes whence the crickets issue. It will effectually destroy them. And cockroaches also.

TO EXPEL FLEAS.—Get some pennyroyal. Having stripped the leaves from the stalks, stuff them into little bags, made of muslin or thin calico, and sewed up all round. Lay these bags among the bedding, and the pennyroyal will send away the fleas. If more convenient, sprinkle the bedding with oil or essence of pennyroyal. When travelling, it is well to take with you some little bags of pennyroyal, in case you should have to sleep in a bed infested with fleas.

Camphor is also a good remedy against fleas.

Pennyroyal will generally expel the small brown cockroaches, if bunches of it are kept constantly in the closets, wardrobes, bureaus, &c. It is likewise an excellent remedy against wood-ticks; keeping some of it about you, if obliged to go into places where these intolerable insects abound. When the wood-ticks fasten on the skin, brush them with a bunch of pennyroyal, and they will fall off immediately.

TO DESTROY BED-BUGS.—Among the numerous ways of destroying bugs, there is none better than to wash carefully, with a solution of corrosive sublimate in spirits of wine, all the cracks and crevices of the bedstead, at least once a week; taking care to throw out directly whatever may remain in the bowl or saucer, which should at once be washed clean in hot water. Corrosive sublimate is a most deadly poison, if even a small quantity is swallowed. One of the best remedies for it, is to take *immediately* a large quantity of sweet oil.

Mercurial ointment, rubbed once a week into all the joints and crevices of the bedstead, is an excellent destroyer of bugs. It can best be rubbed in with the finger. Leave it on the bedstead without wiping off; and do not put on the bedding till evening.

TO DESTROY FLIES.—Get, at a druggist's, some Egyptian or Fly-killing paper. Lay a piece of it on an old plate, and keep it moist by wetting it frequently with water. It will soon be found covered with dead flies. Shake them off, and wet the paper again.

Or mix together a table-spoonful of powdered black pepper, the same quantity of brown sugar, and as much milk as will make it into a thin paste. Set it about on saucers. It will attract the flies, and they will die on eating it.

TO DESTROY GARDEN ANTS.—Mix together half a pound of flour of brimstone, and four ounces of potash. Put them into an iron pot or pan, and stir it over the fire till they are dissolved, and well incorporated. Then pound them to a powder. Put the powder into a glass jar, with a cover, and keep it for use. Infuse some of this powder in a cup of water, and sprinkle with it the places that are infested by ants. They will soon disappear.

TO EXPEL SMALL ANTS.—Mix a tea-spoonful of tartar emetic in two table-spoonfuls of molasses. Stir this into a small saucer of water, and set it where you have seen the ants. Let it remain all night; and in the morning you will find a great number of ants lying dead on the surface of the water, and the others will have been frightened away. Skim off the dead ants, and set the saucer in any other place where these insects have appeared. This we know, by experience, to be an excellent remedy for the little ants with which so many houses are infested, and which swarm over sweet things.

MICE.—An excellent preparation for expelling mice and rats is Levy's Exterminator, spread upon bread or cheese, and laid about the places they frequent. It is a preparation of phosphorus; and after one mouse has eaten it and (of course) died, the others will disappear. It is to be had of most druggists; and will also destroy cockroaches, by spreading it on bits of cake or something similar, and laying it at night on the kitchen hearth, and in the closets. We highly recommend it.

If you propose to destroy a mouse by arsenic spread on bread and butter, sprinkle on the arsenic a drop or two of oil of rhodium, and the mouse will unfailingly be attracted to the poison. Place beside it a saucer of water, and as soon as he has eaten of the poisoned bread and butter, he will drink, and then die on the spot.

Oil of aniseed, spread on the bait, will attract them into a trap.

TO DESTROY CATERPILLARS.—Mix together twelve ounces of powdered quick-lime, two ounces of snuff, two ounces of fine salt, and two ounces of powdered sulphur. Strew this mixture over the caterpillars, or dissolve it in five gallons of water; keep it in a convenient vessel, and sprinkle with it places where they abound.

Any garden insects may be destroyed in this manner.

TO DESTROY WORMS IN GARDEN WALKS.—Pour into the worm-holes a strong lye, made of wood-ashes, lime, and water. Or, if more convenient, use, for this purpose, strong salt and water.

TO DESTROY THE BEE-MILLER.—This insect, whose night-visits are so destructive to bees, may be destroyed by mixing a large wine-glass of vinegar with a pint of water, that has been made very sweet with honey. Set it in a bowl on the top of the hive, or beside it. It will attract the miller, and then drown him.

TO MAKE THE HANDS SMOOTH AND SOFT.—For this purpose there is nothing nicer than the beautiful, fragrant, and delicate composition called Almond Cream, (Crême d'Amandes.) This almond cream (which must not be confounded with another preparation called Amandine) is, when fresh, very soft and white, and resembles ice-cream in appearance. To use it—first dip your hands into a basin of water, and then put on one of the palms a very small portion of the almond cream, (not larger than a grain of indian corn,) and with the other hand rub it to a lather. Rub it well into your hands and all over them before you wash it off. We know, by experience, that this is the best of all preparations for keeping the hands in nice order. If used every day, it will effectually prevent the skin from chapping in cold weather; and will remove any roughness caused by incidental employments, or by putting the hands into salt water. We earnestly recommend it. Keep it closely covered. If you live where it can be easily procured, do not get more than one gallicup at a time, as almond cream is always best when freshly made. Exposure to the air hardens and discolours it.

Another very excellent article for the hands is sand-soap, or sand wash-balls,—a preparation of soap mixed with fine sea-sand. There is nothing superior to it for washing the hands of boys, and of all persons whose business obliges them to use much manual exertion. Also, the hands of the most delicate lady will be rendered still softer and smoother by the daily use of sand-soap. Try it—but not for the face or neck.

Sand-soap is made by shaving down and melting some white soap, and then stirring into it, while warm, an equal quantity of fine dry sea-sand. Put it, warm, into square moulds, or roll portions of the mixture between your hands, so as to form balls. Set them in a dark place to dry gradually.

TO REMOVE CORNS FROM BETWEEN THE TOES.—These corns are generally more painful than any others, and are frequently situated as to be almost inaccessible to the usual remedies. Wetting them several times a day with hartshorn will in most cases cure them. Try it.

TO ALLAY PAIN IN THE FEET WHEN CAUSED BY FATIGUE.—If your feet become painful from walking or standing too long, put them as soon as you can into warm salt and water, mixed in the proportion of two large handfuls of salt to a gallon of water. Sea-water made warm is still better, if you can conveniently procure it. Keep your feet and ankles in the salt water till it begins to feel cool, rubbing them well with your hands. Then wipe them dry, and rub them long and hard with a coarse thick towel, or with a hair glove. Where the feet are tender and easily fatigued, it is an excellent practice to go through this process regularly every night, or every morning, or both; also employing it without fail always on coming home from a walk. With perseverance this has cured neuralgia in the feet.

To prevent any roughness that may ensue after taking your hands out of the brine, wash them immediately with soap; or what is still better, with almond cream, first dipping them into cold water, and then rubbing on a little of the above composition till it forms a lather. Almond cream is much used by gentlemen as a shaving soap, but it is also a very pleasant and useful article for a ladies washing-stand, being excellent for smoothing the hands, and preventing their chopping in cold weather. It is well to get but a small box at a time, as exposure to the air somewhat dries and discolours it. It should be kept closely covered.

Chilblains or frost-bitten feet may be cured or prevented by dipping the feet night and morning into *cold* water. Then taking them out and wiping them dry with a coarse towel. Persevere, and you will find the remedy effectual.

RELIEF FOR RHEUMATIC PAINS.—Bathe the afflicted part at night and morning, and frequently through the day, with warm salt and water, (mixed in the proportion of two handfuls of salt to a quart of water,) rubbing it well into the skin. Do this near the fire, or in a warm room; avoiding exposure to a draught of air. Sea-water heated over the fire will answer the purpose still better.

A table-spoonful of Hopkins's Compound Syrup of Sarsaparilla, taken thrice a day, and persevered in for six or eight weeks, has frequently cured a chronic rheumatism.

Swaim's Panacea has effected wonderful cures in rheumatism of long standing.

RELIEF FOR A SPRAINED ANKLE.—Wash the ankle very frequently with *cold* salt and water, which is far better than warm vinegar or decoctions of herbs. Keep your foot as cool as possible to prevent inflammation; and sit with it elevated on a high cushion. Live on very low diet, and take every day some cooling medicine; for instance epsom salts. By observing these directions *only*, a sprained ankle has been cured in a few days.

BATHING THE FEET.—In bathing the feet of a sick person, use at the beginning, tepid or lukewarm water. Have ready in a tea-kettle or covered pitcher, some *hot* water, of which pour in a little at intervals; so as gradually to increase the temperature of the foot bath, till it becomes as warm as it can be borne with comfort; after which, the feet should be taken out before the water cools. This is a much better way than to put them at first into very warm water, and let it grow cool before they are taken out. Clean stockings, well warmed, should be ready to put on the feet as soon as they are out of the water, and have been rubbed dry with a flannel.

CURE FOR A RUN-ROUND.—That disease of the finger or toe commonly called a *run-round*, may be easily cured by a remedy so simple that persons who have not seen it tried are generally incredulous as to its efficacy. The first symptoms of the complaint are heat, pain, swelling, and redness at the top of the nail. The inflammation, if not checked, will soon go round the whole of the nail, causing intense pain, accompanied by a festering or gathering of yellow matter, and ending in the loss of the nail. To prevent all this, as soon as the first symptoms of swelling and inflammation commence, lay the finger flat on the table, and let the nail be scratched, all over with the sharp point of a pair of scissors, or a penknife. This excoriation must be done first crossways, and then lengthways, so as thoroughly to scratch up the *whole surface* of the nail, leaving it rough and white. This little operation does not give the slightest pain; and we have never, *in a single instance*, known it fail. By next morning the finger will be well. If done before the festering commences, it is a *certain* and speedy cure. And it will even succeed at a later stage of the disease, by first opening with a needle that part of the swelling where the yellow matter has begun to appear; and afterwards by scratching up the surface of the nail with scissors or penknife.

Hard horny warts on the hands can be cured *positively*, and without pain, by touching their tops twice a day or more with a clean quill pen, dipped in aquafortis. The wart, after a few applications of the aquafortis, will turn brown, and crumble till it falls off.

For ring-worms there is no remedy so good as mercurial ointment, rubbed on it at night, and not washed off till morning. It causes no pain, and by repetition will *always* effect a cure.

TO APPLY AN EYE-STONE.—Eye-stones are frequently used to extract motes from the eye, sparks from steam-engines, and other extraneous substances. They are to be procured at the druggists'. They cost but two or three cents a piece; and it is well to get several, that in case one fails you may try another. To give an eye-stone activity, lay it for about five minutes in a saucer of vinegar and water; and if it is a good one it will soon begin to move or swim round in the liquid. Then wipe it dry, and let it be introduced beneath the eye-lid, binding a handkerchief closely round the eye. The eye-stone will make the circuit of the eye, and in its progress take up the mote, which it will bring with it, when on the pain ceasing, the handkerchief is removed. Eye-stones are the eyes of lobsters.

When a mote or spark gets into your eye, immediately pull down the lower eye-lash; and, at the same moment with a handkerchief in your hand, blow your nose violently. This will frequently expel the mote without further trouble. A mote will sometimes come out by merely holding your eye wide open in a cup or glass filled to the brim with clear cold water. Or, take a pin, and wrapping its head in the corner of a soft cambric handkerchief, sweep carefully round the eye with it, above and below, inserting it under the lid. This should be done with a firm and steady hand, and will often bring out the mote. Another way is to take a long clean bristle from a brush, tie the ends together with a bit of thread so as to form a loop, and sweep round the eye with it, so that the loop may catch the mote and bring it out.

A particle of iron or steel, has, *we know*, been extracted from the eye, by holding near it a powerful magnet.

Rail-road sparks, &c., have frequently been removed from the eye by introducing the feather-end of a quill, and sweeping it round beneath the edge of the lid. If done with care and dexterity it will generally succeed.

CURE FOR THE TETTER.—Obtain at a druggist's an ounce of sulphur*et* of potash. Be careful to ask for this article *precisely*. It is a preparation of sulphur and potash. Put the sulphuret into a large glass jar; pour on it a quart of cold soft water; and leave it to dissolve, having first corked it tightly. Afterwards add to it a wine-glass of rose-water. It may be more convenient afterwards to transfer it to smaller bottles, taking care to leave them closely corked. Pour into each a table-spoonful or more of rose-water. To use it, pour a little into a saucer, and dipping in a soft sponge, bathe the eruption five or six times a day. Persist, and, in most cases, it will very soon effect a cure. It is, indeed, a safe and most excellent remedy. Should the tetter re-appear with the return of cold weather, immediately resume the use of this solution. A bath in which sulphuret of potash was dissolved in water (in the above proportions) has succeeded in curing the tetter after the eruption had spread all over the body of a child.

CURE FOR EXCORIATED NOSTRILS.—If, after a severe cold in the head, the inside of the nostrils continue sore and inflamed, rub them lightly with a little kreosote ointment, applied to the interior of your nose with the finger. Do this at night, and several times during the day. It will very soon effect a cure; often in twenty-four hours.

FOR A CHAFED UPPER LIP.—For a chafed upper lip and soreness of the end of the nose, such as generally accompanies a cold in the head or influenza, much relief may be found from the homely remedy of greasing the excoriation, at night on going to bed, with a bit of mutton tallow (that of a candle will do) held to the fire to soften. Extend the application over all the nose and even between the eyes. It is well to keep always in the house some nice tallow, prepared by boiling and skimming a sufficient quantity of fresh mutton fat, (there must not be a particle of salt about it,) and then pouring it warm into gallicups, which should be closely covered as soon as the liquid has congealed.

CURE FOR PRICKLY HEAT.—Mix a *large* portion of wheat bran with either cold or lukewarm water, and use it as a bath twice or thrice a day. Children who are covered with prickly heat in warm weather will be thus effectually relieved from that tormenting eruption. As soon as it begins to appear on the neck, face, or arms, commence using the bran-water on these parts repeatedly through the day, and it may probably spread no farther. If it does, the bran-water bath will certainly cure it, if persisted in.

BROWN MIXTURE FOR A COUGH.—Mix in a large bottle, half an ounce of liquorice; a quarter of an ounce of gum-arabic; two tea-spoonfuls of antimonial wine; sixty drops of laudanum; and half a pint of water. Shake it well, and when the ingredients are thoroughly amalgamated it will be fit for use. For a cold and cough, take a dessert-spoonful three or four times a day, shaking or stirring it first.

RED LIP SALVE.—Mix together equal portions of the best suet and the best lard. There must be no salt about them. Boil slowly, and skim and stir the mixture. Then add a small thin bag of alkanet chips; and when it has coloured the mixture of a fine deep red, take it out. While cooling, stir in, very hard, sufficient rose or orange-flower water to give it a fine perfume. A few drops of oil of rhodium will impart to it a very agreeable rose-scent.

Cold cream for excoriated nostrils, chafed upper lips, or chapped hands may be made nearly as above, but with one-third suet, and two-thirds lard, and no alkanet. When it has boiled thoroughly, remove it from the fire, and stir in, gradually, a large portion of rose-water, or a little oil of rhodium, beating very hard. Put it into small gallicups, with close covers.

MUSTARD PLASTERS.—Mustard plasters are frequently very efficacious in rheumatic or other pains occasioned by cold. It is best to make them entirely of mustard and vinegar without any mixture of flour. They should be spread between two pieces of thin muslin, and bound on the part affected. As soon as the irritation or burning becomes uncomfortable, take off the plaster. They should never remain on longer than twenty minutes; as by that time the beneficial effect will be produced, if at all. When a mustard plaster has been taken off, wash the part tenderly with a sponge and warm water. If the irritation on the skin continues troublesome, apply successive poultices of grated bread-crumbs wetted with lead water.

A mustard plaster behind the ear will often remove a toothache, earache, or a rheumatic pain in the head. Applied to the wrists they will frequently check an ague-fit, if put on as soon as the first symptoms of chill evince themselves.

OPODELDOC.—Take an ounce of gum camphor; half a drachm of oil of rosemary; half a drachm of oil of origanum; two ounces of castile soap cut small; and half a pint of spirits of wine. Boil these all together for half an hour after the boiling has commenced. Let the mixture cool in the vessel, and then bottle it for use. It is a good embrocation for bruises, sprains, stiffness of the neck and shoulder, and for rheumatic pains.

CAMPHOR SPIRITS.—Break up into small bits an ounce of gum camphor, and put it into a pint glass bottle. Then fill up with spirits of wine, cork it, and leave the camphor to dissolve, shaking it occasionally. This will be found quite as good as the camphor spirits obtained at the druggist's, and the cost will be far less. It is well to keep a bottle of it always in the house. When taken to remove faintness or nervous affections, pour a few drops into a wine-glass of water. Camphor kept for external use is best when dissolved in whisky, as it produces less irritation of the skin than when melted in alcohol.

The pain of a fly-blister will be much alleviated by sprinkling powdered gum camphor thickly over the surface of the plaster before it is put on. This should always be done.

REMEDY FOR ARSENIC.—Dissolve a few scruples of sulphuret of potash in half a pint, or a pint of water, and administer it a little at a time, as the patient can bear it; having first given the white of an egg.

Another remedy is to mix two tea-spoonfuls of made mustard with sufficient warm water to thin it, so as to make it easy to swallow. It acts as an emetic, and is good for any poison.

ANTIDOTE TO CORROSIVE SUBLIMATE.—If corrosive sublimate (one of the worst poisons) has been swallowed, immediately drink a large quantity of olive oil, even the whole contents of a flask; or more, indeed, if that is not found sufficient. This remedy, if taken in time, is always efficacious. If it cannot be *immediately* obtained, try white of egg.

REMEDY FOR AN OVER-DOSE OF LAUDANUM.—A cup of the *strongest possible* coffee has been known to keep the patient awake, and effect a positive cure when all other means have failed. After the fatal sleep has been thus prevented, and the patient is thoroughly roused and excited, let an emetic be administered.

MEDICATED PRUNES.—Take a quarter of an ounce of senna and manna (obtained ready mixed from the druggists') and pour on it not quite a pint of boiling water. Cover it; set it by the fire; and let it infuse for an hour. If the vessel in which you prepare it has a spout, stop up the spout with a roll or wad of soft paper. This should always be done in making herb teas, or other decoctions; as a portion of the strength evaporates at the spout. When the infusion of senna and manna has thus stood an hour at the fire, strain it into a skillet or sauce-pan (one lined with porcelain will be best) and stir in a large wine-glass or a small teacup-full of West India molasses. Add about half a pound or more of the best prunes; putting in sufficient prunes to absorb all the liquid during the process of stewing. Then cover the vessel closely, and let it stew (stirring it up occasionally) for an hour; or till you find the stones of the prunes are all loose. If stewed too long, the prunes will taste weak and insipid. When done, put it into a dish to cool; and pick out all the stones. If properly prepared there will be no perceptible taste of the senna and manna. It may be given to children at their lunch or supper.

FINE HOARHOUND CANDY.—Take a large bunch of the herb hoarhound, as green and fresh as you can get it. Having picked it clean, and washed it, cut it up (leaves and stalks) with scissors. Scald, twice, a china tea-pot or a covered pitcher; then empty it of the hot water. Put in the hoarhound, pressing it down with your hands. The pot should be about two-thirds full of the herb. Then fill it up with boiling water; cover it closely, and wedge a small roll of paper tightly into the mouth of the spout, to prevent any of the strength escaping with the steam. Set it close to the fire to infuse, and keep it there till it begins to boil. Then immediately take it away, and strain it into another vessel. Mix with the liquid sufficient powdered loaf-sugar to make it a very thick paste. When the sugar is in, set it over the fire, and give it a boil, stirring and skimming it well. Take a shallow, square tin pan, grease it slightly with sweet oil, and put into it the candy, as soon as it is well boiled; smoothing the surface with a wet knife-blade. Sift over it some powdered sugar. Set it away to cool; and when nearly congealed, score it in squares. It is a well-known remedy for coughs and hoarseness.

If you find it too thin, you may stir in, while boiling, a spoonful of flour, of arrow-root, or of finely-powdered starch.

Another way of making this candy is, to boil the hoarhound in barely as much water as will cover it, and till all the juice is extracted. Then squeeze it through a cloth, and give the strained liquid another boil, stirring in, gradually, sugar enough to make it very thick and stiff. Afterwards sift sugar over a shallow tin pan, fill it with the paste, and leave it to congeal; scoring it in squares before it is quite hard.

Any herb-candy may be made as above.

FINE LAVENDER COMPOUND.—For this purpose, use lavender buds, gathered just before they are ready to blow. As soon as the blossom expands into a flower, a portion of its strength and fragrance immediately evaporates. This is also the case with roses; which, for rose-water, should always be gathered, not after they are blown, but when just about to open.

Having stripped the lavender buds from the stalks, measure a pint of the buds, and mix with them half an ounce of whole mace; half an ounce of whole cloves; two nutmegs broken up, but not grated; and half an ounce of powdered cochineal. Put the whole into a large glass jar, and pour in a quart of the best French brandy. Cover the jar closely; making it completely air-tight by the addition of strong paper, pasted down over the cover. Set it away, and leave the ingredients to infuse, undisturbed, for a month. Then strain it into a pitcher; and from the pitcher pour it through a funnel into bottles; corking them tightly. It is a well-known remedy for flatulence, and pains and sickness of the stomach. To use it, put some loaf-sugar into a spoon, and pour on sufficient lavender to soften the sugar; then eat it.

Instead of cochineal, you may give a fine red colour to lavender compound by tying up a quarter of an ounce of alkanet in a thin muslin bag, (seeing that the alkanet is free from dust,) and putting the bag into the jar while the other ingredients are infusing in the brandy.

BLACKBERRY SYRUP.—Take a sufficient quantity of fine, ripe, sweet blackberries. Put them into a sieve placed over a large broad pan; and with a clean potatoe-masher, (or something similar,) mash the blackberries, and press out all their juice. Or (having bruised them first) put the blackberries into a linen bag, and squeeze out all the juice into a vessel placed beneath. Measure it; and to every quart of the strained juice allow half a pound of powdered loaf-sugar; a heaped tea-spoonful of powdered cinnamon; the same of powdered cloves; and a large nutmeg grated. Mix the spices with the juice and sugar, and boil all together in a porcelain preserving-kettle; skimming it well. When cold, stir into each quart of the syrup half a pint of fourth-proof brandy. Then bottle it for use. This is a good family medicine; and is beneficial in complaints incident to summer. It should be administered, (at proper intervals,) from a tea-spoonful to a wine-glassful, according to the age of the patient.

RHUBARB BITTERS.—Take two ounces of rhubarb root; half an ounce of cardamom seeds; one drachm of Virginia snake-root; and half a drachm of gentian root. Put these articles into a large bottle, and pour on it a quart of good brandy.

It is excellent for children in complaints incident to summer weather.

TO PREVENT A JUG OF MOLASSES FROM RUNNING OVER.—A jug or bottle of molasses frequently causes inconvenience by working over at the top, after coming from the grocer's, and being set in a room or closet that is warmer than the place from which it was brought. To prevent this—as soon as you receive it, pour out a portion into another vessel; for instance, into a pitcher or bowl. Then set the jug of molasses into a deep pan or basin, and leave it *uncorked* till next day. By that time, all danger from fermentation will have subsided. Then cork it tightly, and set it away. Keep always under the bottom of the jug an old plate, or a double piece of thick paper to receive any drippings that may run down the sides. Never bring molasses to table without a plate or saucer under the vessel that contains it.

West India molasses is far more wholesome and nourishing than any other, and is decidedly the best for gingerbread, molasses-candy, indian-puddings, &c. Sugar-house molasses, if used for those articles, will render them hard and tough.

TO EXTINGUISH A COAL FIRE.—Many persons who burn anthracite coal in their chambers, have suffered great inconvenience from not knowing how to extinguish it before they go to bed. The process is very simple, and always successful. Lift off with the tongs any large coals that may lie on the top, and lay them on the iron hearth of the grate; they will make good cinders to burn next day in a close-stove or furnace. Then shut up the tongs, and with them make a hollow or deep cavity just in the centre of the fire, heaping up the coals like a hill on each side, and making the tongs go down to the bottom of the grate. If there are not many coals, you may do this with the poker. The fire will immediately begin to fade and deaden; and in less than ten minutes, it will be entirely out, without farther trouble; unless it has been very large, and then it may require a second stirring.

In the morning, let the grate be cleared *entirely* of all the cinders and ashes, and swept out clean with a brush. Cover the bottom of the grate with a sort of flooring of small fresh coal, before you put in the kindlings; otherwise, after the kindlings (wood or charcoal) are lighted, they will burn away immediately, and fall through the bottom bars of the grate, before they have had time to ignite the coal that has been laid above them; so that the grate will have to be again cleared out, fresh kindlings brought, and the fire built up anew, before it can possibly succeed.

The above way of extinguishing a coal-fire answers equally well for a close-stove or a furnace.

The heat of a grate may be considerably diminished by standing up the blower against it; the bottom of the blower resting on the hearth. To lessen the heat of a close-stove, leave open the large door of the stove. In the same manner diminish the heat of a furnace.

LAUNDRY-WORK, NEEDLE-WORK, ETC.

SODA SOAP.—Take six pounds of the best brown soap, and cut it into pieces. Put it into a large wash-kettle, and pour on seven gallons and a half of clear soft water. Next stir in six pounds of washing-soda, (sub-carbonate,) set it over the fire, and let it boil two hours after it has come to a boil. Then strain it into stone jars; cover it, and put it away. It must be used for *white clothes only*, as it will fade coloured things. Put the clothes in soak the night before, in tubs of cold water; having first rubbed the grease spots with wet fuller's earth, (scraped fine,) and the stains with wet cream of tartar. Allow a pound of the soda soap to a bucket of water, and put it over the fire in a wash-kettle. When the water is warm, put in as many white clothes as convenient; seeing that there is water enough to cover them well. Boil them an hour; occasionally moving them up and down with the clothes-stick. Then take them out, and finish washing them in the usual way. The soda soap will whiten them very much; but if used in a larger quantity than the above proportion, it will injure them greatly. We do not recommend any soda preparation for washing, unless it can be used under the immediate inspection of a good housekeeper; most servants and washerwomen being very apt to employ it too freely, if left to themselves.

SOFT SOAP MADE WITH POTASH.—Put twelve pounds of potash into a barrel, and then pour in water till the barrel is half full. Stir the potash several times, while it is dissolving in the water. Have ready twelve pounds of good soap-fat, and melt it over the fire in a large kettle. Then stir it, gradually, into the barrel with the dissolved potash. After standing a quarter of an hour, fill up the barrel with cold water; and stir it hard. This process will form an excellent soft soap.

COLD STARCH FOR LINEN.—Take a quarter of a pint, or as much of the best raw starch as will half fill a common-sized tumbler. Fill it nearly up with very clear cold water. Mix it well with a spoon, pressing out all the lumps, till you get it thoroughly dissolved, and very smooth. Next add a tea-spoonful of salt to prevent its sticking. Then pour it into a broad earthen pan; add, gradually, a pint of clear cold water; and stir and mix it well. Do not boil it.

The shirts having been washed and dried, dip the collars and wristbands into this starch, and then squeeze them out. Between each dipping, stir it up from the bottom with a spoon. Then sprinkle the shirts, and fold or roll them up, with the collars and wristbands folded evenly inside. They will be ready to iron in an hour.

This quantity of cold starch is amply sufficient for the collars and wristbands of half a dozen shirts. Any article of cambric muslin may be done up with cold starch made as above.

Poland starch is better than any other. It is to be had at most grocery stores.

Cold starch will not do for thin muslin, or for any thing that is to be clapped and cleared. It is very convenient for linen, &c., in summer, as it requires no boiling over the fire. Also, it goes farther than boiled starch.

TO WASH WHITE SATIN RIBBON.—Make a strong lather of clear cold water and the best white soap. Squeeze and press the ribbon through this, till it looks quite clean; but do not rub it, as that will cause it to fray. Then make a fresh lather of white soap and cold water, and squeeze the ribbon through that. Do not rinse it, as the suds remaining in the ribbon will give it the proper stiffness. Pull and stretch it evenly; and then iron it on the wrong side while it is still damp. When quite dry, roll it on a ribbon-block; wrap it closely in coarse brown paper; and put it away till you want to use it. None but plain unfigured white satin ribbon of very good quality, can be washed to advantage. The day before washing it, rub some magnesia upon any grease that may be on the ribbon, and some cream of tartar on the stains.

In winding several pieces of ribbon on the same block, always put the end of each successive piece *under* that of the last, instead of *over* it; and wind the whole tight and smoothly. Secure the last end with two very small minikin pins; as large pins will make conspicuous holes all through, and probably leave a brassy or greenish stain. The ribbon-block should on no account be narrower than the ribbon.

A small white silk handkerchief may be washed as above, if thick and unfigured.

TO CLEAN SILK SHAWLS OR SCARFS.—Mix together a quarter of a pound of soft soap; a tea-spoonful of brandy; and a pint of whisky or gin; stirring them hard. Spread the shawl on a clean *linen* cloth, and with a clean sponge dipped in the mixture, go carefully over it on both sides. The shawl should be kept even, by placing weights along the edges. Dry it in the shade. Then wash (or rather squeeze it) in two or three cold waters without soap; stretch it, and hang it out again; and when almost dry, iron it.

TO CLEAN A SILK DRESS.—Rip the dress entirely apart. Take large raw potatoes, and allow a pint of cold water to each potatoe. Having pared the potatoes, grate them into the basin of water. Cover it; and let it stand three hours, or more. Then pour it carefully off, into a broad pan; leaving the sediment or coarse part of the grated potatoes at the bottom of the basin. Having spread a clean linen cloth on a large ironing table, and put some irons down to the fire, lay the silk (a breadth at a time) upon the cloth, and with a clean sponge dipped in the potatoe-water, go all over it, on the wrong side. Then hang that breadth out upon a line; stretch it evenly, and leave it to dry. Take another breadth; sponge it with the potatoe-water; hang it out; and proceed in the same manner till all the silk is done. By the time the whole has been sponged and hung out, the first breadths will in all probability be dry enough to iron. It must be ironed on the wrong side.

The sleeves must be taken out and ripped open, before sponging them. Each piece of the body must, of course, be done separately.

FRENCH METHOD OF WASHING COLOURED SILK CRAVATS, SCARFS, SHAWLS, &c.—Make a mixture of the following articles in a large flat dish. A large table-spoonful of soft soap, or of hard *brown* soap shaved fine, (white soap will not do,) a small tea-spoonful of strained honey, and a pint of spirits of wine. Have ready a large brush (for instance a clothes-brush) made perfectly clean. Lay the silk on a board or on an ironing-table; stretching the article evenly, and securing it in its place by weights set round upon its edges. Then dip the brush into the mixture, and with it go all over the silk, lengthways of the texture; beginning at that part of the silk which is least seen when worn; and trying a little at a time till you have ascertained the effect. If you find the colour of the silk changed by the liquid, weaken it by adding a little more spirits of wine. Brocaded silks cannot be washed this way.

Having gone carefully over the whole of the article, dip it, up and down, in a bucket of clean water, but do not squeeze or wring it. Repeat this through another clean water, and then through a third. Afterwards spread it on a line to dry, but without any squeezing or wringing. Let it dry slowly. While still damp, take it down; pull it, and stretch it even; then roll or fold it up; and let it rest a few minutes. Have irons ready, and iron the silk; taking care that the iron is not so hot as to change the colour.

The above quantity of the washing-mixture is sufficient for about half a dozen silk handkerchiefs; for a silk apron; or for one shawl; or for two scarfs, if not very long. If there is fringe on the scarfs it is best to take it off and replace it with new; or else to gather the ends of the scarfs, and finish them with a tassel or ball.

Gentlemen's silk or chaly cravats may be made to look very well washed in this manner. Ribbons also, if thick and rich. Indeed whatever is washed by this process should be of excellent quality. A dress must be previously taken apart.

This is also a good method for washing a white blond veil or scarf; using a soft sponge instead of a brush, and making the mixture with rather less soap and honey. When dry, lay the blond in smooth even folds, within a large sheet of smooth nankeen paper. Press it for a few days in a large quarto or folio book. Do not iron it.

TO MAKE THREAD LACE LOOK ALWAYS NEW.—Thread lace should never be sewed fast, or washed upon the article of which it forms the trimming. It should be merely run on, or basted with short stitches; so as to draw out the thread easily, when the lace is taken off for washing. The trouble is nothing in comparison to the advantage. In the first place, thread lace, to look well and last long, should never be touched with starch. Starching thread lace injures the texture, (causing the threads to break,) and gives it a hard, stiff appearance. If sewed fast, and washed and done up with the muslin collar or pelerine, it shrinks and thickens up among the gathers, and partakes of the starch that has been used for the muslin; and, of course, can have no resemblance to new lace that has never been washed at all. Again, it will not last half so long, as if always taken off, and done up separately from the muslin.

Every lady should have at least two lace bottles, as it is not well to wind more than three or four yards of lace upon one bottle. They should be straight black bottles of the largest size, and it is well to buy them new for the purpose; otherwise something of their former contents may come out when boiling, and injure the lace. Also there may be remains of wax, rosin, or some other cement, lingering about the place where the cork was; and this will melt in the water, and cause the lace to look streaked. The bottles being perfectly clean, (inside and out,) cover them with thick, strong, new white linen, sewed on tightly and smoothly, with coarse thread. When not in use, keep them wrapped up in clean paper.

Having taken off the lace from the article on which it was basted, begin near the bottom of the bottle; tack one end of the lace with a needle and strong thread to the linen; and wind it smoothly round with the edge downward; and all the scollops smooth, so that none may be creased or curled inward. Wind the lace on the bottle in such a manner as to leave the scolloped or pattern-edge visible all round; and finish just below the neck of the bottle. Then tack down with the needle and thread the last or terminating end of the lace. Early in the evening put the bottle with the lace into a clean *earthen* or white-ware vessel, filled with clear cold water, and let it soak till bed-time. Then change the water, and let it soak all night.

In the morning, fill a clean porcelain kettle, or a deep earthen pipkin, with a strong suds of clear soft water and the best white soap. Into this, put the bottle with the lace on it; having tied a twine string round the neck of the bottle so as to make it fast to the handles or the rim of the vessel, that it may be kept as steady as possible while boiling. It must on no account be boiled in a tin or iron vessel, as the lace will then certainly be discoloured. Set the vessel over hot coals or in a stove; and keep it boiling regularly till the lace looks quite white. If very dirty, it will be necessary to change the water for a clean fresh suds. It may boil from an hour to an hour and a half; but take it out as soon as it looks clean and white. Then turn up the bottle to drain off the suds, and set it (without rinsing) in the sun. Keep it in the sun till the lace dries on the bottle. When *quite* dry, take it off; stretch or pull down each scollop separately with your thumb and finger; and then wind the lace evenly and smoothly on a ribbon-block of somewhat broader width. You can get ribbon-blocks at the stores where ribbons are sold, and you will find them very useful. Wrap the block with the lace on it in soft *brown* paper, and put it away till you want it for use. If you have no ribbon-block, fold or roll up a piece of smooth clean paper, and roll the lace round it. Never wrap any thing in printed paper.

The above method of cleaning thread lace, (without rubbing, squeezing, rinsing, starching, or ironing,) as it is the most simple and easy, is also the most certain of success. In fact we can confidently assert that there is no other so good; and we only ask a trial of its efficacy; well-assured that every lady who has once had her lace washed in this manner will continue it; as it makes it look always new. Of course, it should be done on a clear bright day, and the hotter the sun the better. If you have more than one lace bottle to boil, they may be put into a brass or bell-metal wash-kettle, (previously made very clean,) but remember that no tin or iron must be used for this purpose. If the coating or lining of an enamelled or porcelain kettle is the least cracked or scaled off, do not boil the lace in it, or it will be stained with iron mould.

Thread lace done *exactly* according to these directions, has the look, feel, transparency, and consistence of new lace that has never been washed at all; and may easily be mistaken for it. Drying in the soap-suds gives it just the right stiffness, and it will last much longer than if washed in the old manner with squeezing, rinsing, starching, clapping, and ironing.

Before your lace is sewed on the bottle, look over it, and see if it requires any mending. There is a lace-stitch done with *very fine* thread, that, when neatly executed, renders a mended place imperceptible. It may be learned in a few minutes by seeing it done, but cannot be described intelligibly. Those who have had no opportunity of learning this stitch may mend lace very neatly by darning it with the finest possible thread; taking care not to make the darn too thick, or close, but imitating as nearly as possible the open texture of the lace. In quilling or setting on the lace, endeavour to conceal the darns under the pleats.

Cotton lace cannot be cleaned in the foregoing manner, as it is too soft and fuzzy, and shrinks up too much. It requires squeezing, starching, clapping, and ironing.

WASHING BLACK LACE.—Every description of black *silk* lace (or of black Scotch blond) may be made to look extremely well by the following process; either veils, shawls, scarfs, capes, sleeves, or trimming-lace. A black lace dress, must be previously taken apart, and all the loose threads or stitches carefully picked out. We will suppose the article that requires washing to be a veil that has been worn long enough to look soiled and rusty. By exactly observing the following directions, it may be made to appear fresh, new, and of an excellent black; provided always that it was originally of good quality, with no mixture of cotton in it. All lace articles of that brownish black, falsely called jet, are now mixed with cotton; and frequently have no silk at all about them.

In a large clean earthen pan, or a small tub, make a strong lather of white soap and clear soft water, warm but not hot. Mix with the suds a large table-spoonful of ox-gall. No family should be without a bottle of ox-gall, which can always be obtained from the butcher at a very trifling cost. The gall as soon as brought home should be opened, its liquid poured through a funnel into a clean black bottle, and tightly corked. You may perfume it by putting in a grain of musk. It is useful in washing all sorts of coloured things, as it materially assists in preventing them from fading. Having stirred the gall well into the suds, put in the black lace veil, and work and squeeze it up and down through the lather for five minutes or more; taking care not to rub it. Then squeeze it out well, open it loose, and shake it a little. Next, transfer it to a second suds of clean warm water and white soap; adding a tea-spoonful of gall. Into this second lather infuse *a large quantity* of blue, pressed into the water from the indigo bag, and well stirred in. Having worked the veil up and down through this second suds for about ten minutes, alternately loosening it out, and squeezing it up, but not rubbing it. Squeeze it finally as dry as you can, and then open it out widely.

Have ready in another pan some glue-stiffening, made as follows: On a bit of glue about the size of a shilling pour two jills, or a half-pint, of boiling water, and let it dissolve. After the glue is entirely melted, add to it a quart of *cold* water; and then make it *very blue* by squeezing into it a large portion of indigo from the blue-bag. Stir it well, and then put in the veil, rinsing and squeezing it up and down through the stiffening water. Having done this sufficiently, squeeze out the veil as dry as you can get it; then open it, stretch it, and clap it all over. Next, fold it evenly; roll it up in a thick clean towel; and let it rest for a quarter of an hour or more.

Spread a large clean *linen* cloth on your clothes-line, and hang the veil (well spread out) upon the cloth. When nearly, but not quite dry, take down the veil, and clap and stretch it again. Have warm irons ready. Lay a clean linen cloth over your blanket, and press the veil smoothly on the wrong side; first trying the irons on an old piece of thin black silk, crape, or gauze; lest they should be too hot for the lace, and scorch or discolour it.

The foregoing process (followed exactly) will restore to any article of *good* black silk lace that has become brown and soft by wearing, the deep black colour and consistence it had when new.

Be careful not to have too much glue, and to put plenty of indigo-blue into the second suds and into the stiffening water.

Before washing the veil, rip open the casing at the top, and remove the string. Afterwards, make a new case, and draw it with a new ribbon.

TO WASH A WHITE LACE SCARF.—Fold up the scarf, and lay it in a thin cambric handkerchief, folded over so as to enclose the scarf, and secured by basting it slightly with a needle and thread. Dip it in cold water. Make a strong lather with white soap and warm water; put the scarf, &c., into it, and let it rest all day. In the evening, make a fresh lather, and leave the scarf in it all night, (having first squeezed it well.) Next morning, make some thin starch. Shave small a quarter of a cake of white wax, and put it into two quarts of soft water; adding six lumps of loaf-sugar, and a table-spoonful of thin-made starch. Put these articles into an earthen pipkin or a porcelain kettle, and set it over the fire. On no account use, for this purpose, a vessel of any sort of metal, as it will discolour the lace. When the mixture has come to a boil, put in the scarf, (still folded in the handkerchief,) and boil it ten minutes. Then take it out, open the handkerchief, and if you do not find it perfectly white, return it to the pipkin, and boil it longer. Afterwards, take it out of the handkerchief, and throw the scarf into cold water. Squeeze and press it, till it drips no longer. Then open it out; stretch it even; and hang it in the sun. When almost dry, take it in, and iron it carefully on a linen cloth.

A veil, a shawl, or a pelerine of white lace may be washed in this manner.

TO CLEAN GOLD OR SILVER EMBROIDERY.—Warm some spirits of wine, and apply it with a bit of clean sponge. Then dry it, by rubbing it with soft, new canton flannel. Gold or silver lace may be cleaned thus. Also, jewelry.

WASHING AMERICAN CHINTZES.—American chintzes, of good quality, (such as are sold at twelve or fourteen cents per yard,) can be washed so as to retain their colours, and look as bright as when quite new. The water must be quite clean, and merely warm, but by no means hot. Rub the soap into the water, so as to form a strong lather, before you put in the dress. Add to the lather a handful of fine salt. Wash the chintz through two warm waters, making a lather in the second also, and adding salt. The salt will keep the colours from running. Then rinse it through two cold waters; putting a table-spoonful of vinegar into each, before the dress goes in. This will brighten the colours. Immediately, wring out the dress, and hang it up to dry; but not in the sun. When nearly dry, (so as to be just damp enough to iron,) have irons ready heated; bring in the dress; stretch it well, and iron it on the wrong side. If allowed to become *quite* dry on the line, and then sprinkled and rolled up, and laid aside to be ironed next day, the colours may run from remaining damp all night.

An imported chintz, a gingham, or a mousseline de laine, may be washed in the above manner; which *we know* to be excellent; substituting, for the salt, a table-spoonful of ox-gall in each water. All sorts of coloured dresses should be washed and ironed as quickly as possible, when once begun. It is well to allot a day purposely to coloured dresses, rather than to do them with all the other things on the regular washing-day. If washed in half-dirty suds, and left soaking in the rinsing-water, the colours will *most assuredly* run and fade, and the dress look dingy all over.

Of course, nothing that has any colour about it should be either scalded, or boiled, or washed in *hot* water. Scalding, boiling, and hot-water washing are only for things *entirely* white.

PRESERVING THE COLOURS OF DRESSES.—Before washing a new dress, try a small piece of the material, and see if the colours are likely to stand of themselves. They are generally fast, if the article is so well printed that the wrong side is difficult to distinguish from the right. If you obtain from the store a small slip for testing the durability of the colours, give it a fair trial, by washing it through two warm waters with soap, and then rinsing it through two cold waters. No colours whatever will stand, if washed in *hot* water. Some colours, (very bright pinks and light greens particularly,) though they may bear washing perfectly well, will change as soon as a warm iron is applied to them; the pink turning purplish, and the green bluish.

The colours of merinoes, mousselines de laine, ginghams, chintzes, printed lawns, &c., may be preserved in washing by mixing a table-spoonful of ox-gall in the first and second waters, (which should not be more than lukewarm,) and making a lather of the soap and water *before* you put in the dress, instead of rubbing the soap on it afterwards. At the last, to brighten the colours, stir into the second rinsing-water a *small* tea-spoonful of oil of vitriol, if the dress is that of a grown person; for a child's dress, half a tea-spoonful will suffice. If washed at home, one of the ladies of the family should herself put in the vitriol, as, if left to the servants, they may injure the dress by carelessly putting in too much. Vitriol is excellent for preserving light or delicate colours.

The colours of a common calico or mousseline de laine may be set by putting into each of the two warm waters a large handful of salt, and into each rinsing water a tea-spoonful of vinegar.

No coloured articles should be allowed to remain in the water, as soaking will cause the colours to run in streaks. As soon as the dress is washed and rinsed, let it be immediately wrung out, hung in the shade, and, as soon as dry enough, taken in and ironed at once. Each dress should be washed separately. The washing of dresses should only be undertaken in fine weather.

PUTTING AWAY WOOLLENS.—The introduction of furnaces, for the purpose of warming houses, is supposed to be one cause of the great increase of moths, cockroaches, and other insects that now, more than ever, infest our dwellings. For moths, particularly, the usual remedies of camphor, tobacco, pepper, cedar-shavings, &c., seem no longer sufficiently powerful; perhaps because their odour so soon evaporates. Still it is well to try them when nothing better can be done; and they are sometimes successful. Camphor and tobacco-shreds will be found much more efficacious if (after interspersing them among the furs or woollens) each fur or woollen article is carefully and closely pinned up in newspapers; so closely as to leave no aperture or opening, however small. The printing-ink has a tendency to keep off moths and other small insects. The papers used for this purpose should be those that are printed with ink of a good quality, not liable to rub off, and soil the things enclosed. We highly recommend this mode of preserving furs and woollens.

But the following method of putting away all the woollen, worsted, and fur articles of the house, will be found an *infallible* preservative against moths; and the cost is trifling, in comparison with the security it affords of finding the things in good order when opened for use on the return of cold weather. Procure at a distiller's, or elsewhere, a tight empty hogshead that has held whisky. Have it well cleaned, (*without washing,*) and see that it is quite dry. Let it be placed in some part of the house that is little used in the summer, where there is no damp, and where it can be shut up in entire darkness.

After the carpets have been taken up, and well shaken and beaten, and the grease spots all removed, let them be folded and packed closely down in the cask, which can be reached by means of a step-ladder. Put in, also, the blankets; having first washed all that were not clean; also the woollen table-covers. If you have worsted or cloth curtains and cushion-covers, pack them in likewise, after they have been thoroughly freed from dust. Also, flannels, merinos, cloaks, coats, furs, and, in short, every thing that is liable to be attacked by the moths. It is well to rip the cloaks from the collars, and the skirts of pelisses from the bodies, before packing, as they can be folded more smoothly, and so as to occupy less space. Fold and pack all the articles closely, and arrange them to advantage, so as to fit in well, and fill up all hollows and vacancies evenly. If well-packed, one hogshead will generally hold all the woollen and fur articles belonging to a house of moderate size, and to a moderate-sized family. But if *one* is not enough, it is easy to get another. When the cask is filled, nail the head on tightly, and let the whole remain undisturbed till the warm weather is over. If the house is shut up, and the family out of town in the summer, you may safely leave your woollens, &c., put away in this manner. Choose a clear, dry day for unpacking them in the autumn; and, when open, expose them all separately to the air, till the odour of the whisky is gone off. If they have been put away clean, and free from dust, it will be found that the whisky-atmosphere has brightened their colours. As soon as the things are all out of the cask, head it up again *immediately*, and keep it for the same use next summer. If more convenient, you may have the cask sawed in two before you pack it. In this case, you must get an extra head for one of the halves.

In putting away woollens for the season, always keep out a blanket for each bed, and some flannel for each member of the family, in case of occasional cold days, or easterly rains in the summer.

Have no *hair* trunks about the house; they always produce moths.

TO CLEAN WHITE FUR.—Take a sufficiency of dry starch, very finely powdered, and sift it, through a fine sieve, into a broad, clean, tin pan. Set the pan near enough the fire for the powdered starch to get warm, stirring it frequently. Then roll and tumble about the white fur among the powdered starch, till it is well saturated. Shut it up closely in a bandbox, and let it remain unopened for a fortnight. It will then look clean.

When you put away white fur in the spring, proceed as above, (using a very large quantity of the pulverized starch,) and put into the box some lumps of camphor tied up in thin white papers. Keep the box closely shut through the summer, and do not open it to look at the fur till you want it for cold weather. It will then be found a good clean white.

In joining pieces of fur or swans-down, lay the two edges together, and pass the needle and thread back and forward on the wrong side, (in the way that carpet-seams are sewed,) so as to unite the edges evenly and flat without making a ridge. Then line every seam by sewing or running strong tape along it, of course on the wrong side. Unless they are strengthened in this manner with tape, the stitches are liable, after a while, to give way, and the seams or joins to gape open, making rents inside that are very difficult to repair.

TO KEEP A MUFF. Always when returning a muff to its box, give it several hard twirls round. This will smooth the fur, and make all the hairs lie the same way. To prevent the wadding inside the muff from sinking downwards, and falling into clods, keep the muff-box always lying on the side, instead of standing it upright. When you put it away till next winter, place within it some lumps of camphor wrapped in papers, and sprinkle the outside of the fur with powdered camphor. Then enclose the muff, completely, in one or two large newspapers, sewing or pinning them entirely over it, sides and ends, so that nothing can possibly get in. Do the same with all your furs; and after putting them away with these precautions, open them no more till the return of cold weather. The printing ink on the papers will assist in keeping out moths.

TAKING CARE OF PICTURES.—An excellent way to preserve an oil-picture from the injuries of damp, mould, and mildew, is to take the precaution of covering the *back* of the canvas (before nailing it on the straining frame) with a coating of common white lead paint; and when that is dry, give it a second coat. If you buy a picture that has been framed without this precaution, do not neglect having the back of it coated as above, before you hang it up.

The simplest way of cleaning an oil-picture, is to mix some whisky and water *very weak*. If the mixture is too strong of the liquid, it may take off the paint, or otherwise injure it. Dip into the mixture a very soft and very clean sponge, which you must first ascertain to be perfectly free from sand, grit, or any extraneous object. A good way to soften and clean a sponge, is to boil it in several successive waters, till there is no longer any appearance of sand at the bottom of the vessel. Having carefully washed the picture with the sponge and whisky-water, dry it by going over it with a clean soft *silk* handkerchief. This is all that can be safely attempted by any one who is not a regular picture cleaner. Therefore, if the picture is smoked or much soiled, it is best to send it to a person who makes picture-cleaning his profession. Many a good picture has been destroyed by injudicious cleaning.

Till it has been made *perfectly clean*, no picture should be re-varnished; otherwise the fresh varnish will work up the dirt, and make it look worse than ever. As long as a picture is the least wet (either with paint or varnish) it should be carefully guarded from dust; the smallest particles of which by drying into the surface will injure it irreparably. No sweeping or dusting should be permitted where there is a picture not *perfectly and thoroughly* dry. If there is a fire in the room it should not be stirred, replenished, or touched in any way till the picture has been previously carried out, lest some of the flying ashes might stick to it.

When a picture is finished, it would always be well for the artist to inscribe on the back of the canvas the subject of the painting, the date of its completion, his own name and that of the person for whom it was painted. In short, a concise history of the picture, arranged somewhat like the title-page of a book. Had this excellent practice always prevailed, there would be no occasion for any doubts and controversies concerning the works of the old masters.

A PORTRAIT PAINTER'S TRAVELLING BOX.—The large wooden box for the easel and other things indispensable to a portrait painter, when travelling professionally, should be made broad, low, and square, so that it may be used as a platform on which to place the chair of the sitter. When unpacked of its contents, and appropriated to this purpose, the box must be turned bottom upwards, and concealed under a cover of carpeting or drugget brought along with it. The cover should fit smoothly and closely, and be so made that it can be lifted off, and folded up, whenever the platform is again to be used as a box.

TRAVELLING BOXES.—As bandboxes are no longer visible among the baggage-articles of *ladies*, the usual way of carrying bonnets, caps, muslins, &c., is in tall square wooden boxes, covered with black canvas or leather, edged with strips of iron and brass nails, and furnished with a tray for small things. They are usually lined with paper or calico pasted all over the inside. This lining, however, is apt to peel off in places where most rubbed; and is then very troublesome; catching the corners of the tray so as to prevent its being lifted out. To obviate this inconvenience, when you bespeak the box, direct that the inside, instead of being lined with pasted paper or calico, shall be planed smooth, and either stained of some colour, or left the natural tint of the wood. It is best that the tray should have a *close* bottom of strong linen. When there are only strips nailed across, (like open lattice-work,) the small articles laid upon them are always falling through.

A small bandbox can be easily carried *inside* of a trunk or box, keeping it steady by filling in heavy articles closely round it. The best way of securing a bandbox-lid, is to have a hole made in the rim or top of the lid, and a corresponding hole in the side of the bandbox, near its cover. Through each of these holes pass a string of ribbon or ferret; securing one end by a large knot inside, and leaving the other end outside; so that you can tie them together in a bow-knot. It is best to have two pair of these strings, one pair on each side of the bandbox.

Let your whole name (not merely the initials) be painted in white or yellow letters on each of your travelling trunks or boxes; and also the name of the town in which you live. Have also your name and residence painted in black on the leather part of your carpet-bag.

If you are clever at lettering, you can mark your trunks yourself with a small brush and a saucer of ready-mixed paint, which you may buy at a paint-shop for a few cents. The more conspicuously your baggage is lettered, the less liable you are to lose it. To make it still more easily distinguished, tie on the handles of each article a bit of ribbon; the same colour on every one—for instance, all blue or all red.

On returning home, let all the travelling cases, bags, straps, keys, &c., be kept together in one trunk; so that when preparing for your next journey you may know exactly where to find them.

A RIBBON SACK.—These bags are quite pretty, and very convenient for a short journey, or a visit of a day or two in the country. While on the journey, they are to be carried in the hand, and may contain whatever is necessary for a short absence from home; for instance, clean night-clothes, tightly rolled up; stockings; handkerchiefs; sewing materials; books, &c. To make a ribbon sack, take five or six pieces of *very* broad, very thick, strong ribbon; each piece at least three-quarters of a yard in length. Sew all these stripes closely together, with very strong sewing-silk. Then fold or double this piece of joined ribbons, leaving one end half a finger longer than the other. Sew up the two sides as you would a pillow-case, so as to form a square sack with a flap to turn over at the top. Round off, with your scissors, both corners of this flap, so as to make its edge semicircular. Then bind the top or mouth all round (flap and straight-sides) with thick velvet ribbon of a dark colour. Cover, with the same velvet ribbon, a very thick strong cotton cord about three quarters of a yard in length; and sew its two ends to the tops of the side-seams; so as to form an arched handle like that of a basket. Work an upright button-hole near the edge of the flap, and sew on a handsome button to meet it, a little below the straight edge of the bag's mouth. If the ribbon is very thick and strong (broad belt-ribbon for instance) no lining will be necessary. Also, no lining is required if the sack is of stout old-fashioned brocade. No other sort of silk will be strong enough without a lining.

A LADY'S SHOE-BAG.—Take a piece of strong linen or ticking. Fold or double it so as to leave a flap to turn over at the top. Then, with very strong thread, stitch the bag into compartments—each division large enough to contain, easily, a pair of shoes. Next sew up the sides, and bind the flap with broad tape. Put strings or buttons to the flap so as to tie it down. The shoes, when put in, must be laid together with the heel of one to the toe of the other; and if they are slippers with strings, tie the strings closely round both. These shoe-bags are very convenient when you are travelling.

A BOOT-BAG.—Take a piece of very strong brown linen or Russia sheeting; about a yard in length, and three-quarters wide. Fold it in the form of a pillow-case, and sew up the sides; leaving it at the open or top-end about a finger's length (or four inches) longer at the back than at the front, so as to turn over like a flap. Hem this flap. Take two pieces of strong twilled tape, each about a yard or more in length. Double each tape in the middle, so as to make a double string. Sew these strings on one edge of the turn-over or flap, about half a quarter of a yard apart. Having rolled up each boot, put them, side by side, into the bag. Pull down the flap over the opening or mouth; bring round the strings; and tie them tightly. The boots can thus be carried in a trunk or carpet-bag, without injuring other articles.

A TOWEL-CASE.—Travellers often complain much of the difficulty of procuring nice towels, in steamboats, at country inns, and at taverns in remote places. This inconvenience may easily be obviated by putting a few of your own towels into your trunk. In case of being obliged to proceed on your journey before your towels are dry, take with you, on leaving home, a square oil-cloth or oiled silk case or bag, made like a large pocket-book with a flap to fold over, and to fasten down with two or more buttons and loops. Having squeezed your wet towels as dry as you can, fold or roll them into as small a compass as possible; and put them into the case. Before you go to bed, take them out, and hang them about your room to dry.

In this towel-case there maybe separate compartments for tooth-brushes, soap, and a sponge.

CONVENIENT HAIR-BRUSHES.—We highly recommend to travellers those hair-brushes that have a looking-glass at the back, with a comb fixed on a pivot, and concealed beneath the mirror, so as to be drawn out when wanted. Those of black buffalo horn are the strongest. With one of these you may always have a comb and a small mirror at hand, all three occupying no more space than a simple hair-brush.

A TRAVELLING-CASE FOR COMBS AND BRUSHES.—Get about three-quarters of a yard of strong oiled silk of the best quality—double it—leaving one side, at the top, about half a quarter longer than the other, so as to fold over like a flap. Sew it strongly up, at the bottom and sides, with a felled seam. Then stitch it lengthways into compartments, like an old-fashioned thread-case—except that the divisions must differ in size; taking care to make each division rather large, that the articles may go in easily, and not rub against each other. Make one compartment large enough to contain a hair-brush; allot another to a comb; others to tooth-brushes; one to a nail-brush; one to a clasp-knife; one to a pair of scissors; one to a vial of lavender or camphor; one to a sponge; and another to a cake of soap; and a large one to hold a towel. In short, make the divisions according to the size and number of useful articles you require in travelling. Sew two pair of strings to the flap, and tie them fast when the articles are all in. Let your name be marked on the outside of the flap.

This bag may be made of strong linen, or ticking. But oiled silk is better, as you can then put into it tooth-brushes and sponges when quite wet. If of oiled silk, let there be one compartment large enough to hold a wet towel. It is well in travelling always to take with you some towels of your own; and if after using them there is no time for drying, you can roll them up and carry them away wet, if you have furnished yourself with an oiled silk bag.

TO CARRY INK WHEN TRAVELLING.—Have ready a small square bag of oiled silk, or thick buckskin, with a narrow tape string sewed on near the top. Buy a small six-cent vial of good ink. The vial must be broad and short with a flat bottom; so that it will stand alone, and answer the purpose of an ink-stand. If the seal on the cork has been cut away, get a longer and better cork, and wedge it in as tightly as possible. Cut off a finger-end from an old kid glove; put it over the cork, and draw it down closely till it covers both the top and the neck of the bottle, tying it on tightly with narrow tape. Then wrap the bottle in double blotting-paper, and put it into the little oil-cloth bag, securing the top well. To prevent all possibility of accidents, from ink stains, do not pack the ink-bottle in a trunk with your clothing, but keep it in your travelling-basket or reticule. *We know* that ink thus secured has been carried many hundred miles, with the convenience of being always at hand to write with, whenever wanted, in a steamboat or at a stopping-place. The best way of carrying quill-pens is in a pasteboard pen-case, to be had at the stationers for a trifle. Steel-pens may be wrapped in soft paper twisted at each end.

We highly recommend a neat and convenient article called a travelling escritoir. It occupies no more space than a cake of scented soap, and is so ingeniously contrived as to contain a small ink-bottle with a lid so close-fitting as to be perfectly safe; a pen-holder; a piece of sealing-wax; a wax taper; and some lucifer matches with sand-paper to ignite them on the bottom of the box. The whole apparatus can be safely carried in the pocket, or in a ladies reticule, or it may be put into a travelling-desk. It is to be purchased in Philadelphia, at Maurice Bywater's stationery store, No. 151 Walnut street, near Fifth. We know nothing better for the purpose; and the cost is trifling.

BONNETS.—Before you send a straw bonnet to be whitened, it will be well to remove whatever stains or grease marks may be upon it. Do this *yourself*, as many professed bonnet-cleaners are either unacquainted with the best methods, or careless of taking the trouble; and will tell you, afterwards, that these blemishes *would not* come out. You can easily remove grease marks from a straw, leghorn, or Florence braid bonnet, by rubbing the place with a sponge dipped in *fresh* camphine oil; or by wetting it with warm water, and then plastering on some scraped Wilmington clay, or grease-ball; letting it rest half an hour, and then repeating the application till the grease has disappeared. Magnesia rubbed on dry will frequently remove grease spots, if not very bad. To take out stains, discoloured marks, or mildew, moisten slightly with warm water some stain powder composed of equal portions of salt of sorrel and cream of tartar, well mixed together. Rub on this mixture with your finger. Let it rest awhile; then brush it off, and rub on more of the powder. When the stain has disappeared, wash off the powder, immediately, and thoroughly, with warm water. By previously using these applications, no trace of grease or stain will remain on the bonnet, after it has undergone the process of whitening and pressing in the usual manner.

In cleaning straw bonnets it is best to give them as much gloss and stiffening as possible. The gloss will prevent dust from sticking to the surface, and the stiffness will render them less liable to get out of shape when worn in damp weather. For a similar reason, the wire round the inside of the edge should *in all bonnets* be very thick and stout. If the wire is too thin, even the wind will blow the brim out of shape.

An excellent way of cleaning and whitening straw or leghorn bonnets may be found in the House Book, page 67.

In lining bonnets, always fit the lining on the *outside* of the brim. It is not only the least troublesome way, but the most certain of success. Nothing is more disfiguring to a bonnet than an uneven puckered lining—left too loose in some places, and stretched too tight in others. If the lining is drawn more to one side than the other, the brim will always set crookedly round the face. The best way, is first to fit upon the *outside* of the bonnet-front, a piece of thin, soft, white paper, pinning it on smoothly and evenly, with numerous pins. Then cut it the proper shape; allowing it rather more than an inch all round larger than the brim. From this paper cut out the silk lining; allowing still more for turning in at the edges, on account of the silk ravelling. Then (having notched the edge of the lining all round) baste it on the inside of the brim, and try it on before the glass, previous to sewing it in permanently. See that it is perfectly smooth and even throughout. A white silk bonnet-lining should be of the most decided white, (a dead white, as it is called,) for if it has the least tinge of pearl, rose, blue or yellowish-white, it will be unbecoming to any face or complexion. Straw bonnets are frequently lined with white crape or tarletane.

The lining of a silk or velvet bonnet should always be put in *before* the brim is sewed to the crown.

In trimming a bonnet, after the bows, bands, &c., have all been arranged with pins, sew them on with a needle and thread; and afterwards withdraw the pins. If pins are allowed to remain in, they leave a greenish speck wherever they have been; besides denting the straw, and probably tearing it. Also, sew on the flowers, after you have arranged them to your satisfaction.

Bonnet strings when somewhat soiled may be cleaned by rubbing them with scraped Wilmington clay, or grease-ball, or else magnesia. Roll them on a ribbon-block with the clay upon them; let them rest a few hours; then brush off that clay, and put on some fresh. Roll the ribbon again on the block, and leave it till next day. You will find it look much cleaner. It is well always to buy an extra yard, or yard and a half of ribbon, to replace with new ones the bonnet strings when soiled.

To keep the bows of a bonnet in shape when put away in the bandbox, fill out each bow by placing rolls of wadding inside of all the loops.

A piece of thin oiled silk introduced between the lining and the outside, partly beneath the upper part of the brim, and partly at the lower part of the crown, will prevent any injury to the bonnet from perspiration of the head, or oiliness of the hair.

In bespeaking a bonnet of a milliner, always request her to send you the frame to try on, before she covers it; that you may see if it fits.

When a bonnet is to be sent to a distant place in wooden box, (*bandboxes* should never *visibly* travel,) to keep the bonnet steady, and prevent its tumbling or knocking about, sew very securely to the brim and back, some bits of strong tape, and fasten the other end of each bit of tape to the floor of the box, with *very small* tack nails. Fill all the loops and bows with wadding as above mentioned. A bonnet thus secured may travel uninjured from Maine to Texas.

TO KEEP A BONNET WHITE. — If you have a white velvet or silk bonnet that looks well enough to wear a second season, lay beside it in the bandbox a cake of white wax, (such as you get at an apothecary's for sixpence or a shilling,) cover the bandbox closely, and do not on any account open it till you are about to take the bonnet again into wear. You will then find the cake of wax much discoloured, but the bonnet as white as ever. Shawls of white silk or canton crape, or indeed any white articles, may be kept in the same manner by putting a cake of white wax in the box with them, and not opening it so as to admit the external air, till the season for wearing them has returned.

In bespeaking bandboxes, desire that they shall not be lined with white paper. A lining of the coarsest brown paper is far preferable for preserving either the colours or the whiteness of any articles that are kept in them. The chloride of lime used in manufacturing white paper is very injurious to the colours of silks, and frequently causes in them spots and stains. The very coarse thick brown paper made of old ropes is far better; as the tar remaining about it partakes somewhat of the qualities of turpentine, and is therefore a preservative to colours.

White ribbons, blonds, &c., should be kept wound on ribbon-blocks, and wrapped in the coarse brown iron-monger's paper.

WHALEBONES AND HOOKS. — The whalebones for dresses should always be perfectly straight, for if crooked they draw the body crooked wherever they are, and give it a warped or puckered look. Let them be stout also; for if thin, they curve and break. In cutting them of the desired length, round off and smooth the edge of both ends; for if left rough, square, or sharp they will very soon pierce through the dress. If you case them in linen or twilled tape, make the covering double, for about an inch at each end; and sew them on to the body-lining with very strong thread or silk. Secure them firmly and steadily at both ends, so that they may not slip up and down, and rub through to the outside of the body. For fastening dresses never use those hooks that have a sort of bulb, or that spread out near the point. They catch very badly, and are troublesome both to fasten and unfasten. Do not put black hooks on dresses that are to be washed, as they cause iron-mould. When a dress comes home from the wash with any of the hooks flattened in ironing, raise or open them by inserting beneath the hook the points of your scissors.

See that not a particle of *coloured* lining is introduced anywhere about a dress that is to be washed. No coloured lining-muslin will wash at all; but its colour or dye will run and streak the outside of the dress so as to spoil it. However dark a washable dress may be, the lining should be *entirely* of white linen or brown holland; the smallest bit of coloured muslin will spoil it when washed.

On no consideration let even a dark or black chintz dress have any black cotton cord about it; as when it comes from the wash it will be ruined with black streaks, from the dye of the cord.

CUTTING OUT PATTERNS.—In taking the pattern or cutting out the shape of a cape, pelerine, mantilla, or any other article of dress, instead of using a newspaper for that purpose, (according to the general custom,) cut the pattern in coarse, low-priced muslin or calico. Then with a needle and thread sew or run all the different parts together, so that you can try it on and see if it fits, or if any alteration will be necessary in suiting it to your own figure. Cut out the *whole* of the pattern, and not merely the half; otherwise you will not be able to try it on conveniently. The stiffness of paper and its liability to tear, render it far less suitable for pattern-cutting than coarse muslin; which, if not already in the house, can be bought for a mere trifle.

TO HEM BOBBINET.—In making a collar, pelerine, cape, scarf, or any article of bobbinet, you may hem it so as to prevent the usual inconvenience and disfigurement of the edges stretching out of shape after being washed, starched, and ironed. After turning down the hem, lay a *very small* cotton cord into the upper or extreme edge of the hem, and with a fine needle and thread secure the cord by running it closely along with short stitches. Having done this, lay a second small cord into the other edge, or the edge that is to be hemmed down. It is well worth the trouble of thus going twice round with a cord at each edge of the hem; which in consequence will remain ever firm and straight after the article has been washed.

When any part of a bobbinet article is cut bias, or rounded in a semicircle, it will be best, instead of hemming, to face the edge with a bias slip of the same material, having a covered cording sewed in; as in binding or facing the edge of a cape or pelerine. Without this precaution, the bias or rounded edge will lose all shape in being ironed. If new bobbinet is very stiff and full of creases, let it be damped and ironed before it is cut out. As bobbinet shrinks much in washing, every thing made of it should be allowed full large. It may be shrunk before cutting out, by dipping it into a pan or tub of cold water. As soon as it is wet all through, take it out and squeeze it with your hands till it ceases entirely to drip. Then open, stretch, and pull it, till you get it all straight and even. Next, fold it up smoothly, and wrap it in a clean towel. It will be ready for ironing by the time an iron can be heated; first trying the iron on something very thin.

A bobbinet, or any clear muslin dress should have the hems and tucks drawn out before washing; renewing them after the dress is done up. The dress will never look well, if washed and clear-starched with the hem, &c., remaining in.

TO STRENGTHEN THE HEM OF A SILK DRESS.—In silk dresses the edge of the hem at the bottom of the skirt is apt to wear out (or cut as it is called) very soon, and look faggled or ravelled. To prevent this, get some broad strong silk braid of the same colour as the dress, or a little darker, (but on no account lighter,) and run it on to the edge, on both sides, like a binding; with strong silk, and short close stitches.

TO MAKE A COAT-DRESS OR GOWN SIT IN CLOSELY TO THE WAIST. — On finishing the dress, take about a yard and a half (more or less) of rather broad twilled tape. Sew the tape strongly in three places to the lower extremity of the inside of the back, exactly where the body joins the skirt; using sewing-silk the colour of the dress. The tape must be fastened precisely in the middle, and at each of the side seams of the back. When you put on the dress, bring the tape round (pulling it downwards as you do so) and tie it in front under the skirt, and just below the termination of the fore-body. By drawing the dress closely into the waist, it makes the back look hollow, and is a great improvement to the figure.

CORDING DRESSES. — A dress that is to be washed, should be corded with the same material. A merino or mousseline de laine, if corded with silk, will be disfigured, after washing, by the silk *always* fading and making the dress look old. But a balzorine or barege had best be corded with silk, as they rarely bear washing, and the material is so slight that, if used for cording, it will fray and wear off almost directly. The silk should be of the darkest colour in the dress. Satin should always be corded with silk, (and silk of the best quality,) as satin cording ravels and frays immediately. Velvet also should have silk cording.

DIRECTIONS FOR WORKING SLIPPERS. — Half a yard of canvas is a full pattern for a large pair of slippers. If the canvas is of extra width, three quarters of a yard will make two pair. It is well to get your shoemaker to cut out for you the size and form, in a piece of paper. They will look *immensely large* before they are made up, but will not be found so afterwards.

Coloured engravings of slipper patterns are for sale in all the worsted and trimming stores. In making your selections, it is best to avoid those patterns that have white in them; as the white crewel will look soiled very soon, and give a dirty appearance to the whole slipper. You may, however, contrive to substitute for the white stitches the palest possible tints of pink, blue, or yellow.

To work one pair of slippers, you will require from fifteen to twenty skeins of crewel. In selecting the crewel, place beside you the pattern, that you may match the tints with it; choosing them so as to correspond precisely with those in the coloured engraving. It is best to go *exactly* by the pattern. If varied according to your own fancy, they will rarely look as well as when done in precise conformity to the taste and judgment of the practised artist, who has designed the plate and its colouring. Generally speaking, you should have *at least* from four to six shades of each colour; the darkest to be nearly black, the lightest nearly white; otherwise the effect will be dull and indistinct. Strong lights and shades are always of importance to brightness and beauty; even in worked slippers.

Wind the crewels, separately, in balls; and have a sufficient number of needles, so as to appropriate a needle to every shade. The needles must be large and blunt-pointed. Keep beside you, while working, something in which to stick the needles you are not using at the moment. A very simple and convenient thing for this purpose, is an empty gallicup, with a blank piece of canvas stretched flat, and tied tightly over the top. Stick the needles into this canvas; it is better than a pin-cushion.

Slippers (like all other worsted work) should be done in a frame, the canvas stretched tightly; and tacked firmly in, with strong thread. Keep the pattern beside you all the time you are working; and follow every stitch precisely. Do the central part first; next the heel part; and then fill up with groundwork all the vacant space within the outline. The usual way is to work them in common cross-stitch; but if done in tent-stitch or queen-stitch, the slippers will be more elastic, much softer, and will take a smaller quantity of crewel. When you have finished working them, have the slippers made up by a very good shoemaker. They will last a long time.

Instead of canvas, you may work slippers on fine broad-cloth, such as is used for gentlemen's coats. Cloth slippers require no filling up with groundwork; having only a cluster of flowers in the centre, and a small running-pattern round the heel. You must baste upon the cloth a bit of canvas, a little larger than the space to be occupied by the flowers. Work the flowers upon this; taking every stitch quite through both the canvas and the cloth beneath it. When done, pull out the threads of the canvas from under the stitches, (they can be drawn out very easily,) and the flowers will remain in their proper form upon the cloth. This method of working slippers saves time, trouble, and crewel; yet they will be found less durable than if worked entirely on canvas, and with the whole ground filled up by crewel-stitches; cloth wearing out much sooner than worked canvas.

When preparing to work slippers, do not have them previously cut out, as it will cause the canvas or cloth to stretch all round, and will spoil their shape; besides being very troublesome to keep straight and even while working. Having obtained from your shoemaker a paper or shape, (allowed *extremely* large,) lay it down on the canvas, and mark out the form and size by a pen or pencil outline.

Cloth slippers braided in a handsome pattern with coloured braid, look much better and are done far more expeditiously than when worked in crewel.

Bands or rims for velvet caps look very well when braided. The braid may be gold or silver.

TO WORK MERINO IN CROSS-STITCH.—If you determine to work merino in cross-stitch, in the common manner of worsted work, have ready a pattern accurately drawn and coloured, so as to represent the place and tint of every stitch; and keep it before you to look at. Having marked out, with a dot, the place for every sprig, baste *over* each place a bit of very fine canvas, leaving the raw edge. On this canvas work the sprigs; carefully taking up with every stitch the merino beneath, as well as the canvas above it. Avoid drawing your hand too tight. When done, pull out, thread by thread, the canvas from under the needle-work; so as to leave the sprig resting on the merino only. This you will find a much more easy process than it appears on description. Have a number of needles, one for every different shade, and thread them all in advance. A tumbler or gallicup with a piece of canvas stretched tightly, and tied down over the top, is a very convenient thing to have beside you to stick your threaded needles in, when working worsted.

TO BRAID MERINO DRESSES OR CLOAKS FOR CHILDREN.—Patterns for braiding should be as continuous as possible, so as to avoid frequent cutting off and fastening on of the braid. These patterns should have nothing in them that stops short; all the parts following and entwining, so as to connect with each other.

For braiding, the dress must be cut out first, and the breadths sewed together, so that the border may run smoothly and regularly along, without any breaks or ill-joined places. Wind your braid upon cards or corks, and reserve a sufficiency for raveling to sew on the rest with; which is far better than to sew it on with silk thread, as, of course, the raveling matches the colour so exactly as to render the stitches imperceptible. The braid reserved for raveling should be cut into the usual length of needle-fulls; then ravelled, and put into long thread-papers.

Having drawn the pattern on a strip of stiff white paper, prick it all along, according to its form or outline, with large, close pin-holes. Then lay or baste it on the merino. Take some pounce, (gum-sandarac finely powdered and sifted,) and with your finger rub it along the pricked outline of the paper-pattern. On removing the paper, you will find that the pounce-powder, going through the pin-holes, will have traced the pattern in small dots on the merino. This will be a guide in sewing on the braid, which should be run on, with short, close stitches. A double row of braid, the inner or right-hand row a *much darker* shade than the first, has a raised or relieved look, which is very pretty; particularly when the second row is of the same colour as the merino or ground, but of an infinitely darker shade.

If you cannot match the merino with a braid exactly similar, select, always, one of a darker rather than a lighter shade. A light-coloured merino looks very well with a braiding of the same colour, but of a shade *considerably* darker. Gray, fawn-colour, or scarlet merino appears to advantage braided with black; so, also, does light blue or pale lilac. Salmon-colour looks well with purple braiding; and dark brown braided with light blue or pink. The lining of a child's cloak should be of the same colour as the braiding.

Braiding can be done with great ease and expedition. A child's dress or cloak may be braided in two days, or less.

Cloth slippers look very well braided in shaded patterns, with the rows of braid so close as to touch each other.

Cloth covers for tabourets or stools can be braided so as to look infinitely handsomer and richer than those worked in worsted on canvas. They should have a border all round, with corner-pieces, and a central pattern in the middle; all which can be done beautifully in close braiding. The pattern must be defined on the cloth by first drawing it with a pen and ink on white paper; then pricking the outline with a large pin, and laying pounce-powder along the pricked outline, so that the powder may fall through the holes, and thus trace it on the cloth, in the manner before mentioned.

DIRECTIONS FOR EMBROIDERING MERINO.—Merino dresses are usually worked in small sprigs, representing a little flower or bud, with two or three green leaves. Blue, lilac, or purple flowers have generally a more tasteful effect for this purpose than red or yellow ones. They will be sufficiently brightened by a shaded yellow spot in the centre. A beautiful sprig may be formed entirely of leaves, some of them comprising different tints of green, and others of brown. Three green leaves, with two brown ones at the bottom of the sprig, look exceedingly well on a gray merino; also, on a scarlet, crimson, or cherry-coloured ground. Mourning-gray should have black sprigs only. Gold-coloured flowers, if properly shaded, look well on purple, dark brown, or dark slate-coloured merino; but blue or lilac will look better still. Blue and brown harmonize well; also very light blue and very dark purple. Pink flowers look best on a dark olive ground. Blue and red should never come together in a dress. The effect of all sprigs, spots, or stars will be greatly improved by working, on the *right hand* of each, a shadow of a colour similar to the merino, but of a *much darker* shade. This dark shade along the right-hand side will give the sprig a relieved or raised appearance; and, if well done, will make it look almost as if you could take it up with your fingers. Executed by a skilful embroidress, or by one who is a proficient in drawing, this mode of producing a shadow, that seems to come from behind the sprig, will be found extremely beautiful. We are surprised that is not more generally known and practised.

Previous to working a dress, it is well to have the breadths of the skirts measured, and cut apart. The remainder, of course, is to be reserved for the body, sleeves, and pelerine; but do not have these parts fitted and cut out before embroidering. Though by that means you may save the trouble of doing a few unnecessary sprigs, you will lose more than you will gain; for the pieces, if cut out, will stretch out of shape, and ravel at the edges, so that it will be very difficult to put them *well* together when wanted. Also, if previously cut out into their respective shapes, the pieces cannot well be worked in a frame, which is always the best way of doing embroidery.

You may work the dress with either soft-twisted silk, (not too fine,) or with Berlin wool or crewel. If worked with silk, it cannot possibly be washed to look well. *Floss* silk should never be used for this or any other embroidery, as, though it fills up well, and looks beautifully at first, it almost immediately wears rough and fuzzy. Embroidery-stitch is far more elegant than cross-stitch, having none of its stiffness, hardness, and ungracefulness; and being, besides, more easy, expeditious, and manageable; and capable of a far greater diversity of forms.

Prepare on a pasteboard drawing-card, an exact pattern of the sprig, drawn and coloured precisely as it is to be worked; and you may put a dark back-ground behind one side of the sprig, of exactly the same tint as the merino. Mark the distances of the sprigs by measuring their places on the merino with a pair of compasses, (often called dividers,) or by means of a piece of card. Designate the place of each sprig by a dot with a red or white chalk pencil; the dot being the centre of the sprig. Rub, on a saucer, some water-colour paint of any colour that will show plainly on the merino, (which should first be stretched in a frame.) If you cannot get a frame, or prefer working on your hand, baste, under the place occupied by each sprig, a small circular bit of stiff writing-paper; and be careful, while working, not to catch up the paper with the stitches of your needle. When done, remove the paper, and the sprigs will look smooth and even. If you attempt to work it merely on your hand, with no paper beneath, it is impossible to prevent its puckering and drawing up.

Fine embroidery must be worked with extremely close stitches in rows or ridges. Every other stitch should be short, and every other one long. In every row, the alternate long and short stitches should fit in, by extending a little beyond those of the neighbouring row, so as to blend well. If you have no knowledge of drawing, get your pattern-sprig done by some person that draws well, and that is familiar with the effect of lights and shades.

If your dress is to have a belt of the same, you may work a long strip of merino for that purpose; the pattern being so arranged that the flowers will form a close row or straight wreath. Allow this strip of merino full wide, so that there may be an ample sufficiency for turning in at the edges. Sleeve-bands, also, may be worked in this way.

A two-yard-square of merino, embroidered in coloured flowers, and trimmed with a deep fringe, makes a beautiful shawl. On a dark brown or purple merino, flowers entirely of shaded blue, with light brown leaves and stalks interspersed among the green ones, will have a beautiful effect; very superior to the common tasteless and gaudy calico-style of introducing flowers of all colours—red, blue, and yellow. An olive merino shawl may have pink flowers entirely; a slate, or dark gray, or a purple will look well with rich gold-coloured flowers. In all flower-borders, the introduction of brown leaves among the green will be a decided improvement. If the merino is *light* brown, or light gray, or *pale* olive, the flowers may be scarlet, cherry-colour, or crimson. For a black merino, the embroidery should be of shaded gray.

Keep beside you, while working, a number of needles threaded with all the different shades of silk, and stuck in a flat pin-cushion, or something similar, so as to be always ready for use.

EMBROIDERY ON BOTH SIDES.—For this purpose, the embroidery-frame must be placed in a perpendicular or upright position, and two persons employed together; both equally skilled in needle-work. Get a carpenter to make an upright stand, somewhat in the form of a towel-rail, and about the usual height of a work-table; having broad feet, that it may stand steadily, and a broad cross-bar just above them, and a shelf at the top, on which to lay the needle-cushions, silk balls, &c., with a raised ledge on each side of the shelf, to prevent their rolling off. At each end of this shelf there must be slits down, into which put the upright ends of the embroidery-frame, secured with wooden pegs.

We will suppose that the article to be embroidered the same on both sides, is a plain canton-crape shawl, or a square of merino *intended* for a shawl. Stretch the shawl tightly in the embroidery-frame, sewing it strongly to the linen; the pattern having been drawn on both sides with a camel's-hair pencil dipped in water-colour paint, of a tint a little darker than the shawl. The two ladies who are to work it, must sit one on each side; and as one sticks in the needle, the other must draw it through, and stick it in for the next stitch; to be drawn through by her companion. The fastenings on and off must be neatly concealed under the stitches. By thus working together, (each alternately sticking in and drawing out the same needle,) both sides will, of course, be embroidered *exactly* alike, so that not the slightest difference can be perceptible. It is in this manner that canton-crape shawls are embroidered in China. The sewing-silk must be of the best quality, not too fine or slack-twisted. Floss-silk will not do at all.

EMBROIDERING STANDARDS.—Military standards have been successfully embroidered in the above manner. They should be made of *very thick*, strong India silk, satin not being the same on both sides. Instead of sewing-silk, standards had best be worked with chenille, such as comes on purpose for embroidering. Have a needle for every shade. An embroidered standard should always be copied from a painted model, executed by an artist; the model to stand in such a position that each of the two embroiderers may see it all the time. An outline of the model must be drawn on the silk. The most durable colour for a standard is deep blue. Part of the embroidery (stars, for instance) may be done in gold or silver thread.

FINE COLOURING FOR ARTIFICIAL FLOWERS.—For light blue and pink, buy, at a drug or paint store, what are called blue saucers and pink saucers. They contain the most beautiful tints of these colours. To use them, take a large clean camel's-hair pencil, and dipping it into some water, liquefy a portion of the paint that is on the saucer, till you get the exact tint you desire. When you have enough, pour off the liquid into a teacup, and add a *small* drop of lemon-juice to each tea-spoonful of the colour. The lemon-juice (if used properly) will brighten and set the colour; and is indeed superior to any thing else for this purpose. But *too much* of this, or any other acid, will destroy the colour entirely. Therefore be very careful in employing it; though no colouring for artificial flowers will be bright and clear without the addition of *some little* acid. Put the book-muslin, jaconet, white silk, or whatever materials the flowers are to be made of, into the cup of liquid dye; and when the muslin has thoroughly imbibed the colour, take it out, stretch it evenly, and dry it in the shade. Then press it with an iron *entirely cold*. A mixture of colour from both the blue and pink saucers will make lilac.

For a yellow colour.—Get six cents' worth of saffron; put it into a bowl, and pour on cold water, in quantity according to the deepness or vividness of the tint that you wish. When it has infused sufficiently, pour off the liquid; and, in proportion to its quantity, add to it, carefully, four, five, or six drops of lemon-juice.

For green.—Buy, at a druggist's, one ounce of French berries. Put a tea-spoonful of them into a common-sized tea-cup of boiling water. Cover it, and let it infuse half an hour or more. Then (having poured it off) add to the liquid (according to its quantity) about five or six drops of lemon-juice. This infusion of French berries makes a bright grass-green. To render it lighter, add some saffron yellow. To make it darker, put to it some blue from the blue saucer.

For a brown dye.—Infuse, in cold water, some pieces of bark from the white or black walnut tree; exposing it for several days to the sun and air, while it is soaking.

Crimson.—You may make a beautiful crimson for shading artificial flowers with a camel's-hair pencil, by taking some of the fresh petals of the piony, when the flower is in full bloom. Lay them on a plate, and mash and press them with the back of a silver spoon, till you have extracted as much of their red juice as you want. To about twelve drops of the piony-juice, add one small drop of lemon-juice; and use the colour for *shading* the flowers, not for dyeing them.

For a bright red shading. — Press out, in the above manner, the juice of full-blown bergamot flowers; adding, also, (as above,) a drop of lemon-juice to brighten and set the colour.

Blue shading. — A beautiful blue shading can be obtained by pressing and mashing on a plate, the flower-leaves of the common blue flag or iris; adding, always, a very little lemon-juice. With this, and a camel's-hair pencil, you can put the shades and streaks into blue flowers, whose first tint has been dyed from the blue saucer.

A mixture of crimson piony-juice, and blue flag-juice, will make a fine purple for shading.

When a little touch of dark brown or black is required for flowers, dip into water the end of a cake of umber, bistre, or indian ink, from a colour-box; rub the paint on a plate, and apply it with a camel's-hair pencil.

All these dyes and shading colours for artificial flowers will (*as we know*) be found beautiful on trial. An exact knowledge of the precise proportions of the colouring materials cannot, however, be correctly obtained without a little practice.

DIRECTIONS FOR MAKING A TABOURET. — A tabouret is a square stool, tall enough for a grown person to sit on, and about the usual height of a chair. Get a carpenter to make a strong square box of well-seasoned wood, planed smooth both inside and out. Instead of having the lid or cover-piece *exactly* at the top, it should be placed below it, four or five inches down the inside, so as to leave a vacant space between itself and the upper edges of the box; to the sides of which it must be well secured, either with glue, or with small headless tack-nails. The wooden bottom of the box must be placed two or three inches up, so as to leave a space at each end of the lower corners for concealed castors, that will cause the tabouret to be moved easily on the carpet.

The carpenter's part of the work being thus accomplished, the remainder of the tabouret can be easily completed by the ladies of the family, and at far less cost than if done by an upholsterer. We have seen beautiful tabourets made in this manner, and looking as if made entirely at a shop.

Get about seven or eight yards of strong, broad, very stout webbing, such as is used by saddlers or trunk-makers. You may either procure it of *them*, or at one of the large fringe stores. Nail the webbing to the upper edges of the box, across the vacant top, so as to interlace in small open squares. This is to give elasticity to the seat when finished. Make a square cushion of thick, strong brown linen; allowing it, each way, three or four inches larger than the top of the box; as the linen will take up that much, at least, in sewing and stuffing. Sew the linen strongly round three sides, and leave the fourth open, for putting in the stuffing. Then stuff it, hard and evenly, with curled horse-hair, which you may obtain at a cabinet-maker's or an upholsterer's. Afterwards, cover this cushion with damask, cloth, velvet, or some other handsome and durable article, and bind the edges all round. Next cover the four sides of the exterior of the box with the same material as the outside covering of the cushion; stretching it on very tightly and smoothly, and securing it to the wood with small tack-nails. While one person is driving in the nails, another must hold the box fast, and stretch and smooth the covering. When this has been neatly accomplished, nail on the cushion to the top edge of the box, above the webbing; hammering the tacks into the binding. Finish by tacking a handsome fringe all round the cushion, so as to conceal the binding. If you cannot get a fringe *exactly* the colour of the outside cover, choose one that is a good contrast,—either much darker or much lighter. A light blue tabouret may have purple, brown, black, or deep orange-coloured fringe. One of crimson or scarlet may have a fringe of black, dark green, or gold-colour. For a green tabouret, the fringe may be black, purple, or lilac. A brown or purple tabouret may have a light blue or gold-coloured fringe. A gray one may be fringed with dark brown, dark green, or purple. Light blue may be fringed with a very dark blue; light green with a very dark green; pink with crimson; light brown with a very dark brown; and bright scarlet with *very deep* crimson. You may suspend, all round, deep festoons of thick, rich cord, corresponding with the fringe; one festoon to hang at each of the four sides. The corners may be finished with long tassels.

In a similar manner, you can make an excellent and handsome footstool, employing a carpenter to construct the frame or box.

The footstool may be covered with rich carpeting, trimmed with worsted fringe.

THE SUMMER HEARTH.—Summer blowers, of handsomely ornamented iron, are now much used to conceal the empty coal-grates, during the season of warm weather. Like chimney-boards, they render the room very close, by entirely excluding the fresh air that may enter from the chimney. Certainly, in a bed-chamber, it is best that the fire-place should always be left entirely open. A frame made to fit in exactly, and having open slats, like a Venetian door, is a good screen for a summer-hearth. These screens are best when divided down the middle, like a pair of Venetian shutters; one or both of which may be left open at night, if in a sleeping room. To sleep in a room from whence all external air is entirely excluded, cannot be otherwise than prejudicial to health; and rarely fails, sooner or later, to undermine the constitution. Many people accustom themselves to sleep with the window-sash farthest from the bed a little open all the year round, (except when the rain or snow comes in that direction;) and in consequence of having acquired this salutary habit, these persons rarely take cold from any exposure to a draught of air. On this subject, the author can adduce the evidence of her personal experience.

Another good chimney-screen is a maple or walnut-wood frame, filled up with open wire-work, painted green like a wire fender, and fitting exactly into the fire-place. These frames should have two brass knobs near the top, for lifting them in and out. Chimney-boards, of course, can only be put into open fire-places, where wood is burnt in cold weather. On the hearth of a vacant Franklin stove it is usual to keep a large jar of flowers, which should be renewed every day or two.

Where there is no summer-blower, it is usual to decorate the empty grate with cut paper. This may be done in a very pretty manner by obtaining a sufficient quantity of coloured, glossy writing-paper, of such tints as will harmonize best with each other. For instance, green and lilac; green and light pink; light blue and dark brown; blue and buff, or cream-colour; purple and yellow; two shades of green—one very dark, the other very light; or two shades of blue—one much lighter than the other. Cut this paper, lengthways, into long, straight strips; in breadth, about three or four inches. Fold these slips lengthways, and evenly; and, while doubled, cut their edges with sharp scissors into a fringe. Then wreathe these double fringes thickly and closely round the bars of the grate, securing them with pins. On each bar there should be two wreaths, each of a different colour or shade. Twist or wrap these two wreaths together, so as to conceal the iron entirely; beginning the first twist or fringe from the left hand, and crossing or entwining it with one of another shade or colour commencing from the right. If well arranged, this mode of decorating an empty grate has an excellent effect. The bars should previously be well cleaned, and the back and whole interior of the grate completely blacked. Tissue-paper is too soft and thin for wreathing the bars of grates. Coloured writing-paper will be found much better; or, indeed, any nice paper that is thick and smooth, and of the same colour on both sides.

TISSUE-PAPER HEARTH CURTAINS.—There is an infinite variety of patterns for tissue-paper drapery to conceal empty coal-grates. The most simple is to take a sufficient number of long sheets of this paper; fold each sheet, lengthways, in four or six; and with scissors cut through the edges of the folds, so as to form scollops or points when opened out; leaving at the bottom of each sheet a space to be cut into a deep fringe. Having opened out the sheets, have ready part of the handle or stick of an old broom, cut to fit the length of the aperture or slit left open at the back of the grate for the draught. This stick must be covered with baize or cloth sewed on tightly. Sew to this covering the long streamers of cut tissue-paper, gathering them at the top so that they may hang down full and double. Then lay the stick nicely in the aperture at the top of the grate-back; fasten it securely, and let the drapery fall over the outside of the bars, so as to conceal them.

The following is a very handsome way of arranging hearth curtains. Have ready a sufficient number of long sheets of tissue-paper. Some of them may be white, others of a delicate pink. They are to be cut out in a handsome open-work pattern. You may take your pattern from muslin-work, flowered ribbon, furniture chintz, wall-paper, or table-covers. The more open it is the better. To render it accurate, first draw the outline on stiff paper, and then cut out that paper accordingly. Lay this cut out model upon a sheet of the pink tissue-paper spread out on a smooth common table, and kept down by weights at each corner. With a pencil, go round the model, and trace its outline upon the tissue-paper. Then with a sharp penknife or scissors, cut it out with great care and nicety. If you use a penknife, keep the tissue-paper stretched out smoothly upon the table, all the time you are doing it.

Next, take two more sheets of the pink paper, and cut the upper part of each sheet into the form of curtain-falls; festooned at the top, and descending long and low at the side. Ornament them with a handsome cut pattern, and scollop the edges.

The white tissue-paper is not to be cut or decorated with an open pattern or flowering. It is to form a lining for the pink, through the open work of which the white is to appear. The form or arrangement of this white paper is to fit or correspond with that of the pink, only that the white must be allowed two or three inches deeper at the edge, that it may project out beyond the pink. These projecting white edges are to be cut into a fringe. Additional fringe must be made of white tissue-paper, and twisted together so as to represent cords; the cords to be finished with tassels made of rolls of white paper fringe, fastened to the cords very neatly by sewing them on with a needle and thread. Observe that none of the *white* paper is to be cut out in flower patterns, or any sort of open work. It is only to furnish lining, fringe, cords, and tassels for the pink. Observe, also, that the fringed edge of this white lining is to appear beyond the scolloped edge of the pink outside.

When all is ready, arrange it handsomely in the fire-place, so as entirely to conceal the whole of the grate. It must be fixed at the top by sewing it to a covered piece of broom-handle, made to fit the draught aperture. The two long straight pieces of pink paper, with their white lining underneath, are to go on first. Then put up the festoons with their falls, having their white lining beneath, with its fringe appearing beyond the pink scollops. Then put on, at proper distances, the white cords and tassels. The effect, when complete, will represent at the back, closed pink curtains, with their white lining appearing through the cut-out flower pattern; over them, two festoons and falls of pink lined with white, opening in front with their white fringe, and white cords and tassels. In these festoons and falls, the cut-out flowers of the pink paper outside, show the white paper lining beneath. If well executed, these hearth curtains will (as we have seen) have a most beautiful effect. The pattern or flowering of the cut work is displayed to great advantage by the white lining. In one parlour you may have hearth curtains of pink and white; in the other of green and white, or blue and white.

Hearth curtains of tissue-paper may be fixed to the front ledge or slab that goes along the top of the grate, provided this ledge is wide enough. Leave, uncut, at the top of the sheets of paper, a plain piece to fit the ledge. To keep down this paper upon the ledge, prepare three heavy weights (for instance smooth stones) covered with thick silk or satin, and decorated with large bows of ribbon of the same colour. In this way, by keeping it down with weights on the top, we have seen a very handsome drapery of cut out tissue-paper entirely concealing a Franklin stove.

MARKING THE KEYS OF A PIANO.—Beginners on the piano (children especially) sometimes find much difficulty in learning the affinity between the keys and the notes. After acquiring the gamut theoretically, it is frequently a long time before they can apply it practically to the keys of the instrument, so as at once to find the right key on looking at the corresponding note. The process may be much accelerated (and indeed made perfectly easy) by some grown person marking on the keys the letters that designate the notes. By the following simple method this can be done without any injury or defacement of the ivory. Take a sheet of thick smooth writing-paper, and cut out of it as many little square pieces as there are white keys on the piano. Paste these papers on the ivory; and when *perfectly* dry, mark on each with common *blue* ink the letter belonging to that key. It will be best to do this in Roman capitals. If the natural keys are thus distinctly designated, the learner will find little difficulty from the flats and sharps, or black keys, being left unmarked.

The learner will thus in a very short time become familiar with the correspondence of the keys of the piano and the notes in the music book; and will soon be at no loss in finding them. It is well, however, not to remove the marks in less than a month or two. Then loosen the papers by wetting them with a little water; take them off, and wipe the keys first with a wet and then with a dry cloth. Blue ink of the common sort will leave no trace upon the ivory; but good black ink might probably leave a slight stain, unless the paper was very thick. Therefore do not use it.

The learner having thus become thoroughly acquainted with the keys while they were lettered, will not find the least difficulty in remembering them after the marks are taken off.

TO USE A PAPER-KNIFE.—In using a paper-knife to cut open the leaves of a new book, keep your left hand firmly pressed down upon the open page, while you hold the knife in your right. This will prevent the edges of the leaves from cutting rough and jagged. Cut open the tops of the leaves before you run the knife up the side-edges, and cut with a short, quick, hard stroke. The most serviceable paper-knives are of ivory, and without a handle; the handles being very apt to break.

The best way of writing your name in a book is on the inside of the cover; but if the paper that lines it seems likely to cause the ink to run or spread, cut out a handsome slip of fine smooth paper, write your name upon that, and paste it on nicely. If you put your name on one of the fly-leaves, it may be torn out; and if written on the corner of the title-page, that corner may be snipped off, should the book fall into the hands of a dishonest person.

HOUSEHOLD TOOLS.—Much inconvenience and considerable expense would be saved, if it was the universal custom to keep in every house a few tools, for the purpose of performing at home what are called small jobs; instead of being always obliged to send for a mechanic, and pay him for executing little things that might be very well done by a man or boy belonging to the family; provided that the proper instruments were at hand. The cost of these articles is very trifling, and the advantages of having them always in the house (particularly in the country) are beyond all price. In a small private family it may not be necessary to keep more than a few of these things; but that few are almost indispensable to comfort. For instance, there should be an axe, a saw, a claw-hammer, a mallet, a screw-driver, a bed-screw, a gimlet, one or two jack-knives, a pair of large scissors or shears, and a trowel. If there were two gimlets, and two screw-drivers, (large and small,) it would be better still. Likewise, an assortment of hooks, and of nails of different sizes, from large spikes down to small tacks; not forgetting a supply of brass-headed nails, some large and some small. Screws, also, will be found very convenient. The nails and screws should be kept in a wooden box, with divisions or partitions to separate the various sorts; for it is very troublesome to select them when all mixed together.

No house should be without glue, chalk, putty, paint, cord, twine, and wrapping-paper of different sorts. And care should be taken that the supply is not suffered to run out, lest the deficiency might cause delay and inconvenience at a time when most wanted.

It is well to have, in the lower part of the house, a deep closet appropriated entirely to tools and things of equal utility, for performing at once such little repairs as convenience may require, without the delay or expense of sending for an artisan. This closet may have one large, broad shelf; and that not more than three feet above the floor. Beneath the shelf may be a deep drawer, divided in two. This drawer may contain cakes of glue; pieces of chalk; hanks of manilla-grass cord; and balls of twine, of different size and thickness. At the sides of the closet may be small shelves for glue-pots, paste-pots, and brushes; pots for black, white, green, and red paint; cans of painting-oil, &c. On the wall above the large shelf, let the tools be suspended, or laid across nails or hooks of proper size to support them. This is much better than to keep them all in a box, where they may be injured by rubbing against each other, and the hand may be hurt by feeling among them to find the one that is wanted. When hung up against the closet-wall, each tool may be seen at a glance. We have been shown an excellent and simple contrivance for designating the exact places of these things. On the wall, directly under the nails that support the tools, is drawn, with a small brush dipped in black paint or ink, an outline representation of the tool or instrument appropriated to that particular place. For instance, under each saw is sketched the outline of the saw; under each gimlet is a sketch of the gimlet; under the screw-drivers are slight drawings of the screw-drivers. So that when any tool is brought back after being taken away for use, the exact spot to which it belongs may be seen in a moment by its representation on the wall; and all confusion in putting them up, or finding them again, is thus prevented. We highly recommend this plan.

Wrapping-paper may be piled on the floor beneath the large shelf. It can be bought very low, by the ream, at the wholesale paper stores; and every house should be supplied with it in several varieties. For instance, coarse brown paper for common things. That denominated ironmongers' paper, being strong, thick, and in large sheets, is useful for enclosing heavy articles. Nankeen-paper is best for putting up nice parcels, such as books, or things of fine quality that are to be sent to a distance. What is called shoe-paper (each ream generally containing a variety of colours, red, blue, buff, &c.) is also very useful for wrapping small articles, as, though soft, it is not brittle. This paper is very cheap, the usual price seldom exceeding 56 cents per ream, (twenty quires.)

Old waste newspapers are unfit for wrapping any articles that can be soiled by the printing-ink rubbing off upon them. But they may be used for packing china, glass, brass, tin, &c. Also for lighting fires, singeing poultry, and cleaning mirrors or windows. Waste written-paper is of little use, except for allumettes or lamp-lighters. It is well to keep a large jar or bag to receive scraps of waste paper, as it sells for a cent a pound, and these cents may be given to poor children.

We have seen persons, when preparing for a journey, or putting up things to send away, "at their wits' end" for want of a sheet of good wrapping-paper; a string of twine; a few nails; or a little paint to mark a box. We have seen a door standing ajar during a whole week, (and in cold weather too,) for want of a screw-driver to fix a disordered lock, the locksmith not coming when he was sent for.

It seems scarcely credible that any respectable house should be without a hammer; yet we have known genteel families, whose sole dependence for that indispensable article was on borrowing it of their neighbours. And when the hammer was obtained, there were, perhaps, no nails in the house; at least none of the requisite size.

The attention of boys should be early directed to the use of common tools. And if there were tools at hand, there are few American boys that would not take pleasure in learning to use them. By seeing carpenters, locksmiths, bell-hangers, &c., at work, they may soon learn to be passably expert in those arts; and a smart and observant boy will soon acquire considerable amateur proficiency in them. Many useful jobs can be done by servant-men, if there are proper tools in the house.

LETTERS.—For letter-writing, always use good paper; it should be fine, smooth, white, and sufficiently thick not to let the writing show through on the other side. Very good letter-paper can seldom be purchased at less than twenty-five cents per quire. That which is lower in price is inferior in quality. If you cannot trust yourself to write straightly without some guide, have printed ruled lines to slip beneath the page; for a letter does not look well if written on paper that is already ruled with pale blue ink. If you write a small hand, your lines should be closer together than if your writing is large. It is well to have several sorts of ruled lines; they are to be bought at any stationer's for a few cents a page.

If you are writing to a relative, or to an intimate friend, and have much to say, and expect to fill the sheet, begin near the top of the first page. But if your letter is to be a short one, commence lower down, several inches from the top. If a *very* short letter, of only a few lines, begin but a little above the middle of the page.

Write the date near the right-hand side, and place it about a line higher than the two or three words of greeting or accosting with which letters usually commence. Begin the first sentence a little below these words, and farther towards the right than the lines that are to follow it. It is well, in dating *every* letter, to give always your exact residence,—not only the town, but the street also, and the number of your house. If your correspondent has had but one notification of your present place of abode, the number, and even the street may have been forgotten; the letter containing it may not be at hand as a reference; and the reply may, in consequence, be misdirected; or directed in so vague a manner that it may never reach you. We have known much trouble, inconvenience, and indeed loss, ensue from not specifying, in the date of *each* letter, the exact dwelling-place of the writer. But if it is always designated at the top of *every one*, a reference to any of your letters will furnish the proper address. It is customary to date letters at the top, and notes at the bottom. If your letter is so long as to fill more than one sheet, number the pages.

As important words are frequently lost by being torn off with the seal in opening a letter, leave always, in the third or last page, two blank spaces where the seal is to come. These spaces should be left rather too large than too small. You can write in short lines between them. If you cannot otherwise ascertain where the sealing is likely to be, fold your sheet into the form of a letter before you begin to write it; and then, with the point of a pin, (or something similar,) trace, as faintly as possible, two circles, one on the turn-over, the other on the corresponding part of the paper that comes beneath it. These faint circles, when you are writing the last page, will show you where the seal is to go, and what space you are to leave for it. In opening a letter, it is best to cut round the seal; rather than to break it, and *tear* the letter open.

In folding a letter let the breadth (from right to left) far exceed the height. A letter the least verging towards squareness looks very awkward. It is well to use a folding-stick (or ivory paper-knife) to press along the edges of the folds, and make them smooth and even. Take care in folding a letter to make *all* the creases *exactly straight* and even. If one is looser than another, or if there is the slightest widening out or narrowing in towards the edge of the turn-over, the letter will have a crooked, unsightly appearance. You may direct it before sealing; slipping your ruled paper under the back of the letter, that you may run no risk of writing the direction crooked. Begin the address rather nearer to the bottom than the top of the folded letter. Write the name of the person to whom you send it about the middle, and very clearly and distinctly. Then give the number and street on the next line a little nearer to the right. Then the town in *large* letters, and extending almost close to the extreme right. Just under the town, add the abbreviation of the name of the state—as, Pa. for Pennsylvania, N. Y. for New York. But if the letter is to go to New York *city*, put the words New York in full, written large. Much confusion is caused by this state and its metropolis having both the same name. It has been well suggested that the name of the state might be changed to Ontario—a beautiful change.

If the letter is to go to a provincial town, put the name of the county in which that town is situated, immediately over the designation of the state. We believe that throughout the union there are more than fifty towns called Washington. If your letter is for the *city* of Washington, direct for Washington, D. C.—these initials implying the District of Columbia.

Another reason for the propriety of designating the state is, that many of our towns are called after places in Europe: and it has chanced (though not very often) that letters not explicitly and fully directed, have found their way into the mail-bags of packet vessels, and been carried across the Atlantic. We know an instance of a gentleman who directed an important letter simply to Boston, without any indication of the state of Massachusetts; and the letter went from Philadelphia to the small town of Boston in Lincolnshire, England. In writing *from* Europe, it is well always to finish the direction with the words United States of North America.

If you send the letter by a private opportunity, it will be sufficient to introduce close to the lower edge of the left-hand corner on the back, simply the name of the gentleman who takes it, written small. It is now considered old fashioned to insert on the back of such a letter, "Politeness of Mr. Smith," "Favoured by Mr. Jones," "Honoured by Mr. Brown." If to cross the sea, write the name of the vessel on the left hand corner of the outside.

If you make a mistake in a word, it will be better to draw your pen through the error, so as to render it entirely illegible, and then interline the correction, rather than attempt scratching out the mistake with a penknife, and afterwards trying to write another word in the identical place; a thing that is rarely, if ever, done well.

At the end of the letter, nearly on a line with your signature, (which should be close to the right side,) it is usual to put, near the extremity of the *left* side of the page, the name of the person to whom the letter is addressed. Write your signature rather larger than your usual hand; and put a dot or period after your name.

In writing a ceremonious and very respectful note, or in addressing a person with whom you are not very intimate, enclose it in an envelope, and put the direction *on the cover only*. It is now customary always to enclose in envelopes invitations to parties; visiting cards sent to strangers; cards left previous to a marriage; and farewell cards on leaving the place. On the latter it is usual to put the initials *t. t. l.* (to take leave,) or *p. p. c.* (*pour prendre congé*, which has the same signification.) We have also seen *p. d. a.* (*pour dire adieu*, to bid adieu.) For a note, always use a very small seal. There are varieties of beautiful little wafers for notes; also of beautiful note-paper. It is not necessary in addressing an intimate friend to follow, particularly, any of these conventional observances.

For sealing letters no light is so convenient as a wax taper. A lamp or candle may smoke and blacken the wax. To seal well, your wax should be of the finest quality. Good red wax is generally the best, and its colour should be of a brilliant scarlet. Inferior red wax consumes very fast; and always, when melted, looks purplish or brownish. When going to melt sealing-wax, rest your elbow on the table to keep your hand steady. Take the stick of wax between your thumb and finger, and hold it a little above the light, so that it barely touches the point of the flame. Then insert a little of the melted wax *under* the turn-over part of the letter, just where the seal is to come. This will make it more secure than if the sole dependence was on the outside seal. Or instead of this little touch of wax, you may slip under the turn-over a small wafer, either white or of the same colour as the wax. Take the stick of wax, hold it over the flame just so as to touch the tip; next turn it round till the end of the stick is equally softened on every side. Then apply it to your letter, beginning on the outer edge of the place you intend for the seal; and moving the wax round in a circle, which must gradually diminish till it terminates in the centre. Put the seal exactly into the middle of the soft wax, and press it down hard, but do not screw it round. Then withdraw it suddenly. Do not use motto seals unless writing to a member of your own family, or to an intimate friend. For common use, (and particularly for letters of business, or in addressing strangers,) a plain seal with the initials of your name will be best.

We subjoin the usual abbreviations of the states, &c.:—

Maine, *Me.* New Hampshire, *N. H.* Vermont, *Vt.* Massachusetts, *Mass.* Rhode Island, *R. I.* Connecticut, *Ct.* New York, *N. Y.* New Jersey, *N. J.* Pennsylvania, *Pa.* Delaware, *Del.* Maryland, *Md.* Virginia, *Va.* North Carolina, *N. C.* South Carolina, *S. C.* Georgia, *Geo.* or *Ga.* Alabama, *Ala.* Mississippi, *Mi.* Louisiana, *La.* Tennessee,

Ten. Kentucky, *Ky.* Ohio, *O.* Indiana, *Ind.* Illinois, *Ill.* Missouri, *Mo.* District of Columbia, *D. C.* Michigan, *Mich.* Arkansas, *Ark.* Florida, *Fl.* Wisconsin, *Wis.* Iowa, *Io.* Texas, *Tex.* Oregon, *Or.*

To these may be added the abbreviations of the British possessions in North America. Upper Canada, *U. C.* Lower Canada, *L. C.* Nova Scotia, *N. S.* New Brunswick, *N. B.* New Providence, *N. P.*

The name of the town to which the letter is to go, should always be superscribed in full. If a country town or village, it will be necessary to designate the county in which it is situated, as there are so many provincial towns of the same name. Finish with the designation of the state under the whole, close to the right-hand corner.

In directing to a clergyman, put *Rev.* (Reverend) before his name. To an officer, immediately after his name, and on the same line with it, put *U. S. A.* for United States Army; *U. S. N.* for United States Navy. To a member of Congress, precede his name with *Hon.* (Honourable.)

In putting up packets to send away, either tie them round and across with red tape (sealing them also) or seal them without tying. Twine or cord may cut through the paper, and is better omitted. Never put up any thing in newspaper. Beside the danger of soiling the articles inside, it looks mean and disrespectful. Keep yourself provided with different sorts of wrapping-paper. A large parcel should have more than one seal, and the seal may be rather larger than for a letter.

CROSSING THE SEA.—The most usual voyage made by American ladies is across the Atlantic; and the time chosen for that voyage is generally in the spring or autumn. A winter passage is seldom attempted by ladies; and few that have tried it once are willing to undertake it a second time. To those who are preparing to traverse the ocean that separates us from Europe, we hope the following hints may not be unacceptable.

We earnestly recommend that every lady who can afford to pay the additional price, should engage, at an early period, a state-room exclusively to herself; unless, indeed, she can share it with a near relation. She will find the money well spent in securing the privacy and comfort of an apartment into which no one has a right to intrude; besides the additional space she will thus obtain for such articles as she would like to have with her in her room. No one who has not been at sea can imagine the perpetual and mutual annoyance of being confined to the small limits of a state-room with a stranger; each incommoding the other all the time, and each feeling herself under the continual *surveillance* of her companion; both expected to make incessant sacrifices to the convenience of each other, and perhaps only one of them having a disposition to submit to these sacrifices; in which case she that is the most amiable is always the sufferer. We believe it to be the rule in packet-ships that the first applicant for a passage is allowed the privilege of being the last to have a stranger put into her apartment. And if the passengers are not numerous, the fortunate first applicant may in this manner have a whole state-room without the extra charge. But by offering this additional price on taking her passage, she can *always* secure the exclusive possession of an entire state-room.

If you have an apartment exclusively to yourself, the place of the second bed can be filled with boxes, books, &c., for which you would not otherwise have room. But as no ship state-room is large enough to contain *much* baggage, you should make your arrangements to wear during the voyage such articles of outside dress as will least require washing. Therefore, let all light-coloured or white dresses be packed away in the trunks that are to remain below, and not to be opened till the close of the voyage.

As ladies can have no washing done at sea, it will be well to begin with such dresses as can be worn all the passage. French silks are not good sea dresses, (even when black,) for the salt-air shrivels, spots, and turns them rusty. Dark-coloured india silks, or dark mousselines de laine, or merinoes, are much better. Dark chintzes, with no white in the figure, are convenient for common wear, at sea as well as on shore.

Muslin or bobbinet collars, to be worn in the ever-damp sea-air, should have no other trimming than an edging sewed on plain; as quilled or pleated frills lose their stiffening immediately. Silk neck-kerchiefs, or little shawls for the neck, will be found very convenient as substitutes for collars; and, if of white silk, they are extremely becoming. Or you may wear a broad, thick white ribbon, shaped with three diminishing pleats, to fit in closely the back of the neck, and crossed in front. Quilled or fluted cap-borders soon become limp and formless with the damp; so also do gauze or *glacé* ribbons. Sea-caps should have borders either simply gathered or laid on plain; and their ribbons should be mantua, lutestring, or soft satin. A cap lined all through with silk of a pretty colour, will be very convenient at sea, as it not only assists in keeping the damp air from the head, but conceals the hair effectually; and there are rough days when the motion of the ship renders it impossible to arrange the hair nicely. A silk or madras handkerchief, pinned up into a sort of small turban, is sometimes worn at sea, instead of caps. They are very convenient, but only becoming to pretty ladies.

It is colder at sea than on shore; and even in summer, the atmosphere of the Atlantic is liable to be chilled for several days by the vicinity of floating icebergs,— even when these icebergs are not seen. Therefore, be careful at any season, to have in your state-room a sufficiency of warm clothing. A spring-passage is generally colder than an autumn one; and even in May it is sometimes found necessary, when on the open ocean, to dress as if it were winter. Flannel, of course, is indispensable; so, also, is a large thick woollen shawl, and a second shawl of lighter texture for mild weather. A very convenient outside sea-dress is the garment or coat that is sometimes called a mandarine. It should be made of very dark India silk, which is soft, strong, and not liable to stain or spot like the silks of Europe. This dress should be very long and wide; wadded and lined all through; and made with large, loose sleeves, large sleeve-holes, and a wrapper-body, confined at the waist by a broad ribbon run into a casing, and tied in front. A mandarine can be put on over another dress without rumpling it; and is far better than a cloak, as it is warmer and more compact, sits closer, and is not so liable to be blown about by the wind. At sea, there are always days when a mandarine will be found very comfortable to wear, even in the cabin.

No dress intended to be worn on a voyage should fasten *behind*, as it is not always that a lady can procure the assistance of another person to do this for her. Gowns, (or coat-dresses, as they are frequently called,) such as fasten in front, are the best habits for sea; and there is now a well-known way of making wrappers that is both handsome and convenient, and universally becoming. Fortunately, corsets are now exploded; and as they are no longer worn on shore, of course no one would be so absurd as to endure them at sea. Jackets of flannel, lined silk, thick cotton, or jean, made without whalebones, and to fasten in front, are best suited to a voyage. A flannel gown and a dark double-wrapper are indispensable in case of sickness. Your upper petticoat should be of dark linen, worsted, or silk. If you have no mandarine, take with you, by all means, a wadded silk petticoat, and a pair of slightly-wadded silk inside-sleeves, to be tied in beneath your gown-sleeves in chilly weather. For this purpose, have four tapes sewed to the top of each sleeve, at equal distances, and four corresponding tapes sewed to the inside of each arm-hole of your gowns.

The best sea-stockings are those of substantial, *unbleached* cotton. No others are so comfortable. Dark satin-ribbed cotton stockings are also good; so are the black raw silk, such as are shaggy inside. Take with you some *very thick* gray yarn stockings, to put on when your feet are cold in bed, and to draw on, occasionally, over your shoes and other stockings. Gaiter-boots, and boots lined with fur, are very comfortable when once on; but at sea, there is often some trouble in lacing or buttoning them. Shoes worn on ship-board should be thin-soled and roomy, so that you may walk the deck easier, and keep your feet better when the vessel rolls. Shoes of wadded silk are very pleasant at sea; so are Indian moccasins, or carpet moccasins lined with wool. Take with you two or three pairs of woolly sheep-skin soles, such as are coated on the under side with india-rubber varnish. They are warm, dry, and water-proof; can be slipped into your shoes or taken out, as occasion may require; and either for sea or shore, are far superior to the cork soles also in use.

A sea-bonnet should have a deep, close front, and a cape or ruffle at the back of the neck. The complexion is always liable to be injured by the salt air, the glare of the sun, and the bleak wind. A quilted close bonnet of dark silk or satin, lined with pink, blue, or lemon-colour, may be made to look very pretty. Cane or whalebone being very apt to break in the wind, it is best to run wired-satin piping-cord into the cases of a sea-bonnet, and round the edge. This will stiffen it sufficiently; and being very elastic, will keep it in shape without danger of breaking. These bonnets should, by all means, have a large wadded cape attached to them. At sea, it is im-portant to keep the back of the neck always covered, for its exposure to the air may produce rheumatic pains in the head, shoulders, and face. Even in the cabin, and at all times when on ship-board, (except in decidedly warm weather,) it is prudent to wear a handkerchief of silk, cashmere, or velvet, tied or pinned round the neck, with a corner covering it closely behind.

Provide yourself, also, with a pair or two of warm gloves. On days when fire is most needed, it is most difficult to have it in the cabin of a ship. If the wind is strong, it impedes the draught of the stove, and fills the cabin with the smoke that is beaten down the chimney. And if the vessel rolls much, (as she always will in rough weather,) there is danger of the fire falling about the floor; and to prevent accidents from this cause, it is deemed safest to extinguish it entirely, or else not to kindle it at all. The passengers must depend chiefly on their clothing for warmth enough to make them tolerably comfortable,—particularly if they cross the ocean early in the spring or late in the autumn. But, as we before observed, a spring-passage is always the coldest. In the autumn, there is no danger of meeting with icebergs. Also, the ocean-water still retains a portion of the warmth communicated to it by the summer sun; while, in the spring, it remains a long while chilled from the cold of the preceding winter.

As dressing on ship-board is always more or less troublesome and inconvenient, on account of the motion of the vessel, and must generally be done in a sitting posture, it is well to make one dressing suffice for the day.

When packing to go on board, select such articles as are indispensable for use during the voyage, and put them all into one trunk, which must not be too large to keep in your state-room. You will find drawers there, in which you can place your caps, collars, handkerchiefs, and other light articles. Have a strong linen clothes-bag, with a drawing-string at the top, to hang up on one of the pegs or hooks in your apartment. The remainder of your baggage must be put below, in the place appropriated to stowing away the trunks of the passengers, with the understanding that they are to remain there all the voyage.

However pleasant you may find it to stay on deck, it is best, as soon as you get on board, to go to your state-room, and make your arrangements there, lest you should be rendered incapable of doing so by the approach of sea-sickness; an event that may usually be expected within an hour after the vessel gets under-way, if she sails from New York or Boston, or any port in the vicinity of the ocean. Take out of your trunk your night-clothes, your easiest slippers, and whatever articles you may require for immediate use; and place them where they can be directly accessible.

Some few ladies, as well as gentlemen, cross the ocean without being in the least troubled with sea-sickness; and very many only suffer from it during the first two or three days, and are then perfectly well during the remainder of the passage, however stormy it may be. If you should incline to be sick, it will be nearly useless to struggle against it the first day or two. You may try as a preventive, or as an early remedy when the first symptoms come upon you, a lump of loaf-sugar placed in the bottom of a wine-glass, with just as much brandy poured on as will be sufficient to dissolve it, so that it can be eaten with a tea-spoon. If taken in time, this frequently succeeds; and it rarely fails in the short sickness that is sometimes felt in excursions down in the bay of New York; or in Boston harbour, when the water is rough; or in going round Point Judith; or in a trip by sea to any of the coast bathing-places.

If you find your sickness increasing, give up to it for a day or two; and you will afterwards feel much the better for it. For the first two days you need take no nourishment but chicken-water. Avoid lemonade, oranges, all other acids, and every sort of warm drink. Be careful, while you are sick, not to taste any thing that you may like to eat afterwards, as it will give you a disgust to it during the remainder of the voyage. For the same reason, it is well not to use cologne-water, or any very fine perfume during your sickness. Liquid camphor, sprinkled over the bed and floor, will be found more refreshing and purifying to the atmosphere than any thing else that you can take with you.

The third day (if not before) you ought to make every possible exertion to go on deck, as you will be losing strength by remaining in bed; and as long as you keep your head in a recumbent posture, you will not become accustomed to the motion of the vessel. Also, on the third day, endeavour to eat a small portion of solid, relishing food—such as a piece of broiled ham, or the lean of salt beef, with a slice of dry toast. We have known what is called the tone of the stomach restored after sea-sickness by a little of the sailors' salt beef and biscuit. Something of this sort is always more effective than light or delicate food.

It will be well before you embark, to provide yourself with a box of that excellent medicine known as Lady Webster's (or Lady Crespigny's) pills. They are called by both names; probably because both these ladies patronized them in England. You may take one every night *immediately after* supper. In Philadelphia they are made according to the best recipe by J. C. Turnpenny, druggist, corner of Spruce and Tenth streets.

You may find a clay-ball for the removal of grease spots very useful to keep in your room; as, when the ship is rolling, greasy substances are frequently spilt on dresses.

Take with you and keep always in your apartment, a life-preserver, in case of being wrecked in sight of land; and it may really save your life by buoying you up, and floating you to the shore. It is said that a man's hat, laid brim downwards, and tied up in a shawl or pocket-handkerchief, and then fastened round the waist, will keep a person above water long enough to prevent drowning, if not far from the beach. The ladies of New York and Boston, and of other cities on the sea-board, have it in their power to learn, without danger or difficulty, the art of swimming; by subscribing to the salt-water baths, and visiting them daily during the summer.

Nothing will make a sea-voyage seem shorter or less monotonous, than to be well provided with occupation—such as amusing and interesting books, and a due portion of needle-work or knitting. By all means take with you one or more blank-books for the purpose of noting down whatever you may wish to remember. If you can keep a regular journal, so much the better. Also, the first day that you are able to write after getting to sea, commence on a *large* sheet of paper, a letter to one of your relations or friends, having previously folded and directed it. Write but a few lines at first; and every day add a little more to it, giving the fresh dates. It will always be ready (requiring only a wafer to seal it) in case you should have an opportunity of sending it by any vessel you may chance to meet, on her way to the land you have left. If no such chance offers during the voyage, this diary-letter will at least be ready to transmit with those you write home directly after arriving at your destined post. And your friends will be glad to have this concise transcript of your sea-life.

BREAKFAST, DINNERS, SUPPERS, ETC.

At the earnest request of numerous young housekeepers, the author has been induced to offer the following hints for the selection of suitable articles in preparing breakfasts, dinners, and suppers. They, of course, may be varied according to convenience, taste, and the size and circumstances of the family. Receipts for them all may be found either in the present work, or in its predecessor, "Miss Leslie's Directions for Cookery."

BREAKFASTS FOR SPRING AND SUMMER.—Fresh shad broiled; hashed mutton; boiled eggs; potatoes fried—Indian cakes; rolls.

Hashed veal; broiled ham; poached eggs; mashed potatoes—Milk toast; rolls.

Fried cat-fish; omelet; cold boiled ham, or smoked tongue—Rolls; buttered toast.

Veal cutlets; stewed clams; ham and eggs; potatoes mashed—Rye batter cakes; rolls.

Clam fritters; hashed veal; cold ham; potatoes—Milk toast; muffins.

Fresh shad broiled; stewed chickens; cream cheese—Indian batter cakes; rolls.

Mutton chops; omelet; boiled potatoes—Rice batter cakes; muffins.

Minced veal; broiled ham; poached eggs; cream cheese—Milk toast; rolls.

Pickled salmon; broiled chickens; eggs—Indian cakes; milk toast.

Stewed chickens; broiled ham with eggs; mashed potatoes—Rye batter cakes; rolls.

Fried egg-plant; tongue or ham toast; pepper-grass—Indian batter cakes; rolls.

Broiled chickens; pork cheese; potatoes sliced and fried—Rye batter cakes; muffins.

Stewed pigeons; young corn omelet; mashed potatoes—Flannel cakes; toast.

Clam fritters; stewed egg-plant; broiled tomatoes—Rice cakes; rolls.

Broiled chickens; mock oysters of corn; cold ham—Milk toast; muffins.

Hashed veal; ham omelet; cucumbers; pepper-grass—Rice cakes; muffins.

Birds with mushrooms; soft omelet; sliced ham or tongue—Flannel cakes; toast.

Tongue or ham toast; stewed mushrooms; cucumbers—Indian batter cakes; rolls.

Fresh mackerel broiled; potatoes; young corn omelet—Rice cakes; rolls.

Broiled ham with poached eggs; fried chickens; cucumbers—Rye batter cakes; toast.

Stewed chickens; fried sweet potatoes; broiled tomatoes—Flannel cakes; rolls.

In warm weather fresh fruit (thoroughly ripe, and eaten with sugar) is an agreeable and wholesome addition to the breakfast table. Fruit-jam, marmalade, and honey may be introduced at any season.

AUTUMN AND WINTER BREAKFASTS.—Pigeons stewed with mushrooms; fried sweet potatoes; broiled tomatoes—Muffins; milk toast.

Fresh fish broiled; cold ham; potatoes—Indian cakes; rolls.

Oysters stewed or fried; broiled ham with poached eggs—Toast; rolls.

Broiled chickens; ham omelet; broiled tomatoes—Indian cakes; toast.

Stewed chickens; egg-plant sliced and fried; potatoes—Rice batter cakes; rolls.

Hashed duck; ham broiled; poached eggs—Flannel cakes; toast.

Oyster fritters; cold ham or tongue; sweet potatoes sliced and broiled—Indian cakes; rolls.

Mutton chops; broiled tomatoes; pickled salmon—Rice batter cakes; toast.

Beef-steaks; stewed oysters; boiled potatoes—Indian cakes; muffins.

Stewed chickens; sausages; mashed potatoes—Rolls; toast.

Broiled chickens; liver pudding sliced; potatoes—Buckwheat cakes; rolls.

Hashed veal; pig's feet fried; potatoes—Buckwheat cakes; toast.

Venison steaks; broiled sweet potatoes; eggs—Indian batter cakes; rolls.

Venison pasty; fried smelts; mashed potatoes—Buckwheat cakes; toast.

Minced cod-fish, drest with eggs, parsnips, onions, butter, &c.; sausages; boiled potatoes—Indian cakes; rolls.

In cold weather, small hominy, boiled, is often introduced at breakfast tables—also indian mush, to be eaten with butter and molasses. We subjoin a receipt for pumpkin mush, an excellent and wholesome breakfast dish.

PUMPKIN MUSH.—Pour into a clean pot, two quarts or more of good milk, and set it over the fire. Have ready some pumpkin stewed very soft and dry; mashed smooth, and pressed in a cullender till all the liquid has drained off. Then measure a large pint of the stewed pumpkin; mix with it a piece of fresh butter, and a tea-spoonful of ground ginger. Stir it gradually into the milk, as soon as it has come to a boil. Add, by degrees, a large pint or more of indian-meal, a little at a time, stirring it in, very hard, with the mush-stick. If you find the mush too thin, as you proceed, add, in equal portions, more pumpkin and more indian-meal, till it becomes so thick you can scarcely stir it round. After it is all thoroughly mixed, and has boiled well, it will be greatly improved by diminishing the fire a little, or hanging the pot higher up, so as to let it simmer an hour or more. Mush can scarcely be cooked too much. Eat it warm with butter and molasses, or with rich milk. It is very good at luncheon in cold weather.

After boiling small hominy, drain off the water, and leave the dish uncovered. If covered up, the condensation of the steam will render the hominy thin and washy.

BREAKFAST PARTIES.—Black tea; green tea; coffee; chocolate; hot cakes of various sorts; omelets; birds; game; oysters, stewed, fried, and pickled; cold tongue; cold ham; biscuit sandwiches; boned turkey, cold; potted or pickled lobster; raised French pie; pigeon, partridge, or moorfowl pie; mushrooms fried, broiled, or stewed; jellies; marmalade; honey; fresh fruit, or sweetmeats, according to the season; a large almond sponge-cake. The table decorated with flowers.

At a breakfast party the dress of the ladies should be more simple than at a dinner or a supper party.

ECONOMICAL DINNERS FOR SMALL FAMILIES.—The receipts for these plain dishes are generally to be found in Miss Leslie's "Directions for Cookery," a work to which the present book is supplemental.

SPRING.—Boiled ham; spinach; asparagus; poke; potatoes[2]—Rhubarb pie.

Veal cutlets; cold ham; spinach; turnips; poke; asparagus—Baked batter pudding.

Broiled halibut cutlets; cold ham; spinach; turnips; asparagus—Boiled indian pudding.

Calf's liver fried with ham; asparagus; turnips; poke; spinach—Rhubarb pudding.

Boiled leg of mutton; stewed onions; turnips; carrots—Baked rice pudding.

Family soup; fried ham and eggs; asparagus; beets; spinach—Baked indian pudding.

Corned beef; cabbage; carrots; stewed onions; beets—Fritters.

Broiled shad; cold corned beef; carrots; spinach; asparagus—Eastern pudding.

Veal pie; fried ham and eggs; asparagus; spinach; turnips—Gooseberry fool.

Roast veal; peas; asparagus; spinach—Gooseberry pudding.

Boiled rock-fish; hashed veal; peas; spinach; asparagus—Farmer's rice pudding.

Boiled ham; peas; beans; spinach—Gooseberry pie.

Veal soup; cold ham; stewed onions; beans; peas—Currant pie.

Roast beef; horse-radish; peas; beans; asparagus—Custard in a dish.

Fresh cod-fish boiled; cold roast beef; horse-radish; peas; beans; spinach—

---

[2] There is no necessity for repeating the mention of potatoes. It will of course be understood that potatoes should constitute a portion of every dinner. Also that pickles should always be on the table with beef and mutton.

Eastern pudding.

Mutton soup; the meat that was boiled in it; stewed onions; turnips; suet dumplings—Currant pie.

Roast lamb with mint-sauce; asparagus; peas; spinach—Custard in a dish.

Boiled black-fish; cold roast lamb; spring salad; beans; peas—Gooseberry pudding.

Green pea-soup; veal cutlets; salad; peas; beans—Currant pie.

Boiled ham; fried chickens; peas; beans; salad—Fritters or pancakes.

Roast fillet of veal; cold ham; peas; beans; salad—Gooseberry pie.

Hashed veal; broiled ham with eggs; peas; beans—Boiled indian pudding.

Boiled sea-bass; beef-steaks; onions; beans; peas—Currant pie.

Stewed breast of veal; fried ham with eggs; peas; beans—Gooseberry pudding.

Fresh cod-fish boiled; mutton chops; stewed onions; beans; peas—Baked batter pudding.

Baked beef with a batter pudding under it; beans; peas—Gooseberry pie.

Broiled mackerel; stewed mutton; stewed onions; beans; peas—Boiled rice pudding.

Boiled halibut; beef-steaks; onions; beans; peas—Currant pudding.

Salt cod-fish; stewed onions; veal cutlets; beans; peas—Baked rice pudding.

PLAIN DINNERS FOR SUMMER.—Clam soup; beef-steaks; stewed onions; peas; beans; summer cabbage—Cherry pie.

Boiled ham; veal cutlets; cucumbers; beans; peas—Custard pudding.

Cat-fish soup; cold ham; cucumbers; peas; beans—Cherry pie.

Stewed fillet of veal; cold ham; squashes; beans; beets—Batter pudding, baked.

Boiled black-fish; beef-steak pie; squashes; beans; beets—Cherry pudding.

Fried sea-bass; stewed knuckle of veal; cucumbers; squashes; beans—Raspberry pudding.

Boiled mackerel; beef-steaks; onions; cucumbers; beans; squashes—Baked rice pudding.

Clam soup; stewed fillet of veal; cucumbers; beets; fried egg-plant—Sweet potatoe pudding.

Beef-steaks with stewed onions; boiled crabs; cucumbers; squashes; boiled corn—Raspberry pie.

Stewed leg of mutton; turnips; squashes; beets; cucumbers—Blackberry pie.

Boiled ham; clam fritters; beans; summer cabbage; corn—Custard pudding.

Clam pie; cold ham; sweet potatoes; lima beans; squashes—Boiled batter pudding.

Boiled fowls; fried ham and eggs; lima beans; sweet potatoes; beets—Raspberry pie.

Roast ducks; stewed egg-plant; lima beans; sweet potatoes; turnips—Custard.

Boiled leg of mutton; nasturtian sauce; turnips; tomatoes; beets—Blackberry pie.

Pilau; clam pie; lima beans; mashed turnips; tomatoes—Boiled indian pudding.

Beef-steak pie; stewed egg-plant; turnips; lima beans; boiled corn—Boiled rice pudding.

Boiled rock-fish; stewed breast of veal; sweet potatoes; tomatoes; lima beans—Green corn pudding.

Roast pig with apple sauce; turnips; lima beans; sweet potatoes—Raspberry pie.

Boiled ham; fried chickens; lima beans; tomatoes; boiled corn—Green gage pie.

Pot-pie; mashed turnips; lima beans; sweet potatoes; cucumbers—Fritters.

Fried sea-bass; boiled fowls; cauliflower; tomatoes; lima beans—Peach pie.

Roast ducks; cauliflower; tomatoes; lima beans—Green gage pudding.

Boiled ham; clam fritters; summer cabbage; lima beans—Apple pie.

Fried chickens; cold ham; cauliflower; tomatoes; sweet potatoes—Sweet potatoe pudding.

Fried calf's liver; cold ham; chitterlings or calf's tripe; tomatoes; cauliflower; sweet potatoes—Peach pie.

Stewed beef's heart; clam fritters; sweet potatoes; tomatoes; squashes—Squash pudding.

Corned beef; cabbage; carrots; stewed onions; tomatoes—Plum pie.

Veal cutlets; cold corned beef; tomatoes; squashes; boiled corn—Blackberry pudding.

Harico of mutton; fried chickens; sweet potatoes; lima beans; beets; boiled corn—Peach pudding.

Chowder; mutton chops; turnips; stewed tomatoes; boiled corn—Huckleberry pudding.

Stewed breast of veal; tomatoes; cauliflower; lima beans—Green gage pudding.

Clam pie; veal cutlet; lima beans; boiled corn—Boiled indian pudding.

Halibut cutlets; roasted beef's heart; tomatoes; sweet potatoes; boiled corn—Plum pie.

Cat-fish soup; chicken pie; beans; peas; tomatoes—Raspberry pudding boiled.

Sea-shore dinner.—Chowder; crabs; broiled mackerel; potatoes—Raisin pudding.

PLAIN DINNERS FOR AUTUMN.—Fresh pork, stewed with sweet potatoes; lima beans; tomatoes; corn—Plum pie.

Roast ducks; stewed egg-plant; tomatoes; lima beans; squashes; turnips—Peach pie.

Ochra soup; beef-steaks; tomatoes; lima beans; sweet potatoes—Sweet potatoe pudding.

Roast leg of pork, with apple sauce; sweet potatoes; lima beans—Custard.

Rabbit soup; boiled ham; cauliflower; lima beans; tomatoes—Peach pie.

Ham pie; veal cutlets; salsify; sweet potatoes; lima beans—Peach pudding.

Rabbit pot-pie; broiled ham with eggs; lima beans; sweet potatoes—Baked bread pudding.

Pigeon soup; beef-steaks; onions; tomatoes; lima beans; sweet potatoes—Apple pie.

Stewed beef; tomatoes; turnips; salsify; sweet potatoes; turnips—Bread and butter pudding.

Ox-tail soup; fried rabbits; lima beans; beets; sweet potatoes—Peach pie.

Roast leg of mutton; stewed onions; russian turnips; beets—Apple rice pudding.

Mutton harico; fried chickens; turnips; salsify; lima beans—Eastern pudding.

Pork and beans; stewed rabbits; tomatoes; sweet potatoes; russian turnips—Boiled indian pudding.

Oyster soup; roast goose with apple sauce; turnips; sweet potatoes—Sweet potatoe pudding.

Boiled fowls with celery sauce; oyster fritters; turnips; sweet potatoes; winter-squash—Apple pie.

Roast pork with apple sauce; turnips; salsify; tomatoes; sweet potatoes—Baked batter pudding.

Roast beef with horse-radish; sweet potatoes; turnips; tomatoes; cold-slaw—Baked apple pudding.

Mutton soup; the meat that was boiled in it; hashed beef; turnips; beets; tomatoes—Baked rice pudding.

Fresh pork stewed with parsnips; turnips; winter-squash or cashaw—Apple dumplings.

Beef bouilli; oyster fritters; turnips; stewed onions; winter-squash—Apple pie.

Stewed leg of mutton; russian turnips; sweet potatoes; salsify—Baked bread pudding.

Hashed mutton; fried ham with eggs; turnips; tomatoes; winter-squash—Apple pudding, boiled.

Beef-steak pot-pie; turnips; tomatoes; stewed pumpkin—Fritters or pancakes.

Boiled corned pork; cabbage; winter-squash; turnips—Bread and butter pudding.

Roast mutton; turnips; cold-slaw; beets; tomatoes—Boiled rice pudding.

Bean soup; cassarole of mutton; turnips; beets; cold-slaw—Apple pie.

Pork pie with apples in it; veal cutlets; turnips; beets; tomatoes—Boiled indian pudding.

Corned beef; cale cannon; tomatoes; beets; turnips; carrots—Indian fritters.

Cold corned beef; tripe and oysters; stewed onions; cold-slaw—Pumpkin pudding.

Fresh beef stewed with parsnips; tomatoes; turnips; beets—Baked rice pudding.

Boiled ham; cabbage; tomatoes; stewed pumpkin; turnips—Apple pie.

Stewed beef's-heart; cold ham; winter-squash; beets—Eastern pudding.

Pigeon pie; smoked tongue; winter-squash; turnips—Apple rice pudding.

Ox-tail soup; veal cutlets; turnips; tomatoes; winter-squash—Dried peach pudding.

PLAIN DINNERS FOR WINTER.—Boiled ham; cabbage; beets; cold-slaw; hominy—Apple pie.

Chicken pie; cold ham; turnips; beets; hominy—Boiled batter pudding.

Pease soup; beef-steaks; onions; turnips; beets; cold-slaw—Baked rice pudding.

Roast goose with apple sauce; turnips; beets; winter-squash—Cranberry pie.

Pork and beans; stewed fowl; winter-squash; turnips—Eastern pudding.

Salt cod-fish with onions and eggs; parsnips; pigeon dumplings; turnips; beets—Apple pie.

Pickled pork with pease-pudding; winter-squash; hominy—Molasses pie.

Roast turkey with cranberry sauce; turnips; winter-squash; salsify—Custard pudding.

Pork pie with apples; oyster fritters; turnips; stewed pumpkin—Boiled bread pudding.

Round of beef stewed; parsnips; cale cannon; carrots; turnips—Baked indian pudding.

Fried rabbits; cold beef; turnips; winter-squash; hominy—Boiled batter pudding.

Pot-pie; winter-squash; turnips; beets—Pumpkin pudding.

Boiled corned pork with indian dumplings; stewed pumpkin; turnips—Baked bread pudding.

Bean soup; beef-steaks; onions; turnips; winter-squash—Squash pudding.

Boiled leg of mutton with nasturtian sauce; turnips; stewed pumpkin; hominy—Pumpkin pudding.

Salt cod-fish; onions; eggs; parsnips; pork-steaks—Apple pot-pie.

Boiled ham; cabbage; winter-squash; hominy—Dried peach pie.

Pilau; mutton chops; turnips; winter-squash; cold-slaw—Apple bread pudding.

Roast fowls; turnips; winter-squash; salsify—Cranberry pie.

Roast beef; horse-radish; winter-squash; turnips; cold-slaw—Pumpkin pudding.

Family soup; veal cutlets; turnips; winter-squash; parsnips—Dried apple pie.

Roast pork; apple sauce; turnips; stewed pumpkin; parsnips—Baked rice pudding.

Beef-steak pudding; fried ham and eggs; turnips; winter-squash—Rice custard.

Boiled fowls; oyster fritters; turnips; winter-squash—Carrageen blanc-mange.

Beef-steak pot-pie; turnips; parsnips; winter-squash—Apple bread pudding.

Corned beef; cabbage; turnips; carrots; beets—Indian fritters.

Stewed rabbits; cold corned beef; cale cannon; winter-squash; parsnips—Boiled indian pudding.

Ox-tail soup; roast leg of mutton; turnips; winter-squash; parsnips—Apple dumplings.

Beef-steaks broiled; mutton harico; onions; hominy; turnips; beets—Indian fritters.

Christmas dinner.—Roast turkey; cranberry sauce; boiled ham; turnips; beets; winter-squash—Mince pies.

New Year's dinner.—A pair of roast geese with apple sauce; smoked tongue; turnips; cold-slaw; winter-squash—Plum pudding.

VERY NICE FAMILY DINNERS FOR SPRING.—Spring soup; roast fillet of veal; (potatoes always;) peas; stewed spinach—Rhubarb pie; custards.

Stewed rock-fish; roast lamb with mint sauce; peas; asparagus; poke—Gooseberry pie; boiled custard.

Clam soup; roast loin of veal; stewed peas; spinach; asparagus—Tapioca pudding; gooseberry fool.

Stewed sea-bass; roast beef; stewed spinach; stewed peas; asparagus; beets—Currant pie; custards.

Stewed halibut; chicken pie; stewed peas; stewed beans; asparagus—Boiled lemon pudding; gooseberry pie.

Green pea soup; roast fillet of veal; beans; peas; asparagus—Gooseberry pudding; boiled custard.

Boiled ham; roast ducks with apple sauce; stewed peas; beans; asparagus—Currant pie; green custard.

Cat-fish soup; roast lamb with mint sauce; peas; asparagus; spinach—Ground rice pudding; gooseberry fool.

Clam pie; roast loin of veal; stewed peas; asparagus; stewed spinach—Currant pudding; red custard.

Maccaroni soup; roast ducks with apple sauce; peas; asparagus; spinach—Currant pie; gelatine custard.

Baked shad; stewed fillet of veal; peas; asparagus; spinach—Soufflé pudding; gooseberry pie.

Roast lamb with mint sauce; clam-sweetbreads; peas; beans; asparagus—Ground rice pudding; currant pie.

Corned fillet of veal; clam pie; stewed peas; spinach; beans; asparagus—Gooseberry pudding; green fritters.

Roast beef; stewed sweetbreads with oysters; beans; peas; asparagus—Gelatine blanc-mange; gooseberry fool.

Halibut cutlets; stewed lamb; peas; beans; asparagus; beets—Maccaroni pudding; currant pie.

Boiled ham; fowl and oysters; asparagus; spinach; peas—Gooseberry pie; custards.

Green pea soup; chicken pie; broiled ham; peas; asparagus; beans—Biscuit pudding; gooseberry fool.

FAMILY DINNERS FOR SUMMER—VERY NICE.—Fresh salmon stewed; roast ducks with stewed currant sauce; beans; peas; turnips—Cherry pie; custards.

Clam soup; roast fowls; peas; turnips; beans—Raspberry charlotte; green fritters.

Boiled ham; sweetbreads with cauliflowers; lima beans; tomatoes; baked egg-plant—Sunderlands; strawberries and cream.

Roast fillet of veal; smoked tongue; lima beans; tomatoes; stewed egg-plant—Sweet potatoe pudding; flavoured curds and whey.

Baked salmon; terrapin veal; chicken pie; sweet potatoes; lima beans; tomatoes—Charlotte pudding; strawberries and cream.

Chickens stewed whole; boiled ham; summer cabbage; beans; sweet potatoes—Maccaroni pudding; raspberries and cream.

Roast beef; fried chickens; cauliflowers; tomatoes; lima beans; sweet potatoes—Cherry pie; custards.

Roast ducks with currant sauce; smoked tongue; stewed onions; lobster salad; stewed beans; peas—Boiled lemon pudding; strawberries and cream.

Boiled ham; tomato chickens; beans; turnips; egg-plant; sweet potatoes—Sweet potatoe pudding; raspberries and cream.

Clam pie; stewed wild ducks; sweet potatoes; turnips; squashes; egg-plant—Peach pie; custards.

Salmon cutlets; chicken pie; smoked tongue; lima beans; sweet potatoes; squashes—Sweet potatoe pudding; floating island.

Chicken gumbo; boiled ham; young corn omelet; lima beans; sweet potatoes—Peach pie; flavoured curds and whey.

Roast pig with apple sauce; chicken pie; lima beans; tomatoes; young corn omelet—Charlotte pudding; custard.

Ochra soup; roast beef; tomatoes; lima beans; squashes; turnips—Squash pudding; fritters.

Stewed sea-bass; boiled ham; clam fritters; sweet potatoes; tomatoes; lima beans—Peach pie; boiled custard.

Baked salmon-trout; pigeon pie; tomatoes; lima beans; sweet potatoes; cucumbers—Sweet potatoe pudding; peaches and cream.

Sea-shore dinner.—Oyster soup; clam pie; stewed rock-fish; crabs; mashed potatoes—Boiled lemon pudding.

VERY NICE AUTUMN DINNERS FOR FAMILIES.—Autumn soup; Roast fowls; smoked tongue; lima beans; squashes; sweet potatoes—Sweet potatoe pudding; apple pie.

Italian pork; roast ducks with apple sauce; squashes; egg-plant; lima beans—Peach pie; gelatine custard.

Oyster soup; roast beef; sweet potatoes; squashes; egg-plant; lima beans—Quince pudding; bread fritters.

Sea-bass with tomatoes; boiled ham; pigeon pie; sweet potatoes; stewed red cabbage; lima beans—Squash pudding; preserved peaches.

Ham pie; sweetbreads with oysters; sweet potatoes; lima beans; egg-plant—Boiled lemon pudding; preserved quinces.

Rabbit soup; roast beef; cold-slaw; lima beans; tomatoes; sweet potatoes—Sago pudding; preserved tomatoes.

Roast pork with apple sauce; sweet potatoes; lima beans; egg-plant—Sweet potatoe pudding; fritters.

Boiled ham; roast fowls; stewed red cabbage; turnips; sweet potatoes; lima beans—Squash pudding; apple pie.

Roast fillet of veal; cold ham; broccoli; turnips; lima beans; sweet potatoes—

Baked rice pudding; preserved peaches.

Stewed pork with sweet potatoes; fried rabbits; onions; turnips; lima beans—Peach pudding; custards.

Roast goose with apple sauce; smoked tongue; onions; turnips; lima beans; sweet potatoes—Eve's pudding; floating island.

Oyster soup; chicken pie; beef-steaks; onion sauce; tomatoes; turnips; sweet potatoes—Sweet potatoe pudding; preserved peaches.

Roast fowls; corned beef; stewed red cabbage; turnips; tomatoes—Apple custard; preserved tomatoes.

Boiled rock-fish; roast pork with apple sauce; sweet potatoes; turnips; tomatoes—Baked apple pudding; fritters.

Oyster soup; venison steaks; tomato sweetbreads; turnips; sweet potatoes—Pumpkin pudding; preserved tomatoes.

Venison pie; smoked tongue; broccoli; sweet potatoes; turnips; winter-squash—Eve's pudding; fritters.

Roast venison; oyster fritters; turnips; sweet potatoes; winter-squash—Apple pie; boiled custard.

Ochra soup; roast fowls; smoked tongue; turnips; sweet potatoes; broccoli—Pumpkin pudding; baked pears.

WINTER DINNERS FOR FAMILIES—VERY NICE.—Winter soup; roast beef; stewed onions; cold-slaw; turnips—Apple pie; custards.

Boiled ham; oyster pie; turnips; parsnips; stewed pumpkin—Baked rice pudding; preserved tomatoes.

Chicken pot-pie; oyster fritters; turnips; parsnips; beets—Pumpkin pudding; preserved peaches.

Boiled turkey with oyster sauce; smoked tongue; turnips; salsify; beets—Cranberry pie; custards.

Roast fowls with cranberry sauce; oyster fritters; turnips; beets; winter-squash—Potatoe pudding; preserved quinces.

Bean soup; roast pork with apple sauce; turnips; pumpkin; beets—Pumpkin pudding; preserved tomatoes.

Roast beef; scolloped oysters; turnips; parsnips; stewed beets; winter-squash—Cranberry pie; boiled custard.

Pease soup; roast fowls; turnips; beets; cold-slaw; hominy; winter-squash—Squash pudding; baked apples.

Roast turkey with cranberry sauce; boiled ham; winter-squash; turnips; salsify—Mince pudding; lemon custards.

Ham pie; oyster fritters; turnips; winter-squash; salsify; stewed beets—Raisin pudding; baked pears.

Venison soup; roast fowls; stewed beets; turnips; winter-squash—Sago pudding; baked apples.

Roast venison with currant jelly; chicken curry; turnips; winter-squash; salsify—Cranberry pie; custards.

Roast fowls; boiled corned beef; cabbage; carrots; parsnips; turnips—Apple pie; boiled custard.

Roast beef; stewed fowls; cold-slaw; stewed beets; turnips; hominy; salsify—Plum pudding; cranberry pie.

Soup à la Julienne; roast goose with apple sauce; scolloped oysters; turnips; stewed onions; stewed beets—Pumpkin pudding; preserved pears.

Roast mutton; chicken curry; cold-slaw; beets; turnips; stewed pumpkin—Eve's pudding; baked apples.

Venison pasty; fricasseed chickens; turnips; salsify; winter-squash—Plum pudding; preserved tomatoes.

Roast beef; fricasseed fowls; cold-slaw; beets; turnips; winter-squash—Mince pie; custards.

Boiled turkey with oyster sauce; boiled ham; stewed beets; turnips; cold-slaw—Pumpkin pudding; baked apples.

Bean soup; cold ham; roast fillet of veal; stewed beets; turnips; winter-squash—Mince pie; boiled custard.

A-la-mode beef; scolloped oysters; turnips; carrots; beets; cold-slaw—Carrot pudding; preserved pears.

Christmas and New Years' dinners.—Boiled turkey with oyster sauce; two roast geese with apple sauce; roasted ham; chicken pie; stewed beets; cold-slaw; turnips; salsify; winter-squash—Plum pudding; mince pie; lemon custards; cranberry pie.

Roast turkey with cranberry sauce; boiled fowls with celery sauce; boiled ham; goose pie; turnips; winter-squash; salsify; cold-slaw; beets—Mince pudding boiled; lemon pudding baked; pumpkin pudding.

Mock turtle soup; roast turkey with cranberry sauce; boiled turkey with celery sauce; roasted ham; smoked tongue; chicken curry; oyster pie; beets; cold-slaw; winter-squash; salsify; fried celery—Plum pudding; mince pie; calves'-feet jelly; blanc-mange.

COMPANY DINNERS—SPRING.—1. Oyster soup; boiled sheep's-head fish; roasted ham; white fricassee; chickens stewed whole; terrapin veal; sweetbread croquettes; asparagus; stewed peas; stewed spinach; fried celery; maccaroni—Lemon pudding; almond pudding; calves'-feet jelly; vanilla ice-cream.

2. Maccaroni soup; stewed rock-fish; boiled ham; brown fricassee; veal rissoles; chicken rice pudding; larded sweetbreads; asparagus loaves; asparagus omelet; French spinach; French peas; stewed beets—Rhubarb cups; transparent pudding; charlotte russe; lemon ice-cream.

3. French white soup; baked sheep's-head fish; boiled ham; lamb cutlets, the French way; roasted sweetbreads; beef's tongue stewed; French chicken pie; maccaroni; stewed peas; stewed beans; asparagus; stewed spinach—Omelet soufflé; orleans pudding; blanc-mange; orange ice-cream.

4. Fine clam soup; halibut cutlets; roasted ham; brown fricassee; broiled sweetbreads; pigeon pie; lobster rissoles; asparagus omelet; maccaroni; lettuce peas; asparagus; French spinach; potatoe snow—Boiled almond pudding; sweetmeat fritters; vanilla flummery; cake syllabub.

5. Green pea soup; stewed sea-bass; French ham pie; baked tongue; cutlets à la Maintenon; fricasseed chickens; maccaroni; asparagus; stewed peas; stewed beans—Marietta pudding; Spanish blanc-mange; calves'-feet jelly; lemon ice-cream.

6. Asparagus soup; stewed halibut; roasted ham; chicken curry; fricasseed sweetbreads; terrapin veal; chicken patties; maccaroni; lettuce peas; potatoe snow; stewed beans; stewed beets—Lady's pudding; green custard; wine fritters; gooseberry water-ice.

7. Friar's chicken; halibut cutlets; boiled ham; French chicken pie; sweetbread croquettes; lamb cutlets, French way; lobster patties; Columbus eggs; French peas; stewed beans; stewed beets; potatoe snow—Orleans pudding; orange tarts; pistachio cream; iced jelly.

8. Rich veal soup; stewed carp; boiled ham; sweetbreads stewed with oysters; roast ducks; soft crabs; chicken rice pudding; stewed peas; stewed beans; stewed beets; potatoe snow—Maccaroni pudding; red custard; chocolate cream; almond ice-cream.

COMPANY DINNERS—SUMMER.—1. Duck soup; fresh salmon stewed; roasted ham; French chicken pie; veal olives; sweetbreads with cauliflowers; baked clams; stewed lobster; fried artichokes; scolloped tomatoes; lettuce peas; stewed beans; lettuce chicken salad—Pine-apple pudding; currant ice; iced jelly; strawberries and cream.

2. Pigeon soup; cream trout; baked tongue; terrapin veal; clam sweetbreads; chicken curry; roast ducks; fried cauliflower; French peas; stewed beans; lobster salad—Lady's pudding; pine-apple tarts; raspberry charlotte; strawberry ice-cream.

3. The best clam soup; roasted salmon; boiled ham; rice pie; tomato chickens; sweetbread croquettes; veal olives; lobster patties; cauliflower maccaroni; lima beans; stuffed egg-plant; sweet potatoes—Charlotte russe; cherry water-ice; vanilla blanc-mange; iced jelly.

4. Lobster soup; baked salmon-trout; tongue pie; roast ducks; fricasseed chickens; sweetbreads with cauliflowers; reed-birds; lettuce peas; stewed beans; stewed beets; Sydney Smith's salad—Almond pudding; orange pudding; vanilla ice-cream; Spanish blanc-mange.

5. Maccaroni soup; salmon steaks; French ham pie; chickens stewed whole; white fricassee; lobster rissoles; tomato sweetbreads; lima beans; sweet potatoes;

young corn omelet; potatoe snow; fried cauliflower; salad — French charlotte; vanilla blanc-mange; lemon custards; raspberry ice-cream.

6. Rich white soup; boiled salmon; roasted ham; stewed ducks; boiled fowls; plovers; scolloped tomatoes; lima beans; sweet potatoes; cauliflower omelet; lobster salad — Marietta pudding; raspberry charlotte; iced jelly; pistachio cream.

7. Normandy soup; roasted salmon; boiled ham; French chicken pie; brown fricassee; sweetbreads with cauliflowers; lobster patties; birds with mushrooms; lima beans; scolloped tomatoes; sweet potatoes; turnips; stewed egg-plant; salad — Orleans pudding; maccaroni pudding; Spanish blanc-mange; peach ice-cream.

8. Mock turtle soup; baked salmon; roasted ham; tongue pie; fricasseed chickens; stewed ducks; plovers; clam sweet breads; broccoli and eggs; sweet potatoes; onion custard; lima beans; salad — Orange tarts; charlotte russe; maccaroni blanc-mange; Marlborough pudding; lemon ice-cream.

Sea-shore dinner. — Clam soup; roast salmon; boiled ham; sea-coast pie; stewed oysters; fried oysters; stewed lobster; crabs; baked clams; mashed potatoes — Biscuit pudding; sweetmeat fritters; cake syllabub; orange flummery.

COMPANY DINNERS — AUTUMN. — 1. Mock turtle soup; stewed rock-fish; roasted ham; boiled fowls; stewed ducks; fried rabbits; stuffed egg-plant; broccoli and eggs; fried artichokes; stewed mushrooms; potatoe snow; sweet potatoes — Chocolate pudding; meringued apples; cake syllabub; peach ice-cream.

2. Venison soup; baked salmon-trout; boiled ham; French chicken pie; roast ducks with cranberry sauce; veal olives; sweetbread omelet; stewed red cabbage; turnips; onion custard; sweet potatoes — Boiled almond pudding; orange tarts; sweetmeat fritters; vanilla ice-cream.

3. Rich brown soup; sea-bass with tomatoes; ham pie; fricasseed chickens; roast goose with apple sauce; oyster omelet; birds with mushrooms; scolloped tomatoes; cold-slaw; sweet potatoes; broccoli and eggs; fried artichokes; onion custard — Lady's pudding; sweetmeat tarts; lemon custards; almond ice-cream.

3. Normandy soup; stewed rock-fish; tongue pie; roast fowls; partridges in pears; stewed ducks; oyster loaves; lima beans; tomatoes broiled; stewed mushrooms; cold-slaw; sweet potatoes — Orleans pudding; orange custards; Spanish blanc-mange; vanilla ice-cream.

4. Soupe à la Julienne; cream trout; roasted ham; stewed wild ducks; tomato sweetbreads; French oyster pie; white fricassee; mushroom omelet; stewed red cabbage; lima beans; winter squash; sweet potatoes; turnips — Marrow pudding; lemon custards; meringued apples; peach ice-cream.

5. The best oyster soup; stewed rock-fish; boiled ham; roast wild ducks with currant jelly; chicken rice pudding; birds in a grove; terrapin veal; sweetbread croquettes; turnips; sweet potatoes; onion custard; broiled tomatoes — Vanilla flummery; omelet soufflé; sweetmeat tarts; lemon ice-cream.

6. Meg Merrilies soup; boiled rock-fish; roasted ham; stewed wild ducks; French oyster pie; roasted pheasants; Columbus eggs; mushroom omelet; lima

beans; sweet potatoes; turnips; winter-squash; beets—Orange flummery; sweet potatoe pudding; calves' feet jelly; lemon ice-cream.

7. Rich white soup; sea-bass with tomatoes; baked tongue; roast goose with apple sauce; fricasseed fowls; venison steaks with currant-jelly; oyster omelet; broiled mushrooms; turnips; sweet potatoes; winter-squash; lima beans—Cocoa-nut pudding; sweetmeat tarts; lemon custards; chocolate ice-cream.

8. Hare or rabbit soup; stewed rock-fish; boiled ham; pigeon pie; roast fowls; brown fricassee; partridges in pears; woodcocks; oyster loaves; turnips; sweet potatoes; winter-squash; beets; cold-slaw—Sweet potatoe pudding; orange tarts; whipped cream; Spanish blanc-mange.

COMPANY DINNERS—WINTER.—1. Mulligatawny soup; fresh cod-fish fried; boiled ham; roast turkey with cranberry sauce; fowls stewed whole; oyster pie; potatoe snow; turnips; parsnips; winter-squash—Cocoa-nut pudding; lemon pudding; mince-pie; calves' feet jelly.

2. Clear gravy soup; stewed rock-fish; roasted ham; boiled turkey with oyster sauce; venison pie; brown fricassee; sweet potatoes; turnips; parsnips; beets—Orange pudding; almond pudding; meringued apples; chocolate cream.

3. Venison soup; fresh cod-fish boiled; smoked tongue; pair of roast geese with apple sauce; oyster pie; French stew of rabbits; turnips; potatoe snow; parsnips; onion custard; beets—Transparent pudding; orange tarts; mince-pie; floating island.

4. Mock turtle soup; boiled rock-fish; ham pie; smoked tongue; roast turkey with cranberry sauce; boiled fowls with celery sauce; oyster loaves; sweetbread croquettes; turnips; parsnips; beets; maccaroni—Charlotte russe; mince-pie; calves' feet jelly; blanc-mange.

5. Rich brown soup; fresh cod-fish stewed; boiled ham; venison roasted; red-head ducks with currant jelly; oyster patties; veal rissoles; turnips; parsnips; beets; winter-squash; cold-slaw—Mince-pudding; omelet soufflé; orange flummery; vanilla ice-cream.

6. Rich white soup; fresh cod-fish fried; roasted ham; venison pie; boiled turkey with oyster sauce; partridges in pears; chicken rice pudding; potatoe snow; beets; turnips; winter-squash; stewed red cabbage—Plum pudding; chocolate blanc-mange; cocoa-nut cream; apple-jelly.

7. Meg Merrilies soup; stewed rock-fish; boiled ham; canvas-back ducks roasted; French oyster pie; fricasseed chickens; veal olives; winter-squash; potatoe snow; beets; turnips; maccaroni—Orange pudding; cocoa-nut pudding; cake syllabub; chocolate ice-cream.

8. Maccaroni soup; fresh cod-fish stewed; smoked tongue; canvas-back ducks stewed; partridge pie; fricasseed fowls; stewed sweetbreads with oysters; turnips; potatoe snow; parsnips; beets; cold-slaw—Orleans pudding; Italian charlotte; apple compote; orange-jelly.

Christmas dinners.—Mock turtle soup; stewed rock-fish; roasted ham; roasted venison with currant-jelly; boiled turkey with oyster sauce; roast geese with apple sauce; French oyster pie; fricasseed chickens; potatoe snow; parsnips; beets; winter-squash; cold-slaw—Plum pudding; mince-pies; orange tarts; cream cocoa-nut pudding; Spanish blanc-mange; apple-jelly; vanilla ice-cream.

New Year's dinner.—Venison soup; stewed fresh cod; boiled ham; roasted turkey with cranberry sauce; roast goose with apple sauce; partridge pie; winter-squash; beets; potatoe snow; cold-slaw—Columbian pudding; lemon tarts; charlotte polonaise; vanilla blanc-mange; trifle.

LARGE DINNER PARTIES.—1. *Spring.*—Rich brown soup at one end; rich white soup at the other; two dishes of sheep's-head fish, one baked, one stewed, or else baked salmon-trout and cream trout; roasted ham; smoked tongue; chickens stewed whole; roast ducks with cranberry-jelly; sweetbreads with oysters; terrapin veal; white fricassee; brown fricassee; sweetbread croquettes; lobster rissoles; oyster loaves; lobster patties; asparagus loaves; French spinach; French peas; cauliflower maccaroni; stewed beans; fried cauliflower; fried artichokes; stewed spinach; asparagus omelet; cauliflower omelet—Columbian pudding; orange tarts; lemon tarts; charlotte polonaise; green custard; red custard; pistachio cream; maccaroon blanc-mange; vanilla blanc-mange; gooseberry-water ice; currant-water ice; almond ice-cream; calves' feet jelly.

2. *Summer.*—Turtle soup; fresh salmon stewed; salmon steaks; baked turtle; boiled ham; baked tongue; roast ducks with cherry-jelly; chicken curry; chicken patties; sweetbreads and cauliflowers; tomatoe sweetbreads; lobster pie; stewed lobster; birds in a grove; thatched house pie; plovers roasted; rice pie; mushroom omelets; broccoli and eggs; fried artichokes; stewed peas; stewed beans; stewed beets; potatoe snow; lettuce peas; scolloped tomatoes; mashed sweet potatoes; stuffed egg-plants; stewed egg-plant; Sydney Smith's salad—Pine-apple tarts; lady's pudding; transparent pudding; marmalade puddings; French charlotte; Italian charlotte; iced jelly; vanilla blanc-mange; almond blanc-mange; orange ice-cream; strawberry ice-cream.

3. *Autumn.*—Meg Merrilies soup; sea-bass with tomatoes; salmon-trout; roasted ham; smoked tongue; roast fowls; partridge pie; birds with mushrooms; partridges in pears; terrapin; young geese with apple sauce; tongue pie; chicken gumbo; woodcocks roasted; rice croquettes; Columbus eggs; onion custard; mushroom omelet; cauliflower omelet; scolloped tomatoes; baked egg-plant; potatoe snow; lima beans; fried sweet potatoes; mashed sweet potatoes—Cream cocoa-nut pudding; chocolate pudding; sweet omelet; preserved pine-apple; preserved citron-melon; Spanish blanc-mange; calves' feet jelly; meringued apples; orange-water ice; peach ice-cream; biscuit ice-cream.

4. *Winter.*—Mock turtle soup; oyster soup; rock-fish stewed; fresh cod-fish fried; boiled ham; baked tongue; roast turkey with cranberry-jelly; boiled turkey with oyster sauce; roasted canvas-back ducks with currant-jelly; stewed canvas-back ducks; partridges in pears; salmi of partridges; French oyster pie; turnips; potatoe snow; winter-squash; fried salsify; fried celery; onion custard—Plum pudding; mince-pie; charlotte polonaise; charlotte russe; calves' feet jelly; pistachio

cream; cocoa-nut cream; chocolate ice-cream; orange ice-cream.

TEA PARTIES.—Have black tea, green tea, and coffee. Immediately after the first cups are sent in, let fresh tea be put into the pots, that the second cups may not be weaker than the first. With the cream and sugar, send round a small pot of boiling water to weaken the tea of those who do not like it strong; or for the convenience of ladies who drink only milk and water, and who otherwise may cause interruption and delay by sending out for it. When tea is handed round, it is not well to have hot cakes with it; or any thing that is buttered, or any sort of greasy relishes. Such things are frequently injurious to the gloves and dresses of the ladies, and can well be dispensed with on these occasions. It is sufficient to send round a waiter with large cakes of the *best* sort, ready sliced but the slices not taken apart. There should be an almond sponge-cake for those who are unwilling to eat cakes made with butter.

Immediately on tea being over, let the servants go round to all the company with waiters having pitchers of cold water and glasses, to prevent the inconvenience of ladies sending out for glasses of water.

In less than an hour after tea, lemonade should be brought in, accompanied by baskets of small mixed cakes, (maccaroons, kisses, &c.,) which it is no longer customary to send in with the tea. Afterwards, let the blanc-mange, jellies, sweet-meats, ice-creams, wines, liquors, &c., be handed round. Next, (after an hour's interval,) the terrapin, oysters, and chicken salad, &c. These are sometimes accompanied by ale, porter, or cider; sometimes by champagne. At the close of the evening, it is usual to send round a large plum-cake.

If the plan is to have a regular supper table, it is not necessary to send in any refreshments through the evening, except lemonade and little cakes.

When the company is not very numerous, and is to sit round a tea-table, waffles or other hot articles may there be introduced. Take care to set a tea-table that will certainly be large enough to accommodate all the guests without crowding them.

SUPPER DISHES FOR A LARGE COMPANY.—[3]Boned turkey with jelly; partridge pie; game dressed in various ways; cold ham glazed thickly all over with a mixture of bread-crumbs, cream, and yolk of egg; two smoked tongues, one placed whole in the centre of the dish, the other cut into circular slices and laid round it; cold alamode beef; French chicken salad; Italian chicken salad; marbled veal; potted lobster; pickled lobster; terrapins; cream oysters; fried oysters; pickled oysters; oyster patties; biscuit sandwiches; charlotte polonaise; charlotte russe; French charlotte; calves' feet jelly; trifle; Spanish blanc-mange; chocolate blanc-mange; coffee blanc-mange; maccaroon blanc-mange; vanilla blanc-mange; pistachio cream; cocoa-nut cream; chocolate cream; vanilla cream; lemon custards; orange custards; green custard; red custard; meringued apples; whipt cream meringues; iced grapes; orange-water ice; damson-water ice; vanilla ice-cream; lemon ice-cream; almond ice-cream; chocolate ice-cream; biscuit ice-cream; macca-

[3] From these may be selected supper dishes for a small assemblage, or for a company of moderate size.

roon ice-cream; preserved pine-apple; preserved citron-melon; preserved limes; preserved oranges; brandy peaches; brandy green gages; port wine-jelly; pink champagne-jelly; frozen punch, &c.; plum-cake; lady-cake; almond sponge-cake; frothed chocolate with dry toast.

An elegant supper table may be decorated with a profusion of real flowers tastefully disposed in pyramids and other forms; or with the sugar temples, obelisks, pagodas, baskets, &c., made by the confectioners. Unless at a very large and splendid supper it is bad taste to introduce these sugar ornaments.

OYSTER SUPPERS.—It is customary at oyster suppers to have a great portion of the oysters roasted in the shell and brought in on large dishes "hot and hot." Near every two chairs should be placed a small bucket to receive the shells. An oyster knife, and a clean coarse towel must be laid beside every plate, for the purpose of opening the oysters; an office that is usually performed by the gentlemen. The oysters should all be of the largest and best kind. Besides those that are roasted, there should be other dishes of them, fried, stewed, and pickled. Also, oysters in pies or patties;—cold-slaw; beets; pickles; and celery; bread in the form of rolls; and butter made up into handsome basket or pine-apple shapes. Ale and porter are frequently introduced at oyster suppers.

ADDITIONAL RECEIPTS.

BUENA VISTA CAKE.—Put half a pound of powdered white sugar into a deep pan, and cut up in it half a pound of fresh butter. Stir them together hard, till perfectly light. Add a nutmeg powdered. (This cake should be highly-flavoured with nutmeg.) Beat four eggs in a shallow pan, till they are very thick and smooth. Then stir them, gradually, into the pan of beaten butter and sugar; in turn with three-quarters of a pound of sifted flour. Add a wine-glass of rose-water. Have ready three large wine-glasses of cream or rich milk, divided equally in two portions, and put into two cups. Take one yeast-powder, of the very best sort; dissolve in one cup of the cream, the contents of the blue paper, (or the carbonate of soda,) and in the other cup the contents of the white paper, (tartaric acid,) and mix the first with the cake-batter; and then, immediately after, stir in the other, lightly and slowly. Transfer the batter to a large well-buttered square pan, and set it immediately into a brisk oven. Bake it steadily an hour, or more. If not thoroughly baked, it will be heavy. When cool, cut it into squares, and sift powdered sugar over it. It will be still better to ice it, adding rose-water or lemon-juice to the icing. It is best when fresh, the day it is baked; though very good the following day.

This cake will be found excellent, if the foregoing directions are *exactly* followed. If wanted fresh for tea, at a short notice, it can be made and baked in two hours. For instance, if commenced at five o'clock in the afternoon it may be on the table at seven. The above quantity of ingredients will make enough to fill a large cake-basket.

If you wish to have a large Buena Vista cake baked in a loaf, take double the above quantity of ingredients, viz., one pound of butter, one pound of powdered sugar, a pound and a half of flour; eight eggs, two nutmegs, and two wine-glasses of rose water; six wine-glasses of cream or milk, and two yeast-powders; that is, two of the blue papers and two of the white. Put the mixture into a circular pan, and setting it directly in a brisk oven bake it from four to five hours in proportion to its thickness, keeping up a steady heat all the time. When done, ice and ornament it; flavouring the icing with rose or lemon. One of the decorations should be the words Buena Vista.

All cakes that have milk or cream in them require longer baking than those that have not; and the heat of the oven must be well kept up.

YEAST-POWDERS.—Get at a druggist's a pound of super-carbonate of soda, and three-quarters of a pound of tartaric acid. Both these articles must be of the very best quality. Prepare an equal number of square blue papers, and square white papers; nicely folded. To be very accurate, weigh the articles alternately. In every blue paper put a hundred grains of the super-carbonate of soda, and in each white paper ninety grains of tartaric acid; and then fold them up so as to secure their contents. If you have not suitable scales and weights, you may guess tolerably well at the proportions of the articles by measuring a full tea-spoonful of the soda for each blue paper, and three-quarters of a tea-spoonful of the acid for each white paper. Put them up in boxes, and keep them in a dry place. The contents of one blue paper and of one white paper are considered as one yeast-powder; half the contents of each paper are called half a yeast-powder.

Yeast-powders of themselves have not sufficient power to raise bread or cakes so as to make them light enough to be wholesome. They should only be employed when real yeast, or eggs, are also used. Then they add greatly to the lightness of the cake. They are also an improvement to batter puddings. They must always be added at the last.

To use them, dissolve first the soda in a wine-glass and a half of milk or luke-warm water, and when thoroughly melted, stir it into the batter. Then melt in another cup the acid, with a similar quantity of milk or water, and stir it in at the last.

These powders entirely destroy the flavour of lemon or orange-juice. But they will convert sour milk into sweet. A yeast-powder added to buckwheat batter that has already been raised by real yeast, will render it surprisingly light. One blue and one white powder will suffice for two quarts of batter.

FINE WAFER CAKES.—Wash and squeeze half a pound of fresh butter in a pan of cold water. Then take it out, and cut it up in another pan, into which you have sifted half a pound of powdered white sugar; and stir them together with a spaddle (a round stick flattened at one end) till they are very light and creamy. Then stir in half a grated nutmeg, a small tea-spoonful of powdered mace, a glass of sherry or Madeira, and a glass of rose or lemon brandy. Put the whites of four eggs into a deep plate, beat them to a stiff froth with a whisk, and add the beaten white of eggs gradually to the mixture. Lastly, stir in as much sifted flour as will make a light soft dough or paste. Divide it into equal portions; flour your hands, and roll each portion in your palms till it becomes round like a small dumpling. Then having heated the wafer-iron, butter the inside, and put in one of the dumplings, making it to fit well. Put the wafer-iron into a clear hot fire, and bake each cake five minutes. When done, take them out carefully and lay them separately on an inverted sieve to cool.

This mixture may be more easily baked in thin flat cakes. Roll out the dough into a thin sheet, and then cut it into round cakes with the edge of a tumbler, or with a tin cutter of that circumference. Butter large square iron pans, and lay the cakes in them, but not so close as to touch. Put them into a quick oven, and bake them brown.

LANCASTER GINGERBREAD.—Cut up a quarter of a pound of fresh butter into two pounds of sifted flour; rub it well in, and add a small teacup of ground ginger, and a tea-spoonful of powdered cinnamon. Stir in a pint and a half of West India molasses, and milk enough to make it into a thick batter. Lastly, add a tea-spoonful of soda dissolved in a little tepid water; and immediately after dissolve in another cup a salt-spoonful of tartaric acid, and stir that in. Stir the whole very hard. Butter square pans, put into them the mixture, and bake it well; seeing that the oven is not so hot as to scorch it. It requires very long baking. When cool, cut it into squares.

Never put allspice into gingerbread or any other cake. It communicates a disagreeably bitter taste. Allspice is now rarely used for any purpose; cloves being far better. Either of them will considerably darken the colour of the cake.

WARM ICING FOR CAKES.—Beat to a stiff froth the whites of four eggs; then beat into them, gradually, (a spoonful at a time,) a pound of finely-powdered loaf-sugar. Next put the beaten white of egg and sugar into a very clean porcelain-lined kettle, (or something that will not discolour it,) and boil and skim it till the scum ceases to rise. Then remove it from the fire; and while it is warm, stir in the juice of two large lemons or oranges, or a tea-spoonful of extract of roses, or a wine-glass of rose-water, or a large table-spoonful of extract of vanilla. Have ready your cake, which must first be dredged with flour all over, and the flour wiped off with a clean cloth. This will make the icing stick. With a spoon, place a large portion of the warm icing on the centre of the top of the cake; and then with a broad-bladed knife, (dipped now and then into a bowl of cold water) spread it thick and evenly all over the surface. When done, let it dry gradually. It is best that the cake, when iced, should be warm from the oven.

This warm icing is now much in use. It spreads easily; rises up high and thick in cooling; and has a fine gloss on the surface.

To give it a fine red or pink colour, use cochineal. For green colouring, pound in a mortar some raw spinach till you have extracted a tea-cup full of green juice. Put the juice into a very clean porcelain or earthen pan, set it over the fire, and give it one boil up, (not more,) and when cold it will be fit for use. This is the best way of preparing green colouring for all culinary purposes.

CINNAMON BREAD.—On a bread-baking day, (having made more than your usual quantity of wheat bread,) when the dough has risen quite light, so as to be cracked all over the surface, take out as much as would suffice for a moderate-sized loaf, (for instance, a twelve-cent one,) and make it into a large round cake. Having dissolved a yeast-powder in two separate cups in a little lukewarm water, the carbonate of soda in one cup, and the tartaric acid in another, mix the first with the dough of the cake, and then mix in the second. Have ready a half-pint of brown sugar, moistened with fresh butter, so as to make it a thick stiff paste, and flavoured with a heaping table-spoonful of powdered cinnamon. Make deep cuts or incisions, at equal spaces, over the cake, and fill them with the above mixture, pressed in hard; and pinch the dough with your thumb and finger, so as to close up each cut, to prevent the seasoning from running out. Set it immediately into the oven with the other bread, and bake it thoroughly. When cool, brush it over with white of egg, in which some sugar has been melted.

This is an excellent plain cake for children, and can be prepared any bread-baking day.

It is much improved by mixing with the dough two large heaped table-spoonfuls of butter that has been melted in a teacup of warm milk, and also one or two beaten eggs. Do this before you add the yeast-powder.

SNOW CREAM.—Take a large pint of very rich cream, and half a pound of the best loaf-sugar, powdered. Rub off, on a lump of sugar, the yellow rind of three large lemons or oranges, (or, four or five, if small;) scraping it off the sugar with a teaspoon as you proceed, and transferring it to a saucer. Then powder this lump of sugar, and add it to the rest. Mix with the sugar the juice of the fruit, and the grated rind; and then mix the whole with two quarts of clean snow, in a broad pan. Set the pan into a tub, and pack it closely all round with coarse salt and snow; taking care that they do not quite reach to the edge of the pan, lest some of the salt should get in, and spoil the whole. While packed in the snow and salt, beat the mixture very hard till it is smooth and stiff. Then set it on ice; or in a very cold place, till wanted for use. Turn it out into a glass bowl.

This is a good and easy way of imitating ice-cream in families that are not provided with the regular apparatus of a freezer and moulds. The pint of cream must be very rich, and the flavouring very high. All flavouring loses much strength in freezing.

You may flavour it with vanilla, by boiling a vanilla bean in half a pint of milk, till the vanilla taste is well infused. Then strain the milk, and mix it with the cream. Or, instead of vanilla, you may boil in the milk a handful of shelled bitter almonds, or peach-kernels, to be afterwards strained out.

LEMON HONEY.—Take three large ripe lemons, (or four or five small ones,) and (having rolled them under your hand on a table, to increase the juice,) rub off on a piece of loaf-sugar the yellow rind or zest, scraping it up with a teaspoon as you proceed, and putting it aside on a saucer. Then squeeze the juice of the lemons through a strainer, upon a pound of loaf-sugar, (broken small or powdered,) and add the zest or grated rind. Cut up, among the sugar, a large quarter of a pound of the best fresh butter. Break six eggs into a shallow earthen pan, and beat them till as light as possible. Then mix in, gradually, the sugar and lemon, stirring all very hard. Put the whole into a porcelain-lined kettle; set it over a moderate fire that has no blaze, and (stirring it all the time) let it boil till it becomes of the consistence of very thick honey. If the weather is warm, you may add to its thickness by stirring in a table-spoonful of ground arrow-root, or of sifted flour. When done, put it warm into glass jars; cover them, closely, and seal the covers. It will keep in a cool dry place a month or more. If made in winter, it will continue good for two months.

ORANGE HONEY is made as above, except that you must have five or six oranges, all of the largest size, using the juice only and none of the rind. Orange peel will give it an unpleasant taste after it has been kept a few days.

RAISIN CURRANTS.—Strip as many ripe currants from the stems as will fill a quart measure when done. Put them into a porcelain-lined kettle; mash them, and add three quarters of a pound of sugar—brown will do. Prepare three quarters of a pound of the largest and best raisins, washed, drained, seeded, and cut in half. Or, use the small sultana or seedless raisins. When the currants and sugar have come to a boil, and been skimmed, mix in the raisins, gradually, and let them boil till quite soft; skimming the surface well; and after each skimming stir the whole down to the bottom of the kettle. When done, take it up in a deep dish, and set it to cool. This is a nice, plain dessert.

For a larger quantity, take two quarts of stripped currants; a pound and a half of sugar; and a pound and a half of raisins. None but raisins of the best quality should be used for this or any other purpose. Low-priced raisins are unwholesome, being always of bad quality.

CURRANT-RAISIN JAM.—Wash, drain, seed, and chop fine two pounds of the best bloom or muscatel raisins, and put them into a large pan till wanted. Having stripped them from the stems, squeeze through a linen bag into a large bowl as many ripe currants as will yield three quarts of juice. Sweeten this juice with two pounds and a half of sugar. Having put the minced raisins into a preserving kettle, pour the currant-juice over them, and give the whole a hard stirring. Set it over the fire, and boil and skim it, (stirring it down after skimming,) till it is thoroughly done, forming a thick smooth jam or marmalade. When cool, put it into jars. Cork them closely, covering the corks with paper tied down over the top, and set them away in a dry place. It is an excellent jam for common use, and very nice with cream.

TO KEEP PINE-APPLES, WITHOUT COOKING.—Take large fine pine-apples—the ripest you can procure. Pare and slice them thin, removing the hard core from the centre. Weigh the slices, and to each pound allow a pound of double-refined powdered loaf-sugar. Spread the slices on large flat dishes, with a layer of sugar both under and over them. Let them stand several hours; then put them up (without any cooking) in large glass tumblers, with the syrup that has issued from them; and put a thick layer of sugar at the top of each tumblerful. Cover the glasses closely, and tie a piece of bladder over each.

If the sugar is of the best quality, and the pine-apples ripe and without blemishes, they will keep perfectly well, done as above, and retain the flavour of the fruit better than when cooked. They must be kept in a dry cool place.

FINE PINE-APPLE MARMALADE.—Take pine-apples of large size, and as ripe as possible. Having removed the green leaves, cut each pine-apple (without paring) into four quarters; and then, with a large coarse tin grater, grate them down as near the rind as you can go. Do this in a large dish, carefully saving the juice. Then weigh the grated pine-apple, and to every pound allow three large quarters of a pound of the best double-refined loaf-sugar, finely powdered. Too much sugar will, after boiling, cause the marmalade to candy in the jars. Mix with the sugar the pine-apple and all its juice, and put them into a preserving kettle over a moderate, but very clear, fire. Boil them slowly together, skimming them when necessary, and frequently stirring them up from the bottom with a silver spoon. Let them boil till they become a very thick smooth mass, of a fine gold colour. Put the marmalade warm into glass jars. Lay upon the surface a double tissue paper, cut circular, and fitting exactly; then cover the jars, and tie a piece of bladder over each.

Instead of grating the pine-apple, you may pare, core, and cut it into small thin pieces; but it will require a longer time to boil, and will be less smooth and beautiful. With a coarse grater the trouble is not much.

MELON MARMALADE.—Take fine large citron melons, and cut them into quarters, having removed the seeds. Weigh the pieces, and to every pound allow a pound of the best double-refined loaf-sugar. To every three pounds of melon allow two lemons, and a tea-spoonful of ground white ginger. Then grate the melon slices on a coarse grater, but not too close to the rind. Grate off the yellow rind of the lemons, and add it with the ginger to the sugar, which must be finely powdered. Then mix the whole with the grated melons in a preserving kettle. Set it over a moderate fire, and boil, skim, and stir it till it is a very thick smooth jam. Put it warm into glass jars, or large tumblers; lay a double round of tissue paper on the surface of the marmalade; cover the jars closely, and tie a piece of bladder over each.

Pumpkin marmalade may be made in the above manner, omitting the ginger.

TOMATO MARMALADE.—Take large fully-ripe tomatoes, and scald them in hot water, so that the skins can be easily peeled off. Weigh the tomatoes; and to every pound, allow a pound of the best sugar; to every three pounds, two lemons and a small tea-spoonful of ground ginger. Grate off the yellow rind of the lemons, and mix it with the sugar and ginger; then add their juice. Put the tomatoes into a preserving kettle, and mash them with the back of a wooden ladle. Then mix in the sugar, &c., stirring the whole very hard. Set the kettle over a moderate fire, and boil it very slowly for three hours, till it is a smooth mass, skimming it well; and stirring it to the bottom after each skimming.

This is an excellent sweet-meat; and as the lemon must on no account be omitted, it should be made when lemons are plenty. The best time is the month of August, as lemons are then to be had in abundance, and the tomatoes are less watery than in the autumn months. For children it may be made with brown sugar, and with less lemon and more ginger. Like all preparations of tomato it is very wholesome.

YANKEE APPLE PUDDING.—Butter the bottom and inside of a deep tin pan. Pare, core, and quarter six or eight large, fine, juicy apples; and strew among them a heaped half-pint or more of broken sugar. Dissolve a tea-spoonful either of soda, sal-eratus, or pearlash, in a pint of *sour* milk. The soda will take off entirely the acid of the milk, and render the whole very light. Stir the milk, and pour it among the apples. Have ready a good pie-crust, rolled out thick. Lay it over the top of the pan of apples, &c.; trim the edge nicely, and notch it neatly. Put the pudding into a hot oven, and bake it brown. It will require at least an hour, or more, according to its depth. Eat it warm.

This is a good plain family pudding. A similar one may be made of peaches; pared; stoned, and quartered.[4]FILET GUMBO.—Cut up a pair of fine plump fowls into pieces, as when carving. Lay them in a pan of cold water, till all the blood is drawn out. Put into a pot, two large table-spoonfuls of lard, and set it over

----

[4] Pronounced Fee*lay*.

the fire. When the lard has come to a boil, put in the chickens with an onion finely minced. Dredge them well with flour, and season slightly with salt and pepper; and, if you like it, a little chopped marjoram. Pour on it two quarts of boiling water. Cover it, and let it simmer slowly for three hours. Then stir into it two heaped tea-spoonfuls of sassafras powder. Afterwards, let it stew five or six minutes longer, and then send it to table in a deep dish; having a dish of boiled rice to be eaten with it by those who like rice.

This gumbo will be much improved by stewing with it three or four thin slices of cold boiled ham, in which case omit the salt in the seasoning. Whenever cold ham is an ingredient in any dish, no other salt is required.

A dozen fresh oysters and their liquor, added to the stew about half an hour before it is taken up, will also be an improvement.

If you cannot conveniently obtain sassafras-powder, stir the gumbo frequently with a stick of sassafras root.

This is a genuine southern receipt. Filet gumbo may be made of any sort of poultry, or of veal, lamb, venison, or kid.

FINE CABBAGE SOUP.—Take a fine large cabbage, and, after removing the outside leaves, and cutting the stalk short, divide the cabbage into quarters, more than half way down, but not quite to the stem. Lay the cabbage in cold water for half an hour or more. Then set it over the fire in a pot *full* of boiling water, and let it boil for an hour and a half, skimming it frequently. Then take it out, drain it, and laying it in a deep pan, pour on *cold* water, and let the cabbage remain in it till cold all through. Next (having drained it from the cold water) cut the cabbage into shreds or small pieces, and put it into a clean pot containing three pints of rich boiling milk, into which you have stirred a quarter of a pound of the best fresh butter; adding a very little salt and pepper. Boil it in the milk about two hours, or till thoroughly done, and quite tender. Then cut up some pieces of bread into small squares. Lay them in a tureen, and pour the soup upon them.

This, being made without meat, is an excellent soup for Lent or fast-days.

It is still better when cauliflowers or broccoli are substituted for cabbage; adding a few blades of mace, or some grated nutmeg.

EXCELLENT PICKLED CABBAGE.—Shred very fine, with a cabbage-cutter, a large fresh red cabbage. Pack it down (with a little salt sprinkled between each layer) in a large stone jar. The jar should be three parts full of the shred cabbage. Then tie up, in a bag of very thin clean muslin, two table-spoonfuls of whole black pepper; the same quantity of cloves; and the same of cinnamon, broken very small, but not powdered. Also a dozen blades of mace. Put two quarts of the best cider-vinegar into a porcelain-lined kettle; throw in the bag of spices, and boil it. Five minutes after it has come to a hard boil, take out the bag of spice, and pour the vinegar hot over the cabbage in the jar; stirring it up from the bottom, so that the vinegar may get all through the cabbage. Then lay the bag of spice on the top, and while the pickle is hot, cover the jar closely. It will be fit for use in two days.

If you find, after awhile, that the pickle tastes too much of the spice, remove the spice-bag.

You may pickle white cabbage in the same way; omitting the cloves, and boiling in the vinegar a second muslin bag, with three ounces of turmeric, which will give the cabbage a fine bright yellow colour. Having put up the cabbage into the jar, lay the turmeric-bag half way down, and the spice-bag on the top. But the turmeric-bag need not be put into the jar if the vinegar has sufficiently coloured the cabbage.

Small onions may be pickled, as above, with turmeric. Always, in preparing onions, for any purpose, peel off the thin outer skin.

MADEIRA HAM.—Take a ham of the very finest sort; a Westphalia one, if you can obtain it. Soak it in water all day and all night; changing the water several times. A Westphalia ham should be soaked two days and nights. Early in the morning of the day it is to be cooked, put it over the fire in a large pot, and boil it four hours, skimming it well. Then take it out; remove the skin, and put the ham into a clean boiler, with sufficient Madeira wine to cover it well. Boil, or rather stew it an hour longer, keeping the pot covered, except when you remove the lid to turn the ham. When well stewed take it up, drain it, and strain the liquor into a porcelain-lined saucepan. Have ready a sufficiency of powdered white sugar. Cover the ham all over with a thick coating of the sugar, and set it into a hot oven to bake for an hour.

Mix some orange or lemon-juice with the liquor, adding sugar and nutmeg. Give it one boil up over the fire, and serve it up in a tureen, as sauce to the ham.

What is left of the ham may be cut next day into thin slices, put into a stew-pan, with the remains of the liquor or sauce poured over it, and stewed for a quarter of an hour. Serve it up all together in the same dish. Instead of Madeira you may use champagne. Bottled cider is also a good substitute.

Fresh venison, pheasants, partridges, grouse, or any other game, (also canvas-back ducks,) cut up and stewed with a mixture of Madeira wine, orange, or lemon-juice, sugar, nutmeg, and a little butter will be found very fine. The birds should first be half roasted, and the gravy saved to add to the stew.

NEW WAY OF DRESSING TERRAPINS.—In buying terrapins, select those only that are large, fat, and thick-bodied. Put them whole into water that is boiling hard at the time, and (adding a little salt) boil them till thoroughly done throughout. Then, taking off the shell, extract the meat, and remove carefully the sand-bag and gall; also *all the entrails*. They are disgusting, unfit to eat; and are no longer served up in cooking terrapin for the best tables. Cut the meat into pieces, and put it into a stew-pan with its eggs, and sufficient fresh butter to stew it well. Let it stew till quite hot throughout, keeping the pan carefully covered that none of the flavour may escape; but shake it over the fire while stewing. In another pan, make a sauce of beaten yolk of egg, highly flavoured with Madeira or sherry, and powdered nutmeg and mace, and enriched with a large lump of fresh butter. Stir this sauce well over the fire, and when it has *almost* come to a boil, take it off. Send the terrapin to table hot in a covered dish, and the sauce *separately* in a sauce-tureen, to be used by those who like it, and omitted by those who prefer the genuine flavour of the terrapin when simply stewed with butter.

This is now the usual mode of dressing terrapins in Maryland and Virginia, and will be found superior to any other.

No dish of terrapins can be good unless the terrapins themselves are of the best quality. It is mistaken economy to buy poor ones. Besides being insipid and tasteless, it takes more in number to fill a dish. The females are the best.

A TERRAPIN POT-PIE.—Take several fine large terrapins, the fattest and thickest you can get. Put them into a large pot of water that is boiling hard; and boil them half an hour or more. Then take them out of the shell, pulling off the outer skin and the toe-nails. Remove the sand-bag and the gall, taking care not to break it, or it will render the whole too bitter to be eaten. Take out also the entrails, and throw them away; as the custom of cooking them is now, very properly, exploded. Then cut up all the meat of the terrapins, taking care to save all the liquid that exudes in cutting up, and also the eggs. Season the whole with pepper, mace, and nutmeg, adding a little salt; and lay among it pieces of fresh butter slightly rolled in flour.

Have ready an ample quantity of paste, made in the proportion of a pound of butter to two large quarts (or pounds) of flour, or a pound and a half of butter to three quarts of flour, and rolled out thick. Butter the inside of an iron pot, and line the sides with paste, till it reaches within one-third of the top. Then put in the pieces of terrapin, with the eggs, butter, &c., and with all the liquid. Lay among the terrapin, square pieces of paste. Then pour in sufficient water to stew the whole properly. Next, cover all with a circular lid, or top-crust of paste, but do not fit it so closely that the gravy cannot bubble up over the edges while cooking. Cut a slit in the top-crust. Place the pot-pie over a good fire, and boil it till the whole is thoroughly done, which will be from three-quarters to an hour, (after it comes to a boil;) taking care not to let it get too dry, but keeping a kettle of *hot* water to replenish it if necessary. When done, take it up in a deep dish, and serve it hot. Then let every one add what seasoning they choose.

It may be much improved by mixing among the pieces of terrapin (before putting them into the pie) some yolks of hard-boiled eggs, grated or minced. They will enrich the gravy.

A BEEF-STEAK POT-PIE.—Take a sufficiency of tender beef-steaks from the sirloin, removing all the fat and bone. Season them slightly with pepper and salt; adding also some nutmeg. Put them into a pot with plenty of water, and par-boil them. Meanwhile, make a large portion of paste, (a pot-pie with but little paste is no better than a mere stew,) and roll it out thick. If you use suet for shortening, allow to every two quarts or two pounds of flour a large half-pound of suet, divested of the skin and strings, and minced as finely as possible with a chopping-knife. Sprinkle in a very little salt. Mix the suet with the flour in a large pan, rubbing it fine with your hands, and adding gradually sufficient cold water to make a stiff dough. Then transfer the lump of dough to the paste-board; knead it well with your hands; and beat it hard on all sides with the rolling-pin. Next roll it out into sheets. Line the sides of a pot with a portion of the dough. Then put in the beef;

adding for gravy the liquid in which it was boiled, and a little hot water. Also, some potatoes sliced or quartered. Intersperse the meat with square slices of paste. Finish by covering it with a lid of paste, having a slit in the top: but do not fit the lid too closely. Then placing the pot over the fire, let it boil from three-quarters to an hour, (after it comes to a boil,) replenishing it, if necessary, with more hot water. This will be found an excellent family dish.

CHICKEN POT-PIE.—Cut up, and par-boil a pair of large fowls, seasoning them with pepper, salt, and nutmeg. You may add some small slices of cold ham; in which case add *no salt*, as the ham will make it salt enough. Or you may put in some pieces of the lean of fresh pork. You may prepare a suet-paste; but for a chicken pot-pie it is best to make the paste of butter, which should be fresh, and of the best quality. Allow to each quart of flour, a small half-pound of butter. There should be enough for a great deal of paste. Line the sides of the pot, two-thirds up, with paste. Put in the chickens, with the liquor in which they were parboiled. You may add some sliced potatoes. Intersperse the pieces of chicken with layers of paste in square slices. Then cover the whole with a lid of paste, not fitting very closely. Make a slit in the top, and boil the pie about three-quarters of an hour or more.

This pie will be greatly improved by adding some clams to the chickens while par-boiling, omitting salt in the seasoning, as the clams will salt it quite enough.

BROILED MUSHROOMS.—Take the largest and finest fresh mushrooms. Peel them, and cut off the stems as closely as possible. Lay the mushrooms on their backs, upon a large flat dish; and into the hollow or cup of each put a piece of fresh butter, and season it with a little black pepper. Set a clean gridiron over a bed of clear hot coals, and when it is well heated, put on the mushrooms, and broil them thoroughly. The gridiron should be one with grooved bars, so as to retain the gravy. When the first gridiron-full of mushrooms is well broiled, put them with their liquor into a hot dish, and keep them closely covered while the rest are broiling. This is an excellent way of cooking mushrooms.

AN EASY WAY TO PICKLE MUSHROOMS.—Take two quarts of small freshly-gathered mushrooms. With a sharp-pointed knife peel off, carefully, their thin outside skin; and cut off the stalks closely. Prepare eight little bags of very thin clear muslin, and tie up in each bag six blades of mace; six slices of root-ginger; and a small nutmeg (or half a large one) broken small, but not powdered. Have ready four glass jars, such as are considered to hold a quart. Lay a bag of spice in the bottom of each; then put in a pint of the mushrooms, laying a second bag of spice on the top. Have ready a sufficiency of the best cider-vinegar, very slightly seasoned with salt; allowing to each quart of vinegar but a salt-spoon of salt. Fill up the jars with the vinegar, finishing at the top with two table-spoonfuls of sweet oil. Immediately close up the jars, corking them tightly; and pasting thick paper, or tying a piece of leather or bladder closely down over the corks.

These mushrooms will be found very fine; and as they require no cooking, are speedily and easily prepared. When a jar is once opened, it will be well to use them fast. They may be put up in small jars, or in glass tumblers, such as hold but a pint altogether; seeing that the proportions of spice in each jar or tumbler are duly divided, as above. Keep them in a very dry place.

If you wish the mushrooms to be of a dark colour when pickled, add half a dozen cloves to each bag of spice; but the clove-taste will most likely overpower that of the mushrooms. On no account omit the oil.

If you cannot obtain button-mushrooms, cut large ones into four quarters, first peeling them and removing the stems.

BREAKFAST ROLLS.—These rolls must be mixed the night before, near bed-time. Sift three quarts of flour into a deep pan, and cut up into it a half-pint cup-full (or a quarter of a pound) of fresh butter. Rub the butter with your hands into the flour till thoroughly incorporated, and add a very small tea-spoonful of salt. Make a hole in the middle of the flour, and pour in four large table-spoonfuls of excellent yeast. Have ready sufficient warm milk; a pint will generally be enough, (heated but not boiling,) to make it into a light dough. Add the milk gradually; and then knead the dough. Put it into a pan, cover it with a clean thick cloth, and set it in a warm place. Early in the morning, add to the dough a small tea-spoonful of pearl-ash or sal-eratus, or a large tea-spoonful of soda, dissolved in a little warm water. Mix it well in, and knead the dough over again. Then divide it into equal portions, and make each portion into an *oval-shaped* roll. Draw a deep mark along the top-surface of each with a knife. Put them into a hot oven, and bake them brown.

If intended for tea, mix them in the forenoon; and previous to baking, make out the dough into *round cakes,* pricking them with a fork.

BUCKWHEAT BATTER PUDDING.—Mix early in the day, a quart of buck-wheat meal with a large tea-cup full of Indian meal or of wheat flour; and add a tea-spoonful of salt. Have ready some water, warm but not boiling; and stir it gradually into the pan of meal till it makes a thick batter. Then add two large ta-ble-spoonfuls of fresh strong yeast from the brewer's. Of home-made yeast you will require three or four spoonfuls. Stir the whole very hard; cover the pan and set it near the fire to rise. When quite light, and covered with bubbles, melt a small tea-spoonful of soda or pearl-ash in a little warm water, and stir it into the batter. This, added to the yeast, will make the mixture light enough for a pudding with-out eggs. Have ready on the fire, a pot of boiling water. Dip in the pudding-cloth, then shake it out, spread it into a bread pan, and dredge it with flour. Pour the batter into the cloth as soon as you have added the soda, and tie it tightly, leaving a vacancy of about one-third, to allow for the swelling of the pudding. Put it into the pot while the water is boiling hard, and boil the pudding fast during an hour or more; buckwheat meal requiring much less time than indian or wheat. While boiling, turn the pudding several times in the water. When done, turn it out on a dish, and send it to table hot. Eat it with butter and sugar, or molasses.

This is a good plain pudding; but the batter must be *perfectly* light before it is tied up in the cloth; and if the water boils away, replenish the pudding-pot with *boiling* water from a kettle. To put *cold* water into a boiling pot will most certainly spoil whatever pudding is cooking in it, rendering it heavy, flat, and unfit to eat.

If you intend having buckwheat cakes at breakfast, and this pudding at dinner, mix at once sufficient batter for both purposes, adding the soda at the last, just before you put the pudding into the cloth.

Yeast-powders will be still better than soda; real yeast having previously been used when first mixing the batter. To use yeast-powders, dissolve the contents of the blue paper (super-carbonate of soda) in a little warm water, and stir it into the batter. Then, directly after, melt in another cup the powder from the white paper, (tartaric acid,) and stir that in also.

BUCKWHEAT PORRIDGE.—Boil a quart of rich milk, and when it has come to a hard boil, stir in, gradually, as much buckwheat meal as will make it of the consistence of very thick mush, adding a tea-spoon of salt, (not more,) and a table-spoonful of fresh butter. Five minutes after it is thick enough, remove it from the fire. If the milk is previously boiling hard, and continues to boil while the meal is going in, but little more cooking will be necessary.

Send it to table hot, and eat it with butter and sugar, or with molasses and butter.

This is sometimes called a Five Minute Pudding, from its being made so soon. It is very good for children, as a plain dessert; or for supper.

Before it goes to table, you may season it with powdered ginger, or nutmeg.

APPLE TAPIOCA.—Take a quart bowl, and half fill it with tapioca: then fill it very nearly to the top with cold water, allowing a little space for the tapioca to swell in soaking. Cover it, and let it stand all night. In the morning, pare and core six or eight fine pippin or bell-flower apples. Put them into a preserving kettle; filling up the holes from whence the cores were extracted with powdered sugar, and the grated yellow rind of one large lemon, or two small ones; and also the juice. Stew among the apples additional sugar, so as to make them agreeably sweet. Add about half enough of water to cover them. This will be sufficient to keep them from burning. Stew them gently till about half done; turning them carefully several times. Then put in the tapioca, and let it simmer with them till perfectly clear, and the apples are tender and well done throughout; but not long enough for them to break and fall to pieces. The tapioca will form a fine clear jelly all round the apples.

This is a nice dessert for children. And also, cooling and nourishing for invalids.

Quinces may be done in the same manner. They require more cooking than apples. For quinces, it is best to use, as flavouring, the grated yellow rind, and the juice of very ripe oranges.

TERRA FIRMA.—Take a piece of rennet about four inches square, and wash it in two or three cold waters to get off all the salt. Then wipe it dry, put it into a cup, and pour on sufficient lukewarm water to cover it well. Let it stand four or five hours, or all night. Then stir the rennet-water into three pints of rich unskimmed milk, flavoured with rose or peach-water. Cover the pan of milk, and set it on the hearth near the fire, till it forms a very firm curd. Then take it out, (draining off the whey,) put it into a clean sieve, (under which set a pan to receive the droppings,) and with the back of a broad flat wooden ladle, press all the remaining whey out of the curd. Next put the mass of curd into a deep bowl to mould it; and set it on ice till tea-time. Then transfer it to a deep glass bowl or dish, and pour all round it some cream sweetened well with sugar, and flavoured with rose or peach like the curd. On the curd lay circles of small sweetmeats, such as preserved strawberries, raspberries, or gooseberries. You may add to the cream that is to surround it, white wine and nutmeg.

TO USE COLD PUDDING.—If you have a large piece of boiled pudding left after dinner, (such as plum pudding, indian pudding, or batter pudding,) and you wish to cook it next day, tie it up in a cloth, and put it into a pot of boiling water, and keep it boiling hard for half an hour or more. It will be found as good as on the first day, and perhaps rather better; and it will be far more palatable, as well as more wholesome than if sliced, and fried, or broiled. Eat it with the same sauce as on the preceding day.

TO KEEP EGGS.—Break some glue into pieces, and boil it in sufficient water to make a thin solution. While warm, dip a brush into it, and go carefully over every egg. They must all be quite fresh. When the eggs are thoroughly glazed with the glue, spread them out to dry. When quite dry, pack them in kegs or boxes, with dry wood-ashes or saw-dust, (of which there must be a plentiful portion,) putting a thick layer of the ashes or saw-dust at the bottom and top of the keg. This is an excellent way of keeping eggs for sea-voyages, and is well worth the trouble. Before using them, soak them in warm water to get off the coating of glue.

Eggs of parrots and other tropical birds preserved in this manner, and the glue-coating soaked off in *cold* water, it is said have afterwards been hatched in the usual way; and the young birds have lived.

FINE FRENCH MUSTARD.—Take a sufficient quantity of green tarragon leaves, (picked from the stalks) and put them into a wide-mouthed glass jar till it is half full; pressing them down hard. Then fill up the jar with the best cider-vinegar, and cork it closely. Let it infuse a week or two. Then pour off the vinegar into a pitcher, remove all the tarragon from the jar, and put in an equal quantity of fresh leaves of the plant, and pour back the same vinegar from the pitcher. Cork it again, and let the last tarragon remain in the jar. In another fortnight the vinegar will be sufficiently flavoured with tarragon to use it for French mustard, or for other purposes. Then peel a clove of garlic, (not more than *one*,) and mince it as fine as possible. Mix it into four ounces (a quarter of a pound) of the best mustard-powder, in a deep white pan. Take a jill, or two large wine-glasses of the tarragon vinegar, (strained from the leaves,) pour it into a mug, and mix with it thoroughly an equal quantity of salad oil. Then with the mixture of vinegar and oil, moisten the mustard-powder, gradually, (using a wooden spoon,) till you get it a very little thicker than the usual consistence of made mustard. Put it into small clean, white jars, and cork them closely.

If you find that the above quantity of oil and vinegar will make the mustard too thin, you need not use the whole of the liquid. If the mustard seems too thick, dilute it gradually with a little more of the oil and vinegar.

This mustard is very superior to the common preparation, and is universally liked; particularly with beef and mutton. It must be kept closely corked. It is usual to bring it to table in the little white jar, with a small spoon beside it.

The herb tarragon may be had green and fresh in July and August. It is much used in French cookery, as a seasoning for stews, soups, &c.

Tarragon vinegar is very good with boiled cabbage or greens. The tarragon leaves of the second infusion should be kept remaining in the jar, pouring off the vinegar from them as it is wanted. A small quantity may be kept in a cruet; retaining the leaves at the bottom.

A WASHINGTON PUDDING.—Pick, and wash clean half a pound of Zante currants; drain them, and wipe them in a towel, and then spread them out on a flat dish, and place them before the fire to dry thoroughly. Prepare about a quarter of a pound or half a pint of finely-grated bread-crumbs. Have ready a heaping tea-spoonful of powdered mace, cinnamon, and nutmeg mixed. When the currants are dry, dredge them thickly on all sides with flour, to prevent their sinking or clodding in the pudding while baking. Cut up in a deep pan half a pound of the best fresh butter, and add to it half a pound of fine white sugar, powdered. Stir the butter and sugar together, with a wooden spaddle, till they are very light and creamy. Then add a table-spoonful of wine, and a table-spoonful of brandy. Beat in a shallow pan eight eggs till perfectly light, and as thick as a good boiled custard. Afterwards, mix with them, gradually, a pint of rich milk and the grated bread-crumbs, stirred in alternately. Next, stir this mixture, by degrees, into the pan of beaten butter and sugar; and add the currants, a few at a time. Finish with a table-spoonful of strong rose-water, or a wine-glass full, if it is not very strong. Stir the whole very hard. Butter a large deep white dish; or two of soup-plate size. Put in the batter. Set it directly into a brisk oven, and bake it well. When cold, dredge the surface with powdered sugar. Serve it up in the dish in which it was baked. You may ornament the top with bits of citron cut into leaves and forming a wreath; or with circles of preserved strawberries.

This will be found a very fine pudding. It must be baked in time to become quite cold before dinner.

For currants, you may substitute raisins of the best quality; seeded, cut in half, and well dredged with flour.

Instead of rose-water you may stir in the yellow rind (finely grated) of one large lemon, or two small ones, and their juice also.

NEW WAY OF WASHING SILK.—For ribbons, cravats, and other small articles of silk, put a sufficiency of the best fresh camphine oil into a large basin, and press and squeeze the things well through it, without either soap or water. Then squeeze them, till as dry as you can get them: open them out; and having washed the basin, put into it some fresh camphine, and wash the articles through that in the same manner as before. Have hot irons ready, and as the things come out of the second camphine, (after well squeezing and shaking them, but not rinsing,) spread them open on the ironing-sheet, and iron them smoothly and evenly on the wrong side. Do each article, as soon as it has had the second washing, as they should remain wet as short a time as possible.

There is no way of washing silk things that will make them look so well as this. It injures no colour, but rather brightens all, and gives the silk just the right degree of stiffness, besides making it very clean and fresh. When done, hang them in the open air for a while. A silk dress may be washed in this manner, putting the camphine into a large queensware-foot-bath. It should not go into a vessel of either wood or metal. The dress must first be taken entirely apart; but it will look so well when washed and ironed, that you will not regret the trouble.

Camphine generally sells at about fifty cents a gallon, sometimes lower.

TO SAVE STAIR-CARPETS.—Stair-carpets always wear out first (and sometimes very soon) at those parts that go against the edges or ledges of the stairs. They will last much longer at the edges, (indeed, as long as any other part of the carpet,) if the following precaution is taken. Get some old carpeting, (first made very clean,) and cut it into strips just the width of the stair-carpet. Each strip must be wide enough to put on double. Nail these strips, carefully and smoothly, on the round edge of each stair, so as to cover it entirely, above and below. Afterwards, put down the stair-carpet. When it is taken up to have the stairs washed, these strips will be found no inconvenience to the cleaning; taking care, however, if any of the nails or tacks get loosened, to drive them in again tightly; and if bent, to replace them by new ones. The slips must have time to get quite dry before the carpet is put down again.

Another way to save a stair-carpet, is to buy enough to make it a yard or more too long. Whenever the carpet is put down again, after it has been taken up for the purpose of cleaning the stairs, shift its position every time, so that the same places of the carpet may not always go against the ledges of the stairs. The extra length must be folded under, sometimes at the top of the staircase, and sometimes at the bottom.

Both these methods of saving a stair-carpet we know to be good. The first is the least expensive; but it is more trouble to nail on all the double slips of old carpeting, than to buy the additional yard of new.

In hotels where there is always plenty of old carpeting, and where there are men who can easily nail on the slips, this is a much better way than to cover the stairs first with oil-cloth, and then with zinc to save the oil-cloth; corners of the zinc frequently getting loose and catching and tearing the ladies' dresses.

Oil spilt on a stair-carpet can generally be taken away by immediately wiping off as much as can thus be removed, and then directly washing the place with cold water; renewing the water with fresh, till the grease disappears. If it will not come out, cover the place thoroughly with scraped fuller's earth. Let it rest an hour or two: then brush that off, and put on a fresh layer of fuller's earth; repeating it till the oil is entirely expelled. Scraped Wilmington clay is still better than fuller's earth.

SPERMACETI, TO EXTRACT FROM CARPETS OR CLOTHES.—There is no better way of removing spermaceti, than, (after scraping off with a knife as much as you can get from the surface of the spot,) to cover it with a piece of clean blotting paper, or any paper that is soft and thin, and press it with a warm iron. By repeating this, (taking each time a clean part of the paper,) any spermaceti spot may be removed from carpets, coats, ladies' dresses, or other similar articles.

When spermaceti has been dropped on a table, lay a blotting paper on the spot, and then hold over it, *carefully*, at a small distance above, a hot coal in the tongs. Pressing it with a warm iron would mark the mahogany.

CHEAP OIL FOR KITCHEN LAMPS.—Let all scraps of fat (including even whatever bits are left on the dinner-plates) and all drippings be carefully saved, and put into an earthen crock, covered, and set in a cold place. When the crock is full, transfer the fat to an iron pot, filling it half-way up with fat; and pour in sufficient cold water to reach the top. Set it over the fire, and boil and skim it till all the impurities are removed. Next pour the melted fat into a large broad pan of cold water, and set it away to cool. It will harden into a cake. Then take out the cake, and put it away in a cool place. When wanted for use, cut off a sufficient quantity, melt it by the fire till it becomes liquid, and then fill the lamp with it, as with lard. It will give a clear bright light, quite equal to that of lard, and better than whale oil; and it costs nothing but the trouble of preparing the fat. We highly recommend this piece of economy.

RELIEF FOR CORNS.—Experience proves that there is scarcely a possibility of removing corns on the feet, so that they will never return. The following remedy *we know* to be an excellent palliative; it will for a time diminish their size, and take away their soreness, and is easily renewed when they again become troublesome. It is peculiarly excellent for corns between the toes, which, of all others, are the most painful when they inflame.

Get at a druggist's a sixpenny box of Simple Cerate, (which is made of white wax, spermaceti, and lard, melted together, and stewed to a salve,) and with your finger, apply a small portion of this to each corn, letting it stay on for two or three hours; and then repeat the application. Do this several times during the day. For corns between the toes, add to the cerate a little soft, open white wool, such as you may pick off the surface of a blanket. Stick this in between the toes—the salve that adheres to it will keep it in its place. Repeat this through the day with fresh cerate and wool; putting on your stockings carefully. At night, before going to bed, wash off the cerate. In the morning renew it, as before. It gives not the least pain, but is soothing and pleasant. Proceed in this manner for a few days or a week, and you will find great relief. Try it, and be convinced.

Stockings with toes too narrow or pointed, are just as apt to produce corns, and to increase their pain and inflammation, as the wearing of narrow-toed shoes.

BROILED CANVAS BACK DUCKS.—To have these ducks with their flavour and juices in perfection, they should be cooked immediately after killing. If shot early in the morning, let them be broiled for breakfast; if killed in the forenoon, they should be dressed for that day's dinner. When they can be obtained quite fresh, broiling is now considered the best way of cooking them.

As soon as the ducks have been plucked, and drawn, and washed, split them down the back, and lay them, spread open, on a very clean gridiron, set over a bed of clear bright coals. The gridiron should have grooved bars to retain as much as possible of the gravy. Broil them well and thoroughly, so that the flesh may not have the least redness when sent to table. They will generally be done in twenty minutes or more. Serve them up as hot as possible. They will be found full of gravy, and require no sauce when cooked in this manner; but you may season them as you please when on your plate.

AUTUMN LEAVES.—The autumnal colours of our American forest trees are justly admired for the brightness, richness, and variety of their tints. Some of our fair countrywomen have worn them in Europe, formed into wreaths for the hair, or trimmings for ball-dresses, and the effect was considered beautiful. They may be preserved for this purpose by the following process. Gather as many varieties of autumn foliage as you can obtain; seeing that every leaf is perfect, and that there is a stem to each. The best time is in the month of October. Include among them those of the crimson maple, the purple beech, the willow oak with its underside of silvery white, the yellow hickory, the aspen, and any others that are richly tinted by the frost. Also, by way of contrast, some green pine sprigs. Lay them separately between the leaves of a large *writing-paper* book, (an old ledger will do very well,) and do not put tree-leaves between all the book-leaves successively, but alternately; otherwise they will not be smooth and flat when pressed. That is, put tree-leaves between the second and third pages of the book, and then no more till between the sixth and seventh pages. Lay the next tree-leaves between the tenth and eleventh pages, and so on, till they are all in. Place several other heavy books upon the ledger so as to press well the leaves beneath.

Stretch a twine across the room, or from the backs of two chairs, and tie a small twine string to each stem. Have ready some very fine clear varnish, (such as is used for maps, &c.) and with a large camels' hair brush, go carefully over both sides of the leaves, including the stem. Fasten them all, separately, to the stretched twine; seeing that none of them are near enough to each other to touch. Then lock the door of the room, that nothing may get in to disturb them, or raise the slightest dust while the varnish is drying. When perfectly dry, and not in the least sticky to the touch of the finger, have ready some sheets of smooth thick white paper. In each sheet cut small double slits to admit the stems, and in this way secure the leaves from slipping about and being injured. Write the name of each leaf above it. Let the other half of the sheet lie upon them. Put these sheets within a double cover of binders-board, (like a port-folio,) which you must then seal up in paper, like a large parcel, and the leaves in all their autumn beauty may be safely transported to any part of the world.

They will be found very useful to landscape-painters.

MADEIRA CHARLOTTE RUSSE.—Take one ounce of gelatine, or of the very best Russia isinglass, and soak it, near half an hour, in as much cold water as will barely cover it. It must merely soften, and not dissolve. Then drain off the water, and put the gelatine or isinglass into a pint of rich cream; adding a vanilla bean split, cut to pieces, and tied closely in a very thin muslin bag. Set the cream over a slow fire in a porcelain preserving-kettle, and let it boil till the gelatine is entirely dissolved, and thoroughly mixed with the cream. Give it a hard stirring, down to the bottom, several times while boiling.

Have ready the yolks only, of eight eggs, beaten till very light and thick; and then beat, gradually, into the yolk of egg three quarters of a pound of the best powdered loaf-sugar. Then take the cream off the fire, and (having first removed the vanilla) stir into it, by degrees, the mixture of beaten yolk of egg and sugar. Set the kettle again over a slow fire, and let it simmer till very thick; but do not allow it to boil hard, or too long, lest it should curdle.

When the mixture is sufficiently thick, take it off, and set it away to cool. Have ready the whites of four of the eight eggs beaten to a stiff froth. Then stir two heaping table-spoonfuls of powdered loaf-sugar into half a tumbler-full of Madeira wine, and beat it slowly into the white of egg; adding a little more powdered sugar if the wine seems likely to curdle the egg.

When the yellow or yolk-of-egg mixture is quite cold, stir gradually into it the white mixture, till all is thoroughly amalgamated. Have ready a mould or moulds lined with very thin slices of almond sponge-cake. Fill them up with the mixture, and set them on ice till the charlotte is wanted. Then turn it out. You may cover the top with icing made in the usual way, and flavoured with extract of vanilla, or extract of bitter almond—or peach-water.

LEMON CHARLOTTE RUSSE.—Is made as in the preceding receipt; substituting for the vanilla and Madeira, the yellow rind and the juice of two large whole lemons, or three if not of the largest size. Rub off the yellow rind (or zest) upon lumps of loaf-sugar, scraping it off with a knife as you proceed, and saving it on a saucer. Then powder these lumps, and mix them with half the remainder of the three-quarters of a pound of sugar, and the scraped yellow rind. Add it (as above) to the beaten yolk of egg, and boil it slowly with the isinglass and cream. Then cut the lemons, and squeeze their juice into the remaining sugar. Having beaten the whites of half the eight eggs to a stiff froth, add to it the lemon-juice and sugar; and when the mixture of cream, egg, and isinglass is cold, mix gradually with it the beaten white of egg, &c. Lastly, line the mould with thin slices of lady-cake, or almond sponge-cake; put in the mixture, and set it on ice. Before it goes to table ice the top; flavouring the icing with lemon-juice.

ORANGE CHARLOTTE RUSSE.—Is made as above—substituting for the lemons three fine large oranges, and flavouring the icing with orange-juice. Line the moulds with almond sponge-cake. Orange cake will be still better for this purpose.

ROSE CHARLOTTE RUSSE.—Take an ounce of Russia isinglass or of gelatine, and soften it by soaking a while in cold water. Then boil it slowly in a pint of cream, sweetened with a quarter of a pound of fine loaf-sugar, (adding a handful of fresh rose-leaves tied in a thin muslin bag,) till it is thoroughly dissolved, and well mixed. Take it off the fire; set it to cool; and beat together till very light and thick, four whole eggs, and the yolks only of four others. Stir the beaten eggs gradually into the mixture of cream, sugar and isinglass, and set it again over the fire. Stir it well, and see that it only simmers; taking it off before it comes quite to a boil. Then, while it is warm, stir in sufficient extract of roses, to give it a high rose-flavour and a fragrant smell. Have ready two moulds lined with lady-cake, or almond sponge-cake. Fill them with the mixture, and set them on ice. Before they go to table, ice the tops of the charlotte, flavouring the icing with rose.

CHOCOLATE CHARLOTTE RUSSE.—Having soaked in cold water an ounce of Russia isinglass, or of gelatine, shave down three ounces of the best chocolate, which must have no spice or sugar in it, (Baker's Prepared Cocoa is excellent for this and all other chocolate purposes,) and mix it gradually into a pint of cream, adding the soaked isinglass. Set the cream, chocolate, and isinglass over the fire, in a porcelain kettle; and boil it slowly till the isinglass is dissolved thoroughly, and the whole is well mixed. Then take it off the fire and let it cool. Have ready eight yolks of eggs and four whites, beaten all together till very light; and stir them gradually into the mixture, in turn with half a pound of powdered loaf-sugar. Simmer the whole over the fire, but do not let it quite boil. Then take it off, and with a chocolate-mill, (or with rods,) whip it to a strong froth. Line your moulds with sponge-cake, and set them on ice.

If you like a strong chocolate flavour, take four ounces of the cocoa.

ALMOND ICE-CREAM.—To every quart of cream, allow two ounces of shelled sweet almonds, and two ounces of shelled bitter almonds. Blanch the almonds in scalding water, and then throw them into cold water; afterwards, put them, one at a time, (bitter and sweet alternately,) into a marble mortar, and pound them to a fine, smooth paste, moistening them with a little cream as you proceed. When the almonds are all done, stir them gradually into the cream you intend to freeze. Set it over a fire, and continue to boil it five minutes after it has come to a boil. Then strain it into a freezer, and while it is warm stir in gradually sufficient powdered loaf-sugar to make it very sweet, allowing three-quarters of a pound to every quart of cream. Freeze it in the usual manner.

ALMOND ICE-CREAM—*Another way.* To each quart of cream, allow three ounces of shelled bitter-almonds, and no sweet ones. Blanch them and break them up slightly. Put them into a porcelain sauce-pan, and pour on water, allowing half a pint of water to each ounce of almonds. Boil them long and slowly, till the water is highly-flavoured, and so reduced in quantity that it barely covers the almonds. Then strain it off; and when cool, stir the almond water into the cream, adding sugar by degrees; allowing three-quarters of a pound to every quart of cream. Put the mixture into a freezer, and proceed as usual.

CHOCOLATE ICE-CREAM.—Chocolate used for this purpose must have neither sugar nor spice in it. Baker's Prepared Cocoa is the best. For each quart of cream, scrape down three large ounces of cocoa or chocolate, put it into a sauce-pan with half a pint of hot water for each ounce, and mix it into a smooth paste with a spoon. Place it over hot coals, and when it has come to a boil, take it off the fire and set it to cool. When it has become lukewarm, stir the chocolate into the cream, and strain it. When strained, add gradually, for each quart of cream, three-quarters of a pound of powdered loaf-sugar; and give the whole a boil up. Then put it into a freezer.

Another way.—To every quart of cream, allow three ounces of Baker's Prepared Cocoa, and half a pound of powdered loaf-sugar. Scrape the cocoa very fine, and stir it into the cream, alternately with the sugar, a little of each at a time. Having well mixed the whole, boil and stir it, continuing to do so five or six minutes after it has come to a boil. Then strain it into the freezer.

ORANGE ICE-CREAM.—To each quart of cream, allow two fine ripe oranges, and three-quarters of a pound of loaf-sugar. Rub the yellow rinds of the oranges upon a large lump of sugar, and scraping it off as you proceed, transfer it to a saucer. Then powder the lump of sugar, and put it, with the rest, all of which must be powdered. Squeeze the juice of the oranges among the sugar, mixing it well in. Then stir it gradually into the cream. Give it one boil up, and then transfer it to the freezer.

LEMON ICE-CREAM.—May be made as in the above receipt. It will require more sugar, as lemons are more acid than oranges.

Never use oil of lemon or essence of lemon for any flavouring. This article is now too generally made of tartaric acid, vitriol, or other drugs that render it unpalatable and unwholesome. Some of it tastes like peppermint. All lemon-flavouring should be obtained from the fruit only.

WINE JELLY.—Take three ounces of Cooper's isinglass or gelatine, and soak it in cold water during five minutes. Then take it out and put it into a preserving kettle, and dissolve it in two quarts of boiling water. Stir into it a pound of loaf-sugar, on part of which has been rubbed off the thin yellow rind of four large lemons. Add two large sticks of cinnamon broken up, and the juice of the lemons mixed with a pint of white wine, (madeira, sherry, or malaga,) and add also the broken shells and beaten whites of four eggs. Having mixed all the ingredients well in the preserving kettle, put on the cover, set the kettle over the fire, and boil it steadily during twenty minutes. Then take it off, and let it stand five minutes or more, to settle. Pour the whole carefully into a thin flannel bag, and let it run into your jelly moulds. On no account squeeze the bag, as that will injure the clearness of the jelly.

This mode of preparing jelly with artificial isinglass saves the trouble of boiling calves' feet the day before. It can be made in a short time.

VERY FINE APPLE JELLY.—Having cut out all blemishes, quarter half a bushel of the best pippin or bell-flower apples, without peeling or coring, and as you cut them, throw them into a pan of cold water to preserve the colour. When all the apples have been thus cut up, take them out of the water, but do not wipe or dry them. Then weigh the cut apples, and to each pound, allow a pound of the best loaf-sugar. Put them with the sugar into a large preserving-kettle and barely enough of water to prevent their burning, mixing among them the yellow rind of half a dozen lemons pared off very thin and cut into pieces. Also the juice of the lemons. When perfectly soft, and boiled to a mash, put the apples, &c., into a large linen jelly-bag, and run the liquid into moulds, if wanted for present use; and into jars if intended for keeping. Lay brandy paper on the top of each jar, and cover them closely.

PEAR MARMALADE.—Take large fine juicy pears. Pare, core, and cut them up into small pieces. Weigh the pieces; and to every two pounds allow a pound and a half of sugar, and the grated peel and juice of a large orange or lemon, adding a tea-spoonful of powdered ginger. Put the whole into a preserving-kettle and boil it over a moderate fire, till it becomes a very thick, smooth marmalade, stirring it up from the bottom frequently, and skimming the surface before each stirring. When quite done, put it warm into jars—and cover it.

For children, or for common family use, it may be made with large pound pears and brown sugar; but it always requires the acid of orange or lemon to make it palatable; pears, when cooked, having no acid of their own.

FIG-MARMALADE.—Take fine fresh figs that are perfectly ripe, such as can only be obtained in countries where they are cultivated in abundance. Weigh them, and to every two pounds of figs allow a pound and a half of sugar, and the yellow rind of a large orange or lemon, pared very thin. Cut up the figs, and put them into a preserving-kettle with the sugar, and orange or lemon-rind, adding the juice. Boil them till the whole is reduced to a thick, smooth mass, frequently stirring it up from the bottom. When done, put it warm into jars, and cover it closely.

TOMATA MARMALADE.—This is the best sort of tomata sweetmeat. Take ripe tomatas in the height of the season. In autumn they become watery, and insipid. Weigh them; and to every pound of tomatas allow a pound of sugar. Put the tomatas into a large pan, or a small tub, and scald them with boiling water, so as to make the skin peel off easily. When you have entirely removed the skins, put the tomatas (without any water) into a preserving-kettle, mash them, and add the sugar, with spoonfuls of ground ginger to your taste; also fresh lemon-peel finely grated, and sufficient lemon-juice to give it a fine flavour. Stir up the whole together, and set it over a moderate fire. Boil it gently for two or three hours, till the whole becomes a thick, smooth mass—skimming it well, and stirring it to the bottom after every skimming. When done, put it warm into jars; cover it tightly, (pasting paper over the lids,) and keep it in a dry place. This will be found a very fine sweetmeat. There should be enough of ginger and lemon to overpower the tomata flavour.

For children, this sweetmeat is better than any other; and it may be made for them very economically with good brown sugar, (always allowing a pound of sugar to a pound of tomatas,) and with no other flavouring than ginger. The natural taste of the tomatas must not be perceptible, it is their substance only that is wanted, and their wholesome properties.

RED FLUMMERY.—Boil a pound of ground rice in as much water as will cover it. When it is thoroughly boiled, and very thick and smooth, stir into the rice (while hot) a half pound of powdered white sugar, and about three jills, or six large wine-glasses of fresh currant or cherry juice, that has been pressed through a linen bag. Next replace it on the fire, and boil the whole together for about ten minutes, stirring it well. Then put it into moulds, and set it on ice. When cold, turn it out, and eat it with sweetened cream, or with boiled custard.

You may use the juice of fresh strawberries or raspberries, stirred in while the flummery is hot, but not boiled afterwards. The flavour of strawberries and rasp-berries is always impaired and weakened by cooking.

RICE BLANCMANGE.—Boil half a pint of whole rice in as little water as pos-sible, till all the grains lose their form and become a soft mass. Next put it into a sieve, and drain and press out all the water. Then return it to the sauce-pan, and mix with it a large half pint of rich milk, and a quarter of a pound of powdered sugar. Boil it again till the whole is reduced to a pulp. Then remove it from the fire, and stir in, (while hot,) a wine-glass of rose-water. Dip your moulds into cold water, and then fill them with the rice; set them on ice, and when quite firm and cold, turn out the blancmange, and serve it up on dishes with a sauce-tureen of sweetened cream flavoured with nutmeg. Or you may eat it with a boiled custard, or with wine sauce.

You may mould it in large breakfast cups. Always dip your moulds for a mo-ment in lukewarm water before you turn out their contents.

FARINA.—Farina is a very fine and delicate preparation made from the inner part of the grain of new wheat. It is exceedingly nutritious, and excellent, either for invalids or for persons in health. It is now much in use, and is to be had in packages of a pound or half a pound at the best grocers' and druggists', or in large quantities at No. 101 South Front Street, Philadelphia; and 201 Cherry Street, New York. It is highly recommended by physicians.

FARINA GRUEL.—Have some water boiling on the fire, and slowly sprinkle in sufficient farina to thicken it to the desired consistence. Continue the boiling twenty minutes afterwards. Sweeten it with loaf-sugar.

FARINA PANADA.—Soak the farina for several hours in milk. Then drain it, and put it into a vessel that has a close lid. Set this vessel in a kettle of water, raising it on a trivet or something similar. Place it over the fire, and make it boil all round the outside of the inner vessel. This will cook the farina very nicely. Keep it boiling till it becomes a thick, smooth mass. When done, sweeten it with white sugar; and, if permitted, you may flavour it with a little nutmeg and white wine. Some fresh lemon peel may be boiled with it, to be removed when the farina is taken up.

BAKED FARINA PUDDING.—Boil a quart of milk, gradually stirring into it, while boiling, a quarter of a pound of farina. Then take it up; and, while warm, mix into it a quarter of a pound of sugar; half a nutmeg grated; and a wine-glass of rose-water, or of white wine, or half a glass of brandy. Then beat four eggs very light, and stir them gradually into the farina mixture. Bake it in a buttered, deep dish, and grate sugar over it when done.

FARINA FLUMMERY or BLANCMANGE.—From a quart of rich milk take out a half pint. Put the half-pint into a small sauce-pan, and add to it a handful of bitter almonds broken up; or a bunch of fresh peach-leaves; or a vanilla bean split and cut into pieces, and tied up in a bit of thin muslin. Having boiled the milk till it is very highly-flavoured, strain it, and add it to the pint and a half. Then set it over the fire in a porcelain or delft-lined vessel, and boil it well. When it has come to a boil, begin to sprinkle in gradually a quarter of a pound (or four large heaping table-spoonfuls) of farina, stirring it well. Let it boil a quarter of an hour after all the farina is in. When done, remove it from the fire, and stir in (if you have used bitter almond or peach-leaf flavouring) a wine-glass of rose-water; add four large table-spoonfuls of powdered sugar. Put the flummery into a blancmange mould, set it on ice, and turn it out when wanted for dinner. Have ready to eat with it, a boiled custard, flavoured either with bitter almond or vanilla.

Another way.—Grate on a lump of sugar the yellow rind of a large lemon or orange, scraping it off with a tea-spoon as you proceed, and saving it on a saucer. Then mix it with a quarter of a pound of powdered loaf-sugar. Boil a quart of water, and when it has come to a boil, stir in alternately the sugar and four large heaping table-spoonfuls of farina. Let it boil a quarter of an hour longer. Then add the juice of the lemon or orange. Then put it into a mould and set it on ice to congeal. Eat with it boiled custard, flavoured with lemon or orange.

Another way.—Mix with a pint of water a pint of ripe currant-juice, strained through a sieve or bag, and well sweetened. In winter you may substitute the juice of stewed cranberries made very sweet. Boil the water and juice together. Then stir in gradually a quarter of a pound of farina, and boil it fifteen minutes longer. Transfer it to a mould, and set it on ice to congeal. Eat it with sweetened cream.

FARINA PLUM PUDDING.—Having extracted the seeds from half a pound of the best raisins, cut them in half, and dredge them well with sifted flour, to prevent their clodding, or sinking in the pudding. Pick, wash, and dry half a pound of Zante currants, and dredge them also with flour. Prepare a heaped teaspoonful of powdered spice; nutmeg, mace, and cinnamon, mixed together. Boil three pints of milk, and while it is boiling, sprinkle in a half pound of farina. Next add the spice, and let it boil a quarter of an hour longer. Then take it up, and set it to cool. When it is lukewarm, stir in gradually, six well-beaten eggs, in turn with the raisins and currants; a large piece of fresh butter; and a small glass of brandy. You may add some slips of citron, dredged with flour. Stir the mixture very hard. Put it into a buttered pudding-mould. Tie a double cloth tightly over the top, and place it in a pot of boiling water. Boil it three or four hours; and then turn it out on a dish. Eat it with wine-sauce; or with cold butter and sugar stirred together to a cream, and flavoured with nutmeg and lemon.

ROXBURY TEA CAKE.—On bread-making day take a pound or a quart of very light wheaten bread-dough, just before the loaves are put into the oven. Lay it in an earthen pan, and mix in, gradually, and alternately, three well-beaten eggs; a half-pint of powdered white sugar; half a pint of rich milk or cream; half a pint or a half-pound of fresh butter; and a tea-spoonful of mixed spice, powdered mace, nutmeg and cinnamon; with a wine-glass of rose-water. Mix the whole thoroughly, beating and stirring it well. Lastly, add a yeast powder; dissolving in one cup the portion of soda in a little lukewarm water, and mixing it into the dough; and melting in another cup the tartaric acid, and then stirring *that* in. Sprinkle some flour on your paste-board, and make the dough into small round cakes. Having pricked the tops with a fork, lay them in a buttered pan, set them immediately into the oven, and bake them brown. Eat them fresh, the day they are baked. You may bake the dough all in one loaf.

This cake will be improved by the addition of some raisins of the best quality, seeded and cut in half; and well-dredged with flour to prevent their sinking into a clod.

For a larger quantity, you must have two quarts of risen bread-dough; six eggs; a pint of powdered sugar; a pint of milk; a pound of fresh butter; and a table-spoonful of mixed spice; two wine-glasses of rose-water; and two yeast powders, or a full tea-spoonful of soda, and somewhat less than a tea-spoon of tartaric acid.

ALPISTERAS. (*Spanish cakes.*)—To one pound of fine flour, (well sifted and dried,) add half a pound of powdered loaf-sugar, (also sifted,) and mix them well together. In a shallow pan beat your eggs very light, and then gradually wet with them the mixed flour and sugar, adding a wine-glass of rose-water, or orange-flower water, or else the juice of two large oranges or lemons. Work the whole into a stiff dough, and knead it well. Roll it out into a very thin sheet, and cut it into squares of about five inches in size each way. Divide each square (half way down) into slips, so as to resemble a hand with fingers. Then curl or bend up the slips or fingers; or twist and twirl them so as to look like bunches of ribbons. Have ready, in a pot over the fire, a large portion of boiling lard. Put the alpisteras carefully into it, a few at a time, and fry them a light brown. Take them up on a perforated skimmer, draining back the lard into the pot. Spread them to cool on a large dish; and when cool, sift powdered sugar over them.

PISTO OMELETTE.—This is a favourite omelette in Spain. Mince together cold turkey or chicken, and an equal quantity of cold ham or tongue; adding a chopped onion or two, and sufficient sweet marjoram and sweet basil to season it well: also a little cayenne. No salt, as the ham will render it quite salt enough. Have ready sufficient well-beaten eggs to make it into a good omelette mixture; and stir the whole very hard at the last. Have ready over the fire, a broad pan of boiling lard. Put in the mixture with a ladle, and fry it in flat cakes. Serve it up hot.

GUISADA OR SPANISH STEW.—Take hare, rabbit, partridges, pheasants, or chickens. Cut them up as in carving; and save the giblets. Do not wash the pieces, but dry them in a cloth. Put them into a pan in which there is a sufficiency of hot sweet oil, (adding a sliced onion,) and fry them brown. Then transfer them (with the gravy) to an earthen stew-pan or pipkin. Add some bits of cold ham cut thin and small, and a bunch of sweet herbs chopped fine; also a little cayenne. Pour in wine and broth in equal portions, sufficient to cover the pieces well; adding the giblets. Let it simmer gently, till thoroughly done, carefully skimming off all the grease, and stirring the meat up from the bottom with a wooden spoon. Serve it hot in a covered dish.

It will be improved by the juice of one or two oranges, squeezed in toward the last.

POLLO VALENCIANO.—This is also a Spanish dish. Cut up a large fine fowl into pieces. Wipe them clean and dry, but do not wash them or lay them in water. Put into a broad sauce-pan, a tea-cup of sweet oil, and a bit of bread. Let it fry, (stirring it about with a wooden spoon,) and when the bread is browned take it out, and throw it away. Then put in a sliced onion, and fry that; but take care not to let it burn or it will become bitter, and spoil the stew. Then put in the pieces of fowl, and let them brown for a quarter of an hour. Then transfer it to a stew-pan, adding a little bit of chili or red pepper minced small, and some chopped sweet herbs. Also half a dozen large tomatas quartered; and two tea-cups of *boiled* rice. Add a little salt, and stir the whole well together, having poured on sufficient hot broth to cover it. Place it over the fire, and when it has come to a hard boil, put the lid on the pan and set it aside to simmer till the whole is completely cooked, and the gravy very thick. About ten minutes before the stew goes to table, take off the lid of the stew-pan, lest the steam should condense on it and clod the rice, or render it watery. Serve it up *un*covered.

GAZPACHO.—In Spanish countries this is a common luncheon or supper for working people. Take onions, cucumbers, and a small chili or red pepper. Peel them, chop them fine, and mix them with plenty of bread crumbs, and a little salt. Mix equal quantities of vinegar and water, and add an ample portion of sweet oil. Put the whole into a pipkin, and stir it well. Set it on hot coals, and simmer it till well cooked. Eat slices of bread with it.

In summer it is usual to serve up this mixture in a large bowl without any cooking.

SPANISH SALAD.—A Spanish proverb says that for compounding a *good* salad, four persons are required—a spendthrift for oil; a miser for vinegar; a counsellor for salt, (or a man of judgment;) and a madman for stirring up the whole, hard and furiously. Get a very large salad-bowl, that there may be ample room for stirring well. Prepare in separate vessels the lettuce and the seasoning. They should not be put together till a few minutes before the salad is to be eaten; otherwise it will be tough and sodden instead of crisp and fresh. Do not cut it with a knife, but tear or strip off the leaves of the lettuce, and throw all the stalk away. Then wash the leaves through several cold waters, and dry them in a clean napkin. Put them into the large bowl; and in a smaller bowl mix the seasoning, for which you must have equal quantities of mixed vinegar and water; a small tea-spoonful of mixed cayenne and salt; and four times as much sweet oil as the mixed vinegar and water. Mix all the seasoning thoroughly, stirring it very hard. Have ready on a plate some tarragon finely minced or powdered.

Just before the salad is to be eaten, pour the dressing over the lettuce and strew the surface with tarragon. You may decorate the top with nasturtion flowers; they are very nice to eat.

CAROLINA WAY OF BOILING RICE.—Pick the rice carefully, and wash it through two or three cold waters till it is quite clean. Then (having drained off all the water through a cullender) put the rice into a pot of boiling water, with a very little salt; allowing as much as a quart of water to half a pint of rice. Boil it twenty minutes or more. Then pour off the water, draining the rice as dry as possible. Lastly, set it on hot coals with the lid off, that the steam may not condense upon it and render the rice watery. Keep it drying thus for a quarter of an hour. Put it into a deep dish, and loosen and toss it up from the bottom with two forks one in each hand, so that the grains may appear to stand alone.

A NICE WAY OF COOKING ASPARAGUS.—Where asparagus is plenty, there is no better way of cooking it than the following. Take it as nearly of a size as possible, wash it, and cut off the stalks very short; leaving them not more than half an inch in length. Two quarts of water will be sufficient to boil one quart of asparagus tops; allow a tea-spoonful of salt to this quantity of water, and set it over the fire to boil. When the water is boiling hard, put in the asparagus; and boil it fast for at least half an hour. To see if it is done, take up two or three of the largest pieces and taste them. While it is boiling, prepare two slices of bread cut half an inch thick, and (having removed the crust) toast the bread brown on both sides. Have ready a large jill of melted (or drawn) fresh butter. When the asparagus is done, take it up with a perforated skimmer, and lay it on a sieve to drain. Dip the slices of toast (one at a time) first in the hot asparagus liquor, and then in the melted butter. Lay the slices, side by side, in a deep dish and cover it with the asparagus, laid evenly over and round the toast. Then add the remainder of the drawn butter, and send the asparagus to table hot, in a covered dish.

This is a much nicer way than that of boiling and serving it up with the long stalks left on. And where you have asparagus in abundance, (for instance in a country garden,) it may always be cooked in this manner.

This is from the receipt of Mr. N. Darling of New Haven.

FRENCH WAY OF DRESSING ASPARAGUS.—Having boiled the asparagus-tops as above; drain them on a sieve, and put them into a deep dish with a large lump of the best fresh butter. Mix the butter well among the asparagus, till it is melted throughout, and sprinkle in (if you like) a very little pepper. Cover the dish, and keep it hot by the fire till it is time to send it to table. You may lay in the bottom, of the dish two thin slices of toast, spread over with butter, after being first dipped in the asparagus water.

Another way is to substitute salad oil for butter, mixed among the asparagus.

ONION EGGS.—Boil a dozen eggs quite hard. Slice and fry in fresh butter five or six onions. Slice (whites and yolks together) ten of the eggs, reserving two for the seasoning. Drain the sliced onions, and lay them on a dish with the sliced eggs placed upon them. Cover the dish, and keep it hot. Take the two remaining eggs; grate the yolks; and mix them with cream and grated nutmeg, and a very little cayenne. Put this mixture into a very small sauce-pan; give it one boil up; pour it over the eggs and onions; and send it to table hot. For those who have no objection to onions, this is a nice side dish.

EGG BALLS.—Boil eight eggs till quite hard; and when done, throw them directly into cold water. Then put the yolks into a mortar, and pound them to a paste, moistening them as you proceed with the beaten yolks of three *raw* eggs, seasoned with as much salt as will lie *flat* upon a shilling, and a little cayenne, and powdered nutmeg and mace. Mix the whole well together, and make it up into small, round balls. Throw them into mock-turtle soup, or into stewed terrapin, about two minutes before you take it up.

CURRY BALLS.—Take a sufficiency of finely-grated bread-crumbs; hard-boiled yolk of egg, grated; fresh butter; and a little curry powder. Pound the whole in a mortar, moistening it with raw yolk of egg (well-beaten) as you proceed. Make it into small balls, and add them to stewed chicken or stewed rabbit, about five minutes before you take it up.

TOMATA PASTE.—Scald and peel as many ripe tomatas as will fill a large, deep, stone jar. Set them into a warm oven for an hour. Then skim off the watery liquid that has risen to the top, and press and squeeze the tomatas in a sieve. Afterwards add salt, cayenne, pounded mace, and powdered cloves to your taste; and to every quart of tomatas allow a half a pint of cider vinegar. Stew the whole slowly in a porcelain kettle for three hours, (stirring it frequently from the bottom,) till it becomes a smooth, thick paste. Then put it into small jars or glasses, and cover it closely; pasting paper over each. It is an excellent sauce, at the season when fresh tomatas are not to be had, and is very good to thicken soup.

DRIED OCHRAS.—Take fine large fresh ochras; cut them into thin, round slices; string them on threads, and hang them up in festoons to dry in the store-room. Before using, they must be soaked in water during twenty-four hours. They will then be good (with the addition of tomata paste) to boil in soup or gumbo.

BEEF GUMBO.—Put into a large stew-pan some pieces of the lean of fresh beef, cut up into small bits, and seasoned with a little pepper and salt. Add sliced ochras and tomatas, (either fresh, or dried ochras and tomata paste.) You may put in some sliced onions. Pour on water enough to cover it well. Let it boil slowly, (skimming it well,) till every thing is reduced to rags. Then strain and press it through a cullender. Have ready a sufficiency of toasted bread, cut into dice. Lay it in the bottom of a tureen, and pour the strained gumbo upon it.

FRIED CAULIFLOWER.—Having boiled the cauliflower in milk till thoroughly done; take it out, drain it, and cut it up into very small pieces, adding a *very little* salt and cayenne. Have ready in a frying-pan, sufficient fresh butter; and when it comes to a boil and is bubbling all over, put in the cauliflower and fry it, but not till it becomes brown. Make a slice or two of toast, dip it in hot water, butter it; lay it on a dish; and put the fried cauliflower upon it.

FRIED CABBAGE.—Parboil a fine cabbage. Then take it out, drain it, and lay it a while in cold water to remove the cabbage smell. Next put it into a clean pot of fresh water, and boil it again till thoroughly done. Afterwards chop it small, season it with a little pepper and salt, and fry it in fresh butter.

A less delicate way is to fry it in boiling lard.

TO PREPARE LARD.—As soon it is cut off from the newly-killed pork, put the fat into a crock; cover it; and let it stand all night in a cool place. Next day, cut it into small bits, (carefully removing all the fleshy particles of lean,) and put the fat into a pot without either water or salt. The pot should not be more than half-full. Let it boil slowly (stirring it frequently from the bottom lest it burn) till it becomes quite clear, and transparent. Then ladle it out into clean pans. When almost cold, put it into stone jars, which must be closely covered, and kept in a cool place. If to go to a distance, tie it up in bladders.

There are two sorts of pork fat for lard. The leaf fat, which is the best; and the fat that adheres to the entrails. These two fats should be boiled separately.

The entrails, whose skins are to be used for sausage-cases, must be well scraped and cleaned out, and thrown into strong salt and water for two days, and afterwards into strong lye for twenty-four hours. This lye, when strained, will afterwards be good to assist in soap-making.

BRINE FOR HAM OR BACON.—To every four gallons of water, allow four pounds of salt; two ounces of salt-petre; three pounds of sugar, and two quarts of molasses. Boil the whole together; skimming it well. When clear, let it cool. Rub the meat all over with ground red pepper. Then put as much meat into the pickling tub as can be very well covered by the brine, which must be poured on cold. Let it remain six weeks in the pickle, turning each piece every day. Afterwards, smoke it well for a fortnight, hanging the large end downward. The fire in the smoke-house should be well kept up. Hickory or oak is the best wood for this purpose. On no account use pine, spruce, fir, or hemlock. Corncobs are excellent for smoking meat.

Sew up the hams closely in thick cotton cloth—or canvas covers, and then white-wash them.

Tongues may be pickled and smoked as above. Also beef.

HOG'S HEAD CHEESE.—Hog's head cheese is always made at what is called "killing-time." To make four cheeses of moderate size, take one large hog's head, two sets of feet, and the noses of all the pigs that have been killed that day. Clean them well, and then boil them to rags. Having drained off the liquid through a cullender, spread out the things in a large dish, and carefully remove all the bones, even to the smallest pieces. With a chopper, mince the meat as small as possible, and season it to your taste with pepper, salt, powdered cloves, and some chopped sage or sweet marjoram. Having divided the meat into four equal parts, tie up each portion tightly in a clean coarse towel, and press it into a compact cake, by putting on heavy weights. It will be fit for use next day. In a cool dry place it will keep all winter. It requires no farther cooking, and is eaten sliced at breakfast, or luncheon.

FRYING FISH.—Fish should be fried in fresh butter or lard; a large allowance of which must be put by itself into the frying-pan, and held over a clear fire till it becomes so hot as to boil hard in the pan. Till it bubbles, the fish must not be put in. They must first be dried separately, in a clean cloth, and then scored on the back, and slightly dredged with flour. Unless the butter or lard for frying is sufficient in quantity to cover the fish well, and bear them up, they will sink heavily to the bottom of the pan, and perhaps stick there and burn. Also, if there is not fat enough, the fish will absorb all of what there is, and be disagreeably greasy.

AXJAR PICKLES.—Take a variety of young fruits or vegetables, and put them into strong salt and water for three days; stirring them well, night and morning. Then take them out, and spread them on trays, or old servers, or large flat dishes; taking care that they do not touch each other. Set them out in the sun every fine morning, and let them remain till sunset; but not if it becomes damp, or even cloudy. Do this till they are perfectly dry. Then wash them well in cold water, drain them, and wipe them separately with a coarse cloth. Put them into large jars. To a three gallon jar, put in half a pound of horse-radish, sliced, and two cloves of garlic; half a hundred small white onions; two ounces of mace; one ounce of cloves; two nutmegs powdered; two pounds of the best crushed sugar; half a bottle of the best ground mustard; one pound of yellow mustard seed; and half a pound of green ginger, sliced or scraped. Then take half an ounce of turmeric powder; mix it with sufficient vinegar to render it liquid, and pour it over the pickles in the jar, which must not be more than half full of them. Have ready some boiling vinegar of the best cider kind, and pour it scalding hot into the jar, till it is three parts full. The pickles will expand to their natural size. When they are perfectly cold, cork the jar tightly, and seal the cork. These pickles will be fit for use in a month; but they improve by keeping.

For this pickle you may use plums, small peaches; grapes picked from the stems; cherries; barberries; nasturtion seeds; button tomatas; radish-pods; beans, cauliflowers sliced; white cabbages sliced, small cucumbers; and limes or small lemons—mixed together in any proportion you like. The turmeric powder gives the whole a yellow tinge, and is indispensable to this pickle.

Axjar is an East Indian word.

FINE PEACH MANGOES.—Take fine, large, free-stone peaches. They should be ripe, but not the least bruised. The best for this purpose are the large white free-stones. Having rubbed off the down with a clean flannel, cut the peaches in half, and remove the stones. Prepare a mixture, in equal portions, of mace, nutmeg, and root-ginger; all broken up small, but not powdered. Fill with this the cavities of the peaches whence the stones were extracted. Then put together the two halves of each peach, (making them fit exactly,) and tie them round with coarse thread or fine twine. If you choose, you may stick the outside of the peaches all over with cloves. Put them into stone jars, filling each jar rather more than three-quarters full; and laying among them little thin muslin bags of turmeric to colour them yellow. If you prefer to colour them red, tie up some cochineal in thin muslin bags.

Fill up the jars to the top with cold vinegar of the best quality—real white wine vinegar, if you are sure it *is* real. If the pickles are to be sent to a distant place, or to a warmer climate, boil the vinegar, and pour it on, scalding hot. Close the jars immediately; sealing the corks with red cement, and tie a bladder tightly over the top of each.

These peach mangoes will be fit for use in two months.

TO PICKLE PEPPERS, SMALL CUCUMBERS, AND BEANS.—Put all these vegetables together into a brine strong enough to bear up an egg to the surface; and let them stay in it for three days. Then take them out, and lay them in cold water for an hour. Change that water for fresh, and let them remain another hour. Do this a third or fourth time.

Having washed them well in a fresh water, put them into a preserving-kettle, (one lined with delft-porcelain is best,) and surround and cover them with fresh cabbage leaves, or vine-leaves. Fill up the kettle with cider-vinegar mixed with an equal quantity of water; and during four hours let them simmer without boiling.

Then take them off the fire; take them out of the kettle, transfer them to broad pans, and pour the vinegar over them. When they are cold, return the pickles to the kettle, (having first washed it out clean,) and scald them four times with fresh vinegar boiled for the purpose in another vessel. When cold, put them into jars, (three parts full,) and pour on fresh vinegar till it reaches the top. Lay among the pickles, mace; nutmegs broken small; mustard seed; and whole white-pepper-corns, tied up in thin white muslin bags.

PICKLED ONIONS.—Take small button-onions; remove the outer skin, and lay the onions in dry salt for twenty-four hours. Then soak off the salt, in several waters; wash them well; and put them into a porcelain kettle, with equal quantities of vinegar and water. Simmer them till tender. Then take them out; drain them; and, returning them to the kettle, scald them with fresh vinegar boiled in another vessel. When cold, take them out, drain them again; put them into wide-mouthed jars, and fill up with cold vinegar. Place among them thin muslin bags with mace and broken nutmegs. On the top of each jar, put a table-spoonful of sweet oil. Cover them tightly.

PICKLED PLUMS or DAMSONS.—The fruit must be large, fine, fully ripe, and with no blemishes. To every quart of plums allow a quarter of a pound of loaf-sugar powdered, and a pint of the best cider vinegar. Damsons being more acid will require half a pound of sugar. Put the fruit with the sugar and vinegar into a preserving kettle, adding little bags with some broken pieces of cinnamon and some blades of mace, and, if you choose, a few cloves. Give them one boil up, and skim them well. Put them warm into stone jars, and cover them closely at once. By winter they will be fit for use.

Another way.—Is to pack a jar more than three-fourths full with layers of ripe plums or damsons; and thick layers of powdered sugar between. Fill up with cold vinegar, and cover them tightly.

PICKLED CHERRIES.—Take large, fine, red cherries, perfectly ripe, and cut the stems about an inch long. Put the cherries into jars with layers of powdered sugar between each layer of fruit, interspersing them with little, thin muslin bags of broken cinnamon, mace, and nutmeg. The jars should be three-quarters full of cherries and sugar. Fill up with cold vinegar, and cover them closely.

TO KEEP STRING BEANS AND GREEN PEAS.—String the beans, (which should be full grown but not old,) and cut them into *three* pieces—not more. Pack them in wide-mouthed stone-jars; a layer of beans and a thin layer of fine salt. The day before they are to be cooked, take out a sufficient quantity, and soak them at least twenty-four hours in a pan of cold water, changing the water several times, till it no longer tastes salt. Having drained them well, boil the beans till quite tender. Then take them up, drain off the water thoroughly, so as to have the beans as dry as possible. Next put them into a sauce-pan, with a piece of fresh butter and a little black pepper. Cover the pan, and stew them in the butter till they almost come to a boil.

Green peas may be kept in a similar manner. They should be fresh and young. When you take them out of the salt, soak them, as above, for twenty-four hours or more; changing the water till it tastes quite fresh. Boil them soft; then drain them, and stew them a while with butter and pepper.

You may, while boiling, add a *very little* soda to the peas or beans. This will green and soften them. Too much soda will give them a disagreeable taste, and render them unfit to eat.

SCOTCH SHORT-CAKE.[5]—Take a pound of Zante currants; and, after they are well picked and washed, dry them on a large dish before the fire, or on the top of a stove. Instead of currants, you may use sultana or seedless raisins cut in half. When well dried, dredge the fruit profusely with flour to prevent its clodding while baking. Have ready a tea-spoonful of mixed spice, powdered mace, nutmeg, and cinnamon. Sift two quarts of flour, and spread it to dry at the fire. Cut up a pound of the best fresh butter; put it into a clean sauce-pan, and melt it over the fire; shaking it round and taking care that it does not burn. Put the flour into a large pan, and mix with it a pound of powdered white sugar. Pour the melted butter warm into the midst of the flour and sugar; and with a large spoon or a broad knife mix the whole thoroughly into a soft dough or paste, *without using a drop of water*. Next sprinkle in the fruit, a handful at a time, (stirring hard between each handful) and finish with a tea-spoonful of spice, well mixed in. Let all the ingredients be thoroughly incorporated.

Strew some flour on your paste-board; lay the lumps of dough upon it, flour your hands, and knead it a while on all sides. Then cut it in half, and roll out each sheet about an inch thick. With a jagging-iron cut it into large squares, ovals, triangles, or any form you please, and prick the surface handsomely, with a fork. Butter some square pans, put in the cakes, and bake them brown.

For currants and raisins, you may substitute citron cut into slips and floured. This cake will be found very fine if the receipt is *exactly* followed. In cold weather it keeps well; and packed in a tin or wooden box, may be sent many hundred miles, for Thanksgiving-day, Christmas, or New Year's.

It is still more Scotch made of fine fresh oatmeal, sifted and dried. When in London, the author has eaten Scotch cake sent from Edinburgh, and made as above, but of oatmeal.

RICE WAFFLES.—Take a tea-cup and a half, or a common sized tumbler-full and a half, of rice that has been well boiled, and warm it in a pint of rich milk, stirring it till smooth and thoroughly mixed. Then remove it from the fire, and stir in a pint of cold milk and a small teaspoonful of salt. Beat four eggs very light, and stir them into the mixture, in turn with sufficient rice flour to make a thick batter. Bake it in a waffle-iron. Send them to table hot; butter them; and eat them with powdered sugar and cinnamon, prepared in a small bowl for the purpose.

---

[5] This receipt, though inserted somewhat out of place, is too good to be omitted.

THE INDIAN MEAL BOOK.

HINTS ON HEATING OVENS, AND BAKING.—Brick ovens are generally heated with dry fagots or small branches, or with light split wood. For baking bread, the oven-wood must be heavier than for pies. A heap of wood should be placed in the centre of the oven on the brick floor, and then set on fire. While the wood is burning, the door of the oven must be left open. When the wood is all burnt down, and reduced to a mass of small red coals, the oven will be very hot. Then shovel out all the coals and sweep the oven floor with a broom, till it is perfectly clean, and entirely free from ashes. Try the heat within. For baking bread, the floor of the oven should look red; and a little flour thrown in should burn brown immediately. If you can hold your hand within the mouth of the oven as long as you can distinctly count twenty, the heat is about right. Pies, puddings, &c., require less heat. When a brick oven is used, a peel, or large broad-bladed, long-handled wooden shovel is necessary for putting in the bread, pies, &c., placing them on the broad or shovel-end of the peel, and then depositing them on the oven floor. Then close up the door of the oven, and leave the things to bake. When done, slip the peel beneath them, and hand them out on it.

To bake in an iron Dutch oven, (a large deep, cast-iron pan, with a handle, a close-fitting lid, and standing on three or four feet,) you must first stand the lid upright before a clear fire to heat the inside; and it will be best if the oven itself is also stood up before the fire for the same purpose. This should be done while the article to be baked is preparing, that it may be put in as soon as it is ready. The oven may be suspended to the crane, and hung over the fire, or it may be set on a bed of hot wood-coals in the corner of the hearth. As soon as the loaf or pie is in, put on the lid of the oven, and cover it all over with hot coals, replenishing it with more live coals as the baking proceeds. If you find it too hot on the top, deaden it with ashes. If the oven stands on the hearth, keep up the heat at the bottom, by additional live coals placed beneath it. Whether the oven is hung over the fire, or stood on the hearth, there must always be hot coals all over the lid, the hottest near the edge.

To bake on a griddle, you may either hang it over the fire, or set it over hot coals on the hearth. Most griddles have feet. The fire must be quite clear and bright, and free from smoke, or the cakes will be blackened, and have a disagreeable taste. The griddle must be perfectly clean; and while you are baking, it will require frequent scraping, with a broad knife. If it is well scraped after every cake is taken off, it will not want greasing, as there will be no stickiness. Otherwise, some butter tied up in a clean rag and laid on a saucer, must be kept at hand all the time, to rub over the griddle between the baking of each cake; for butter, lard, or nice beef or veal-dripping may be substituted, but it will not be so fine. Never grease with mutton-fat, as it will communicate the taste of tallow. A bit of the fat of *fresh* pork may do, (stuck on a fork,) but salt pork will give the outside of the cakes a disagreeable saltiness, and therefore should not be used.

A griddle may be placed in the oven of a hot stove. Some close stoves have a hole in the top with a flat lid or cover, which lid can be used as a griddle.

The tin-reflecting-ovens (with shelves for the pies and cakes) that are used for baking in the summer, and that, having a furnace beneath, and a chimney-pipe, can be set out of doors, so that the kitchen may not be kept hot, are very good for things that will bake soon, and that do not require what is called a strong, solid heat. But they are not effective unless the inside is kept *very bright*; otherwise it will not reflect the heat. These tin ovens should (as well as tin roasters) be cleaned thoroughly and scoured bright with sand every time they are used.

The art of baking with anthracite, (or any other mineral coal,) can only be acquired by practice. The above hints on baking, refer exclusively to wood fires.

When a charcoal furnace is used for baking, stewing, or any sort of cooking, it should either be set out in the open air, or the door of the kitchen must be kept open all the time. The vapor of charcoal in a close room is so deleterious as to cause death.

DRIED CORN MEAL YEAST CAKES.—Half a pound of fresh hops.—Four quarts of water.—A pint of wheat or rye flour.—Half a pint of strong fresh yeast, from the brewer or baker.—Three pints, or more of Indian meal. Boil half a pound of fresh hops in four quarts of water, till the liquid is reduced to two quarts. Strain it into a pan, and mix in sufficient wheat flour to make a thin batter; adding half a pint of the best yeast you can procure. Leave it to ferment; and when the fermentation is over, stir in sufficient Indian meal to make a moderately stiff dough. Cover it, and set in a warm place to rise. When it has become very light, roll it out into a square sheet an inch thick, and cut it into flat cakes, about four inches square. Spread them out separately, on a large dish; and let them dry slowly, in a cool place where there is no sun. While drying, turn them five or six times a-day. When they are quite dry and hard, put them separately into brown paper bags, and keep them in a box closely covered, and in a place not the least damp.

When you want them to use for yeast, dissolve in a little warm water, one or more of the cakes, in proportion to the quantity of bread you intend making. When it is quite dissolved, stir it hard, thicken it with a little wheat flour, cover it, and place it near the fire to rise, before you use it. Then mix it with the flour, according to the usual manner of making bread. One yeast cake is enough for two quarts of meal or flour.

This way of preserving yeast is very convenient for keeping through the summer; or for conveying to a distance.

EXCELLENT HOME-MADE YEAST.—Yeast should always be kept in a glass bottle or a stone jug, and never in earthen or metal. Before you make fresh yeast, empty entirely the vessel that has contained the last; and if of stone, scald it twice with boiling water, in which it will be well to mix a little clear lye. Then rinse it with cold water, till perfectly clean. If you have not used lye in scalding it, dissolve some potash or pearlash in the rinsing-water, to remove any acidity that may linger about the vessel, and may therefore spoil the new yeast. If you keep your yeast in glass bottles, the water must be warm, but not hot; as scalding water may crack them: also melt some potash or pearlash in this water. The vessel for keeping it being purified, proceed to make your yeast. Have ready, in a kettle over the fire, two quarts of boiling water; put into it a very large handful of hops, (as fine and fresh as possible,) and let the water boil again with the hops in it, for twenty minutes or more. Sift into a pan three pints of wheat flour. Strain the liquor from the hops into a large bowl, and pour half of it hot over the flour. Stir it well, and press out all the lumps till it is quite smooth. Let the other half of the liquid stand till it is cool, and then pour it gradually to the rest; mixing it well, by stirring as you proceed. Then take half a pint of good strong yeast—brewers' or bakers' yeast, if you can get it fresh; if not, you must use some that has been left from your last making, provided it is not the least sour; stir this yeast into the mixture of hop-water and flour; put it immediately into your jug or bottles, and cork it loosely till the fermentation is over, (which should be in an hour,) and it will then be fit for use. Afterwards cork it tightly. It will keep better if you put a raisin or two into the bottom of each bottle, before you pour in the fresh yeast. Into a stone jug put half a dozen raisins.

All yeast is better and more powerful for being fresh. It is better to make it frequently, (the trouble being little,) than to risk its becoming sour by endeavouring to keep it too long. When sour, it becomes weak and watery, and tastes and smells disagreeably, and will never make light bread; besides being very unwholesome. The acidity may be somewhat corrected by stirring in some dissolved pearlash, sal-eratus, or soda, immediately before the yeast is used; but it is better to have it good and fresh, without the necessity of any corrective. Yeast should always be kept in a cool place.

Those who live in towns where there are breweries have no occasion to make their own yeast during the brewing season; and in summer they can every day supply themselves with fresh yeast from the baker's. It is only in country places where there are neither brewers nor bakers that it is expedient to make it at home. For home-made yeast, we know the above receipt to be excellent.

Sweet cakes, buns, rusks, &c., require stronger and fresher yeast than bread; the sugar will otherwise retard their rising.

INDIAN BREAD, OR PONE.—Four quarts of Indian meal sifted.—A large half pint of wheat flour.—A heaping table-spoonful of salt.—Half a pint of strong fresh yeast.—A quart of warm water.—Sift into a large deep pan, the Indian meal and the wheat flour; mixing them well. Make a hole in the centre. The water must be warm, but not hot. Mix it with the yeast, and pour them into the hole in the midst of the meal. Take a spoon, and with it mix into the liquid enough of the surrounding meal to make a thin batter, which you must stir till it is quite smooth, and free from lumps. Then strew a handful of wheat flour over the surface, scattering it thinly, so as to cover the whole. Warm a clean cloth, and lay it folded over the top of the pan. Then set it in a warm place to rise, nearer the fire in winter than in summer. When it is quite light; and has risen so that the flour on the surface is cracked, strew on the salt, and begin to form the whole mass into a dough; commencing round the hole that contains the batter, and adding, gradually, sufficient luke-warm water (which you must have ready for the purpose) to mix it of the proper consistence. When the whole is completely mixed, and the batter in the centre is thoroughly incorporated with the dough, knead it hard for at least half an hour. Then, having formed the dough into a round lump in the middle of the pan, strew a little more flour thinly over it. Cover it, and set it again in a warm place for half an hour. Then flour your paste-board, divide the dough equally, and make it into two loaves. Have the oven ready. Put in the loaves directly, and bake them about two hours or more. Indian meal requires always more baking than wheat. When you take them out, it is well to wrap each loaf in a clean, coarse towel, previously sprinkled with cold water; and rolled up damp till the bread is baked. Having thus wrapped up the loaves, stand them on end to cool slowly. The damp cloths will prevent the crust from hardening too much while the loaves are cooling.

All Indian bread, and every sort of Indian cake is best when quite fresh.

Excellent bread may be made of equal proportions of wheat, rye flour, and Indian; or of three parts wheat and one part Indian. All bread should be kept closely secluded from the air, wrapped in cloths, and put away in boxes or baskets with tightly-fitting lids.

Should you find the dough sour, (either from the heat of the weather, or from standing too long,) you may recover it, by dissolving in a little lukewarm water, a tea-spoonful of pearlash, sal-eratus, or soda. Sprinkle this water all over the dough. Then knead it in, so that it may be dispersed throughout. Then put it into the oven as soon as possible; first tasting the dough, to discover if the sourness is entirely removed. If not, mix in a little more pearlash, and then taste it again. Take care not to put too much of any of these alkaline substances, lest they communicate a disagreeable, soapy taste to the bread.

When you buy corn meal, it will keep better if the whole is sifted as soon as you get it. Avoid buying much at a time, unless you can keep it in a very cool place. When sour it is unfit to eat.

INDIAN RYE BREAD. — Two quarts of Indian meal. Two quarts of rye meal. — Three pints of milk or water. Two teaspoonfuls of salt. — Half a pint of strong fresh yeast. Having sifted the rye and Indian meal into a large pan, mix them well together, adding the salt. Boil the milk or water in a sauce-pan, and when scalding hot pour it on the meal, and stir the whole very hard. If too stiff, add a little more warm water. Let it stand till it becomes only of a lukewarm heat, and then stir in the yeast. Knead the mixture into a stiff dough, and knead it long and hard for at least half an hour. Then cover the pan with a thick cloth that has been previously warmed, and set it near the fire to rise. When the dough is quite light, and cracked all over the top, take it out of the pan; divide the mass in half; make it into two loaves; knead each loaf well for ten minutes or more; and then cover and set them again near the fire, for about half an hour. By this time have the oven ready, put in the loaves directly, and bake them at least an hour and a half. This bread is considered very wholesome.

Should you find the dough sour, you may rectify it by kneading in a tea-spoonful of soda or pearlash, dissolved in a little warm water.

INDIAN WHEAT BREAD.—This is made in the above manner, substituting wheat for rye flour.

In any sort of home-made bread (either white or brown) a handful or more of Indian meal will be found an improvement, rendering it moist and sweet.

BOSTON RYE AND INDIAN BREAD.—Two quarts of Indian meal.—Two quarts of rye meal.—Half a pint of strong fresh yeast.—Half a pint of West India molasses.—A small table-spoonful of salt. Sift the rye and Indian meal into a large pan or wooden bowl; and mix them, well together, adding the salt. Have ready half a pint of water, warm but not hot. Mix with it the molasses, and then stir into it the yeast. Make a hole in the middle of the pan of meal; pour in the liquid; and then with a spoon work into it a portion of the flour that surrounds the hole, till the liquid in the centre becomes a thick batter. Sprinkle the top with rye meal; lay a thick cloth over the pan; and set it in a warm place to rise. In three or four hours it should be light enough to appear cracked all over the surface. Then pour into the middle (by degrees) about a pint of warm water, (it must not be hot,) and as you pour, mix it well all through the dough, till the whole becomes a round mass. Sprinkle some rye flour on the dough, and having floured your hands, knead it long and hard, (at least half an hour, and after it ceases to stick to your hands,) turning it over as you proceed. Then sprinkle the dough again with flour, cover it, and again set it in a warm place to rise. Have the oven ready, and of the proper heat, so that the bread may be put in as soon as it has completely risen the second time. When perfectly light, the dough will stand high, and the surface will be cracked all over. This quantity will be sufficient for a common-sized loaf. Set it directly into the oven, and bake it about two hours. When bread has done rising, it will fall again if not put into the oven. As soon as it is done, wrap it immediately in a clean coarse towel wrung out of cold water, and stand it up on end till it is cool.

This is a palatable, cheap, and wholesome bread.

It may be mixed thinner, with a larger portion of water, and baked in a deep tin or iron pan.

If the dough should have stood so long as to become sour (which it will, if mixed over night) restore it by kneading in a small tea-spoonful of pearlash or sal-eratus melted in a little warm water.

EGG PONE.—Three eggs.—A quart of Indian meal.—A large table-spoonful of fresh butter.—A small tea-spoonful of salt.—A half-pint (or more) of milk. Beat the eggs very light, and mix them with the milk. Then stir in, gradually, the Indian meal; adding the salt and butter. It must not be a batter, but a soft dough, just thick enough to be stirred well with a spoon. If too thin, add more Indian meal; if too stiff, thin it with a little more milk. Beat or stir it *long and hard*. Butter a tin or iron pan. Put the mixture into it; and set the pan immediately into an oven, which must be moderately hot at first, and the heat increased afterward. A Dutch oven is best for this purpose. It should bake an hour and a half or two hours, in proportion to its thickness. Send it to table hot, and cut into slices. Eat it with butter, or molasses.

INDIAN MUSH.—Have ready on a clear fire, a pot of boiling water. Stir into it, by degrees, (a handful at a time,) sufficient Indian meal to make a very thick porridge, and then add a very small portion of salt, allowing not more than a level tea-spoonful to a quart of meal. You must keep the pot boiling all the time you are stirring in the meal; and between every handful stir hard with the mush-stick, (a round stick about half a yard long, flattened at the lower end,) as, if not well stirred, the mush will be lumpy. After it is sufficiently thick and smooth, keep it boiling an hour longer, stirring it occasionally. Then cover the pot closely, and hang it higher up the chimney, or set it on hot coals on the hearth, so as to simmer it slowly for another hour. The goodness and wholesomeness of mush depends greatly on its being long and thoroughly boiled. It should also be made very thick. If well made, and well cooked, it is wholesome and nutritious; but the contrary, if thin, and not sufficiently boiled. It is not too long to have it three or four hours over the fire, first boiling, and then simmering. On the contrary it will be better for it. The coarser the corn meal the less cooking it requires. Send it to table hot, and in a deep dish. Eat it with sweet milk, buttermilk, or cream; or with butter and sugar, or with butter and molasses; making a hole in the middle of your plate of mush; putting some butter into the hole, and then adding the sugar or molasses.

Cold mush that has been left, may be cut into slices, or mouthfuls, and fried next day, in butter, or in nice drippings of veal, beef, or pork; but not mutton or lamb.

INDIAN HASTY PUDDING.—Put two quarts of milk into a clean pot or sauce-pan. Set it over the fire, adding a level tea-spoonful of salt, and, when it comes to a boil, stir in a lump of fresh butter about the size of a goose-egg. Then add (a handful at a time) sufficient Indian meal to make it very thick, stirring it all the while with a mush-stick. Keep it boiling well, and continue to throw in Indian meal till it is so thick that the stick stands upright in it. Then send it to table hot, and eat it with milk, cream, or molasses and butter. What is left may be cut into slices, and fried next day, or boiled in a bag.

INDIAN MEAL GRUEL.—This is an excellent food for the sick. Having sifted some Indian meal, mix in a quart bowl three table-spoonfuls of the meal with six of cold water. Stir it smooth, and press out the lumps against the side of the bowl. Have ready a very clean sauce-pan, entirely free from grease, with a pint of boiling water. Pour this, scalding hot, on the mixture in the bowl, a little at a time, and stir it well, adding a pinch of salt. Then put the whole back into the sauce-pan. Set it on hot coals, and stir it till it boils, making the spoon go down to the bottom, to prevent the gruel from burning. After it has come to a boil, let it continue boiling half an hour, stirring it frequently, and skimming it. Give it to the invalid warm, in a bowl or tumbler, to be eaten with a teaspoon. It may be sweetened with a little sugar. When the physician permits, some grated nutmeg may be added; also a very little wine.

RYE MUSH.—To make smooth rye mush, sift a quart or more of rye meal into a pan, and gradually pour in sufficient cold water to make a very thick batter, stirring it hard with a spoon as you proceed, and carefully pressing out all the lumps against the side of the pan. Add a very little salt. The batter must be so thick at the last that you can scarcely stir it. Then thin it with a little more water, and see that it is quite smooth. Rye, and also wheat flour, have a disposition to be more lumpy than corn meal, when made into mush. When thoroughly mixed and stirred, put it into a pot, place it over the fire, and boil it well, stirring it with a mush-stick till it comes to a hard boil; then place it in a diminished heat, and simmer it slowly till you want to dish it up. Eat it warm, with butter and molasses, or with sweet milk, or fresh buttermilk. Rye mush is considered very wholesome, particularly in cases of dyspepsia.

COMMON HOE-CAKE.—Take an earthen or tin pan, and half fill it with coarse Indian meal, which had best be sifted in. Add a little salt. Have ready a kettle of boiling water. Pour into the Indian meal sufficient hot water (a little at a time) to make a stiff dough, stirring it with a spoon as you proceed. It must be thoroughly mixed, and stirred hard. If you want the cakes for breakfast, mix this dough over night; cover the pan, and set it in a *cool* place till morning. If kept warm, it may turn sour. Early next morning, as soon as the fire is burning well, set the griddle over it, and take out the dough, a handful at a time. Flatten and shape it by patting it with your hands, till you form it into cakes about the size of a common saucer, and half an inch thick. When the griddle is quite hot, lay on it as many cakes as it will hold, and bake them brown. When the upper side is done, slip a bread knife beneath, and turn them over. They must be baked brown on both sides. Eat them warm, with buttermilk, sweet milk, butter, molasses, or whatever is most convenient. If you intend these cakes for dinner or supper, mix them as early in the day as you can, and (covering the pan) let them stand in a cool place till wanted for baking. In cold weather you may save trouble by mixing over night enough to last the next day for breakfast, dinner, and supper; baking them as they are wanted for each meal. Or they may be all baked in the morning, and eaten cold; but they are then not so palatable as when warm. They will be less liable to stick, if before each baking the griddle is dredged with wheat flour, or greased with a bit of fat pork stuck on a fork. You may cover it all over with one large cake, instead of several small ones.

In America there is seldom a house without a griddle. Still, where griddles are not, these cakes may be baked on a board standing nearly upright before the fire, and supported by a smoothing-iron or a stone placed against the back. Where wood fires are used, a good way of baking these cakes is to clear a clean place in the hottest part of the hearth, and, having wrapped the cake in paper, lay it down there, and cover it up with hot red ashes. It will bake very well, (replenishing the heat by throwing on from time to time a fresh supply of hot ashes,) and when taken out of the paper they will be found sweet and good. The early settlers of our country frequently baked their Indian cakes under the ashes of their wood fires; and the custom is still continued by those who cannot yet obtain the means of cooking them more conveniently.

This cake is so called, because in some parts of America it was customary to bake it on the iron of a hoe, stood up before the fire. It is better known by that name than by any other.

COMMON GRIDDLE CAKE.—A quart of Indian meal.—Sufficient warm water to make a soft dough.—A small tea-spoonful of salt.—Put the Indian meal into a pan, and add the salt. Make a hole in the centre of the meal, and pour in a little warm water. Then mix it with a large, strong spoon, adding, by degrees, water enough to make a soft dough. Flour your hands, and knead it into a large lump— divide it into two equal portions. Flour your paste-board, lay on it the first lump of dough, and roll it out about an inch thick. Then, (having already heated your griddle,) lay the cake upon it, spreading it evenly, and make it a good round shape. It should cover the whole surface of the griddle, which must first be greased, either with butter or lard tied in a rag, or with a bit of fat fresh pork. Butter it well; and when one side is well browned, turn it on the other, taking care not to break it. Send it to table hot, cut into three-cornered pieces—split and butter them. As soon as the first cake is sent in, put the other to bake.

This is one of the plainest and simplest preparations of Indian cake, and is very good when warm.

PLAIN JOHNNY CAKE.—A quart of Indian meal.—A pint of warm water.—A level tea-spoonful of salt.—Sift a quart of Indian meal into a pan. Make a hole in the middle, and pour in a pint of warm water, adding the salt. With a spoon mix the meal and water gradually into a soft dough. Stir it very hard for a quarter of an hour or more, till it becomes light and spongy. Then spread the dough; smooth and evenly, on a stout, flat board. A piece of the head of a flour barrel will serve for this purpose. Place the board nearly (but not quite) upright, and set a smoothing-iron or a stone against the back to support it. Bake it well. When done, cut it into squares, and send it hot to table, split and buttered. You may eat molasses with it.

NICE JOHNNY CAKE.—A quart of sifted Indian meal.—A small teacup of molasses, (West India is best.)—Two large table-spoonfuls of fresh butter.—A tea-spoonful of ground ginger.—Some boiling water. Having sifted the meal into a pan, rub the butter into it; add the molasses and ginger, and pour on, by degrees, sufficient boiling water to make a moderately soft dough. It must be stirred very hard. Then grease with fresh butter a board of sufficient size, spread the dough thickly upon it, and stand it nearly upright to bake before the fire, placing a flat-iron against the back of the board. The cake must be very well baked, taking care that the surface does not burn, while the inside is soft and raw. Cut it into squares when done, and send them hot to table, split and buttered.

The johnny-cake board had best be placed so as *slightly* to slant backwards; otherwise the upper part of the cake, being opposite to the hottest part of the fire, may bake too fast for the lower part.

VERY PLAIN INDIAN DUMPLINGS.—Sift some Indian meal into a pan; add about a salt-spoon of salt to each quart of meal; and scald it with sufficient boiling water to make a stiff dough. Pour in the water gradually; stirring as you pour. When the dough becomes a stiff lump, divide it into equal portions; flour your hands, and make it into thick, flat dumplings about as large round as the top of a glass tumbler, or a breakfast cup. Dredge the dumplings on all sides with flour, put them into a pot of boiling water (if made sufficiently stiff they need not be tied in cloths,) and keep them boiling hard till thoroughly done. Try them with a fork, which must come out quite clean, and with no clamminess sticking to it. They are an excellent appendage to salt pork or bacon, serving them up with the meat; or they may be eaten afterwards with butter and molasses, or with milk sweetened well with brown sugar, and flavoured with a little ground spice.

VERY PLAIN INDIAN BATTER CAKES.—A quart of warm water, or of skim milk.—A quart of Indian meal and half a pint of wheat flour, sifted.—A level tea-spoonful of salt. Pour the water into a pan; add the salt; and having mixed together the wheat and Indian meal, stir them gradually into the water, a handful at a time. It should be about the consistence of buckwheat cake or muffin batter. Beat it long and hard. If you find it too thick, add a little more water. Have ready a hot griddle, grease it, and bake the cakes on it. They should not be larger than the top of a tumbler, or a small saucer. Send them to table hot, in even piles, and eat them with butter or molasses.

These are the plainest sort of Indian batter cakes; but if well beaten and properly baked, they will be found very good, as well as economical. It is an improvement to mix them with milk instead of water.

INDIAN MUFFINS.—A pint and a half of yellow Indian meal, sifted.—A handful of wheat flour.—A quarter of a pound of fresh butter.—A quart of milk.—Four eggs.—A very small tea-spoonful of salt. Put the milk into a saucepan. Cut the butter into it. Set it over the fire and warm it till the butter is very soft, but not till it melts. Then take it off, stir it well, till all mixed, and set it away to cool. Beat four eggs very light; and when the milk is cold, stir them into it, alternately with the meal, a little at a time, of each. Add the salt. Beat the whole very hard after it is all mixed. Then butter some muffin-rings on the inside. Set them in a hot oven, or on a heated griddle; pour some of the batter into each; and bake the muffins well. Send them hot to table, continuing to bake while a fresh supply is wanted. Pull them open with your fingers, and eat them with butter, to which you may add molasses or honey. These muffins will be found excellent, and can be prepared in a very short time; for instance, in three quarters or half an hour before breakfast or tea.

This mixture may be baked in waffle-irons, as waffles. Butter them, and have on the table a glass bowl with powdered sugar and powdered cinnamon, to eat with these waffles.

VIRGINIA GRIDDLE CAKES.—A quart of Indian meal.—Two large table-spoonfuls of wheat flour.—A heaped salt-spoon of salt.—A piece of fresh butter, about two ounces.—Four eggs.—A pint, or more, of milk. Sift the Indian meal into a large pan; mix with it the wheat flour; and add the salt. Warm the milk in a small saucepan, but do not let it come to a boil. When it begins to simmer, take it off, and put the butter into it, stirring it about till well mixed. Then stir in the meal, a little at a time, and let it cool while you are beating the eggs. As soon as they are beaten very light, add them gradually to the mixture, stirring the whole very hard. It must be a light batter, and may require more milk.

Having heated the griddle well by placing it over the fire or in the oven of a hot stove, rub it over with some fresh butter, tied in a clean white rag, and pour on a large ladle-full of the batter. When the cake has baked brown, turn it, with a cake-turner, and bake the other side. Then take it off, and put it on a hot plate. Grease the griddle again, and put on another cake; and so on till you have three or four ready to send to table for a beginning. Continue to bake, and send in hot cakes as long as they are wanted. Eat them with butter; to which you may add molasses or honey.

MISSOURI CAKES.—Three large pints of yellow Indian meal.—A pint of cold water.—A tea-spoonful of salt.—A level tea-spoonful of sal-eratus or soda dissolved in a little warm water.—A large table-spoonful of beef-dripping, or lard.—A small pint and a half of warm water. Sift three large pints (a little more than three pints) of Indian meal into a pan; add a tea-spoonful of salt, a large table-spoonful of lard, or nice dripping of roast-beef; and a tea-spoonful of sal-eratus or soda melted in a little warm water. Make it into a soft dough with a pint of cold water. Then thin it to the consistence of a moderate batter, by adding, gradually, not quite a pint and a half of warm water. When it is all mixed, beat or stir it well, for half an hour. Then have a griddle ready over the fire. When hot, grease it with beef-suet, or with lard or butter tied in a clean white rag. Put on a large ladle-full of the batter, and bake the cakes fast. Send them hot to table, about half a dozen at a time, seeing that the edges are nicely trimmed. Eat them with butter, to which you may add honey or molasses.

These cakes are excellent; and very convenient, as they require neither eggs, milk, nor yeast. They may be baked as soon as mixed, or they may stand an hour or more.

INDIAN SLAP-JACKS.—A quart of yellow Indian meal.—Half a pint or more of boiling water.—Half a pint of wheat flour.—Three large table-spoon-fuls of strong fresh yeast.—A heaping salt-spoon of salt.—A level tea-spoonful of pearlash, soda, or sal-eratus, dissolved in warm water.—Lard for frying. Sift the Indian meal into a pan, and add the salt. Then pour on the boiling water, and stir it well. When it has cooled a little, and become only milk-warm, stir in the wheat flour, and add the yeast. Stir it long and hard. Cover the pan, and set it near the fire. When the mixture has risen quite light, and is covered with bubbles, add the dissolved pearlash to puff it still more. Have ready a hot frying-pan over the fire; grease it with a little lard, and put in a portion of the mixture, sufficient for one large cake nearly the size of the pan, or two small ones. Spread the mixture thin, and fry it brown. Send the cakes hot to table, and eat them with butter or molasses.

This is one of the plainest sorts of Indian cake, but if properly made, and baked, will be found very good.

INDIAN FLAPPERS.—A quart of sifted Indian meal.—A handful of wheat flour.—A quart of milk.—Four eggs.—A heaping salt-spoon of salt. Mix together the Indian and wheat meal, adding the salt. Beat the eggs light in another pan, and then stir them a little at a time into the milk, alternately with the meal, a handful at a time. Stir the whole very hard at the last. Have ready a hot griddle, and bake the cakes on it in the manner of buckwheat cakes, or crumpets; greasing or scraping the griddle always before you put on a fresh ladle-full of batter. Make all the cakes the same size, and when done trim the edges nicely with a knife. Send them to table hot, laid one on another evenly, buttered and cut in half. Or they may be buttered after they go to table.

INDIAN CRUMPETS.—A quart of Indian meal.—Half a pint of wheat flour.—A quart of milk.—A heaping salt-spoonful of salt.—Three eggs.—Two large table-spoonfuls of strong fresh yeast.—Warm the milk. Sift the Indian meal and the flour into a pan, and mix them well. Then stir them into the milk, a handful at a time; adding the salt. Beat the eggs very light in another pan, and then stir them, gradually, into the milk and meal. Lastly, add the yeast. Stir the whole well; then cover it, and set it to rise in a warm place, such as a corner of the hearth. When it has become very light, and is covered with bubbles, have the griddle ready heated to begin to bake the cakes; first greasing the griddle. For each crumpet pour on a large ladle-full of batter. Send them to table several on a plate, and as hot as possible. Eat them with butter, to which you may add molasses or honey.

If the batter should chance to become sour by standing too long, you may remedy it by stirring in a level tea-spoonful of pearlash, soda, or sal-eratus, dissolved in a very little lukewarm water. Then bake it.

CORN MEAL BREAKFAST CAKES.—A quart of Indian meal.—A handful, or more, of wheat flour.—A large salt-spoon of salt.—A quart of warm water.—An additional pint of lukewarm water.—A bit of pearlash the size of a hazel-nut, or the same quantity of soda or sal-eratus. Mix over night, in a large pan, the Indian meal, the wheat flour and salt. Pour on gradually a quart of warm water, (warm but not hot,) and stir it in with a large wooden or iron spoon, so as to form a very soft dough. Cover the pan, and set it on the dresser till morning. In the morning thin the dough with another pint of warm water, so as to make it into a batter, having first dissolved in the water a salt-spoonful of powdered pearlash or sal-eratus, or a bit the size of a hazel-nut. Beat the mixture hard. Then cover it, and let it stand near the fire for a quarter of an hour before you begin to bake it. Bake it in thin cakes on a griddle. Send them to table hot, and eat them with butter, and molasses or honey.

INDIAN RICE CAKES.—Take equal quantities of yellow Indian meal and well boiled rice. Mix them together in a pan, the meal and rice alternately, a little at a time of each. The boiled rice may be either hot or cold; but it will be rather best to mix it hot. Having first mixed it with a spoon, knead it well with your hands; moistening it with a little milk or water, if you find it too stiff. Have ready, over the fire, a heated griddle. Grease it with fresh butter tied in a clean white rag; and having made the mixture into flat round cakes, bake them well on both sides. Eat them with butter and sugar, or butter and molasses, or with butter alone.

PUMPKIN INDIAN CAKES.—Take equal portions of Indian meal, and stewed pumpkin that has been well mashed and drained very dry in a sieve or cullender. Put the stewed pumpkin into a pan, and stir the meal gradually into it, a spoonful at a time, adding a little butter as you proceed. Mix the whole thoroughly, stirring it very hard. If not thick enough to form a stiff dough, add a little more Indian meal. Make it into round, flat cakes, about the size of a muffin, and bake them over the fire on a hot griddle greased with butter. Or lay them in a square iron pan, and bake them in an oven.

Send them to table hot, and eat them with butter.

EXCELLENT BUCKWHEAT CAKES.—A quart of buckwheat meal, sifted.—A level tea-spoonful of salt.—A small half-pint, or a large handful of Indian meal.—Two large table-spoonfuls of strong fresh brewer's yeast, or four table-spoonfuls of home-made yeast.—Sufficient lukewarm water to make a moderate batter. Mix together the buckwheat and Indian meal, and add the salt. Make a hole in the centre of the meal, and pour in the yeast. Then stir in gradually, from a kettle, sufficient tepid or lukewarm water to make a moderately thick batter when united with the yeast. Cover the pan, set it in a warm place, and leave it to rise. It should be light in about three hours. When it has risen high and is covered with bubbles, it is fit to bake. Have ready a clean griddle well heated over the fire. Grease it well with a bit of fresh butter tied in a clean white rag, and kept on a saucer near you. Then dip out a large ladle-full of the batter, and bake it on the griddle; turning it when brown, with the cake-turner, and baking it brown on the other side. Grease the griddle slightly between baking each cake; or scrape it smooth with a broad knife. As fast as you bake the cakes, lay them, several in a pile, on a hot plate. Butter them, and if of large size cut them across into four pieces. Or send them to table to be buttered there. Trim off the edges before they go in.

If your batter has been mixed over night, and is found sour in the morning, dissolve a salt-spoon of pearlash or sal-eratus in a little lukewarm water, stir it into the batter, let it stand a quarter of an hour, and then bake it. The alkali will remove the acidity, and increase the lightness of the batter. If you use soda for this purpose it will require a tea-spoonful.

If the batter is kept at night in so cold a place as to freeze, it will be unfit for use. Do not grease the griddle with meat-fat of any sort.

NICE RYE BATTER CAKES.—A quart of lukewarm milk.—Two eggs.—A large table-spoonful of fresh brewer's yeast, or two of home-made yeast.—Sufficient sifted rye meal to make a moderate batter.—A salt-spoon of salt. Having warmed the milk, beat the eggs very light, and stir them gradually into it, alternately with the rye meal, adding the salt. Put in the meal, a handful at a time, till you have the batter about as thick as for buckwheat cakes. Then stir in the yeast, and give the batter a hard beating, seeing that it is smooth and free from lumps. Cover the pan, and set it in a warm place to rise. When risen high, and covered with bubbles, the batter is fit to bake. Have ready over the fire a hot griddle, and bake the cakes in the manner of buckwheat. Send them to table hot, and eat them with butter, molasses, or honey.

Yeast powders, used according to the directions that accompany them, and put in at the last, just before baking, are an improvement to the lightness of all batter cakes, provided that real yeast or eggs are also in the mixture. But it is not well to depend on the powders exclusively, particularly when real yeast is to be had. The lightness produced by yeast powders alone, is not the right sort; and though the cakes are eatable, they are too tough and leathery to be wholesome. As *auxiliaries* to genuine yeast, and to beaten eggs, yeast powders are excellent.

Indian batter cakes may be made as above—or rye and Indian may be mixed in equal proportions.

INDIAN LIGHT BISCUIT.—A quart of sifted Indian meal.—A pint of sifted wheat flour.—A very small tea-spoonful of salt.—Three pints of milk.—Four eggs. Sift the Indian and wheat meal into a pan, and add the salt. Mix them well. Beat the whites and the yolks of the eggs separately in two pans. The yolks must be beaten till very thick and smooth; the whites to a stiff froth that will stand alone of itself. Then stir the yolks gradually, (a little at a time,) into the milk. Add by degrees the meal. Lastly, stir in the beaten white of egg, and give the whole a long and hard stirring. Butter a sufficient number of cups, or small, deep tins—nearly fill them with the batter. Set them immediately into a hot oven, and bake them fast. Turn them out of the cups. Send them warm to table, pull them open, and eat them with butter.

They will puff up finely if, at the last, you stir in a level tea-spoonful of soda, melted in a little warm water.

INDIAN CUPCAKES.—A pint and a half of yellow Indian meal.—Half a pint of wheat flour.—A pint and a half of *sour* milk; buttermilk is best.—A small tea-spoonful of sal-eratus or soda, dissolved in warm water.—Two eggs.—A level tea-spoonful of salt. Sift the Indian and wheat meal into a pan and mix them well, adding the salt. If you have no butter-milk or other sour milk at hand, turn some sweet milk sour by setting a pan of it in the sun, or stirring in a spoonful of vinegar. Take out a small teacupful of the sour milk, and reserve it to be put in at the last. Beat the eggs very light, and then stir them, gradually, into the milk, alternately with the meal, a little at a time of each. Lastly, dissolve the soda or sal-eratus, and stir it into the cup of sour milk that has been reserved for the purpose. It will effervesce; stir it while foaming into the mixture, which should be a thick batter. Have ready some teacups, or little deep tins. Butter them well; nearly fill them with the batter, and set them immediately into a rather brisk oven. The cakes must be thoroughly baked all through. When done, turn them out on large plates, and send them hot to the breakfast or tea-table. Split them into three pieces, and eat them with butter.

The soda will entirely remove the acidity of the milk, which will effervesce the better for being sour at first, adding therefore to the lightness of the cake. Taste the milk, and if you find that the slightest sourness remains, add a little more dissolved soda.

All the alkalies, pearlash, sal-eratus, soda, and sal-volatile, will remove acidity, and increase lightness; but if too much is used they will impart a disagreeable taste. It is useless to put lemon or orange juice into any mixture that is afterwards to have one of these alkalies, as they will entirely destroy the flavour of the fruit.

KENTUCKY SWEET CAKE.—A pint of fine yellow Indian meal, sifted.—Half a pint of wheat flour.—Half a pound of powdered white sugar.—Half a pound of fresh butter.—Eight eggs.—A powdered nutmeg.—A large tea-spoonful of powdered cinnamon.—A glass of white wine.—A glass of brandy. Having powdered the spice, and mixed together the wine and brandy, put the spice to steep in the liquor. Mix well the Indian meal and the wheat flour, putting them into a broad pan. In another pan, stir together the butter and sugar (as for a pound cake) till they are very light and creamy. Break the eggs into a shallow earthen pan, and beat them till very thick and light. Then, by degrees, stir into the beaten butter and sugar, the spice and the liquor, a little at a time of each. Afterwards, add alternately the meal and the beaten egg, also a little of each at a time. Stir the whole very hard when all the ingredients are in. Butter a straight-sided tin pan, put the mixture into it; set it immediately into a rather brisk oven; and bake it well for three or four hours or more, in proportion to its thickness.

This is a very nice cake. It should be eaten the same day that it is baked; as when stale (even one day old) all Indian cakes become dry, hard, and rough.

It will be improved by the addition of a pound of raisins, stoned, cut in half, and well dredged with wheat flour to prevent their sinking to the bottom. Sultana or seedless raisins are best for all sorts of cakes and puddings.

CAROLINA RICE CAKES.—Having picked and washed half a pint of rice, boil it by itself till the grains lose all form and are dissolved into a thick mass, or jelly. While warm, mix into it a large lump of the best fresh butter, and a salt-spoonful of salt. Pour into a bowl, a moderate sized teacupful of ground rice-flour; and add to it as much milk as will make a tolerably stiff batter. Stir it till it is quite smooth, and free from lumps. Then mix it thoroughly with the boiled rice. Beat six eggs as light as possible, and stir them, gradually, into the mixture. Bake it on a griddle, in cakes about as large round as a saucer. Eat them warm with butter; and have on the table, in a small bowl, some powdered white sugar and nutmeg, for those who like it.

CAROLINA CORN CAKES.—Mix together in a pan, a pint and a half of sifted corn meal, and a half pint of wheat flour, adding a heaped salt-spoon of salt. Beat three eggs very light. Have ready a quart of *sour* milk. (You can turn sweet milk sour by stirring into it a very little vinegar.) Put into a teacup a small tea-spoonful of carbonate of soda, and dissolve it in a little lukewarm water. In another teacup melt a salt-spoonful of tartaric acid. Add, alternately, to the milk, the beaten eggs and the mixed meal, a little at a time of each; stirring very hard. Then stir in the melted soda, and lastly the dissolved tartaric acid. Having stirred the whole well together, butter some square pans; fill them with the batter; set them immediately into a hot oven; and bake them well. Serve them up hot, and eat them with butter or molasses, or both. These cakes may be baked in muffin rings. All hot cakes in the form of muffins should be pulled open with the fingers when about to be eaten; and not split with a knife, the pressure of the knife tending to make them heavy.

MADISON CAKE.—A pint and a half of sifted yellow corn meal.—Half a pint of wheat flour.—Half a pint of sour milk.—Half a pint of powdered white sugar.—Half a pound of fresh butter.—Six eggs.—A gill, or two wine-glasses of brandy.—A pound of raisins of the best quality.—A large tea-spoonful of mixed spice, powdered mace, nutmeg, and cinnamon.—A large salt-spoon of sal-eratus, or a small tea-spoonful of soda. If you have no sour milk at hand, turn half a pint of rich milk sour by setting it in the sun, or stirring in a tea-spoonful of vinegar. For this cake the milk must be sour, that the sal-eratus or soda may act more powerfully by coming in contact with an acid. The acidity will then be entirely removed by the effervescence, and the cake will be rendered very light, and perfectly sweet. Having powdered the spice, put it into the brandy, and let it infuse till wanted. Prepare the raisins by stoning them, and cutting them in half; dredging them well with flour. They should be muscadel, or bloom raisins, or sultana; if the latter, they will require no seeding. Low-priced raisins, of inferior quality, should never be used for cooking or for any purpose, as they are unwholesome.

Sift the corn meal and the wheat flour into a pan, and mix them well. In another pan mix the butter and sugar, and stir them together with a hickory spaddle (which is like a short mush-stick, only broader at the flattened end) till they are light and creamy. Then add the brandy and spice. In a broad, shallow pan, beat the eggs till very thick and smooth. Then stir them gradually into the butter and sugar in turn with the meal. Dissolve the sal-eratus or soda in a very little lukewarm water, and stir it into the sour milk. Then, while foaming, add the milk to the rest of the mixture, and stir very hard. Lastly, throw in the raisins, a few at a time, and give the whole a hard stirring.

Butter a deep square pan or a turban-mould. Put in the mixture. Set it *directly* into a brisk oven, and bake it at least three hours; or four if in a turban-mould. When half done, the heat should be increased. This cake should be eaten the day it is baked.

NANTUCKET PUDDING.—Six large ears of Indian corn; full grown, but young and soft.—A pint of milk.—A quarter of a pound of fresh butter.—A quarter of a pound of sugar.—Four eggs.—Half a nutmeg grated, and five or six blades of mace powdered.—Having first boiled the corn for a quarter of an hour, grate the grains off the cob with a coarse grater. Then add the butter (cut into little bits) and the sugar. Having stirred them well into the corn, thin it with milk. Beat the eggs very light, and add them to the mixture, a little at a time, and finish with the spice. Stir the whole very hard. Butter a deep white dish, put in the pudding, set it directly into the oven, and bake it two hours. Send it to table warm, and eat it with butter and sugar, or molasses. It is not good cold. What is left may be put into a small dish, and baked over again next day, for half an hour; or tied in a cloth, and boiled a while.

SAMP PUDDING.—A pint of samp that has been boiled, and grown cold.—A pint of milk.—Three large table-spoonfuls of fresh butter.—Three large table-spoonfuls of sugar, or half a pint of West India molasses.—Six eggs.—A table-spoonful of powdered cinnamon and nutmeg mixed, or a table-spoonful of ground ginger. Boil the milk; and just after you take it from the fire stir in the butter and sugar; or instead of the sugar half a pint of West India molasses. Then add the spice, and set the milk, &c., to cool. Beat the eggs till thick and smooth. Then stir them, gradually, into the mixture, a little at a time, in turn with the samp. Butter a deep dish; put in the mixture, and bake it well. Eat it warm, with butter, sugar, and nutmeg beaten together to a cream; or with molasses and butter.

A rice pudding may be made as above; the rice being previously boiled by itself, and well drained.

A samp pudding may be tied in a cloth and boiled.

A FARMER'S INDIAN PUDDING.—Three small pints of sifted Indian meal, the yellow sort.—A quart of rich milk.—A pint of West India molasses.—A table-spoonful of ground cinnamon, or ginger. Before you begin, set over the fire a large pot filled with water, which must boil hard by the time the pudding is mixed. Put the milk by itself, into another pot or sauce-pan, and give it a boil. When it has come to a boil, pour it into a deep pan, and stir into it a pint of the best West India molasses. Then add, by degrees, the Indian meal, a handful at a time; and lastly, the spice. Stir the whole very hard. Have ready a square pudding-cloth; dip it in boiling water; shake it out; dredge it with flour, and spread it open in a broad pan. Then pour the pudding-batter into the cloth; and, leaving near one-third vacant, as room for it to swell, tie it firmly with tape. Make a morsel of stiff dough with flour and a little water, and with it stop closely the little aperture at the tying-place, to prevent water from getting in there. Plaster it on well. Put the pudding into the large pot of boiling water; cover it closely with the lid; and let it boil steadily for at least three hours; four will not be too long. While boiling, turn it frequently. As the water boils away, replenish it with some more water, kept boiling hard for this purpose, in a kettle. On no account pour in *cold* water, as that will render the pudding heavy. Turn it out of the cloth immediately before it goes to table, and eat it with butter and molasses. It will be found excellent. The West India molasses will make it as light as if it had eggs.

You may add with the spice, the yellow rind of a large lemon or orange, finely grated.

A VERY NICE BOILED INDIAN PUDDING.—Three pints of sifted Indian meal.—Half a pound of beef-suet, minced as fine as possible.—A quart of milk.—Half a pint of West India molasses.—Six eggs.—Three or four sticks of cinnamon, broken small.—A grated nutmeg. Having cleared the suet from the skin and strings, chop it as fine as possible, and mix it with the Indian meal. Boil the cinnamon in the milk till it is highly flavoured. Then strain the milk (boiling hot) into the pan of Indian meal and suet, and add the molasses. Stir the mixture very hard. Cover it and set it away in a cool place. Beat the eggs till quite light, and add them, gradually, to the mixture as soon as it is quite cold. Then grate in the nutmeg. Dip a thick square cloth into boiling water, shake it out, dredge it with flour, and then spread it open in a deep pan, and pour in the mixture. Leaving one-third of the space vacant allowing for the pudding to swell, tie the cloth very securely, and to guard against water getting into it, plug up the little crack at the tying place by plastering on a bit of dough made of flour and water. Put the pudding into a large pot of boiling water, (having an old plate in the bottom,) and boil it six hours or more, turning it often, and replenishing the pot, when necessary, with boiling water from a kettle. If you dine early, the pudding should be mixed before breakfast. Serve it up hot.

Eat it with wine sauce, with butter and molasses, or with a sauce of butter, sugar, lemon-juice and nutmeg, beaten together to a cream. What is left of the pudding, may next day be tied in a cloth, and boiled over again for an hour.

BAKED CORN MEAL PUDDING.—A pint of sifted Indian meal.—Half a pint of West India molasses.—A quarter of a pound of fresh butter.—A pint of milk.—Four eggs.—The yellow rind of a large fresh orange or lemon grated.—A tea-spoonful of powdered cinnamon and nutmeg mixed. Boil the milk. Sift the Indian meal into an earthen pan, pour the boiling milk over it, and stir them well together. Cut up the butter into a small sauce-pan; pour the molasses over it; set it on the fire, and let them warm together till the butter is soft, but not oiled. Stir them well, and mix them with the milk and Indian meal. Set the pan in a cool place. In a separate pan beat the eggs very light, and when the mixture has become cold, add the eggs to it, gradually. Then stir in the spice, and grated orange or lemon peel. Stir the whole very hard. Put the mixture into a buttered white dish, and bake it well. Serve it up hot, and eat it with a sauce made of powdered white sugar, and fresh butter seasoned with nutmeg and lemon or orange juice, and stirred together to a cream; or with a liquid sauce of melted butter, wine and nutmeg.

This quantity of ingredients will make a small pudding. For a large one, allow a double portion of each article, and bake it longer.

It will be improved by gradually stirring in at the last, a pound of Zante currants or of sultana raisins, well dredged with flour.

PUMPKIN INDIAN PUDDING.—Take a pint and a half of cold stewed pumpkin, and mix into it a pint and a half of Indian meal, adding a table-spoonful of ground ginger. Boil a quart of milk, and as soon as you take it from the fire, stir into it a pint of West India molasses. Then add to it gradually the mixture of pumpkin and corn meal, and stir the whole very hard. It will be much improved by adding the grated yellow rind of a large orange or lemon. Have ready over the fire a large pot of boiling water. Dip your pudding-cloth into it; shake it out; spread out the cloth in a broad pan: dredge it with flour; pour the mixture into it, and tie it fast, leaving about one-third of the space for the pudding to swell. Boil it three hours or more—four hours will not be too long. Turn it several times while boiling. Replenish the pot as it boils, with hot water from a kettle kept boiling for the purpose. Take up the pudding immediately before it is wanted for table—dip it a moment in cold water, and turn it out into a dish. Eat it with butter and molasses.

This pudding requires no eggs in the mixture. The molasses, if West India, will make it sufficiently light.

What is left may be tied in a cloth, and re-boiled next day.

A BACKWOODS POT-PIE.—Put a large portion of yellow Indian meal, (with a very little salt,) into a deep pan, and pour on scalding water, (stirring it in as you proceed,) till you have a soft dough. Beat and stir it long and hard, adding more corn meal, till the dough becomes stiff. It will be improved by mixing in a little wheat flour. When it is cool enough to handle, knead it a while with your hands. Take off portions of the dough or paste, and form them into flat, square cakes. Take a large pot; grease the sides with a little good dripping or lard, and line them with the cakes of corn meal. Have ready some fresh venison cut into pieces, and seasoned with a little salt and pepper. Put some of it into the pot, (adding some water to assist in the gravy,) and cover it with a layer of corn cakes. Then more venison, and then more cakes, till the pot is nearly full. The last layer must be a large cake with a slit in the middle. Set it over the fire, and let it boil steadily till the whole is thoroughly done. Then take it up, and dish it together, meat and paste.

The paste that is to line the sides of the pot should be thinner than that which is to be laid among the meat. Put no paste at the bottom.

If you have any cold drippings of roast venison, you may mix some of it with the corn meal, as shortening.

Sweet potatoes sliced, and laid among the meat, will improve this pie.

TO BOIL INDIAN CORN.—Corn for boiling should be full grown, but young and tender, and the grains soft and milky. If its grains are becoming hard and yellow, it is too old for boiling. Strip the ears of their leaves and the silk. Put them into a large pot of boiling water, and boil it rather fast for half an hour or more, in proportion to its size and age. When done, take it up, drain it, dish it under a cover, or napkin, and serve it up hot. Before eating it, rub each ear with salt and pepper, and then spread it with butter. Epicures in corn consider it sweetest when eaten off the cob. And so it is; but *before company* few persons like to hold an ear of Indian corn in their hands, and bite the grains off the cob with their teeth. Therefore, it is more frequently cut off the cob into a dish; mixed with salt, pepper, and butter, and helped with a spoon.

It is said that young green corn will boil sufficiently in ten minutes, (putting it *of course* into a pot of boiling water.) Try it.

Another way.—Having pulled off the silk, boil the corn, without removing the leaves that enclose the cob. With the leaves or husk on, it will require a longer time to cook, but is sweeter and more nutritious.

GREEN CORN DUMPLINGS.—A quart of young corn grated from the cob.— Half a pint of wheat flour, sifted.—Half a pint of milk.—Six table-spoonfuls of butter.—Two eggs.—A salt-spoonful of salt.—A salt-spoonful of pepper.—Butter for frying. Having grated as fine as possible, sufficient young fresh corn to make a quart, mix with it the wheat flour, and add the salt and pepper. Warm the milk in a small saucepan, and soften the butter in it. Then add them gradually to the pan of corn, stirring very hard; and set it away to cool. Beat the eggs light, and stir them into the mixture when it has cooled. Flour your hands and make it into little dumplings. Put into a frying-pan a sufficiency of fresh butter, (or lard and butter in equal proportions,) and when it is boiling hot, and has been skimmed, put in the dumplings; and fry them ten minutes or more, in proportion to their thickness. Then drain them, and send them hot to the dinner-table.

CORN PORRIDGE.—Take young corn, and cut the grains from the cob. Measure it, and to each heaping pint of corn, allow not quite a quart of milk. Put the corn and milk into a pot; stir them well together: and boil them till the corn is perfectly soft. Then add some bits of fresh butter dredged with flour, and let it boil five minutes longer. Stir in at the last, some beaten yolk of egg; and in three minutes remove it from the fire. Take up the porridge, and send it to table hot, and stir some fresh butter into it. You may add sugar and nutmeg.

CORN OYSTERS.—Three dozen ears of large young Indian corn.—Six eggs.—Lard and butter in equal portions for frying. The corn must be young and soft. Grate it from the cob as fine as possible, and dredge it with wheat flour. Beat very light the six eggs, and mix them gradually with the corn. Then let the whole be well incorporated by hard beating. Add a salt-spoon of salt.

Have ready, in a frying pan, a sufficient quantity of lard and fresh butter mixed together. Set it over the fire till it is boiling hot, and then put in portions of the corn-mixture, so as to form oval cakes about three inches long, and nearly an inch thick. Fry them brown, and send them to table hot. In taste they will be found to have a singular resemblance to fried oysters, and are universally liked if properly done. They make nice side-dishes at dinner, and are very good at breakfast.

SUMMER SACCATASH.—String a quarter of a peck of young green beans, and cut each bean into three pieces (not more) and do not split them. Have by you a pan of cold water, and throw the beans into it as you cut them. Have ready over the fire a pot or saucepan of boiling water, put in the beans, and boil them hard near twenty minutes. Afterwards take them up, and drain them well through a cullender. Take half a dozen ears of young but full-grown Indian corn (or eight or nine if they are not all large) and cut the grains down from the cob. Mix together the corn and the beans, adding a very small tea-spoonful of salt, and boil them about twenty minutes. Then take up the saccatash, drain it well through a sieve, put it into a deep dish, and while hot mix in a large piece of butter, (at least the size of an egg,) add some pepper, and send it to table. It is generally eaten with salted or smoked meat.

Fresh Lima beans are excellent cooked in this manner, with green corn. They must be boiled for half an hour or more before they are cooked with the corn.

Dried beans and dried corn will do very well for saccatash, but they must be soaked all night before boiling. The water poured on them for soaking should be hot.

WINTER SACCATASH.—This is made of dried shelled beans, and hard corn. Take equal quantities of shelled beans and corn; put them over night into separate pans, and pour boiling water over them. Let them soak till morning. Then pour off that water, and scald them again. First boil the beans by themselves. When they are soft, add the corn, and let them boil together till the corn is quite soft, which will require at least an hour. Take them up, drain them in a sieve; then put them into a deep dish, and mix in a large piece of fresh butter, and a little pepper and salt.

This is an excellent accompaniment to pickled pork, bacon; or corned beef. The meat must be boiled by itself in a separate pot.

HOMINY.—Hominy is Indian Corn shelled from the cob, divested of the yellow or outer skin by scalding in hot lye, and then winnowed and dried. It is perfectly white. Having washed it through two or three waters, pour boiling water on it, cover it, and let it soak all night, or for several hours. Then put it into a pot or saucepan, allow two quarts of water to each quart of hominy, and boil it till perfectly soft. Then drain it, put it into a deep dish, add some butter to it, and send it to table hot, (and *uncovered*,) to eat with any sort of meat; but particularly with corned beef or pork. What is left may be made next day into thick cakes, and fried in butter. To be *very good*, hominy should boil four or five hours.

CAROLINA GRITS, or SMALL HOMINY.—The small-grained hominy must be washed and boiled in the same manner as the large, only allow rather less water for boiling. For instance, put a pint and a half of water to a quart of small hominy. Drain it well, send it to table in a deep dish *without a cover*, and eat it with butter and sugar, or molasses. If covered after boiling, the vapour will condense within the lid, and make the hominy thin and watery.

SAMP.—This is Indian corn skinned, and then pounded or ground till it is still smaller and finer than the Carolina grits. It must be cooked and used in the same manner. It is very nice eaten with cream and sugar.

For invalids it may be made thin, and eaten as gruel.

HOMINY CAKES.—A pint of small hominy, or Carolina grits.—A pint of white Indian meal, sifted.—A salt-spoonful of salt.—Three large table-spoonfuls of fresh butter.—Three eggs, or three table-spoonfuls of strong yeast.—A quart of milk. Having washed the small hominy, and left it soaking all night, boil it soft, drain it, and while hot, mix it with the Indian meal; adding the salt, and the butter. Then mix it gradually with the milk, and set it away to cool. Beat the eggs very light, and add them, gradually, to the mixture. The whole should make a thick batter. Then bake them on a griddle, in the manner of buckwheat cakes, greasing or scraping the griddle, always before you put on a fresh cake. Trim off their edges nicely, and send them to table hot. Eat them with butter.

Or you may bake them in muffin rings.

If you prefer making these cakes with yeast, you must begin them earlier, as they will require time to rise. The yeast should be strong and fresh. If *not* very strong, use four table-spoonfuls instead of two. Cover the pan, set it in a warm place; and do not begin to bake till it is well risen, and the surface of the mixture is covered with bubbles.

TO KEEP INDIAN CORN FOR COOKING.—Take the corn when it is young and tender, and barely full-grown. Let it remain on the cob till you have boiled it ten or fifteen minutes (not more) in a large pot of slightly-salted water that must be boiling hard when the corn is put in. When thus parboiled, take it out, and when cool enough to handle, cut down the grains from the cob, into a deep pan, with a knife. Then spread out the grains in large flat dishes or shallow pans, and set them in an oven, after the bread, pies, &c., are done, and have been taken out. Let the corn remain in the oven till it is all well dried. If your oven is heated every day, you may put the corn into it a second time. When quite dry, and after it has cooled, put it into a large thick bag; tie the bag tightly, and hang it up in a cool store-room. When wanted for use, corn thus prepared will be found excellent for boiling in winter soup; or boiled by itself and drained, and sent to table in a vegetable-dish to eat with meat; first mixing with it some butter, and a little pepper and salt. It will boil as soft, and taste as well as when fresh from the garden. It will be better for soaking all night in water, before cooking.

Bakers who heat their ovens every day, would find it profitable to buy Indian corn in large quantities, and prepare it as above, to sell afterwards for table use. If the corn is not young and fresh, it will require half an hour's boiling before it is dried in the oven.

What is called sweet corn is excellent for this purpose.

EXCELLENT RECEIPT FOR PORK AND BEANS. — Take a good piece of pick-led pork (not very fat) and to each pound of pork allow a quart of dried white beans. The bone should be removed from the pork, and the beans well picked and washed. The evening before they are wanted for cooking, put the beans and pork to soak in *separate pans*; and just before bed-time, drain off the water, and replace it with fresh. Let them soak all night. Early in the morning, drain them well from the water, and wash first the beans, and then the pork in a cullender. Having scored the skin in stripes or diamonds, put the pork into a pot with fresh cold water, and the beans into another pot with sufficient cold water to cook them well. Season the pork with a little pepper, but of course no salt. Boil them separately and slowly till the pork is thoroughly done (skimming it well) and till the beans have all burst open. Afterwards take them out, and drain them well from the water. Then lay the pork in the middle of a tin pan, (there must be no liquid fat about it) and the beans round it; and over it, so as nearly to bury it from sight. Pour in a very little water, and set the dish into a hot oven, to bake or brown for half an hour. If kept too long in the oven the beans will become dry and hard. If sufficiently boiled when sep-arate, half an hour will be long enough for the pork and beans to bake together. Carefully skim off any liquid fat that may rise to the surface. Cover the dish, and send it to table hot.

For a small dish, two quarts of beans and two pounds of pork will be enough. To this quantity when put to bake in the oven you may allow half a pint of water.

This is a good plain dish, very popular in New England, and generally liked in other parts of the country.

INDEX

B

C

D

E

G

H

Lector House believes that a society develops through a two-fold approach of continuous learning and adaptation, which is derived from the study of classic literary works spread across the historic timeline of literature records. Therefore, we aim at reviving, repairing and redeveloping all those inaccessible or damaged but historically as well as culturally important literature across subjects so that the future generations may have an opportunity to study and learn from past works to embark upon a journey of creating a better future.

This book is a result of an effort made by Lector House towards making a contribution to the preservation and repair of original ancient works which might hold historical significance to the approach of continuous learning across subjects.

HAPPY READING & LEARNING!

LECTOR HOUSE LLP
E-MAIL: lectorpublishing@gmail.com